2ND EDITION

Managing and Using Information Systems

A Strategic Approach

KERI E. PEARLSON
Research Board

CAROL S. SAUNDERS
University of Central Florida

www.wiley.com/college/pearlson

COMP: S. HANLON

Acquisitions Editor   *Beth Lang Golub*
Assistant Editor   *Lorraina Raccuia*
Editorial Assistant   *Ailsa Manny*
Marketing Manager   *Gitti Lindner*
Managing Editor   *Kevin Dodds*
Associate Production Manager   *Kelly Tavares*
Production Editor   *Sarah Wolfman-Robichaud*
Illustration Editor   *Jaye Joseph*

This book was set in New Caledonia by Leyh Publishing LLC and printed and bound by Courier Corp. The cover was printed by Lehigh Press.

This book is printed on acid-free paper. ∞

STAFFORDSHIRE
UNIVERSITY
LIBRARY

SITE: NELSON

19 MAR 2004

CLASS No.
658·403811

Copyright 2004 © John Wiley & Sons, Inc. All rights reserved.

No part of this publication may be reproduced, stored in a retrieval system or transmitted in any form or by any means, electronic, mechanical, photocopying, recording, scanning or otherwise, except as permitted under Sections 107 or 108 of the 1976 United States Copyright Act, without either the prior written permission of the Publisher, or authorization through payment of the appropriate per-copy fee to the Copyright Clearance Center, 222 Rosewood Drive, Danvers, MA 01923, (978) 750-8400, fax (978) 750-4470. Requests to the Publisher for permission should be addressed to the Permissions Department, John Wiley & Sons, Inc., 605 Third Avenue, New York, NY 10158-0012, (212) 850-6008, E-Mail: PERMREQ@WILEY.COM. To order books please call 1(800) 225-5945.

ISBN 0-471-34644-6

Printed in the United States

10 9 8 7 6 5 4 3 2

04893192

To Yale & Hana

To Rusty, Russell & Kristin

Contents

▶ **CHAPTER 2**   Strategic Use of Information Resources   38

▶ **CHAPTER 3**   Organizational Impacts of Information Systems Use   59

► **CHAPTER 4** Information Technology and the Design of Work **81**

► **CHAPTER 5** Information Technology and Changing Business Processes **104**

▶ **CHAPTER 6** Architecture and Infrastructure **127**

▶ **CHAPTER 7** Doing Business on the Internet **153**

► **CHAPTER 8** The Management Information Systems Organization **183**

▶ CHAPTER 9   Funding IT   215

▶ CHAPTER 10   Project Management   239

▶ **CHAPTER 11**   Knowledge Management   **274**

▶ **CHAPTER 12** Using Information Ethically **306**

Preface

"Information technology is a business force now. It amounts to one-half of U.S. firms' annual capital expenditures and increasingly affects how firms organize, do business, and compete. Business managers who choose not to reckon with it do so at their and their firm's peril."

> Peter G. W. Keen
> in *Every Manager's Guide to Information Technology*

"I'm not hiring MBA students for the technology you learn while in school, but for your ability to learn about, use and subsequently manage new technologies when you get out."

> John Post
> Federal Express

Give me a fish and I eat for a day; Teach me to fish and I eat for a lifetime.

> Proverb

Managers are no longer able to afford the luxury of abdicating participation in information systems decisions. Managers who choose to do so risk having their business decisions compromised. With the proliferation of the Web and e-business, information systems are at the heart of virtually every business interaction, process, and decision. Managers who let someone else make decisions about their information systems are letting someone else make decisions about the foundation of their business. This is a textbook about using and managing information, written for current and future managers.

The goal of this book is to assist managers in becoming knowledgeable participants in information systems decisions. Becoming a knowledgeable participant means learning the basics and feeling comfortable enough to ask questions. No text will provide managers with everything they need to know to make important information systems decisions. Some texts instruct on the basic technical background of information systems. Some texts discuss applications and their life cycle. Some texts take a comprehensive view of the MIS field and offer the reader snapshots of current systems along with chapters describing how those technologies are designed, used, and integrated into business life.

This book takes a different approach. This text is intended to provide the reader with a foundation of basic concepts relevant to using and managing information. It is not intended to provide a comprehensive treatment on any one aspect of MIS, for certainly each aspect is itself a topic for many books. It is not intended to provide the reader with enough technological knowledge to make them MIS experts.

It is not intended to be a source of discussion of any particular technology. This textbook is written to help managers begin the discussion of how information systems will help, hinder, and create opportunities for their organizations.

The idea for this text grew out of discussions with colleagues in the MIS area. Many faculty use a series of case studies and current readings from trade and popular press sources to teach their core MIS courses. Others simply rely on one of the classic texts, which include dozens of pages of diagrams, frameworks, and technologies. This text is based on a core MIS course taught for over five years at the University of Texas at Austin. The course was an "appetizer" course—a brief introduction into the world of MIS for MBA students, lasting only ten class sessions. The course had two main topics: using information and managing information. And the course was structured around providing the general MBA with enough knowledge of the field of MIS so they could recognize opportunities to use the rapidly changing technologies in new and creative ways. The course was an appetizer to the "main dish" of a host of specialty courses that went much deeper into the various topics. But completion of this course meant that students were able to feel comfortable listening to, contributing to, and, ultimately, participating in information systems decisions.

This book includes an introduction, twelve chapters of text and minicases, and a set of case studies and supplemental readings on a Web site. The introduction makes the argument that managers must be knowledgeable participants in information systems decisions. The first few chapters build a basic framework of the relationship between a business strategy, an information systems strategy, and an organizational strategy. The links of these strategies are explored in subsequent chapters on the relationship between information technology and, respectively, the organization, the individual, and the business strategy. Readers will also find a chapter on how information technology relates to business transformation.

General managers will find it difficult to discuss their creative applications for information technology without some foundation of how it is managed in organizations. Therefore, the remaining chapters describe the basics of an information architecture, e-business and the Internet, the organization of the MIS function, IT funding, project management, the management of knowledge, and moral/ethical implications of using information and information systems.

This text is written for use with supplemental materials and case studies. In order to keep the case studies current, they were not printed in the text itself, but are available without additional charge to those who have the textbook. For this edition of the book, the cases are available on the Web. These cases come from all over the globe and are written about many different managerial situations. Each provides a rich contextual setting for the discussion of several issues raised in the book chapters. Please visit the book's Web site at www.wiley.com/college/pearlson for more information on the cases.

No text in the field of MIS is current. The process of writing the chapters, coupled with any publication process, makes the text somewhat out-of-date prior to delivery to its audience. With that thought in mind, this text is written to summarize the "timeless" elements of using and managing information. While this text is complete in and of itself, learning is enhanced when the text is supplemented with a series of case studies, current readings, and Web links. The format of this text is such that each chapter provides the basic language used for a set of important management issues. Cases take these issues and put them in a business example for discussion by students. Current readings and Web links bring the foundation issues up-to-date with examples of how successful managers implement these ideas.

Who should read this book? General managers interested in participating in information systems decisions will find this book a good reference resource for the language and ideas of MIS. Managers in the information systems field will find this book a good resource for beginning to understand the general manager's view of how information systems can affect their business decisions. And MIS students will be able to use the readings and concepts in this book as a beginning point in their journey to become informed and productive business people in the twenty-first century.

The information revolution is here. Where do you fit in?

Keri E. Pearlson and Carol S. Saunders

Acknowledgments

Books of this nature are written only with the support of many individuals. We would like to personally thank several individuals who helped with this text. While we've made every attempt to include everyone who helped make this book a reality, there is always the possibility of unintentionally leaving someone off. We apologize in advance if that is the case here.

Early versions of the chapters of this book were researched and drafted by students from the Information Management (IM) program at the University of Texas at Austin Graduate School of Business. These amazingly bright students provided incredible inspiration for this book, and several of them pitched in to help write initial drafts of some of the chapters.

Case studies included with this text came from MIS colleagues all over the globe. A special acknowledgment goes to Professor Jonathan Trower at Baylor University who spent many hours managing the cases for this text. Thank you to Epsen Andersen, Janis Gogan, Ashok Rho, Yvonne Lederer Antonucci, E. Jose Proenca, Bruce Rollier, Dave Oliver, Celia Romm, Ed Watson, D. Guiter, S. Vaught, Kala Saravanamuthu, Ron Murch, Tom Rohleder, Sam Lubbe, Thomas Kern, and Mark Dekker for sending us such great cases.

This text has benefited from the insights and suggestions of several faculty. The first edition of this text was tested and reviewed by Dr. Kathy Hurtt and her students at the University of Wisconsin. The second edition was reviewed by Dr. Kay Nelson at the University of Utah and Dr. John Butler at Ohio State. Both the first and second editions were reviewed by several anonymous reviewers who gave us suggestions that helped improve our manuscript. Thanks!

Thanks to the students of the Fall 2002 Information Resources Management class at the University of Central Florida: Joseph Alcala, Theodore Bill, Kanesha Bryant, Nathan Cain, Omar Cortes, David Emel, Debbi Furrie, Kenneth Garrow, Karina Ledesma, Harold Miles, Stella Otto, Jason Polstein, and Darren Shipp. Their many helpful comments on the proposed revisions really helped to clarify our thinking and make the text more readable. Thanks also to Virginia Ilie for working on those pesky permissions, and to Paul Cheney at the University of Central Florida for creating a supportive environment in which to write this book.

This book would not have been started were it not for the initial suggestion of a wonderful editor at John Wiley & Sons, Inc., Beth Lang Golub. Her persistence and patience have helped shepherd this book through many months of creation, modification, evaluation, and production. Thanks also to Lorraina Raccuia, Ailsa Manny, and Gitti Lindner, who helped us through the updating process. And a special thank you to Kris Pauls and her colleagues at Leyh Publishing, who made the production process so manageable for us. Others at Wiley and at partner companies have provided valuable help. Thank you to each and every one of them.

From Keri: And thank you to my husband, Dr. Yale Pearlson, and my daughter, Hana Pearlson. Their patience with me while I worked on this project was incredible. They celebrated and commiserated the ups and downs that came with the process of writing this book. I love you guys!

From Carol: Thank you, Rusty, for always being there for me with love and support! And Russell and Kristin, your love and encouraging words were (and still are) very important to me! I love you all!

About the Authors

Keri E. Pearlson

Dr. Keri E. Pearlson is Research Director at the Research Board, a private, global think tank for CIOs. She is also president of KP Partners, a consultancy specializing in research and teaching managers and business students through executive education programs, seminars, briefings, and management coaching in the area of strategic use of information systems and organizational design.

Dr. Pearlson has held various positions in academia and industry. She was a member of the information systems faculty at the Graduate School of Business at the University of Texas at Austin, where she taught management information systems courses to MBAs and executives. She was also a research affiliate with CSC-Research Services, where she conducted several studies, including one on the design and execution of mobile organizations and another on e-learning. She has also held positions at the Harvard Business School, CSC-Index's Prism Group, AT&T, and Hughes Aircraft Company.

Her research activities involve topics spanning management of information systems and organizational design. She is co-author of *Zero Time: Providing Instant Customer Value—Every Time, All the Time* (John Wiley & Sons, July 2000) and has published articles and case studies on a variety of MIS issues, including mobility, telecommuting, virtual organizations, e-learning, business process redesign, outsourcing, and customer service support systems. Her work has been published in *Sloan Management Review, Academy of Management Executive, Information Resources Management Journal*, and *Beyond Computing*. Many of her case studies have been published by Harvard Business School Publishing and are used all over the world.

Dr. Pearlson holds a Doctorate in Business Administration (DBA) in Management Information Systems from the Harvard Business School and both a Masters Degree in Industrial Engineering Management and a Bachelors Degree in Applied Mathematics from Stanford University.

Carol S. Saunders

Dr. Carol S. Saunders is professor of MIS at the University of Central Florida in Orlando, Florida. She served as General Conference Chair of the International Conference on Information Systems (ICIS) in 1999 and Telecommuting in 1996. She was the chair of the ICIS Executive Committee in 2000. Currently she is a senior editor of *MIS Quarterly* and *e-Service Journal*, and is an associate editor of

Decision Sciences Journal, Information Systems Research, and *Communications of the AIS.* Her current research interests include electronic commerce, the impact of information systems on power and communication, virtual teams, and interorganizational linkages. Her research is published in a number of journals including *MIS Quarterly, Information Systems Research, Journal of MIS, Communications of the ACM, Academy of Management Journal, Academy of Management Review, Communications Research,* and *Organization Science.*

Dr. Saunders holds a Ph.D. in Organizational Behavior and Management from the University of Houston. Her M.B.A. is from the University of North Carolina at Chapel Hill and her Bachelors Degree in Mathematics and German is from Florida State University. In addition to her academic positions, Dr. Saunders has worked for IBM and EXXON Company, U.S.A.

INTRODUCTION

Why do managers need to understand and participate in the information decisions of their organizations? After all, most corporations maintain entire departments dedicated to the management of information systems (IS). These departments are staffed with highly skilled professionals devoted to the field of technology. Shouldn't managers rely on experts to analyze all the aspects of IS and to make the best decisions for the organization? The answer to that question is no. Managing information is a critical skill for success in today's business environment. All decisions made by companies involve, at some level, the management and use of IS. Managers today need to know about their organization's capabilities and uses of information as much as they need to understand how to obtain and budget financial resources. The explosive growth of personal computers (PCs) and the Internet highlights this fact, because together they form the backbone for virtually all new business models. A manager who does not understand the basics of managing and using information cannot be successful in this business environment.

Consider the now historic rise of companies such as Amazon.com and Expedia. Amazon.com started out as an online bookseller and rapidly outpaced traditional brick-and-mortar businesses like Barnes and Noble, Borders, and Waterstones. Management at the traditional companies responded by having their IS support personnel build Web sites to compete. But upstart Amazon.com moved on ahead, keeping its leadership position on the Web by leveraging its new business model into other marketplaces, such as music, electronics, health and beauty products, lawn and garden products, auctions, tools and hardware, and more. It cleared the profitability hurdle in the fourth quarter of 2001 by achieving a good mix of IS and business basics: capitalizing on operational efficiencies derived from inventory software and smarter storage, cost cutting, and effectively partnering with such companies as Toys "R" Us Inc. and Target Corporation.[1] Likewise, Expedia is playing an important role in revolutionizing the travel industry by simultaneously getting the business basics right and implementing information systems. In 2001 it invested heavily in information technology—about $120 million—to allow customers to bundle airfares, car rentals, hotel reservations, and other travel arrangements. Just a year earlier, it moved from an agent model to a merchant-based model that books

[1] Robert Hof, "How Amazon Cleared the Profitability Hurdle," *BusinessWeek Online* (February 4, 2002), available at http://www.businessweek.com/magazine/content/02_05/b3768079.htm. (accessed on May 23, 2002)

1

hotel rooms and airline seats on consignment. This shift allowed Expedia to earn much higher profits per transaction as a result.[2]

E-businesses were able to succeed where traditional companies were not, in part because their management understood the power of information, IS, and the Internet. They did not succeed because their managers could build Web pages or assemble an IS network. Quite the contrary. The executives in these new businesses understood the fundamentals of managing and using information and could marry that knowledge with a sound, unique business vision to achieve domination of their intended market spaces.

The goal of this book is to provide the foundation for making the general business manager a knowledgeable participant in IS decisions, because any IS decision in which the manager does not participate can greatly affect the organization's ability to succeed in the future. This introduction outlines the fundamental reasons for taking the initiative to participate in IS decisions. Moreover, because effective participation requires a particular set of managerial skills, this introduction identifies the most important ones, recognizing that they will be helpful not just in making IS decisions, but all business decisions. It describes how a manager should participate in the decision-making process, and outlines how the remaining chapters of this book develop this point of view. Finally, the introduction presents current models for understanding the nature of a business and that of an information system in order to provide a framework for the discussions that follow in subsequent chapters.

▶ THE CASE FOR PARTICIPATING IN DECISIONS ABOUT INFORMATION SYSTEMS

Experience shows that business managers have no problem participating in most organizational decisions, even those outside their normal business expertise. For example, ask a plant manager about marketing problems and the result will probably be a detailed opinion on both key issues and recommended solutions. Dialogue among managers routinely crosses all business functions in formal as well as informal settings, with one general exception: IS. Management continues to tolerate ignorance in this area relative to other specialized business functions. Culturally, managers can claim ignorance of IS issues without losing prestige among colleagues. On the other hand, admitting a lack of knowledge regarding marketing or financial aspects of the business will earn colleagues' contempt.

These attitudes are attributable to the historic role that IS played in businesses. For many years, technology was regarded as a support function and treated as administrative overhead. Its value as a factor in important management decisions was minimal. And it often took a great deal of technical knowledge to understand even the most basic concepts. However, in today's business environment, maintaining this back-office view of technology is certain to cost market share and could ultimately lead to the failure of the organization. Technology has become entwined

---

[2] Eric Hellweg, "It's Not Just Amazon. These Net Businesses Are Profitable," *Business2.0* (February 12, 2002), available at http://www.business2.com/articles/web/print/0,650,37921,00.html. (accessed on May 23, 2002)

with all the classic functions of business—operations, marketing, accounting, finance—to such an extent that understanding its role is necessary for making intelligent and effective decisions about any of them. Furthermore, a general understanding of key IS concepts is possible without the extensive technological knowledge required just a few years ago.

Therefore, understanding basic fundamentals about using and managing information is worth the investment of time. The reasons for this investment are summarized in Figure I.1 and discussed next.

A Business View

Information technology (IT) is a critical resource for today's businesses. It both supports and consumes a significant amount of an organization's resources. Just like the other three major types of business resources—people, money, and machines—it needs to be managed wisely. IT now accounts for more than 50 percent of the capital-goods dollars spent in the United States. According to a recent Gartner Group survey, this expenditure translates into more than $7,500 annually per employee. In addition, high-growth firms continue to increase their investments in IS and other types of IT investments. These resources must return value, or they will be invested elsewhere. The business manager, not the IS specialist, decides which activities receive funding, estimates the risk associated with the investment, and develops metrics for evaluating the performance of the investment. Therefore, the business manager needs a basic grounding in managing and using information. On the flip side, IS managers need a business view.

People and Technology Work Together

In addition to financial issues, a manager must know how to mesh technology and people to create effective work. Technology facilitates the work that people do. Correctly incorporating IS into the design of a business enables people to focus their time and resources on issues that bear directly on customer satisfaction and other revenue and profit-generating activities. Adding IS to an existing organization, however, requires the ability to manage change. The skilled business manager must balance the benefits of using new technology with the costs associated with changing existing behaviors of people in the workplace. Making this assessment does not require a detailed technical knowledge. It does require an understanding

Reasons

IS must be managed as a critical resource.

IS enable change in the way people work together.

IS integrate with almost every aspect of business.

IS enable business opportunities and new strategies.

IS can be used to combat business challenges from competitors.

FIGURE I.1   Reasons why business managers should participate in information systems decisions.

of what the short-term and long-term consequences are likely to be and why adopting new technology may be more appropriate in some instances than in others. Understanding these issues also helps managers know when it may prove effective to replace people with technology at certain steps in a process.

Integrating Business with Technology

IS are now integrated with almost every aspect of business. For example, as CEO of Wal-Mart Stores' International, Bob L. Martin described IS's role, "Today technology plays a role in almost everything we do, for every aspect of customer service to customizing our store formats or matching our merchandising strategies to individual markets in order to meet varied customer preferences."[3] IS place information in the hands of Wal-Mart associates so that decisions can be made closer to the customer. IS help simplify organizational activities and processes such as moving goods, stocking shelves, or communicating with suppliers.

Rapid Change in Technology

The proliferation of new technologies creates a business environment filled with opportunities. Even today, new uses of the Internet produce new types of e-businesses that keep every manager and executive on alert. New business opportunities spring up with little advanced warning. The manager's role is to frame these opportunities so that others can understand them, to evaluate them against existing business needs, and finally to pursue any that fit with an articulated business strategy. The quality of the information at hand affects the quality of both the decision and its implementation. Managers must develop an understanding of what information is crucial to the decision, how to get it, and how to use it. They must lead the changes driven by IS.

Competitive Challenges

Competitors come from both expected and unexpected places. General managers are in the best position to see the emerging threats and utilize IS effectively to combat ever-changing competitive challenges. Further, general managers are often called upon to demonstrate a clear understanding of how their own technology programs and products compare with those of their competitors.

▶ WHAT IF A MANAGER DOESN'T PARTICIPATE?

Decisions about IS directly impact the profits of a business. The basic formula PROFIT = REVENUE – EXPENSES can be used to evaluate the impact of these decisions. Adopting the wrong technologies can cause a company to miss business opportunities and any revenues they would generate. Inadequate IS can cause a breakdown in servicing customers, which hurts sales. On the expense side, a poorly calculated investment in technology can lead to overspending and excess capacity.

[3] "The End of Delegation?: Information Technology and the CEO," *Harvard Business Review* (September–October 1995), p. 161.

Inefficient business processes sustained by ill-fitting IS also increase expenses. Lags in implementation or poor process adaptation each reduce profits and therefore growth. IS decisions can dramatically affect the bottom line.

Failure to consider IS strategy when planning business strategy and organizational strategy leads to one of three business consequences: (1) IS that fail to support business goals, (2) IS that fail to support organizational systems, and (3) a misalignment between business and organizational strategies. These consequences are discussed briefly in this section and in more detail in later chapters. While examining IS-related consequences in greater detail, consider their potential effects on an organization's ability to achieve its business goals. How would each consequence change the way people work? Which customers would be most affected and how? Would the organization still be able to implement its business strategy?

Information Systems Must Support Business Goals

IS represent a major investment for any firm in today's business environment. Yet poorly chosen IS can actually become an obstacle to achieving business goals. If the systems do not allow the organization to realize its goals, or if IS lack the capacity needed to collect, store, and transfer critical information for the business, the results can be disastrous. Customers will be dissatisfied or even lost. Production costs may be excessive. Worst of all, management may not be able to pursue desired business directions that are blocked by inappropriate IS. Toys "R" Us experienced such a calamity when its well-publicized Web site was unable to process and fulfill orders fast enough. It not only lost those customers, it had a major customer relations issue to manage as a result. Consider the well-intended Web designer who was charged with building a Web site to disseminate information to investors, customers, and potential customers. If the business goal is to do business over the Web, then the decision to build an informational Web site, rather than a transactional Web site, is misdirected and could potentially cost the company customers by not taking orders online. Even though it is possible to redesign the Web site, the task requires expending additional resources that might have been saved if business goals and IS strategy were discussed together.

Information Systems Must Support Organizational Systems

Organizational systems represent the fundamental elements of a business—its people, work processes, and structure—and the plan that enables them to work efficiently to achieve business goals. If the company's IS fail to support its organizational systems, the result is a misalignment of the resources needed to achieve its goals. It seems odd to think a manager might put a computer on the desk of every employee without providing the training these same employees need to use the tool effectively, and yet this mistake—and many more costly ones—occur in businesses every day. Managers make major decisions, such as switching to new major IS, without informing all the affected staff of necessary changes in their daily work. For example, when companies put in an enterprise resource planning (ERP) system, the system often dictates how many business processes are executed.

Deploying technology without thinking through how it actually will be used in the organization—who will use it, how they will use it, how to make sure the applications chosen actually accomplish what is intended—results in significant expense without a lot to show for it. The general manager, who, after all, is charged with ensuring that company resources are used effectively, must ensure that the company's IS support its organizational systems and that changes made in one system are reflected in other related systems. For example, a company that plans to institute a wide-scale telecommuting program needs an information system strategy compatible with that organization strategy. Desktop PCs located within the corporate office are not the right solution for a telecommuting organization. Instead, laptop computers, applications that are accessible anywhere and anytime, and networks that facilitate information sharing are needed. If the organization only allows the purchase of desktop PCs and only builds systems accessible from desks within the office, the telecommuting program is doomed to failure.

▶ WHAT SKILLS ARE NEEDED TO PARTICIPATE EFFECTIVELY IN INFORMATION TECHNOLOGY DECISIONS?

Participating in IT decisions means bringing a clear set of skills to the table. Managers are asked to take on tasks that require different skills at different times. Those tasks can be divided into visionary tasks, or tasks that provide leadership and direction for the group; informational/interpersonal tasks, or tasks that provide information and knowledge the group needs to have to be successful; and structured tasks, tasks that organize the group. Figure I.2 lists basic skills required of managers who wish to participate successfully in key IT decisions. This list emphasizes understanding, organizing, planning, and solving the business needs of the organization. Individuals who want to develop fully as managers will find this an excellent checklist for professional growth.

These skills may not look much different from those required of any successful manager, which is the main point of this book: General managers can be successful participants in IS decisions without an extensive technical background. General managers who understand a basic set of IS concepts and who have outstanding managerial skills, such as those in Figure I.2, are ready for the digital economy.

How to Participate in Information Systems Decisions

Technical wizardry is not required to become a knowledgeable participant in the IS decisions of a business. What a manager needs includes curiosity, creativity, and the confidence to question in order to learn and understand. A solid framework that identifies key management issues and relates them to aspects of IS provides the background needed to participate.

The goal of this book is to provide this framework. The way in which managers use and manage information is directly linked to business goals and the business strategy that drive both organizational and IS decisions. Business,

Managerial Role	Skill
Visionary	**Creativity**—the ability to transform resources and create something entirely new to the organization
	Curiosity—the ability to question and learn about new ideas, applications, technologies, and business models
	Confidence—the ability to believe in oneself and assert one's ideas at the proper time
	Focus on Business Solutions—the ability to bring experience and insight to bear on current business opportunities and challenges
	Flexibility—the ability to change rapidly and effectively, such as by adapting work processes, shifting perspectives on an issue, or adjusting a plan to achieve a new goal
Informational and Interpersonal	**Communication**—the ability to share thoughts through text, images, and speech
	Information gathering—the ability to gather thoughts of others through listening, reading and observing
	Interpersonal skills—the ability to cooperate and collaborate with others on a team, among groups, or across a chain of command to achieve results
Structured	**Project management**—the ability to plan, organize, direct, and control company resources to effectively complete a project
	Analytical skills—the ability to break down a whole into its elements for ease of understanding and analysis
	Organizational skills—the ability to bring together distinct elements and combine them into an effective whole
	Planning skills—the ability to develop objectives and to allocate resources to ensure objectives are met

FIGURE I.2 Skills of successful managers.

organizational, and information strategies are fundamentally linked in what is called the Information Systems Strategy Triangle. Failing to understand this relationship is detrimental to a business. Failing to plan for the consequences in all three areas can cost a manager his or her job. This book provides managers with a foundation for understanding business issues related to IS from a managerial perspective.

Organization of the Book

In order to be a knowledgeable participant, managers must know about both using information and managing information. Part I offers basic frameworks to make this understanding easier. Chapter 1 explains the Information Systems Strategy Triangle and provides a brief overview of relevant frameworks for business strategy and organizational strategy. It is provided as background for those who have not formally studied organization theory or business strategy. For those who have studied these areas, this chapter is a brief refresher of major concepts used throughout the remaining chapters of the book. Subsequent chapters provide frameworks and sets of examples for understanding the links between IT and business strategy (Chapter 2), organizational forms (Chapter 3), individual work (Chapter 4), and business process transformation (Chapter 5).

Part II looks at issues related to building IS strategy itself. Chapter 6 provides a framework for understanding the four components of IS architecture: hardware, software, networks, and data. Chapter 7 discusses doing business on the Internet. Chapter 8 looks at ways in which people are organized to run an IS department. Chapter 9 focuses on the economics of managing IT. Chapter 10 discusses what IS projects are, why they need managing, and how to manage them. Chapter 11 provides an overview of how to manage knowledge and why managing knowledge is different from managing information. Finally, Chapter 12 presents some of the ethical issues that need to be considered.

▶ BASIC ASSUMPTIONS

Every book is based on certain assumptions, and understanding those assumptions makes a difference in interpretating the text. The first assumption made by this text is that managers must be knowledgeable participants in the IS decisions made within and affecting their organizations. That means that the general manager must have a basic understanding of the business and technology issues related to IS. Because technology changes rapidly, this text also assumes that the technology of today is different from the technology of yesterday, and, most likely, the technology available to readers of this text today differs significantly from that available when the text was written. Therefore, this text focuses on generic concepts that are, to the extent possible, technology independent. It provides a framework on which to hang more current information, such as new uses of the Internet or new networking technologies. It is assumed that the reader will seek out current sources to learn about the latest and greatest technology.

A second assumption is that the role of a general manager and the role of an IS manager are distinct. The general manager must have a basic knowledge of IS in order to make decisions that may have serious implications for the business. In addition to a general business knowledge, the IS manager must have a more in-depth knowledge of technology in order to manage the IS and to be of assistance to general managers who must use the information. Assumptions are also made about how business is done, and what IS are in general. Knowing what assumptions are made about each will support an understanding of the material to come.

Assumptions about Management

The classic view of managing describes four activities, each dependent on the others: planning, organizing, leading, and controlling (see Figure I.3). A manager performs these activities with the people and resources of the organization in order to attain the established goals of the business. Conceptually, this simple model provides a framework of the key tasks of management, which is useful for both general business as well as IS management activities. Although many books have been written describing each of these activities, organizational theorist Henry Mintzberg offers a view that most closely details the perspective relevant to IS management.

Mintzberg's model describes management in behavioral terms by categorizing the three major roles a manager fills: interpersonal, informational, and decisional (see Figure I.4). This model is useful because it considers the chaotic nature of the environment in which managers actually work. Managers rarely have time to be reflective in their approaches to problems. They work at an unrelenting pace, and their activities are brief and often interrupted. Thus, quality information becomes even more crucial to effective decision making. The classic view is often seen as a tactical approach to management, while some describe Mintzberg's view as a more strategic view.

Assumptions about Business

Everyone has an internal understanding of what constitutes a business, which is based on readings and experiences in different firms. This understanding forms a

Classic Management Model	
Planning	Managers think through their goals and actions in advance. Their actions are usually based on some method, plan, or logic, rather than a hunch or gut feeling.
Organizing	Managers coordinate the human and material resources of the organization. The effectiveness of an organization depends on its ability to direct its resources to attain its goals.
Leading	Managers direct and influence subordinates, getting others to perform essential tasks. By establishing the proper atmosphere, they help their subordinates do their best.
Controlling	Managers attempt to assure that the organization is moving toward its goal. If part of their organization is on the wrong track, managers try to find out why and set things right.

FIGURE I.3 Classic management model.
Source: Adapted from James A. F. Stoner, *Management,* 2nd ed. (Upper Saddle River, N.J.: Prentice–Hall, 1982).

Type of Roles	Manager's Roles	IS Examples
Interpersonal	Figurehead	CEO greets touring dignitaries.
	Leader	IS manager puts in long hours to help motivate project team to complete project on schedule in an environment of heavy budget cuts.
	Liaison	Chief information officer works with the marketing and human resource vice presidents to make sure that the reward and compensation system is changed to encourage use of new IS supporting sales.
Informational	Monitor	Division manager compares progress on IS project for the division with milestones developed during the project's initiation and feasibility phase.
	Disseminator	Chief information officer conveys organization's business strategy to IS department and demonstrates how IS strategy supports the business strategy.
	Spokesperson	IS manager represents IS department at organization's recruiting fair.
Decisional	Entrepreneur	Division manager suggests an application of a new technology that improves the division's operational efficiency.
	Disturbance handler	Division manager, as project team leader, helps resolve design disagreements between division personnel who will be using the system and systems analysts who are designing it.
	Resource allocator	CEO allocates additional personnel positions to various departments based upon business strategy.
	Negotiator	IS manager negotiates for additional personnel needed to respond to recent user requests for enhanced functionality in a system that is being implemented.

FIGURE I.4 Manager's roles.
Source: Adapted from H. Mintzberg, *The Nature of Managerial Work* (New York: Harper & Row, 1973).

model that provides the basis for comprehending actions, interpreting decisions, and communicating ideas. Managers use their internal model to make sense of otherwise chaotic and random activities. This book uses several conceptual models of business. Some take a functional view and others take a process view.

Functional View

The classical view of a business is based on the functions that people perform, such as accounting, finance, marketing, operations, and human resources. The business organizes around these functions to coordinate them and to gain economies of scale within specialized sets of tasks. Information first flows vertically up and down between line positions and management; after analysis it may be transmitted across other functions for use elsewhere in the company (see Figure I.5).

Process View

Michael Porter of Harvard University describes a business in terms of the primary and support activities that are performed to create, deliver, and support a product or service (see Figure I.6). The primary activities of inbound logistics, operations, outbound logistics, marketing and sales, and service are chained together in sequences that describe how a business transforms its raw materials into value-creating products. This value chain is supported by common activities shared across all the primary activities. For example, general management and legal services are distributed among the primary activities. Improving coordination among activities increases business profit. Organizations that effectively manage core processes across functional boundaries will be winners in the marketplace. IS are often the key to this process improvement and cross-functional coordination.

Both of the process and functional views are important to understanding IS. The functional view is useful when similar activities must be explained, coordinated, executed, or communicated. For example, understanding a marketing information system means understanding the functional approach to business in general and the marketing function in particular. The process view, on the other hand, is useful when examining the flow of information throughout a business. For example, understanding the information associated with order fulfillment or product development or customer service means taking a process view of the business. This text assumes that both views are important for participating in IS decisions.

Assumptions about Information Systems

Consider the components of an information system from the manager's viewpoint, rather than from the technologist's viewpoint. Both the nature of information and the context of an information system must be examined to understand the basic assumptions of this text.

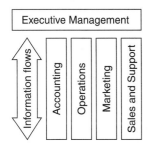

FIGURE I.5 Hierarchical view of the firm.

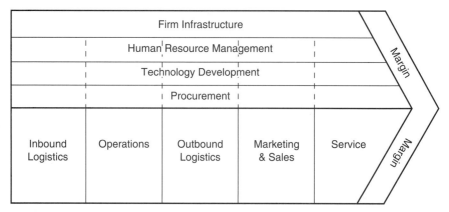

FIGURE I.6 Process view of the firm: the value chain.
Source: M. Porter, *Competitive Advantage* (New York: Free Press, 1985).

Information Hierarchy

The terms *data, information,* and *knowledge* are often used interchangeably, but have significant and discrete meanings within the knowledge management domain. Tom Davenport, in his book *Information Ecology,* points out that getting everyone in any given organization to agree on common definitions is difficult. However, his work (summarized in Figure I.7) provides a nice starting point for understanding the subtle, but important differences.

The information hierarchy begins with data, or simple observations. **Data** are a set of specific, objective facts or observations, such as "inventory contains 45 units." Standing alone, such facts have no intrinsic meaning, but can be easily captured, transmitted, and stored electronically.

Information is data endowed with relevance and purpose.[4] People turn data into information by organizing it into some unit of analysis (e.g., dollars, dates, or customers). Deciding on the appropriate unit of analysis involves interpreting the context of the data and summarizing it into a more condensed form. Consensus must be reached on the unit of analysis.

To be relevant and have a purpose, information must be considered within the context that it is received and used. Because of differences in context, information needs vary across the function and hierarchical level. For example when considering functional differences related to a sales transaction, a marketing department manager may be interested in the demographic characteristics of buyers, such as their age, gender, and home address. A manager in the accounting department probably won't be interested in any of these details, but instead will want to know details about the transaction itself, such as method of payment and date of payment. Similarly, information needs may vary across hierarchical level. These needs

[4] Peter F. Drucker, "The Coming of the New Organization," *Harvard Business Review* (January–February 1988), pp. 45–53.

	Data	Information	Knowledge
Definition	Simple observations of the state of the world	Data endowed with relevance and purpose	Information from the human mind (includes reflection, synthesis, context)
Characteristics	• Easily structured • Easily captured on machines • Often quantified • Easily transferred • Mere facts	• Requires unit of analysis • Data that have been processed • Human mediation necessary	• Hard to structure • Difficult to capture on machines • Often tacit • Hard to transfer
Example	Daily inventory report of all inventory items sent to the CEO of a large manufacturing company	Daily inventory report of items that are below economic order quantity levels sent to inventory manager	Inventory manager knowing which items need to be reordered in light of daily inventory report, anticipated labor strikes, and a flood in Brazil that affects the supply of a major component.

FIGURE I.7   Comparison of Data, Information, and Knowledge
Source: Adapted from Thomas Davenport, *Information Ecology* (New York: Oxford University Press, 1997).

are summarized in Figure I.8 and reflect the different activities performed at each level. At the supervisory level, activities are narrow in scope and focused on production or the execution of the business's basic transactions. At this level, information is focused on day-to-day activities that are internally oriented and accurately defined in a detailed manner. The activities of senior management are much broader in their scope. Senior management performs long-term planning and needs information that is aggregated, externally oriented, and more subjective. The information needs of middle managers in terms of these characteristics fall between the needs of supervisors and senior management. Because information needs vary across levels, a daily inventory report of a large manufacturing firm may serve as information for a low-level inventory manager, whereas the CEO would consider such a report to be merely data. A report does not necessarily mean information. The context in which the report is used must be considered.

Knowledge is information synthesized and contextualized to provide value. It is information with the most value. Knowledge consists of a mix of contextual information, values, experiences, and rules. It is richer and deeper than information, and more valuable because someone thought deeply about that information and added his or her own unique experience, judgment, and wisdom. Knowledge

	Top Management	Middle Management	Supervisory and Lower-Level Management
Time Horizon	Long: years	Medium: weeks, months, years	Short: day to day
Level of Detail	Highly aggregated	Summarized	Very detailed
	Less accurate	Integrated	Very accurate
	More predictive	Often financial	Often nonfinancial
Orientation	Primarily external	Primarily internal with limited external	Internal
Decision	Extremely judgmental	Relatively judgmental	Heavy reliance on rules
	Uses creativity and analytical skills		

FIGURE I.8 Information characteristics across hierarchical level.

also involves the synthesis of multiple sources of information over time.[5] The amount of human contribution increases along the continuum from data to information to knowledge. Computers work well for managing data, but are less efficient at managing information.

System Hierarchy

An information system comprises three main elements: technology, people, and process (see Figure I.9). When most people use the term *information system,* they actually refer only to the technology element as defined by the organization's infrastructure. In this text the term **infrastructure** refers to everything that supports the flow and processing of information in an organization, including hardware, software, data, and network components, while **architecture** refers to the strategy implicit in these components. These ideas will be discussed in greater detail in Chapter 6. **Information system** is defined more broadly as the *combination* of technology (the "what"), people (the "who"), and process (the "how") that an organization uses to produce and manage information. In contrast, information technology (IT) focuses only on the technical devices and tools used in the system. We define **information technology** as all forms of technology used to create, store, exchange, and use information.

Above the information system itself is management, which oversees the design and structure of the system and monitors its overall performance. Management develops the business requirements and the business strategy that the information system is meant to satisfy. The system's architecture provides a blueprint that translates this strategy into components, or infrastructure.[6]

[5] Thomas H. Davenport, *Information Ecology* (New York: Oxford University Press, 1997), pp. 9–10.
[6] Gordon Hay and Rick Muñoz, "Establishing an IT Architecture Strategy," *Information Systems Management* (Summer 1997).

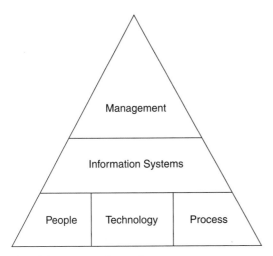

FIGURE I.9 System hierarchy.

▶ SUMMARY

The explosive growth of Internet-based businesses highlights the need for all managers to be skilled in managing and using IS. It is no longer acceptable to delegate IS decisions to the management information systems (MIS) department alone. The general manager must be involved to both execute business plans and protect options for future business vision. This chapter makes the case for general managers' full participation in strategic business decisions concerning IT. It outlines the skills required for such participation, and it makes explicit certain key assumptions about the nature of business, management, and IS that will underlie the remaining discussions. Subsequent chapters are designed to build on these concepts by addressing the following questions:

PART I. FRAMEWORKS AND FOUNDATIONS

- How should information strategy be aligned with business and organizational strategies? (Chapter 1)
- How can a business achieve competitive advantages using its IS? (Chapter 2)
- What does it mean to align IT decisions with organizational decisions? (Chapter 3)
- How is the job of the individual in an organization affected by decisions concerning IS? (Chapter 4)
- How might IS enable business transformation? (Chapter 5)

PART II. IS MANAGEMENT ISSUES

- What are the components of an IT architecture? (Chapter 6)
- How can electronic commerce contribute to business goals? (Chapter 7)
- What is an IS organization? What are the components of IS strategy? How can a manager effectively manage IS? (Chapter 8)

- How are IS funded within an organization? What are the total costs of ownership of IS? (Chapter 9)
- What does it mean to manage a project? (Chapter 10)
- How should knowledge be managed within an organization? (Chapter 11)
- What ethical and moral considerations bind the uses of information in business? (Chapter 12)

▶ KEY TERMS

architecture (p. 14)	information system (p. 14)	infrastructure (p. 14)
data (p. 12)	information technology	knowledge (p. 13)
information (p. 12)	(p. 14)	

▶ DISCUSSION QUESTIONS

1. Why is it important for a general manager to be knowledgeable about information technology?

2. Indicate whether each of the following is information, data, or knowledge:

   a. A daily sales report of each sales transaction that is sent to the chief operating officer

   b. A daily sales report of each sales transaction over $100,000 that is sent to the division marketing manager

   c. A monthly production report that is sent to shop floor supervisors who don't use the report because they believe the figures reported are outdated and inaccurate

   d. An exception report of all accounts that are more than 90 days past-due, which is sent to the Accounts Receivable Manager

   e. A list of Social Security numbers

CASE STUDY I-1

PAT CANNON, MBA*

Pat Cannon, a typical MBA, was about to graduate from a top-ten business school with an MBA and a desire to change the world while growing a significant savings account. Pat was debating among three job opportunities, each of which would be a big step up the professional ladder from the associates job he held when working for Impressive Consulting Group (ICG) prior to returning to school to get an MBA. Pat wasn't sure which job to take, in part because he didn't feel the MBA classes at the business school had been enough preparation in information systems.

Pat started business school after four years' of experience at Impressive Consulting Group (ICG), a global consulting organization with practices in virtually every major city

*The names in this case are fictitious. This case is written to highlight administrative issues relevant to general managers, and any resemblance to real individuals or organizations is coincidental.

in the world. Pat worked in the Dallas office as an associate right out of undergraduate school. Pat's undergraduate degree was in business with a concentration in marketing, and he had worked on a number of interesting strategic marketing projects while at ICG. Pat was just completing a standard MBA program after two years of full-time study, and a summer working for MFG Corporation, a large manufacturing company in the Midwest. The internship at MFG Corporation involved working with the new Web marketing group, which Pat chose in order to see just how a company like MFG takes advantage of the Web. At the same time, Pat hoped to become more proficient in Web and Internet technologies. The experience at MFG's Web marketing group, however, only made Pat more anxious, highlighting to him how much more was involved in information systems and the Web than he had previously thought. Pat returned to business school in the fall of the second year wondering just how much information systems knowledge would be needed in future jobs. Further, he felt that becoming a knowledgeable participant in information decisions was critical to success in the fast-paced Internet-based business world awaiting him after graduation.

Pat wondered just what type of information systems knowledge was needed for each of the three jobs he was considering. All three jobs involved competitive salary, signing bonus, and stock/retirement benefits, so the decision came down to the knowledge needed to be a success on the job. The three jobs are summarized as follows.

1. *Return to ICG as a consultant.* This job was attractive to Pat because it meant returning to his former employer. Pat had left in good standing and liked the company that rewarded innovation and supported learning and growth among consultants. Pat figured a partnership was possible in the future if he joined ICG after business school. As a consultant, Pat could live wherever he desired, and travel to the client site four days a week. The fifth day each week, Pat would be able to work at home, or if desired, in a company office. As a consultant, Pat initially thought engagements in strategic marketing would be the most interesting. ICG had a strong programming group that was brought into each engagement to do the programming and systems analysis work. The consultant role involved understanding client concerns and assisting in building a marketing strategy. Virtually all of the projects would have some Internet component, if not entirely about building an Internet presence. This challenge interested Pat, but based on his summer job experience, he wondered just how much technical skill would be required of the consultants in this arena.

2. *Join start-up InfoMicro.* Several of Pat's friends from business school were joining together to form a new start-up company on the Internet. This business plan for this company projected that InfoMicro would be one of only two Internet start-ups in their marketplace, giving the company good position and great opportunity for growth. The business plan showed the company intending to go public through an IPO as early as three years after inception, and Pat believed they could do it. Pat would join as VP of marketing, supplementing the other three friends who would hold president, VP of finance, and VP of operations positions. The friends who would be president and finance VP were just completing a techno-MBA at Pat's school, and would provide the technical competence needed to get InfoMicro on the Web. Pat would focus on developing customers and setting marketing strategy, eventually building an organization to support that operation as necessary. Because InfoMicro was a Web-based business, Pat felt a significant amount of information systems knowledge would be required of a successful marketing executive.

3. *Return to MFG Corporation.* The job would be to join the marketing department as a manager responsible for new customer development. Many of MFG corporation's customers were older, established companies like MFG Corporation itself, but new customers were likely to be start-ups, newer, up-and-coming companies, or highly successful new companies like Cisco or Dell. Pat felt that some knowledge of information systems would be necessary simply to provide innovative interaction mechanisms such as customer Web pages. Pat knew that discussions with the MFG information systems group would be necessary in order to build these new interfaces. How knowledgeable must Pat be of information systems issues in order to hold this job?

As spring break approached, Pat knew a decision had to be made. Recruiters from all three companies had given Pat a deadline of the end of break week, and Pat wasn't at all sure which job to take. All sounded interesting, and all were reasonable alternatives for Pat's next career move.

Discussion Questions

1. For each position Pat is considering, what types of information systems knowledge do you think Pat would need?

2. How could Pat be a knowledgeable participant in each of the three jobs? What would it mean to be a knowledgeable participant in each job? Give an example for each job.

3. As a marketing major and an MBA, is Pat prepared for the work world awaiting? Why or why not?

CHAPTER ▶ 1

THE INFORMATION SYSTEMS STRATEGY TRIANGLE

National Linen Service, a supplier of linen for restaurants and hotels, found itself facing poor earnings due to increased competition and a weak economy. The company decided to create a strategic systems department in an attempt to increase its competitiveness and lower costs. The new systems department installed a program called Boss. Unfortunately, rather than notifying the contract department when customer contracts expired, Boss was programmed to simply drop expired customers from the database. Needless to say, National Linen's bottom line worsened. National Linen Service failed to take into account the unintended consequences of installing an information system and the effects it would have on its business strategy and organizational design.

This case emphasizes the point made in the Introduction: It is imperative that general managers take a role in decisions about information systems (IS). Even though it is not necessary for a general manager to understand all technologies, it is necessary to aggressively seek to understand the consequences of using technologies relevant to the business's environment. General managers who leave the IS decisions solely to their IS professionals often put themselves and their companies at a disadvantage. Although IS can facilitate the movement and exchange of information, an information system that is inappropriate for a given operating environment can actually inhibit and confuse that same exchange. A management information system (MIS) is not an island within a firm. MIS manages an infrastructure that is essential to the firm's functioning.

This chapter introduces a simple framework for understanding the impact of IS on organizations. This framework is called the **Information Systems Strategy Triangle** because it relates business strategy with IS strategy and organizational strategy. This chapter also presents key frameworks from organization theory that describe the context in which MIS operates, as well as the business imperatives that MIS supports. Students with extensive background in organizational behavior and business strategy will find this a useful review of key concepts. The Information Systems Strategy Triangle presented in Figure 1.1 suggests three key points about strategy.

19

FIGURE 1.1   The Information Systems Strategy Triangle

Successful firms have an overriding business strategy that drives both organizational strategy and IS strategy. The decisions made regarding the structure, hiring practices, and other components of the organizational strategy, as well as decisions regarding applications, hardware, and other IS components, are all driven by the firm's business objectives, strategies, and tactics. Successful firms carefully balance these three strategies—they purposely design their organization and their IS strategies to complement their business strategy.

IS strategy can itself affect and is affected by changes in a firm's business and organizational strategies. In order to perpetuate the balance needed for successful operation, changes in the IS strategy must be accompanied by changes in both the organizational and overall business strategy. If a firm designs its business strategy to use IS to gain strategic advantage, the leadership position in IS can only be sustained by constant innovation. The business, IS, and organizational strategies must constantly be adjusted.

IS strategy always involves consequences—intended or not—within business and organizational strategies. Avoiding harmful unintended consequences means remembering to consider business and organizational strategies when designing IS deployment. For example, placing computers on employee desktops without an accompanying set of changes to job descriptions, process design, compensation plans, and business tactics will fail to produce the anticipated productivity improvements. Success can only be achieved by specifically designing all three components of the strategy triangle.

A word of explanation is needed. This chapter and subsequent chapters in this book address questions of IS strategy squarely within the context of business strategy. Studying business strategy alone is something better done in other texts and courses. However, to provide foundation for IS discussions, this chapter summarizes several key business strategy frameworks, as well as organizational theories. Studying IS alone does not provide general managers with the appropriate perspective. In order to be effective, managers need a solid sense of how IS are used and managed within the organization. Studying details of technologies is also outside the scope of this text. Details of the technologies are relevant, of course, and it is important that any organization maintain a sufficient knowledge base to plan for and operate applications. However, because technologies change so rapidly, keeping a text current is impossible. Therefore this text takes the perspective that understanding what questions to ask is a skill more fundamental to the general manager than understanding any particular technology. This text provides readers with an appreciation of the need to ask questions, a framework from which to derive the questions to ask, and a foundation sufficient to understand the answers received. The remaining book chapters all build upon the foundation provided in the Information Systems Strategy Triangle.

▶ BRIEF OVERVIEW OF BUSINESS STRATEGY FRAMEWORKS

A strategy is a plan. A **business strategy** is a well-articulated vision of where a business seeks to go and how it expects to get there. It is the form by which a business communicates its goals. Management constructs this plan in response to market forces, customer demands, and organizational capabilities. Market forces create the competitive situation for the business. Some markets, such as those faced by airlines, makers of personal computers, and issuers of credit cards, are characterized by many competitors and a high level of competition such that product differentiation becomes increasingly difficult. Other markets, such as those for package delivery, automobiles, and petroleum products, are similarly characterized by high competition, but product differentiation is better established. Customer demands comprise the wants and needs of the individuals and companies who purchase the products and services available in the marketplace. Organizational capabilities include the skills and experience that give the corporation a currency that can add value in the marketplace.

Several well-accepted models frame the discussions of business strategy. We review (1) the Porter generic strategies framework and two variants of its differentiation, and (2) D'Aveni's hypercompetition model.[1] The end of this section introduces key questions a general manager must answer in order to understand the strategy of the business.

The Generic Strategies Framework

Companies sell their products and services in a marketplace populated with competitors. Michael Porter's framework helps managers understand the strategies they may choose to build a competitive advantage. In his book *Competitive Advantage,* Porter claims that the "fundamental basis of above-average performance in the long run is sustainable competitive advantage."[2] Porter identifies three primary strategies for achieving competitive advantage: (1) cost leadership, (2) differentiation, and (3) focus. These advantages derive from the company's relative position in the marketplace, and they depend on the strategies and tactics employed by competitors. Figure 1.2 summarizes these three strategies for achieving competitive advantage.

Cost leadership results when the organization aims to be the lowest-cost producer in the marketplace. The organization enjoys above-average performance by

---

[1] Another popular model by Michael Porter, the value chain, provides a useful model for discussing internal operations of an organization. Some find it a useful model for understanding how to link two firms together. This framework is used in Chapter 4 to examine business process design. For further information, see Michael E. Porter, *Competitive Advantage* (New York: Free Press, 1985).

[2] Michael E. Porter, *Competitive Advantage* (New York: Free Press, 1985).

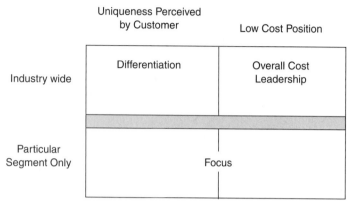

FIGURE 1.2 Three strategies for achieving competitive advantage
Source: M. Porter, *Competitive Strategies* (New York: Free Press, 1998).

minimizing costs. The product or service offered must be comparable in quality to those offered by others in the industry so that customers perceive its relative value. Typically, only one cost leader exists within an industry. If more than one organization seek advantage with this strategy, a price war ensues, which eventually may drive the organization with the higher cost structure out of the marketplace. Through mass distribution, economies of scale, and IS to generate operating efficiencies, Wal-Mart epitomizes the cost-leadership strategy.

Through **differentiation,** the organization qualifies its product or service in a way that allows it to appear unique in the marketplace. The organization identifies which qualitative dimensions are most important to its customers, and then finds ways to add value along one or more of those dimensions. In order for this strategy to work, the price charged customers by the differentiator must seem fair relative to the price charged by competitors. Typically, multiple firms in any given market employ this strategy. Progressive Insurance is able to differentiate itself from other automobile insurance companies by breaking out of the industry mold. Its representatives are available 24/7 (i.e., 24 hours a day, 7 days a week) to respond to accident claims. They arrive at an accident scene shortly after the accident with powerful laptops, intelligent software, and the authority to settle claims on the spot. This strategy spurred Progressive's growth and widened its profit margins.

Focus allows an organization to limit its scope to a narrower segment of the market and tailor its offerings to that group of customers. This strategy has two variants: (1) *cost focus*, in which the organization seeks a cost advantage within its segment, and (2) *differentiation focus*, in which it seeks to distinguish its products or services within the segment. This strategy allows the organization to achieve a local competitive advantage, even if it does not achieve competitive advantage in the marketplace overall. As Porter explains:

The focuser can thus achieve competitive advantage by dedicating itself to the segments exclusively. Breadth of target is clearly a matter of degree, but the essence of focus is the exploitation of a narrow target's differences from the balance of the industry. Narrow focus in and of itself is not sufficient for above-average performance.[3]

Marriott International demonstrates focus in the business and related IS strategies of two of its ten hotel chains. To better serve its business travelers and, at the same time, cut operational expenses, the Marriott chain is considering expanding the Marriott Reward system to include check-in kiosks. A guest could swipe a Marriott Rewards card at the kiosk in the lobby and receive a room assignment and keycard from the machine. The kiosk system would be integrated with other systems such as billing and customer relationship management (CRM) to generate operating efficiencies and enhanced corporate standardization. The kiosks would help the Marriott chain implement its cost focus.

In contrast, kiosks in the lobby would destroy the homey feeling that the Ritz-Carlton chain, acquired by Marriott in 1995, is trying to create. To the Ritz-Carlton chain, CRM means capturing and using information about guests, such as their preference for wines, a hometown newspaper, or a sunny room. Each Ritz-Carlton employee is expected to promote personalized service by identifying and recording individual guest preferences. To demonstrate how this rule could be implemented, a waiter, after hearing a guest exclaim that she loves tulips, could log the guest's comments into the Ritz-Carlton CRM system called "Class." On her next visit to a Ritz-Carlton hotel, tulips could be placed in the guest's room after querying Class to learn more about her as her visit approaches. Class, the CRM, is instrumental in helping the Ritz-Carlton chain implement its differentiation focus.[4]

Variants on the Differentiation Strategy

Porter's generic strategies are fundamental to an understanding of how organizations create competitive advantage. Several variations of his differentiation strategy, including the shareholder value model and the unlimited resources model, are useful for further analyzing sources of advantage. D'Aveni also describes these "arenas of competition" as the timing and knowledge advantage and the deep pockets advantage.

The **shareholder value model** holds that the timing of the use of specialized knowledge can create a differentiation advantage as long as the knowledge remains unique.[5] This model suggests that customers buy products or services from an organization to have access to its unique knowledge. The advantage is static, rather than dynamic, because the purchase is a one-time event.

[3] Michael E. Porter, *Competitive Strategies* (New York: Free Press, 1998).

[4] Scott Berinato, "Room for Two," CIO.com (May 15, 2002), available at http://www.cio.com/archive/051502/two_content.html.

[5] William E. Fruhan, Jr., "The NPV Model of Strategy—The Shareholder Value Model." In *Financial Strategy: Studies in the Creation, Transfer, and Destruction of Shareholder Value* (Homewood, IL: Richard D. Irwin, 1979).

The **unlimited resources model** utilizes a large base of resources that allow an organization to outlast competitors by practicing a differentiation strategy. An organization with greater resources can manage risk and sustain losses more easily than one with fewer resources. This deep-pocket strategy provides a short-term advantage only. If a firm lacks the capacity for continual innovation, it will not sustain its competitive position over time.

Porter's generic strategies model and its variants are useful for diagnostics or understanding how a business seeks to profit in its chosen marketplace, and for prescriptions, or building new opportunities for advantage. They reflect a careful balancing of countervailing competitive forces posed by buyers, suppliers, competitors, new entrants, and substitute products and services. As is the case with many models, they offer managers useful tools for thinking about strategy. However, the Porter models were developed at a time when competitive advantage was sustainable because the rate of change in any given industry was relatively slow and manageable. Since the late 1980s when this framework was at the height of its popularity, several newer models were developed to take into account the increasing turbulence and velocity of the marketplace. In particular, the hypercompetition model offers managers an especially useful tool for conceptualizing their organization's strategy in turbulent environments.

Hypercompetition and the New 7 Ss Framework

Discussions of hypercompetition[6] take a perspective different from the previous models. Those models focus on creating and sustaining competitive advantage, whereas **hypercompetition** models suggest that the speed and aggressiveness of the moves and countermoves in any given market create an environment in which advantages are "rapidly created and eroded."[7] This perspective works from the following assumptions:

- Every advantage is eroded. Advantages only last until competitors have duplicated or outmaneuvered them. Once an advantage is no longer an advantage, it becomes a cost of doing business.

- Sustaining an advantage can be a deadly distraction. Some companies can extend their advantages and continue to enjoy the benefits, but sustaining an advantage can take attention away from developing new ones.

- The goal of advantage should be disruption, not sustainability. A company seeks to stay one step ahead through a series of temporary advantages that erode competitors' positions, rather than by creating a sustainable position in the marketplace.

- Initiatives are achieved with a series of small steps. Competitive cycles are shorter now, and new advantages must be achieved quickly. Companies focus on creating the next advantage before the benefits of the current advantage erode.

[6] R. D'Aveni, *Hypercompetition: Managing the Dynamics of Strategic Maneuvering* (New York: Free Press, 1994).
[7] Ibid.

D'Aveni identified four arenas in which firms seek to achieve competitive advantage under hypercompetition: (1) cost/quality, (2) timing/know-how, (3) strongholds, and (4) deep pockets. His framework suggests seven approaches an organization can take in its business strategy. Figure 1.3 summarizes this model.

D'Aveni's model describes the strategies companies can use to disrupt competition, depending on their particular capabilities to seize initiative and pursue tactics that can create a series of temporary advantages. For the purposes of this book, we briefly summarize his 7 Ss[8] in Figure 1.4.

The 7 Ss are a useful model for identifying different aspects of a business strategy and aligning them to make the organization competitive in the hypercompetitive arena of business in the millennium. This framework helps assess competitors' strengths and weaknesses, as well as build a roadmap for the company's strategy itself. Using this model, managers can identify new organizational responses to their

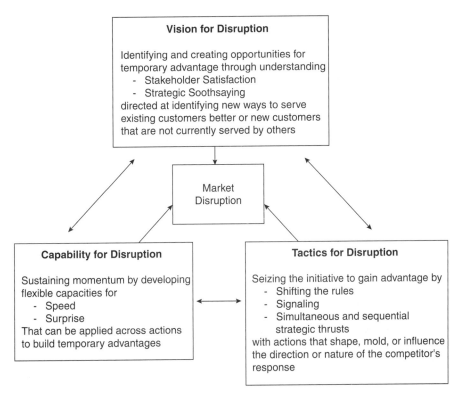

FIGURE 1.3 Disruption and the new 7 Ss

Source: R. D'Aveni, *Hypercompetition: Managing the Dynamics of Strategic Maneuvering* (New York: Free Press, 1994).

[8] The "old" 7 Ss of competitive advantage—structure, strategy, systems, style, skills, staff, and superordinate goals—entered business literature in a paper by R. Waterman, T. Peters, and J. Phillips, "Structure Is Not Organization," in *Business Horizons* (June 1980). D'Aveni used these as a point of reference in deriving his "new" 7 Ss under hypercompetition.

Approach	Definition
Superior stakeholder satisfaction	Understanding how to maximize customer satisfaction by adding value strategically
Strategic soothsaying	Seeking out new knowledge that can predict or create new windows of opportunity
Positioning for speed	Preparing the organization to react as quickly as possible
Positioning for surprise	Preparing the organization to respond to the marketplace in a manner that will surprise competitors
Shifting the rules of competition	Finding new ways to serve customers which transform the industry
Signaling strategic intent	Communicating the intended actions of a company, in order to stall responses by competitors
Simultaneous and sequential strategic thrusts	Taking a series of steps designed to stun and confuse competitors in order to disrupt or block their efforts

FIGURE 1.4   D'Aveni's new 7 Ss.

competition, as well as new opportunities that extend their current strengths. This model is particularly useful in markets where the rate of change makes sustaining a business strategy difficult. It suggests that a business strategy must be continuously redefined in order to be successful.

An application of the hypercompetition model is the destroy your business (DYB) approach to strategic planning that was implemented by Jack Welch at General Electric (GE). Welch recognized that GE could only sustain its competitive advantage for a limited time as competitors attempted to outmaneuver GE. He knew that if GE didn't identify its weaknesses, its competitors would relish doing so. DYB is an approach that places GE employees in the shoes of their competitors. Through the DYB lenses, GE employees develop strategies to destroy GE's competitive advantage. Then, in light of their revelations, they apply the grow your business (GYB) strategy to find fresh ways to reach new customers and better serve existing ones. The goal of the DYB planning approach is the complete disruption of current practices, so that GE can take actions to protect its business before competitors hone in on its weaknesses. The implicit assumption underlying DYB is that GE would not be able to sustain its position in the marketplace over the long term.

GE's Medical Systems Division used DYB to respond to the challenges posed by the Internet.[9] In doing so it applied four of D'Aveni's 7 Ss: positioning for speed,

[9] M. Levinson, "Destructive Behavior," *CIO Magazine* (July 15, 2000), available at http://www.cio.com/archive/071500_destructive_content.html.

superior stakeholder satisfaction, shifting the rules of competition, and strategic soothsaying. In 1999, this manufacturer was leading its industry in sales of MRI, CT scan, ultrasound, and mammography machines. Web sites such as WebMD, Neoforma, and MediBuy were aggregating unbiased information about machines manufactured by GE Medical Systems and its competitors into a single Web site that reached both current and potential GE customers. In the Web sites of these dot-coms, GE appeared to be just another vendor. To offer an alternative to these third-party Web sites, GE Medical Systems reacted as quickly as possible (positioning for speed) to bring GEMedicalSystems.com online with services specifically designed for the Internet. For example, the Web site allowed medical technicians to download and test software for upgrading their MRIs. If pleased at the end of the 30-day trial period, these customers could buy the upgrade. The Web site also enabled GE Medical Systems to monitor the productivity of its customers' equipment in real time via the Web, to provide personalized capacity management analysis, and to offer the services of its specialists to remedy mechanical problems that they observed. These services created superior stakeholder satisfaction and shifted the rules of competition in their industry.

Strategic soothsaying was demonstrated when Tip TV, GE Medical Systems' satellite television network that broadcasts programs to teach doctors and clinicians how to use GE equipment to perform medical procedures, went online. Prior to December 1999, doctors and clinicians signed up six weeks prior to a Tip TV class and then waited several weeks to get their exam results at the end of the course. After Tip TV went online, those seeking to take the class could sign up online anytime, take tests in real-time, and get their results immediately. More importantly, content was expanded by partnership with an Internet start-up, Health Dream, to provide access to educational material offered by the *New England Journal of Medicine*.

Why Are Strategic Advantage Models Essential to Planning for Information Systems?

A general manager who relies solely on IS personnel to make IS decisions may not only give up any authority over IS strategy, but also may hamper crucial future business decisions. In fact, business strategy should drive IS decision making, and changes in business strategy should entail reassessments of IS. Moreover, changes in IS potential should trigger reassessments of business strategy—as in the case of the Internet, where companies that failed to understand or consider its implications for the marketplace were quickly outpaced by competitors who had. For the purposes of our model, the Information Systems Strategy Triangle, understanding business strategy means answering the following questions:

1.   What is the business goal or objective?
2.   What is the plan for achieving it? What is the role of IS in this plan?
3.   Who are the crucial competitors and cooperators, and what is required of a successful player in this value net?

Porter's generic strategies and D'Aveni's hypercompetition and 7 Ss frameworks (summarized in Figure 1.5) are revisited in the next few chapters. They are especially helpful in discussing the role of IS in building and sustaining competitive advantages (Chapter 2), and for incorporating IS into business strategy. The next section of this chapter establishes a foundation for understanding organizational strategies.

▶ BRIEF OVERVIEW OF ORGANIZATIONAL STRATEGIES

Organizational strategy includes the organization's design as well as the choices it makes to define, set up, coordinate, and control its work processes. The organizational strategy is a plan that answers the question: "How will the company organize in order to achieve its goals and implement its business strategy?" A few of the many models of organizational strategy are reviewed in this section.

A simple framework for understanding the design of an organization is the business diamond, introduced by Leavitt and embellished by Hammer and Champy.[10] Shown in Figure 1.6, the **business diamond** identifies the crucial components of an organization's plan as its business processes, its values and beliefs, its management control systems, and its tasks and structures. This simple framework is useful for designing new organizations and for diagnosing organizational troubles. For example, organizations that try to change their cultures but fail to change the way they manage and control cannot be effective.

A complementing framework to the business diamond for organizational design can be found in the book by Cash, Eccles, Nohria, and Nolan, *Building the Information Age Organization*.[11] This framework, shown in Figure 1.7, suggests that the successful execution of a business's organizational strategy comprises the best combination of organizational, control, and cultural variables. Organizational variables include decision rights, business processes, formal

Framework	Key Idea	Application to Information Systems
Porter's generic strategies framework	Firms achieve competitive advantage through cost leadership, differentiation, or focus.	Understanding which strategy is chosen by a firm is critical to choosing IS to complement that strategy.
D'Aveni's hypercompetition model	Speed and aggressive moves and counter-moves by a firm create competitive advantage.	The 7 Ss give the manager suggestions on what moves and countermoves to make. IS are critical to achieve the speed needed for these moves.

FIGURE 1.5   Summary of key strategy frameworks.

[10] M. Hammer and J. Champy, *Reengineering the Corporation*. (New York: HarperBusiness, 1994).

[11] Cash, Eccles, Nohria, and Nolan, *Building the Information Age Organization* (Homewood, IL: Richard D. Irwin, 1994).

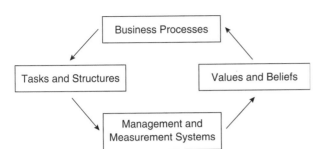

FIGURE 1.6 The business diamond.
Source: M. Hammer and J. Champy, *Reengineering the Corporation* (New York: Harper Business, 1994).

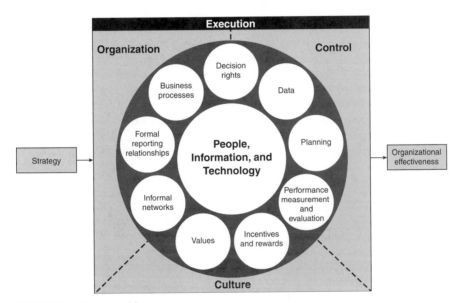

FIGURE 1.7 Managerial levers
Source: Cash, Eccles, Nohria, and Nolan, *Building the Information Age Organization* (Homewood, IL: Richard D. Irwin, 1994).

reporting relationships, and informal networks. Control variables include the availability of data, the nature and quality of planning, and the effectiveness of performance measurement and evaluation systems, and incentives to do good work. Cultural variables comprise the values of the organization. These organizational, control and cultural variables are **managerial levers** used by decision makers to effect changes in their organizations.

Our objective is to give the manager a set of frameworks to use in evaluating various aspects of organizational design. Using these frameworks, the manager can review the current organization and assess which components may be missing and what options are available looking forward. Understanding organizational strategy means answering the following questions:

1. What are the important structures and reporting relationships within the organization?
2. What are the characteristics, experiences, and skill levels of the people within the organization?
3. What are the key business processes?
4. What control systems are in place?
5. What is the culture of the organization?

The answers to these questions inform any assessment of the organization's use of IS. Chapters 3, 4, and 5 use the organizational theory frameworks, summarized in Figure 1.8, to assess the impact of MIS on the firm.

▶ BRIEF OVERVIEW OF INFORMATION SYSTEMS STRATEGY

IS strategy is the plan an organization uses in providing information services. IS allows a company to implement its business strategy. Business strategy is a function of competition (What does the customer want and what does the competition do?), positioning (In what way does the firm want to compete?), and capabilities (What can the firm do?); IS help determine the company's capabilities. An entire chapter is devoted to IT architecture, but for now a more basic framework will be used to understand the decisions related to IS that an organization must make.

Framework	Key Idea	Usefulness in IS Discussions
Business diamond	There are 4 key components to an organization: business processes, values and beliefs, management control systems, and tasks and structures.	Using IS in an organization will affect each of these components. Use this framework to identify where these impacts are likely to occur.
Managerial levers	Organizational variables, control variables, and cultural variables are the levers managers can use to affect change in their organization.	This is a more detailed model than the Business diamond and gives specific areas where IS can be used to manage the organization and to change the organization.

FIGURE 1.8   Summary of organizational strategy frameworks.

The purpose of the matrix in Figure 1.9 is to give the manager a high-level view of the relation between the four IS infrastructure components and the other resource considerations that are key to IS strategy. Infrastructure includes hardware, such as desktop units and servers. It also includes software, such as the programs used to do business, to manage the computer itself, and to communicate between systems. The third component of IS infrastructure is the network, which is the physical means by which information is exchanged among hardware components, such as through a modem and dial-up network (in which case the service is actually provided by a vendor such as AT&T), or through a private digital network (in which case the service is probably provided by an internal unit). Finally, the fourth part of the infrastructure is the data. The data are the actual information, the bits and bytes stored in the system. In current systems, data are not necessarily stored alongside the programs that use them; hence, it is important to understand what data are in the system and where they are stored. Many more detailed models of IS infrastructure exist, and interested readers may refer to any of the dozens of books that describe them. For the purposes of this text, the matrix will provide sufficient information to allow the general manager to assess the critical issues in information management.

	What	Who	Where
Hardware	List of physical components of the system	Individuals who use it Individuals who manage it	Physical location
Software	List of programs, applications, and utilities	Individuals who use it Individuals who manage it	What hardware it resides upon and where that hardware is located
Networking	Diagram of how hardware and software components are connected	Individuals who use it Individuals who manage it Company from whom service is obtained	Where the nodes are located, where the wires and other transport media are located
Data	Bits of information stored in the system	Individuals who own it Individuals who manage it	Where the information resides

FIGURE 1.9 Information systems strategy matrix.

▶ FOOD FOR THOUGHT: ECONOMICS OF INFORMATION VS. ECONOMICS OF THINGS

In their book, *Blown to Bits,* Evans and Wurster argue that every business is in the information business.[12] Even those businesses not typically considered to be information businesses have business strategies in which information plays a critical role. The physical world of manufacturing is shaped by information that dominates products as well as processes. For example, a high-end Mercedes automobile contains as much computing power as a midrange personal computer. Information-intensive processes in the manufacturing and marketing of the automobile include market research, logistics, advertising, and inventory management.

As our world is reshaped by information-intensive industries, it becomes even more important for business strategies to differentiate the timeworn economics of things from the evolving economics of information. Things wear out; things can be replicated at the expense of the manufacturer; things exist in a tangible location. When sold, the seller no longer owns the thing. The price of a thing is typically based on production costs. In contrast, information never wears out, though it can become obsolete or untrue. Information can be replicated at virtually no cost without limit; information exists in the ether. When sold, the seller still retains the information, but this ownership provides little value if the ability of others to copy it is not limited. Finally, information is often costly to produce, but cheap to reproduce. Rather than pricing it to recover the sunk cost of its initial production, its price is typically based on the value to the consumer. Figure 1.10 summarizes the major differences between the economics of goods and the economics of information.

Evans and Wurster suggest that traditionally the economics of information has been bundled with the economics of things. However, in this Information Age, firms are vulnerable if they do not separate the two. The Encyclopædia Britannica story serves as an example. Bundling the economics of things with the economics of information made it difficult for Encyclopædia Britannica to gauge the threat posed by Encarta, the encyclopedia on CD-ROM that was given away to promote the sale of computers and peripherals. Britannica focused on its centuries-old tradition of

Things	Information
Wear out	Doesn't wear out, but can become obsolete or untrue
Are replicated at the expense of the manufacturer	Is replicated at almost zero cost without limit
Exist in a tangible location	May exist in the ether
When sold, seller ceases to own	When sold, seller may still possess and sell again
Price based on production costs	Price based on value to consumer

FIGURE 1.10   Comparison of the economics of things with the economics of information.

[12] Philip Evans and Thomas Wurster, *Blown to Bits* (Boston, MA: Harvard Business School Press, 2000).

providing information in richly bound tomes sold to the public through a well-trained sales force. Only when it was threatened with its very survival did Encyclopædia Britannica grasp the need to separate the economics of information from economics of things, and sell bits of information online. Clearly Encyclopædia Britannica's business strategy, like that of many other companies, needed to reflect the difference between the economics of things from the economics of information.[13]

▶ SUMMARY

The Information Systems Strategy Triangle represents a simple framework for understanding the impact of IS on businesses. It relates business strategy with IS strategy and organizational strategy and implies the balance that must be maintained in business planning. The Information Systems Strategy Triangle suggests the following management principles:

Business Strategy

Business strategy drives organizational strategy and IS strategy. The organization and its IS should clearly support defined business goals and objectives.

- Definition: A well-articulated vision of where a business seeks to go and how it expects to get there
- Models: Porter's generic strategies model; D'Aveni's hypercompetition model

Organizational Strategy

Organizational strategy must complement business strategy. The way a business is organized either supports the implementation of its business strategy or it gets in the way.

- Definition: The organization's design, as well as the choices it makes to define, set up, coordinate, and control its work processes
- Models: Business diamond; managerial levers

IS Strategy

IS strategy must complement business strategy. When IS support business goals, the business appears to be working well. IS strategy can itself affect and is affected by changes in a firm's business and organizational strategies. Moreover, information systems strategy always has consequences—intended or not—on business and organizational strategies.

- Definition: The plan the organization uses in providing information systems and services
- Models: A basic framework for understanding IS decisions relating architecture (the "what") and the other resource considerations ("who" and "where") that represent important planning constraints

Strategic Relationships

Organizational strategy and information strategy must complement each other. They must be designed so that they support, rather than hinder each other. If a decision is made to change one corner of the triangle, it is necessary to evaluate the other two corners to ensure

[13] Ibid.

that balance is preserved. Changing business strategy without thinking through the effects on the organizational and IS strategies will cause the business to struggle until balance is restored. Likewise, changing IS or the organization alone will cause an imbalance.

▶ KEY TERMS

business diamond (p. 28)
business strategy (p. 21)
cost leadership (p. 21)
differentiation (p. 22)
focus (p. 22)
hypercompetition (p. 24)

IS strategy (p. 30)
Information Systems
   Strategy Triangle (p. 19)
managerial levers (p. 29)
organizational strategy
   (p. 28)

shareholder value model
   (p. 23)
unlimited resources
   model (p. 24)

▶ DISCUSSION QUESTIONS

1. Why is it important for business strategy to drive organizational strategy and IS strategy? What might happen if business strategy was not the driver?

2. Suppose managers in an organization decided to hand out laptop computers to all sales-people without making any other formal changes in organizational strategy or business strategy. What might be the outcome? What unintended consequences might occur?

3. Consider a traditional manufacturing company that wanted to take advantage of the Internet and the Web. What might be a reasonable business strategy and how would organizational and IS strategy need to change?

4. This chapter describes key components of an IS strategy. Describe the IS strategy of a consulting firm using the matrix framework.

5. What does this tip from *Fast Company* mean: "The job of the CIO is to provide organizational and strategic flexibility"?[14]

CASE STUDY 1-1

ROCHE'S NEW SCIENTIFIC METHOD

For years, the Swiss pharmaceutical giant, Roche Group, pitted veteran scientific teams against one another. The competing teams were mandated to fight one another for resources. That proud, stubborn culture helped Roche develop blockbuster drugs such as Valium and Librium. But, Roche's ultracompetitive approach made it almost impossible to abandon faltering projects, because scientists' careers were so wrapped up in them. Researchers were tempted to hoard the technical expertise they picked up along the way, since sharing might allow others to catch up. In 1998, the company replaced its gladiator

---

[14] "20 Technology Briefs: What's New? What's Next? What Matters," *Fast Company* (March 2002), available from http://www.fastcompany.com/online/56/fasttalk.html.

mentality with a more collaborative style of teamwork—especially in the chaotic, booming new field of genomics. So Roche began running ads in the back pages of *Science* magazine, looking for a new breed of researcher—people who were starting out, who could reinvent themselves as job opportunities changed.

For Roche, these are thrilling times. Week by week, new breakthroughs in genomics and molecular biology are upending the way it hunts for new drugs. It's now possible to pursue new drug targets with a speed and gusto that would have been unimaginable a few years ago. It's possible to size up toxicity risks earlier than ever. And it's becoming possible to match up drugs with the people who are best suited for them, ushering in an era of customized medicines.

But the genomics revolution is incredibly jarring as well. In fact, reckoning with its impact demands a fresh start in the fundamentals of innovation and R&D. Old ways of managing projects don't make sense. Roche can now run *1 million* genomics experiments a day, churning out enough data to overwhelm every computer it owns. Research teams that once spent years looking for a single good idea now face hundreds or even thousands of candidates. Without a clear way to handle all of this information, it's possible to drown in the data.

Still, at the highest levels of Roche, there is real excitement about what lies ahead. At a media briefing last August, Roche Group chairman and CEO Franz Humer declared, "Look at this revolution of genetics, genomics, and proteomics. It's becoming ever clearer that we will be able to identify early the predisposition of people to disease—and to monitor and treat them more effectively. We'll develop markers for cancer. That will lead to better test kits and to new pharmaceuticals."

So what is the right way to reconfigure a company when breakthrough technology shows up on its doorstep? Step inside Roche's U.S. pharmaceuticals headquarters, and you'll see how that adjustment is taking place. It begins with something as basic—and hard—as embracing the excitement of having way too much data, too fast. It goes on to include new thinking about the best ways to build teams, hire people, and create a culture where failure is all right, as long as you fail fast. The only way to embrace a technological revolution, Roche has discovered, is to unleash an organizational revolution.

Learning to Swim in a Deluge of Data

In the genomics explosion, think of the GeneChip as the detonator. To the unaided eye, it is merely a carefully mounted piece of darkened glass, barely bigger than your thumbnail. Look closely, though, and you can see countless tiny markings on that glass. Each mark represents the essence of a human gene—assembled one amino acid at a time on to the glass. All told, there may be as many as 12,000 different genes on a single chip. Run the right experiments, and the GeneChip will light up the specific genes that are activated in a medically interesting tissue sample. Suddenly, hundreds of brilliant white and blue dots burst forth against the chip's dark background. Each time a chip lights up, you behold a glimpse of which genes might be markers for disease. Yet for all of the ingenuity involved in making the GeneChip, it has required cleverness on Roche's part to use the chips effectively within a big organization.

Take something as basic as computer capacity. Each sample run on a GeneChip set generates 60 million bytes of raw data. Analyze that data a bit, and you need another 180 million bytes of computer storage. Run 1,000 GeneChip experiments a year, which Roche did in both 1999 and 2000, and pretty soon you run the risk of collapsing your data systems. "Every six months, the IT guys would come to us and say, 'You've used up all of your storage,'" recalls Jiayi Ding, a Roche scientist. Some of those encounters were outright testy. At one point in early 1999, Roche's computer-services experts pointed out that they were supposed to support 300 researchers in Nutley—and that the 10 people working on GeneChips were hogging 90% of the company's total computer capacity.

Fail Fast, So You Can Succeed Sooner

One of the biggest challenges in drug research—or in any field—is letting go of a once-promising idea that just isn't working anymore. Without strict cutoff rules, months and even years can slip away as everyone labors to keep a doomed project from dying. Meanwhile, much brighter prospects sit dormant, with no one able to give them any attention.

New hire, Lee Babiss, head of preclinical research, arrived from arch rival Glaxo with a simple message: Fail fast. Babiss wanted successes as much as anyone. But he also knew that the best hope of finding the right new drugs involved cutting down the time spent looking at the wrong alternatives.

For example, screening was becoming a bottleneck for Roche. An ultra-high-throughput screening was installed at a cost of more than $1 million. "We can test 100,000 compounds a day," says Larnie Myer, the technical robotics expert who keeps the system running. Nearly all of those compounds will turn out to be useless for the mission at hand. But that's fine. If his team can get the losers out of consideration for that trial in a hurry and identify a handful of "hits" within a few weeks of testing, that speeds Roche's overall efforts.

What's more, the Zeiss machine represents the gradual retooling of Roche's overall research efforts. Processes farther down the pipeline must be upgraded and reworked in order to handle much greater volume. That is hard and disruptive work—but it is vital.

Change Everything—One Piece at a Time

Peek into almost any aspect of Roche's business, and you will find someone who is excited about the ways that genomics could change things. In Palo Alto, researcher Gary Peltz has built a computerized model of the mouse genome that allows him to simulate classical lab studies in a matter of minutes.

In Iceland, Roche is teaming with a company called Decode, which researches genealogical records from the Icelandic population. That data has helped Decode identify and locate genes that are associated with stroke as well as schizophrenia and other diseases, giving Roche new research leads that otherwise might never have surfaced with such clarity.

And in Nutley, there is talk that genomic data will make it possible to size up a drug's side effects with much greater clarity before embarking on lengthy animal experiments. It will be possible to run simulations or GeneChip experiments with potential new drugs to find out whether they might interact in troublesome ways with the functioning of healthy genes.

Each of those initiatives is running on a different timeline. Some parts of Roche's business will be aggressively reshaped in the next year or two; others may take five years or more to feel the full effects of the most recent genomics breakthroughs. "This isn't just a matter of turning on a light switch," says Klaus Lindpaintner, Roche's global head of genetics research.

Yet eventually, Roche executives believe, all of the retooling within their company will be mirrored by even bigger changes in the ways that all of us get our medical care.

Discussion Questions

1. How does the business strategy affect information systems and organizational decisions?
2. What generic strategy does Roche appear to be using based upon this case? Provide a rationale for your response.
3. Apply the hypercompetition model to Roche? Which of the 7 Ss are demonstrated in this case?
4. How do information systems support Roche's business strategy?

Source: Excerpted from G. Anders, "Fresh Start 2002: Roche's New Scientific Method," *Fast Company* (January 2002), available at http://www.fastcompany.com/online/54/roche.html.

CHAPTER 2

STRATEGIC USE OF INFORMATION RESOURCES[1]

In 1994, Dell Computer Corporation formally stopped selling personal computers (PCs) in retail stores because reaching customers in this way was expensive, time consuming, and did not fit with Michael Dell's vision of the direct business model. Information technology (IT) enabled this vision. The Internet, combined with Dell's well-designed information systems (IS) infrastructure, allowed customers to electronically contact Dell who would then design a PC for a customer's specific needs. Dell's ordering system is integrated with its production system and shares information automatically with each supplier of PC components. This IS enables the assembly of the most current computers without the expense of storing large inventories. Cost savings are passed on to the customer, and this business model allows Dell to focus its production capacity on building only the most current products. With small profit margins and new products arriving quickly to replace existing products, this creative use of IS is critical to Dell's strategic leadership. This strategic use of IS ultimately results in cost savings, reflected in the price of systems. In addition, Dell executives achieve a strategic advantage in reducing response time, building custom computers for reasonable costs, and eliminating inventories that could become obsolete before they are sold.

Dell used its information resources to achieve high volumes without the high costs of the industry's traditional distribution channels. This approach led to continued profitable results and a competitive advantage. As with most strategic advantages, other companies followed suit and adopted Dell's direct-to-the-customer model, but antiquated IS make this task difficult, if not an impossible. As the competitive landscape of the PC industry changes, Dell continues to innovate using information resources and now offers customized order configuring, sales inventory management, kiosks in shopping malls, and technical support directly from the Internet.

As the Dell example illustrates, innovative use of a firm's information resources can provide companies with substantial advantages over competitors. This chapter uses

---

[1] The authors wish to acknowledge and thank W. Thomas Cannon, MBA 1999 for his help in researching and writing earlier drafts of this chapter.

the business strategy foundation from Chapter 1 to help general managers visualize how to use information resources for competitive advantage. This chapter briefly recounts the evolving strategic use of information resources, and highlights the difference between simply using IS and using IS strategically. Then, this chapter explores the use of information resources to support the strategic goals of an organization.

The material in this chapter enables a general manager to understand the link between business strategy and information strategy on the Information Systems Strategy Triangle. General managers want to find answers to questions: Does using information resources provide a sustainable competitive advantage? What tools are available to help shape their strategic use? What are the risks of using information resources to gain strategic advantage?

▶ EVOLUTION OF INFORMATION RESOURCES

The Eras model shows how organizations have used IS over the past decades. Figure 2.1 summarizes this view and provides a road map for a general manager to use in thinking strategically about the current use of information resources within the firm.

	Era I 1960s	Era II 1970s	Era III 1980s	Era IV 1990s	Era V 2000+
Primary role of IT	Efficiency	Effectiveness	Strategic	Strategic	Value creation
	Automate existing paper-based processes	Solve problems and create opportunities	Increase individual and group effectiveness	Transform industry/ organization	Create collaborative partnerships
Justify IT expenditures	ROI	Increasing productivity and better decision quality	Competitive position	Competitive position	Adding value
Target of systems	Organization	Organization/ group	Individual manager/ group	Business processes ecosystem	Customer/ supplier ecosystem
Information models	Application specific	Data-driven	User-driven	Business-driven	Knowledge-driven
Dominate technology	Mainframe, "centralized intelligence"	Minicomputer, mostly "centralized intelligence"	Microcomputer, "decentralized intelligence"	Client Server, "distributed intelligence"	Internet, global "ubiquitous intelligence"
Basis of value	Scarcity	Scarcity	Scarcity	Plentitude	Plentitude
Underlying economics	Economics of information bundled with economics of things	Economics of information bundled with economics of things	Economics of information bundled with economics of things	Economics of information separated from economics of things	Economics of information separated from economics of things

FIGURE 2.1 Eras of information usage in organizations.

IS strategy from the 1960s to the 1990s was driven by internal organizational needs. First came the need to lower existing transaction costs. Next was the need to provide support for managers by collecting and distributing information. An additional need was to redesign business processes. As competitors built similar systems, organizations lost any advantages they held from their IS, and competition within a given industry once again was driven by forces that existed prior to the new technology. As each era begins, organizations adopt a strategic role for IS to address not only the firm's internal circumstances but its external circumstances as well. Thus, in the ubiquitous era, companies seek those applications that again provide them with advantage over competition. They also seek applications that keep them from being outgunned by start-ups with innovative business models or traditional companies entering new markets. For example, a plethora of "dot-coms" have challenged all industries and traditional businesses by entering the marketplace armed with Internet-based innovative systems. The Information System Strategy Triangle introduced in Chapter 1 reflects the link between IS strategy and organizational strategy and the internal requirements of the firm. The link between IS strategy and business strategy reflects the firm's external requirements. Maximizing the effectiveness of the firm's business strategy requires that the general manager be able both to identify and use information resources. This chapter looks at how information resources can be used strategically by general managers.

▶ INFORMATION RESOURCES AS STRATEGIC TOOLS

Crafting a strategic advantage requires the general manager to cleverly combine all of the firm's resources, including financial, production, human, and information resources. Information resources are more than just the infrastructures. This generic term, **information resources,** is defined as the available data, technology, people, and processes within an organization to be used by the manager to perform business processes and tasks. Seen in this way, an IS infrastructure (a concept that is discussed in detail in Chapter 6) is an information resource, as is each of its constituent components. The relationship between a firm's IS managers and its business managers is another type of information resource. This relationship can create a unique advantage for a firm. The following list highlights some of the information resources available to a firm:

- IS infrastructure (hardware, software, network, and data components)
- Information and knowledge
- Proprietary technology
- Technical skills of the IT staff
- End users of the IS
- Relationship between IT and business managers
- Business processes

Committing and developing information resources require substantial financial resources. Therefore, a general manager evaluating an information resource might consider the following questions to better understand the type of advantage the information resource can create:[2]

- *What makes the information resource valuable?* In Eras I through III, the value of information was tied to the physical delivery mechanisms. In these eras, value was derived from scarcity reflected in the cost to produce the information. Information, like diamonds, gold, and MBA degrees, was more valuable because it was found in limited quantities. However, the networked economy prevalent in Era IV drives a new model of value—value from plentitude. **Network externality** offers a reason for value derived from plentitude. The value of a network node to a person or organization in the network increases when another joins the network. For example, a single fax machine has no value without another fax machine that could receive the fax. As fax machines become relatively ubiquitous, the individual fax machine is driven up in value as its potential for use increases. As the cost of producing an additional copy of an information product becomes trivial, the value of the network that invents, manufactures, and distributes it increases.[3] Rather than using the extremely low production costs to guide the determination of price, information products or services must be priced to reflect their value to the buyer. Different organizational buyers have different information needs depending upon their competitive position within an industry.

- *Who appropriates the value created by the information resource?* The value chain model can help determine where a resource's value lies and how the appropriation can be improved in a firm's favor.

- *Is the information resource equally distributed across firms?* A general manager is unlikely to possess a resource that is completely unique. However, by surveying the firms within an industry, he or she may establish that such a resource is distributed unequally. The value of a resource that is unequally distributed tends to be higher because it can create strategic advantage. The value of information mushrooms under conditions of information asymmetries. The possessor of information may use it against, or sell it to, companies or individuals who are not otherwise able to access the information.

- *Is the information resource highly mobile?* A reliance on the individual skills of IT professionals exposes a firm to the risk that key individuals

[2] Adapted from: David J. Collis and Cynthia A.Montgomery, "Competing on Resources: Strategy in the 1990s." *Harvard Business Review,* July-August 1995, reprint no. 95403.

[3] Kevin Kelly, "New Rules for the New Economy," *Wired* (September 1997), available at http://www.wired.com/wired/5.09/newrules_pr.html.

will leave the firm, taking the resource with them. Developing unique knowledge-sharing processes and creating an organizational memory can help reduce the impact of the loss of a mobile employee. Recording the lessons learned from all team members after the completion of each project is one attempt at lowering this risk.

- *How quickly does the information resource become obsolete?* As noted in Chapter 1, "things" wear out, whereas information does not. However, information can become obsolete, untrue, or even unfashionable. Like most other assets, information resources lose value over time. A general manager should understand the rate of this decline of value, as well as what factors may speed or slow it. For example, consider a database of customer information. How long, on average, is the current address of each customer valid? What events in the customers' lives might change their purchasing pattern and reduce the forecasting capability of the current information?

Information resources exist in a company alongside other resources. The general manager is responsible for organizing all resources so that business goals are met. Understanding the nature of the resources at hand is a prerequisite to using them effectively. By aligning the organization's IS strategy with its business strategy, the general manager maximizes its profit potential. Meanwhile, the firm's competitors are working to do the same. In this competitive environment, how should the information resources be organized and applied to enable the organization to compete most effectively?

▶ HOW CAN INFORMATION RESOURCES BE USED STRATEGICALLY?

The general manager confronts many elements that influence the competitive environment of his or her enterprise. Overlooking a single element can bring about disastrous results for the firm. This slim tolerance for error requires the manager to take multiple views of the strategic landscape. We discuss two such views that can help a general manager align IS strategy with business strategy. The first view uses the five competitive forces model by Michael Porter to look at the major influences on a firm's competitive environment. Information resources should be directed strategically to alter the competitive forces to benefit the firm's position in the industry. The second view uses Porter's value chain model to assess the internal operations of the organization and partners in its supply chain. Information resources should be directed at altering the value-creating or value-supporting activities of the firm. This chapter explores this view further to consider the value chain of an entire industry to identify opportunities for the organization to gain competitive advantage. These two views provide a general manager with varied perspectives from which to identify strategic opportunities to apply the firm's information resources.

Using Information Resources to Influence Competitive Forces

Porter provides the general manager with a classic view of the major forces that shape the competitive environment of a firm. These five competitive forces are shown in Figure 2.2, along with some examples of how information resources can be applied to influence each force. This view reminds the general manager that competitive forces do not derive only from the actions of direct competitors. Each force now will be explored in more detail from an IS perspective.

Potential Threat of New Entrants

Existing firms within an industry often try to reduce the threat of new entrants to the marketplace by erecting barriers to entry. Barriers to entry help the firm create a stronghold by offering products or services that are difficult to displace in the eyes of customers based on apparently unique features. Such barriers include controlled access to limited distribution channels, public image of a firm, and government regulations of an industry. Information resources also can be used to build barriers that discourage competitors from entering the industry. For example,

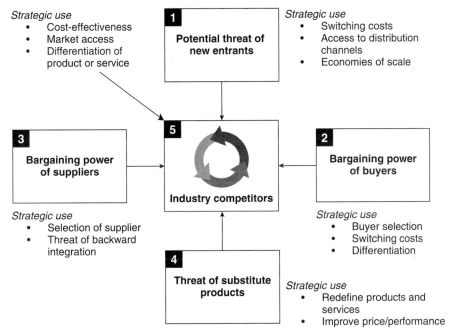

FIGURE 2.2 Five competitive forces with potential strategic use of information resources.
Source: Adapted from Michael Porter, *Competitive Strategy* (New York: The Free Press, 1998); and Applegate, McFarlan, and McKenney, *Corporate Information Systems Management: The Issues Facing Senior Executives,* 4th ed. (Homewood, IL: Richard D. Irwin, 1996).

Massachusetts Mutual Life Insurance Company created an IS infrastructure that connects the local sales agent with comprehensive information about products and customers. An insurance company entering the marketplace would have to spend millions of dollars to build the telecommunications and IS required to provide its sales force with the same competitive advantage. Therefore, the system at Mass Mutual may be a barrier to entry for new companies.

Bargaining Power of Buyers

Customers often have substantial power to affect the competitive environment. This power can take the form of easy consumer access to several retail outlets to purchase the same product or the opportunity to purchase in large volumes at superstores like Wal-Mart. Information resources can be used to build switching costs that make it less attractive for customers to purchase from competitors. Switching costs can be any aspect of a buyer's purchasing decision that decreases the likelihood of "switching" his or her purchase to a competitor. Such an approach requires a deep understanding of how a customer obtains the product or service. For example, Amazon.com's One Click encourages return purchases by making buying easier. Amazon.com stores buyer information including contact information and credit card numbers so that it can be accessed with one click, saving consumers the effort of data reentry. Honeywell hopes to "lock in" building industry customers with the increased responsiveness, better service, and streamlined record keeping made available through its Field Automation Service Technology (FAST) initiative. Honeywell is equipping 1,400 building system service technicians across North America with handheld computers so that they can make sure that repairs are done right the first time and that customers have up-to-date, accurate information about equipment status.

Bargaining Power of Suppliers

Suppliers' bargaining power can reduce a firm's profitability. This force is strongest when a firm has few suppliers from which to choose, the quality of supplier inputs is crucial to the finished product, or the volume of purchases is insignificant to the supplier. For example, steel firms lost some of their power over the automobile industry because car manufacturers developed technologically advanced quality control systems. Manufacturers can now reject steel from suppliers when it does not meet the required quality levels. Through the Internet, firms continue to provide information for free as they attempt to increase their share of visitors to their Web sites. This decision reduces the power of information suppliers and necessitates finding new ways for content providers to develop and distribute information. Many Internet firms are integrating backward within the industry by creating their own information supply and reselling it to other Internet sites. Well-funded firms simply acquire these content providers, which is often quicker than building the capability from scratch.

Threat of Substitute Products

The potential of a substitute product in the marketplace depends on the buyers' willingness to substitute, the relative price-to-performance of the substitute, and the level of switching costs a buyer faces. Information resources can create advantages by reducing the threat of substitution. In the financial services industry, Merrill Lynch used innovative IS to create a product called the Cash Management Account. This account combined the benefits of a brokerage account, a money market account, a Visa credit card, and a checking account into a single product. Other firms lacking Merrill Lynch's IS were unable to provide all these services in a single account. The Cash Management Account helped attract 450,000 new brokerage accounts and allowed Merrill Lynch to build customer relationships that helped retain each account. Customers and potential customers could not easily find substitutes. Other brokerage firms took years to develop similar products. Even when substitutes became available, Merrill Lynch still enjoyed an advantage because competitors had to overcome the cost to the customer of switching accounts. For competitors to be successful, they needed to offer not just a substitute, but a better product. So far none has.

Industry Competitors

Rivalry among the firms competing within an industry is high when it is expensive for a firm to leave the industry, the growth rate of the industry is declining, or products have lost differentiation. Under these circumstances, the firm must focus on the competitive actions of a rival in order to protect market share. Intense rivalry in an industry assures that competitors respond quickly to any strategic actions. The banking industry illustrates this point. When a large Philadelphia-based bank developed an ATM network, several smaller competitors joined forces and shared information resources to create a competing network. The large bank was unable to create a significant advantage from its system and had to carry the full costs of developing the network by itself. Information resources were committed quickly to achieve neutralizing results due to the high level of rivalry that existed between the local bank competitors in Philadelphia.

As firms within an industry begin to implement standard business processes and technologies—often using enterprise-wide systems such as those of SAP and PeopleSoft—the industry becomes more attractive to consolidation through acquisition. Standardizing IS lowers the coordination costs of merging two enterprises and can result in a less competitive environment in the industry.

One way competitors differentiate themselves with an otherwise undifferentiated product is through creative use of IS. Information provides advantages in such competition when added to an existing product. For example, FedEx adds information to its delivery service helping it differentiate its offerings from those of other delivery services. FedEx customers are able to track their packages, know exactly where their package is in-transit, see who signed for the package, and know exactly when it was delivered. Competitors offer some of the same information, but FedEx was able to take an early lead by using information to differentiate their services.

Let's look at an example of these five competitive forces at work simultaneously. The five competitive forces model could be applied by a grocery chain that is considering the use of shopping cards and automated checkouts. Shopping cards allow the grocery chain to compete on price by offering its regular customers reduced rates. They make it possible for the chain to track individual buying habits, fine-tune buying based upon the analysis of sales, and offer card-holding customers the ability to check themselves out at automated checkout lines. Figure 2.3 demonstrates how the five competitive forces could shape the grocery chain's competitive environment through the application of these information technologies. These technologies may be especially helpful in responding to regular customers' needs and locking them in. Although this example conceivably could affect all forces, other technologies or IS may affect only some of these forces, though their impact could be major.

General managers can use the five competitive forces model to identify the key forces currently affecting competition, to recognize uses of information resources to influence forces, and to consider likely changes in these forces over time. The changing forces drive both the business strategy and IS strategy, and this model provides a way to think about how information resources can create competitive advantage. The alternative perspective presented in the next section provides the general manager with an opportunity to select the proper mix of information resources and to apply them to achieve strategic advantage by altering key activities.

Using Information Resources to Alter the Value Chain

The value chain model addresses the activities that create, deliver, and support a company's product or service. Porter divided these activities into two broad categories, as shown in Figure 2.4: support and primary activities. Primary activities relate directly to the value created in a product or service, while support activities make it possible for the primary activities to exist and remain coordinated. Each activity may affect how other activities are performed, suggesting that information resources should not be applied in isolation. For example, more efficient IS for repairing a product may increase the possible number of repairs per week, but the customer does not receive any value unless his or her product is repaired, which requires that the spare parts be available. Changing the rate of repair also affects the rate of spare parts ordering. If information resources are focused too narrowly on a specific activity, then the expected value increase may not be realized, as other parts of the chain are not adjusted.

The value chain framework suggests that competition stems from two sources: lowering the cost to perform activities and adding value to a product or service so that buyers will pay more. To achieve true competitive advantage, a firm requires accurate information on elements outside itself. Lowering activity costs only

Competitive Force	IT Influence on Competitive Force
Threat of New Entrant	Automated checkout technology is expensive to implement. A new entrant might be Peapod, a Web-based delivery service directly connected to the customers through the Internet.
Bargaining Power of Buyers	Card "locks in" customer because of low prices; analysis of buying patterns derived from card use can lead the chain to localize inventory purchases to better fit the buying patterns of regular customers (i.e., stores near new affordable subdivisions with young families may stock more diapers and baby food, or stores near universities may purchase more Oriental or Indian foods, etc.); analysis of buying patterns may allow individual stores to better identify "loss leaders" and target marketing campaigns; analysis of buying patterns may lead store to introduce items that are well received in other stores in the chain where the customers share similar demographics; automated checkouts may lower "switching costs" of customers who like the shorter checkout lines with the automated technology.
Bargaining Power of Suppliers	Analysis of buying patterns derived from card use helps chain to fine-tune its inventory needs, allowing chain to be more specific and to reap economies of scale for items that are more heavily purchased across the chain; buying patterns can be shared with leading suppliers so that they can better manage their inventories.
Threat of Substitute Products	Improved price/performance makes other stores look less appealing to regular customers.
Industry Competitors	Card and automated checkout allows chain to compete on the basis of price for regular customers; automated checkout offers operational efficiencies; analysis of buying patterns allows chain to differentiate its offerings for regular customers.

FIGURE 2.3   Application of five competitive forces model.

achieves advantage if the firm possesses information about its competitors' cost structures. Even though reducing isolated costs can improve profits temporarily, it does not provide a clear competitive advantage unless a firm can lower its costs below a competitor's. Doing so enables the firm to lower its prices so as to grow its market share.

Adding value can be used to gain strategic advantage only if a firm possesses accurate information regarding its customer. Which product attributes are valued,

	Organization			
Support activities	**Human Resources**			
	Technology			
	Purchasing			

	Inbound Logistics	Operations	Outbound Logistics	Marketing and Sales	Service
Primary activities	Materials handling Delivery	Manufacturing Assembly	Order processing Shipping	Product Pricing Promotion Place	Customer service Repair

FIGURE 2.4   Value chain of the firm.
Source: Adapted from Michael Porter and Victor Millar, "How Information Gives You Competitive Advantage," *Harvard Business Review* (July–August 1985, reprint no. 85415).

and where can improvements be made? Improving customer service when its product fails is a goal behind Otis Elevator's Otisline system. The customer's service call is automatically routed to the field technician with the skill and knowledge to complete the repair. Otis Elevator knows that customers value a fast response to minimize the downtime of the elevator. This goal is achieved by using information resources to move the necessary information between activities. When customers call for service, their requests are automatically and accurately entered and stored in the customer service database and communicated to the technician linked to that account. This technician is then contacted immediately over the wireless handheld computer network and told of the problem. That way the service technician can make sure he or she has both the parts and knowledge to make repairs. This approach provides Otis with an advantage because no time is wasted and the technician arrives at the job properly prepared to fix the problem.

Although the value chain framework emphasizes the activities of the individual firm, it can be extended, as in Figure 2.5, to include the firm in a larger value system. This value system is a collection of firm value chains connected through a business relationship. From this perspective a variety of strategic opportunities exist to use information resources to gain a competitive advantage. Understanding how information is used within each value chain of the system can lead to the formation of new businesses designed to change the information component of value-added activities.

Opportunity also exists in the transfer of information across value chains. Amazon.com began by selling books directly to customers over the Internet and bypassing the traditional industry channels. Customers who valued the time saved by shopping from home rather than driving to physical retail outlets flocked to Amazon.com's Web site to buy books. Industry competitors Barnes and Noble and Borders Books were forced to develop their own Web sites, thus driving up their

Supplier's value chains | Firm's value chain | Channel's value chains | Buyer's value chains

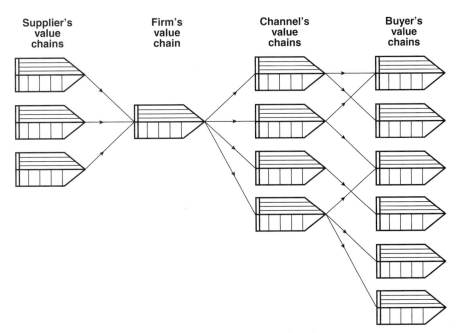

FIGURE 2.5 The value system: interconnecting relationships between organizations.

cost of doing business. The new paradigm for Barnes and Noble and Borders means rethinking how their value chain works with the value offered to their customers through their traditional business.

CRM is a natural extension of applying the value chain model to customers. **Customer relationship management (CRM)** includes management activities performed to obtain, enhance relationships with, and retain customers. CRM is a coordinated set of activities designed to learn more about customers' needs and behaviors in order to develop stronger relationships with them and to enhance their value chains. CRM consists of technological components, as well as a process that brings together many pieces of information about customers, sales, marketing effectiveness, responsiveness, and market trends. CRM can lead to better customer service, more efficient call centers, product cross-selling, simplified sales and marketing efforts, more efficient sales transactions, and increased customer revenues. In Chapter 1 we described the Ritz-Carlton's CRM, Class, which captures information about guest preferences and enables providing enhanced customized service during future visits.

In an application of the value chain model to the grocery chain example discussed earlier in the chapter, Figure 2.6 describes the value added to primary and support activities from the shopping card and automated checkout for the grocery chain and its suppliers. A number of activities in the value chains of both the grocery chain and its suppliers may benefit from the shopping cards and automated checkout. In addition to the value chains of the grocery chain and its supplier, these

Activity	Grocery Chain's Value Chain	Supplier's Value Chain
	Primary Activities	
Inbound Logistics	Analysis of buying patterns suggests items that should be stocked at local stores, including amounts and optimum delivery times.	Analysis of buying patterns can aid grocery chain in better determining demand, leading to better forecasting of demand for both the chain and its supplier.
Operations	Automated checkout can speed checkout operations; may lead to reduced staffing of registers and lower operational costs.	Analysis of buying patterns can help the grocery chain reduce "last-minute" orders and improve suppliers processing of orders.
Outbound Logistics		Sharing analysis of buying patterns by grocery chain can aid supplier in scheduling deliveries.
Marketing and Sales	Analysis of buying patterns can aid chain in developing promotional strategies and marketing campaigns at the local stores; analysis of buying patterns can highlight products to be stocked to best meet customer preferences.	Supplier may be able to offer economies of scale in its purchases.
Service	Automated checkout lanes shorten customers' waiting time.	Sharing analysis of buying patterns allows supplier to offer better service to grocery chain.
	Secondary Activities	
Organization	Shopping card can provide data to help grocery chain plan for trends and demographic changes in its target market.	Shopping card can provide data to help supplier plan for trends and demographic changes in its target market.
Human Resources	Staffing needs for cash registers may be reduced with automated checkout.	
Technology	Shopping card can provide data for market research.	Grocery chain can provide information to help supplier's marketing research.
Purchasing	Grocery chain may be able to capture more discounts for volume purchases.	Supplier chain may be able to capture more discounts for volume purchases.

FIGURE 2.6 Application of value chain model.

systems can add value to the customers' inbound logistics. Because of the analysis of buying patterns, the items that the customers may wish to purchase are more likely to be in stock—and at lower prices.

Unlike the five competitive forces model, the focus of the value chain is on activities. Yet, in applying the value chain, competitive forces may be affected to the extent that the proposed technology may add value to suppliers, customers, or even competitors and potential new entrants.

▶ STRATEGIC ALLIANCES

The value chain helps a firm focus on adding value to the chains of its partners. This latest era of Information Resources Evolution emphasizes the importance of collaborative partnerships. These partnerships can take many forms including joint ventures, joint projects, trade associations, buyer-supplier partnerships, or cartels. Often such partnerships use information technologies to support strategic alliances and integrate data across partners' information systems. A **strategic alliance** is an interorganizational relationship that affords one or more companies in the relationship a strategic advantage. IT can help produce the product developed by the alliance, share information resources across the partners' existing value systems, or facilitate communication and coordination among the partners. For example, Delta recently formed a strategic alliance with e-Travel Inc., a travel service software company that targets large corporations, to promote Delta's online reservations system. The alliance was strategic because it helped Delta reduce agency reservation fees and offered e-Travel new corporate leads. Two other frequently discussed types of IT-facilitated strategic alliances are SCM and virtual corporations.

Supply Chain Management

Supply chain management (SCM) is an approach that improves the way a company finds raw components it needs to make a product or service, manufactures that product or service, and delivers it to customers. Technology, especially Web-based technology, allows the supply chains of a company's customers and suppliers to be linked through a single network that optimizes costs and opportunities for all companies in the supply chain. By sharing information across the network, guesswork about order quantities for raw materials and products can be reduced and suppliers can make sure they have enough on hand if demand for their products unexpectedly rises.

Collaboration paid off for supply-chain partners Wal-Mart and Procter & Gamble (P&G). Until these two giants linked their software systems in the 1980s, they shared little information. Now their integrated systems automatically alert P&G to ship more P&G products when Wal-Mart's distribution centers run low. The SCM system also allows P&G to monitor shelves at individual Wal-Mart stores through real-time satellite linkups that send messages to the factory whenever a

P&G item is scanned at the register. This real-time information aids P&G in manufacturing, shipping, and displaying products for Wal-Mart. Invoicing and payments are automatically processed. Because of high volumes and operating efficiencies derived from the SCM software, P&G can offer discounted prices to help Wal-Mart offer its "low, everyday prices."

Virtual Corporations

A **virtual corporation** is a temporary network of companies linked by information technology to exploit fast-changing opportunities. Suppliers, customers, or even rivals can be linked by communication and computer technologies to share skills, costs, and access to one another's markets. The growth of virtual corporations is spurred by high-speed communications networks, common standards, and an increasingly dynamic, complex environment. The type of environment in which virtual corporations thrive is the same that underlies the concept of hypercompetition. Many of the industry business-to-business (B2B) exchanges that were formed to respond to customer demand and subsequently disbanded were virtual corporations. An example is the short-lived MetalSpectrum, a consortia of companies such as Alcoa, Kaiser Aluminum, Olin Corporation, and Reynolds Aluminum Supply Company in the metals industry.

Co-opetition

Clearly, not all strategic alliances are formed with suppliers or customers as partners. Rather, co-opetition is becoming increasingly popular alternative model. As defined by Brandenburger and Nalebuff in their book of the same name, **co-opetition** is a strategy whereby companies cooperate and compete at the same time with companies in its value net.[4] The value net includes a company and its competitors and complementors, as well as its customers and suppliers, and the interactions among all of them. A complementor is a company whose product or service is used in conjunction with a particular product or service to make a more useful set for the customer. For example, Goodyear is a complementor to Ford and GM because tires are a complementary product to automobiles. Likewise, hardware and software companies are complementors.

Co-opetition, then, is the strategy for creating the best possible outcome for a business by optimally combining competition and cooperation. It frequently creates competitive advantage by giving power in the form of information to other organizations or groups. For example, Covisint, the auto industry's e-marketplace, is backed by competitors General Motors, Ford, and DaimlerChrysler. Further, Nissan and Peugot are equity partners. By addressing multiple automotive functional needs across the entire product life cycle, Covisint offers support for collaboration, supply chain management, procurement, and quality management. Thus, co-opetition as demonstrated by Covisint, not only streamlines the

---

[4] A. Brandenburger and B. Nalebuff, *Co-opetition* (New York: Doubleday, 1996).

internal operations of its backers, but also has the potential to transform the automotive industry.

► RISKS

As demonstrated throughout this chapter, information resources may be used to gain
strategic advantage, even if that advantage is fleeting. When information systems
are chosen as the tool to outpace their firm's competitors, executives should be aware
of the many risks that may surface. Some of theses risks include the following:

- *Awaking a sleeping giant.* A firm can implement IS to gain competitive
  advantage, only to find that it nudged a larger competitor with deeper
  pockets into implementing an IS with even better features. FedEx
  offered its customers the ability to trace the transit and delivery of their
  packages online. FedEx's much larger competitor, UPS, rose to the challenge. UPS not only implemented the same services, but also added a
  new set of features. Both the UPS and FedEx sites passed through multiple Web site iterations as the dueling delivery companies continue to
  struggle for competitive advantage.

- *Demonstrating bad timing.* Sometimes customers are not ready to use
  the technology designed to gain strategic advantage. For example,
  Momenta Corp. experienced monumental failure when it attempted to
  sell pen-based technology in the early 1990s. A decade later Pen-based
  computing is well accepted by PDA users.

- *Implementing IS poorly.* Stories abound of information systems that fail
  because they are poorly implemented. Typically these systems are complex and often global in their reach. In its zeal to implement a system to
  streamline supply chain communications and lower operating costs,
  Nike's implementation team allegedly performed customization that
  extended beyond the recommendations of its software supplier, i2
  Technologies. The resulting missed and duplicated orders may have cost
  Nike as much as a $100 million. Another implementation fiasco took
  place at Hershey Foods when it attempted to implement its supply and
  inventory system. Hershey developers brought the complex system up
  too quickly, and then failed to test it adequately. Related systems problems crippled shipments during the critical Halloween shopping season,
  resulting in large declines in sales and net income.

- *Failing to deliver what users want.* Systems that do not meet the needs
  of the firm's target market are likely to fail. Streamline.com (also called
  Streamline Inc.) experienced this risk when using the Web to provide
  home delivery of groceries and pick-up/drop-off services for movie
  rentals, dry cleaning, and film. Streamline charged a $30-per-month
  subscription fee and worked from "personal shopping lists" customers

submitted through its Web site. But Streamline failed to convince a large number of shoppers that Streamline's services matched their lifestyle. Streamline may have failed because its once-a-week delivery was too infrequent, or because its customers wanted to inspect the produce when bags were dropped off.

- *Running afoul of the law.* Using IS strategically may promote litigation if the IS results in the violation of laws or regulations. Years ago, American Airlines' reservation system, Sabre, was challenged by American Airlines' competitors on the grounds that it violated antitrust laws. More recently Napster filed for bankruptcy as a consequence of BMG Entertainment, AOL Time Warner, EMI, Sony, and Vivendi International jointly suing it for copyright infringement. The suit led to Napster's court-ordered shutdown.

▶ FOOD FOR THOUGHT: TIME-BASED COMPETITIVE ADVANTAGE

In the Internet economy, the pace of technological change continues to accelerate. Classical strategic advantages are created and destroyed based on which actions competitors take, how soon they take them, and how long each action takes. Classic strategies take time to develop and implement. The twenty-first century will see organizations increasingly seeking to use technology to neutralize the competition as quickly as possible. Reaching individual customers and meeting their needs as close to instantaneously as possible will leave no time for competitive actions to change the customer's mind. The moment the need is expressed, the product or service offer and exchange take place. This focus on time-based competition has already begun. Consider the role that Dell Computers played in compressing the time between the customer wanting a specific computer system and receiving that exact system on the doorstep. Dell's process can be executed in as little as five days from the time the customer places an order until he or she receives a custom-built system.

At the strategic level, the organization is confronted with increasing flows of information between itself, its stakeholders, its environment, and its competitors. The combination of technology and information enables each of these information "partners" to quickly change its expectations of the future. The result is a change from one set of activities to another set that aligns more closely with the new expectations. Each of these realignments from an information partner requires a response from the organization. Typical planning cycles are thrown out the window, because the organization needs to respond quickly to customer, competitor, and environmental changes. The speed at which an organization can adapt its business processes to these changes will dictate the true competitive advantage that it holds in the market.

Information resources are the key to achieving a time-based advantage. Understanding how to use them is critical to the strategic success of business today. For example, every organization has been forced to build Web-based applications.

Some embraced this opportunity as a chance to reinvent themselves to create a new business strategy—one that responds instantly. Others simply post a basic Web page with no thought of the lost window of opportunity. The latter group missed the point—time is of the essence and customers no longer accept slow, unresponsive service.

▶ SUMMARY

- Using IS for strategic advantage requires an awareness of the many relationships that affect both competitive business and information strategies.
- The five competitive forces model reminds us that more than just the local competitors influence the reality of the business situation. Analyzing the five competitive forces—new entrants, buyers, suppliers, industry competitors, and substitute products—from both a business view and an information view helps general managers use information resources to minimize the effect of these forces on the organization.
- The value chain highlights how information systems add value to the primary and support activities of a firm's internal operations, as well as to the activities of its customers, and other components of its supply chain.
- IT can facilitate strategic alliances.
- SCM and virtual corporations are two mechanisms for strategic alliances.
- Numerous risks are associated with using information systems to gain strategic advantage: awaking a sleeping giant, demonstrating bad timing, implementing poorly, failing to deliver what customers want, and running afoul of the law.

▶ KEY TERMS

customer relationship management (CRM) (p. 49)
co-opetition (p. 52)
information resources (p. 40)

network externalities (p. 41)
strategic alliance (p. 51)
supply chain management (SCM) (p. 51)

virtual corporation (p. 52)

▶ DISCUSSION QUESTIONS

1. How can information itself provide a competitive advantage to an organization? Give two or three examples. For each example, describe its associated risks.

2. Use the five competitive forces model as described in this chapter to describe how information technology might be used to provide a winning position for each of these businesses:

   a. A global airline

   b. A local dry cleaner

   c. An appliance service firm (provides services to fix and maintain appliances)

   d. A bank

3. Using the value chain model, describe how information technology might be used to provide a winning position for each of these businesses:

a. A global airline

b. A local dry cleaner

c. An appliance service firm (provides services to fix and maintain appliances)

d. A bank

4. Some claim that no sustainable competitive advantages can be gained from IT other than the capability of the IT organization itself. Do you agree or disagree? Defend your position.

5. Cisco Systems has a network of component suppliers, distributors, and contract manufacturers that are linked through Cisco's extranet. When a customer orders a Cisco product at Cisco's Web site, the order triggers contracts to manufacturers of printed circuit board assemblies when appropriate and alerts distributors and component suppliers. Cisco's contract manufacturers are aware of the order because they can log on to Cisco's extranet and link up with Cisco's own manufacturing execution systems. What are the advantages of Cisco's strategic alliances? Does this Cisco example demonstrate SCM? Why or why not?

6. In March 2000, procurement software maker Ariba, a supply chain specialist, i2, and IBM's consulting division formed an alliance. It was agreed that IBM would provide the interface between Ariba's and i2's products to create an integrated software package. While proclaiming its allegiance to the alliance, Ariba tried to buy Agile, a supply chain vendor that competed with i2, and i2 bought RightWorks, a procurement software vendor that competed directly with Ariba. Further, i2 and Ariba actively competed for each other's customers. The shaky alliance ended in 2001. How does this case demonstrate the advantages and disadvantages of co-opetition?

CASE STUDY 2-1

LEAR WON'T TAKE A BACKSEAT

For decades, Lear Corp. made car seats. Today, with the help of virtual reality and other digital technologies, Lear makes a whole lot more—and makes it a whole lot faster. Lear Corp used virtual reality to envision the interior of the Chevrolet Express LT, a new luxury van that Lear helped design and build. Within two years, the first models started coming off a GM assembly line near St. Louis.

In the automotive world, that kind of turnaround time is almost impossibly quick. Even when the shell of a vehicle already exists, as it did in this case, the vehicle design schedule traditionally spans about three years. Between the initial concept and the production-ready design lies a painstaking clay-modeling process that typically involves at least a half-dozen costly iterations. But by shifting much of that process to a virtual reality environment, Lear cut the product development period to a year and a half.

GM awarded Lear the lucrative contract for the Express LT largely because of the speed and flexibility that Lear's use of technology makes possible. "We always thought of Lear as a great seating company," says Linda Cook, 45, GM's planning director for commercial trucks and vans. "We didn't realize how much else it could do. Lear really needed that technology to get our attention."

Lear, based in Southfield, Michigan, has roots that go back to 1917. By the 1990s, it had become the world's biggest manufacturer of automotive seating. (If you've sat in anything from a Chevy to a Ferrari recently, then you've probably enjoyed the comfort of a Lear product.) But in the mid-1990s, the auto parts industry entered a period of aggressive consolidation. Instead of relying on thousands of small vendors to make each part separately, automakers wanted to buy complete systems from a few big suppliers. So Lear snapped up smaller companies and combined them into an operation that was capable of making an entire vehicle interior. It also invested heavily in the latest computer-aided design (CAD) software and in other new technologies. By 2000, thanks to acquisitions and expansion into new product areas, sales had climbed to $14.1 billion.

CAD first appeared in the auto industry in the late 1970s, but it didn't reach a critical mass of power and capability until the mid-1990s. That's when Lear decided to invest in an animated virtual reality package from Alias|Wavefront, a software subsidiary of Silicon Graphics. By 1998, the Reality Center was under construction, complete with a triple-projection screen and three digitized drawing boards. Out went the chisel; in came the cursor. Thanks to this technology, Lear has all but eliminated the slow, muck-filled process of building prototype after prototype from brownish-orange sculpting clay. However, Lear typically makes at least one physical prototype of every product that it develops in the Reality Center in order to test tactile issues.

In exploring new technologies, the Lear team was tempted at first by the prospect of using them to change long-standing ways of working together. Take the Internet. By digitizing much of the design process, Lear made it possible for designers to send their work back and forth over the Net—thereby creating a virtual workplace that brings together people from all around the world. In November 1998, for example, Rothkop traveled to a Volvo design center in Sweden and used the Net to work with colleagues at the Reality Center back in Southfield. Where the Internet extends or enhances communication, the Lear team has embraced it. For the most part, though, the real work of designing auto parts remains an up-close-and-personal business.

For that reason, when it came to building the Reality Center, Lear put a premium on creating an environment that would foster collaboration. The team considered a stereoscopic "cave," a space in which people can sit and be completely surrounded by a screen. While that arrangement simulates being in a car, "it can kind of make people nauseated," Rothkop says. Worse yet, only one or two people at a time can sit in the cave—a situation that has dismal implications for collaboration. Instead, the Lear team chose a simpler design for its virtual reality room, one that has a flatter screen and a more open space. There's even room in front of the screen for a full-sized truck, so Lear designers can bring together the real and the virtual whenever their work calls for that.

Another temptation that Lear executives faced was to think that CAD and VR would let them break down traditional job barriers and combine the roles of designer, sculptor, and animator into a single worker. But, in Lear's experience, the seemingly artificial barriers between jobs often turn out to be quite natural. So Lear drew back from the notion of combining jobs.

Discussion Questions

1. What is the strategic advantage afforded to Lear from virtual reality? How does this technology help it compete?

2. How long is Lear's window of opportunity for the strategic advantage given by the virtual reality system? That is, do you think that competitors will follow suit and implement a similar system. If yes, when?

3. Do you think the CAD system offers Lear strategic advantage? Explain.

4. Apply the value chain to demonstrate how the virtual reality system adds value for Lear and for General Motors.

5. What other types of competitive advantages might Lear executives seek from IS in general?

Source: Fara Warner, "Lear Won't Take a Backseat," *Fast Company*, 47 (June 2001), pp. 178, available at http://www.fastcompany.com/online/47/bestpractice.html.

CHAPTER 3

ORGANIZATIONAL IMPACTS OF INFORMATION SYSTEMS USE

At Diamond Technology Partners, a management consulting firm headquartered in Chicago, Illinois, every consultant has a laptop with applications that allow him or her to tap into the company databases, complete administrative functions, work on projects, and communicate with others. Every staff member also has a computer at his or her disposal. Using the computer is fundamental to the way the company is organized, because every piece of information generated by every person in the organization is created, stored, and retrieved from the IS. Everyone can access the work done by everyone else, regardless of position or status in the company. Information needed to do a task is available to whoever needs it at the time and place they need it. For example, a consultant working with a major bottling company in Florida can access computer routines developed for a similar project for a utility company in Oregon. IS are integrated into every work function, which enables Diamond Technology Partners to operate under an organizational form different from its low-tech counterparts. Employees can sustain organizational activities usually reserved for colleagues collocated at the same physical site even when they are traveling around the world. They also can share information as if everyone was in the same office.

Consider another example. One of the earliest companies to make use of IS as part of designing its organization was Mrs. Fields Cookies. In the early 1980s, this company was managing cookie and bakery stores all over the world with a fraction of the management staff of other fast-food chain stores. Every store had a computer system that told the manager how many cookies batches to make, when to bake them, and when they would lack sufficient freshness for sale. The effect was a control mechanism similar to having founder Debbie Fields in each store ensuring the quality of her cookies. The information system went even further. It allowed Mrs. Fields to hire people whose skills were in selling cookies and not worry about

59

whether those people could calculate baking cycles. The money spent for labor at Mrs. Fields stores paid for sales skills, not for baking skills. With store controllers at the headquarters offices in Park City, Utah, examining the numbers for each store within twelve hours of the end of each business day, the computer system helped frame an organizational design that gave Mrs. Fields the ability to sell gourmet cookies at a reasonable price.

The point is simple: IS comprise a fundamental organizational component that affects the way managers design their organizations. When used appropriately, IS and information technology (IT) leverage human resources, capital, and materials to create an organization that optimizes performance. A synergy results from designing organizations with IT in mind, which cannot be achieved when IT is just added on.

Chapter 1 introduced a simple framework for understanding the impact of IS on organizations. The Information Systems Strategy Triangle relates business strategy with IS strategy and organizational strategy. In an organization that operates successfully, an overriding business strategy drives both organizational strategy and information strategy. The most effective businesses optimize the interrelationships between the organization and IT, maximizing efficiency and productivity.

Organizational strategy includes the organization's design, as well as the managerial choices that define, set up, coordinate, and control its work processes. As discussed in Chapter 1, many models of organizational strategy are available, such as the business diamond that identifies four primary components of an organization: its business processes, its tasks and structures (or organizational design), its management control systems, and its values and culture. Figure 3.1 summarizes complementary design variables from the managerial levers framework. Optimized organizational design and management control systems support optimal business processes, and they, in turn, reflect the firm's values and culture.

This chapter builds on these models. Of primary concern is the ways in which IT can improve organizational design and management control systems. This chapter considers how IT can best affect organizational and management control variables. It looks at some innovative organizational designs that made extensive use of IT and concludes with some ideas about how organizations of the future will organize with the increasingly widespread use of the Internet and electronic linkages with suppliers, customers, and the world. This chapter focuses on organizational-level issues related to structure. The next two chapters complement it with a discussion of the individual worker and organizational processes.

▶ INFORMATION AGE ORGANIZATIONS

In 1988, three professors at the Harvard Business School predicted what would be key characteristics for the Information Age organization. Their predictions were close to what actually happened. The following summary of these characteristics

Variable	Description
Organizational variables	
Decision rights	Authority to initiate, approve, implement, and control various types of decisions necessary to plan and run the business.
Business processes	The set of ordered tasks needed to complete key objectives of the business.
Formal reporting relationships	The structure set up to ensure coordination among all units within the organization.
Informal networks	Mechanism, such as ad hoc groups, which work to coordinate and transfer information outside the formal reporting relationships.
Control variables	
Data	The information collected, stored, and used by the organization.
Planning	The processes by which future direction is established, communicated, and implemented.
Performance measurement and evaluation	The set of measures that are used to assess success in the execution of plans and the processes by which such measures are used to improve the quality of work.
Incentives	The monetary and nonmonetary devices used to motivate behavior within an organization.
Cultural variables	
Values	The set of implicit and explicit beliefs that underlie decisions made and actions taken.

FIGURE 3.1 Organizational design variables.
Source: Cash, Eccles, Nohria, and Nolan, *Building the Information Age Organization* (Homewood, IL: Richard D. Irwin, 1994).

relates them to three dimensions: (1) organizational structure, (2) human resources, and (3) management processes.

These characteristics, shown in Figure 3.2, serve as the basis for this and the next two chapters, which describe how information systems affect organizations. Information Age organizations use a different organization structures because they achieve benefits of small and large scale simultaneously, because they have flexible structures, because they blur the lines of controls, and because they focus on projects and processes. Human resources are different because individuals are better trained and therefore are able to work more autonomously. The work environment is increasingly engaging and exciting due to the velocity at which business happens. Finally, Information Age organizations follow management processes designed with information systems in mind. Control is separated from reporting relationships, keeping information flowing throughout the organization. Decision making and creativity are supported by information systems, which retain corporate history, experiences, and expertise in ways non-information-based organizations cannot achieve.

Dimension	Characteristics
Organizational Structure	Companies have benefits of small scale and large scale simultaneously. Large organizations adopt flexible and dynamic structures. The distinctions between centralized and decentralized control blur. Focus is on projects and processes instead of tasks and standard procedures.
Human Resources	Workers are better trained, more autonomous, and more transient. The work environment is exciting and engaging. Management is a shared, rotated, and sometimes part-time job. Job descriptions tied to narrowly defined tasks are non-existent. Compensation is tied directly to contribution.
Management Processes	Decision making is well understood. Control is separated from reporting relationships. Computers support creativity at all levels of the organization. Information systems retain corporate history, experience, and expertise.

FIGURE 3.2   Key characteristics for the Information Age organization.
Source: Applegate, Cash, and Mills, "Information Technology and Tomorrow's Manager," *Harvard Business Review* (November–December 1988), pp. 128–136.

▶ INFORMATION TECHNOLOGY AND ORGANIZATIONAL DESIGN

This section examines how IT enables or inhibits the design of an organization's physical structure. Ideally an organization is designed to facilitate the communication and work processes necessary for the organization to accomplish its goals. The structure of reporting relationships typically reflects the flow of communication and decision making throughout the organization. Traditional organization structures are hierarchical, flat, or matrix (see Figure 3.3). The networked structure is a newer organizational form. A comparison of these four types of organization structures may be found in Figure 3.4.

Hierarchical Organization Structure

As business organizations entered the twentieth century, they found themselves growing and needing to devise systems for processing and storing information. A new class of worker—the clerical worker—flourished. From 1870 to 1920 alone, the number of clerical workers mushroomed from 74,200 to more than a quarter of a million.[1] Factories and offices structured themselves using the model that Max Weber observed when studying the Catholic Church and the German army. This model, called a bureaucracy, was based on a hierarchical organization structure

Hierarchical organization structure is an organizational form based on the concepts of division of labor, specialization, and unity of command. When work needs to be done, it typically comes from the top and is segmented into smaller and smaller pieces until it reaches the level of the business in which it will be done. Middle managers do the primary information processing and

[1] Frances Cairncross, *The Company of the Future* (London: Profile Books, 2002).

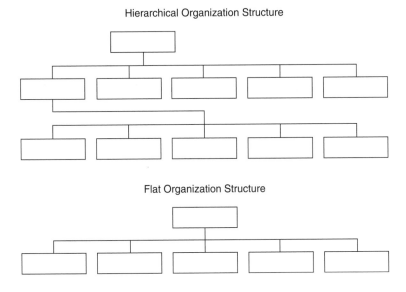

FIGURE 3.3 Hierarchical, flat, and matrix organization structures.

communication function, telling their subordinates what to do and telling senior managers the outcome of what was done. Jobs within the organization are specialized and often organized around particular functions, such as marketing, accounting, manufacturing, and so on. Unity of command means that each person has a single supervisor, who in turn has a supervisor, and so on. A number of rules are established to handle the routine work performed by employees of the organization. When in doubt about how to complete a task, workers turn to rules. If a rule doesn't exist to handle the situation, workers turn to the hierarchy for the decision. Key decisions are made at the top and filter down through the organization in a centralized fashion. IS are typically used to store and communicate information along the lines of the hierarchy and to support the information management function of the managers. Hierarchical structures are most suited to

	Hierarchical	Flat	Matrix	Networked
Description	Bureaucratic form with defined levels of management	Decision making pushed down to the lowest level in the organization	Workers assigned to two or more supervisors in an effort to make sure multiple dimensions of the business are integrated	Formal and informal communication networks that connect all parts of the company
Characteristics	Division of labor, specialization, unity of command, formalization	Informal roles, planning and control; often small and young organizations	Dual reporting relationships based on function and purpose	Known for flexibility and adaptability
Type of Environment Best Supported	Stable Certain	Dynamic Uncertain	Dynamic Uncertain	Dynamic Uncertain
Basis of Structuring	Primarily function	Primarily function	Functions and purpose (i.e., location, product, customer)	Networks
Power Structure	Centralized	Centralized	Distributed (matrix managers)	Distributed (network)
Key Technologies Supporting This Structure	Mainframe, centralized data and processing	Personal computers	Networks	Intranets and Internet

FIGURE 3.4 Comparison of organizational structures.

relatively stable, certain environments where the top-level executives are in command of the information needed to make critical decisions.

Flat Organization Structure

In contrast, in the **flat organization structure,** decision making is centralized, with the power often residing in the owner or founder. In flat organizations, everyone does whatever needs to be done in order to complete business. For this reason, flat organizations can respond quickly to dynamic, uncertain environments. Entrepreneurial organizations often use this structure because they typically have fewer employees, and even when they grow they initially build on the premise that everyone must do whatever is needed. As the work grows, new individuals are added to the organization, and eventually a hierarchy is formed where divisions are responsible for segments of the work processes. Many companies strive to keep the "entrepreneurial spirit," but in reality work gets done in much the same way as with the hierarchy described previously. Flat organizations often use IS to off-load certain routine work in order to avoid hiring additional workers. As a hierarchy develops, the IS become the glue tying together parts of the organization that otherwise would not communicate.

Matrix Organization Structure

The third popular form, the **matrix organization structure,** typically assigns workers to two or more supervisors in an effort to make sure multiple dimensions of the business are integrated. Each supervisor directs a different aspect of the employee's work. For example, a member of a matrix team from marketing would have a supervisor for marketing decisions and a different supervisor for a specific product line. The team member would report to both, and both would be responsible in some measure for that member's performance. In some cases the matrix reflects a third dimension (or more), such as the customer relations segment. IS reduce the operating complexity of matrix organizations by allowing information sharing among the different managerial functions. For example, a salesperson's sales would be entered into the information system and appear in the results of all of the managers to whom he or she reports. The matrix structure allows organizations to concentrate on both functions and purpose. It is especially suited to dynamic, uncertain environments.

Matrix organizations often fail to enable managers to achieve their business strategies, however. Applegate, McFarlan, and McKenney describe the problem as follows:

> The inability to cope with the increased information processing demands was a major cause of the failure of the matrix organization. In the 1960s, mainframe system architectures, with their centralized control of information processing, mirrored the centralized intelligence and control of the hierarchy. The microcomputer revolution of the 1980s provided tools to decentralize information processing control that mirrored organizational attempts to decentralize decision authority and responsibility to small entrepreneurial units. While these decentralized IT resources helped improve local decision making, the debates and conflicts concerning whether to centralize or decentralize IT resource management reflected organizational arguments concerning the centralization or decentralization of organizational decision authority. However, the network revolution of the 1990s enables distributed information processing and intelligence that make the IT centralization/decentralization debates of the 1980s irrelevant.[2]

---

[2] L. M. Applegate, W. McFarlan, and J. McKenney, *Corporate Information Systems Management: Text and Cases,* 4th ed. (Boston: Richard D. Irwin, Inc., 1996).

Networked Organization Structure

Made possible by new IS, a fourth type of organizational structure emerged: the **networked organization structure** (see Figure 3.5). Networked organizations characteristically feel flat and hierarchical at the same time. An article published in the *Harvard Business Review* describes this type of organization: "Rigid hierarchies are replaced by formal and informal communication networks that connect all parts of the company. . . . [This type of organizational structure] is well known for its flexibility and adaptiveness."[3] It is particularly suited to dynamic, unstable environments.

Networked organization structures are those that utilize distributed information and communication systems to replace inflexible hierarchical controls with controls based in IS. Networked organizations are defined by their ability to promote creativity and flexibility while maintaining operational process control. Because networked structures are distributed, many employees throughout the organization can share their knowledge and experience, and participate in making key organizational decisions. IS are fundamental to process design; they improve process efficiency, effectiveness, and flexibility. As part of the execution of these processes, data are gathered and stored in centralized data warehouses for use in analysis and decision making. In theory at least, decision making is more timely and accurate because data are collected and stored instantly. The extensive use of communications technologies and networks also renders it easier to coordinate across functional

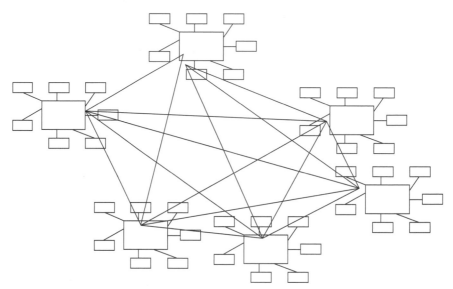

FIGURE 3.5   The networked organization.

[3] L. M. Applegate, J. I. Cash, and D. Q. Mills, "Information Technology and Tomorrow's Manager," *Harvard Business Review* (November–December 1988), pp. 128–136.

boundaries. In short, the networked organization is one in which IT ties together people, processes, and units.

The organization feels flat when IT is used primarily as a communication vehicle. Traditional hierarchical lines of authority are used for tasks other than communication when everyone can communicate with everyone else, at least in theory. The term used is *technological leveling,* because the technology enables individuals from all parts of the organization to reach all other parts of the organization.

Some organizations take the networked structure one step further. When IT is used extensively as a design tool for the organization, a different organizational form called the T-form organization is possible. The "T" stands for "technology-based" or "technology-oriented." In T-form organizations, IT is combined with traditional organizational components to form new types of components, such as electronic linking, production automation, electronic workflows, electronic customer/supplier relationships, and self-service Internet portals. While the original T-form organization was created long before the Internet was popular, this structure has been adopted by many Internet-based companies today.

Work is often coordinated automatically in the T-form organization. Systems enable information to more easily move around an organization and among individuals, making decisions possible wherever they are needed, rather than only at senior levels of the organization. Business processes are typically designed differently, relying on the technology for more mundane, repetitive tasks, and enabling employees to take on more people-oriented and unstructured responsibilities. These types of organizations are increasingly broadening their electronic network to include suppliers and customers. For example, Procter & Gamble works closely with Wal-Mart to make sure shelves are stocked and inventories replenished automatically. Technology is integrated with all components of the business, not just communications networks, as in a traditional networked organization.

▶ INFORMATION TECHNOLOGY AND MANAGEMENT CONTROL SYSTEMS

Not only does IT change the way organizations are structured, it also profoundly affects the way managers control their organizations. By control, we mean how people and processes are monitored, evaluated, given feedback, and compensated or rewarded. Figure 3.6 summarizes the activities of management control.

Traditional hierarchical organizations require managers to tightly control operating processes. To do so, they must understand the standard operating procedures for the primary activities of the organization.[4] The complexity of the activities is handled by creating divisions and subdivisions and dividing the work among them. The subdivision continues until individual jobs are specified and tasks are assigned to individual workers. Then begins the work of the control systems: to ensure that the work is done on time, properly, and within budget.

[4] Robert Simons, *Levers of Control: How Managers Use Innovative Control Systems to Drive Strategic Renewal* (Boston: Harvard Business School Press, 1995).

Control Activities	Brief Definition
Monitoring	Observing and keeping track of the progress, quality, cost, time, and other relevant parameters.
Evaluating	Comparing the data collected through monitoring to standards or historical data.
Providing Feedback	Communicating the results of evaluation to the individuals responsible for the activities and tasks.
Compensating	Deciding on salary or other forms of payment to those individuals who performed the tasks.
Rewarding	Deciding and delivering bonuses, recognition, or other types of prize for exemplary work.

FIGURE 3.6   Model of management control activities.

IS play three important roles in management control processes:

1. *Collection:* They enable the collection of information that may not be collectible other ways.
2. *Communication:* They speed the flow of information from where it is generated to where it is needed.
3. *Evaluation:* They facilitate the analysis of information in ways that may not be possible otherwise.

These roles played by IS are subsumed in various management control activities that we outline in Figure 3.6 and discuss next.

Information Technology Changes the Way Managers Monitor

Monitoring work can take on a completely new meaning with the use of information technologies. IS make it possible to collect such data as the number of keystrokes, the precise time spent on a task, exactly who was contacted, and the specific data that passed through the process. For example, a call center that handles customer service telephone calls is typically monitored by an information system that collects data on the number of calls each representative received and the length of time each representative took to answer each call and then to respond to the question or request for service. Managers at call centers can easily and nonintrusively collect data on virtually any part of the process. In contrast, a manager of field representatives might also use IS to monitor work, but the use may be more obvious and thus present an intrusion. For example, having field sales personnel complete documents detailing their progress adds work for them.

The organizational design challenge is twofold: (1) to embed monitoring tasks within everyday work, and (2) to reduce the negative impacts to workers being monitored. Workers perceive their regular tasks as value-adding, but have difficulty in seeing how value is added by tasks designed to provide information for management control. Often these tasks are avoided, or worse, data recorded are inaccurate, falsified, or untimely. Collecting monitoring data directly from work tasks—or embedding the creation and storage of performance information into software used to perform work—renders them more reliable.

Employee monitoring systems may be intrusive and can hurt morale. Employees should receive prior notice that they are being monitored, but this awareness often heightens their stress levels. Also, tracking job performance in terms of discrete, measurable tasks can serve to disconnect the worker from the larger business process in which he or she is involved, giving him or her less opportunity to broaden his or her skills and advance in the organization. Breaking down jobs into simple tasks counters an organizational philosophy that seeks to empower individuals to make significant contributions to the company as a whole.

Information Technology Changes the Way Managers Evaluate

IS make it possible to evaluate data against reams of standard or historical data as desired. Models can be built and simulations designed. Thus, managers can more easily and completely understand the progress and performance of work. In fact, the ready availability of so much information catches some managers in "analysis paralysis:" analyzing too much or too long. In our example of the call center, a manager can compare a worker's output to that of colleagues, to earlier output, to historical outputs reflecting similar work conditions at other times, and so on.

Even though evaluation constitutes an important use of IS, how the information is used has significant organizational consequences. Information collected for evaluation may be used to provide feedback so the worker can improve personal performance; it also can be used to determine rewards and compensation. The former use—for improvement in performance—is nonthreatening and generally welcome. Using the same information for determining compensation or rewards, however, can be threatening. Suppose the call center manager is evaluating the number and duration of calls service representatives answer on a given day. The manager's goal is to make sure all calls are answered quickly, and he or she communicates that goal to his or her staff. Now think about how the evaluation information is used. If the manager simply provides the workers with information about numbers and duration, then the evaluation is not threatening. Typically, each worker will make his or her own evaluation and respond by improving call numbers and duration. A discussion may even occur in which the service representative describes other important dimensions, such as customer satisfaction and quality. Perhaps the representative takes longer than average on each call because of the attention devoted to the customer. On the other hand, if the manager uses the information about number of calls and duration to rank workers so that top workers are rewarded, then workers may feel threatened by the evaluation and respond accordingly. The representative not on the top of the list may shorten calls, deliver less quality, or cause a decrease in customer satisfaction. The lesson for managers is to take care concerning what is monitored and how the information the systems make available is used. Metrics for performance must be meaningful in terms of the organization's broader goals, but these metrics are harder to define when work is decentralized and monitored electronically.

Information Technology Changes the Way Managers Provide Feedback

Using evaluation information for rewards will drive organizational behavior. How feedback is communicated in the organization also plays a role in affecting behavior.

Some feedback can be communicated via IS themselves. A simple example is the feedback built into an electronic form that will not allow it to be submitted until it is properly filled out. For more complex feedback, IS may not be the appropriate vehicle. For example, no one would want to be told they were doing a poor job via e-mail or voice mail. Negative feedback of significant consequence often is best delivered in person or over the telephone in real time.

IS can allow for feedback from a variety of participants who otherwise could not be involved. Many companies do a "360-degree" feedback, into which the individual's supervisors, subordinates, and coworkers all provide input. IS make it relatively easy to solicit feedback from anyone who has access to the system. Because that feedback is received more quickly, improvements can be made faster.

Information Technology Changes the Way Managers Compensate and Reward

Compensation and rewards are the ways organizations create incentives to good performance. A clever reward system can make employees feel good without paying them more money. IS can affect these processes, too. Some organizations use their Web sites to recognize high performers. Others reward them with new technology. At one organization, top performers get new computers every year, while lower performers get the "hand-me-downs."

IS make it easier to design complex incentive systems, such as shared or team-based incentives. An information system facilitates keeping track of contributions of team members and, in conjunction with qualitative inputs, can be used to allocate rewards according to complex formulas. For example, in the call center example, tracking metrics, such as "average time per call" and "number of calls answered," allows the manager to monitor agents' performance. This quantitative data makes for useful comparisons, but it cannot account for qualitative variables: for example, agents who spend more time handling calls may be providing better customer service. Agents who know they will be evaluated by the volume of calls they process may rush callers and provide poorer service in order to maximize their performance according to the narrow metric. Agents providing the poorest service could in fact be compensated best if the firm's performance evaluation and compensation strategy is linked only to such metrics. The manager must consider both the metrics and qualitative data in assigning compensation and rewards.

Information Technology Changes the Way Managers Control Processes

The preceding section primarily addresses the control of individuals. Managers also need to control work done at the process level. At the individual level, IS can streamline the process of monitoring, evaluating, and compensating. Process control is a different matter.

Process control refers to the levers available to a manager to ensure that operational processes are carried out appropriately. A percentage of that control lies in making sure individuals perform appropriately. The process itself needs continuous improvement, and although the various methods of process improvement lie outside the scope of this book, it is important to understand that IS can play a crucial role. IS provide decision models for scenario planning and evaluation. For example, the airlines routinely use decision models to study the effects of changing routes or schedules. IS collect and analyze information from automated processes, and they can be used to make automatic adjustments to the processes. For example, a paper mill uses IS to monitor the mixing of ingredients in a batch of paper and to add more ingredients or change the temperature of the boiler as necessary. IS collect, evaluate, and communicate information, leaving managers free to make decisions.

▶ VIRTUAL ORGANIZATIONS

The virtual organization provides a clear example of how organizations can be designed differently using information. A **virtual organization** is a structure that makes it possible for individuals to work for an organization and live anywhere. The Internet and corporate intranets create the opportunity for individuals to work from anyplace they can access a computer—from home, satellite offices, customer sites, and hotel rooms.

Just to clarify terms, the *virtual organization* is not to be confused with the *virtual corporation* introduced in Chapter 2, which features some similar characteristics. Like the virtual organization, the virtual corporation is made possible by extensive use of IS to create a virtual whole. However, the virtual corporation, unlike the virtual organization, requires an external orientation. It describes a business strategy for allying with complementary businesses so that the combined businesses respond to customers as a single entity. Each company in the virtual corporation brings a set of strengths to the combined group and relies on the other partners for their core strengths; each company alone would be at risk if other partners did not provide the complementary strengths.

The structure of a virtual organization is networked. Everyone has access to everyone else using the technology. Hierarchy may be present in the supervisory roles, but work is done crossing boundaries. For work that can be done on a computer or work that makes extensive use of telecommunications, technologies such as ISDN, the Internet, Lotus Notes, and Microsoft Outlook make it possible to design a work environment anywhere. E-mail is the most widely used means of communication, making it possible for even the newest member of a team to communicate with the most senior person in the organization. The basis of success in a virtual organization is the amount of collaboration that takes place between individuals. In a traditional organization, individuals mainly collaborate by holding face-to-face meetings. They use IS to communicate and to supplement these meetings, but the culture requires "looking at eyeballs" to get work done. By contrast, a virtual organization uses its IS as the basis for collaboration. For example, Diamond Technology Partners, the consulting firm discussed earlier, uses Lotus Notes as the basis for collaborative work, thus giving its consultants access to the entire knowledge of the organization from the "portal" of its computers.

In the virtual organization, management processes, support processes, and business processes are designed differently. These processes must reflect the assumption that not everyone will be in the office when they happen. For example, a bigger office may not be a useful reward for an employee in such an organization, so the reward system may have to be different. In fact, all management processes must be reexamined. If managers require personal observation to conduct evaluations, then the process may have to change. Managers in a virtual organization often monitor results, rather than the behavior needed to perform the process. It becomes the responsibility of the individual worker to keep the manager informed of problems and to seek assistance. Managers must design ways to monitor performance electronically.

Support functions also differ. For example, a virtual organization might not require individuals to fill out paper expense forms, but rather electronic forms that are accessible from anywhere. IT support might not mean bringing a broken system to the technicians or a visit from the technicians. Instead, technical support might comprise a Web site with a chat room or a posting of frequently asked questions. Perhaps the virtual worker can call a toll-free support center. Also, virtual companies can hire firms to provide on-site service to their workers.

Business processes themselves must be accessible anyplace and anytime. Often they are built on the Internet or made accessible on company computers using other forms of telecommunication. For example, an insurance company put its customer service and ordering processes online so that its teleworkers can take calls and complete these processes from anywhere. Many of its representatives now work from home.

VeriFone, a leading manufacturer of credit verification systems, is well known for its virtual organization.[5] The company was founded in 1981 by an entrepreneur who hated bureaucracy. By 1990, it was the leading company for transaction automation with products and services used in more than 80 countries. VeriFone's office building in northern California houses a nominal corporate headquarters. In several plants around the world, its processing systems are actually made, and its distribution centers facilitate rapid delivery to customers. Most corporate functions, however, occur at multiple global locations, including Texas, Hawaii, India, and Taiwan. The company seeks to put its people in close proximity to customers and emerging markets, which results in about a third of the employees traveling roughly half of the time. This strategy gives VeriFone first-hand information about business opportunities and competitive situations worldwide.

At the heart of the company culture is constant and reliable sharing of information. It is a culture that thrives on the chief executive officer's ban on secretaries and paper correspondence. Everyday the chief information officer (CIO) gathers yesterday's results and measures them against the company's plans. Systems post

---

[5] Hossam Galal, Donna Stoddard, Richard Nolan, and Jon Kao, "VeriFone: The Transaction Automation Company," Harvard Business School case study 195-088.

travel itineraries of everyone in the company and track which people speak what languages. Using IS for simulation and analysis, the CIO pulls together information from databases around the company for an e-mail newsletter to everyone in the company. The newsletter describes the latest products, competitive wins, and operating efficiencies. The top 15 salespeople are often listed, along with their sales figures. More than just managing the IS, VeriFone's CIO provides the "information glue" that holds the virtual organization together.

A story is told of a new salesperson who was trying to close a particularly big deal. He was about to get a customer signature on the contract when he was asked about the competition's system. Being new to the company, he did not have an answer, but he knew he could count on the company's information network for help. He asked his customer for 24 hours to research the answer. He then sent a note to everyone in the company asking the questions posed by the customer. The next morning, he had several responses from others around the company. He went to his client with the answers and closed the deal.

What is interesting about this example is that the "new guy" was treated as a colleague by others around the world, even though they did not know him personally. He was also able to collaborate with them instantaneously. It was standard procedure, not panic time, because of the culture of collaboration in this virtual organization. The information infrastructure provided the means, but the organization built on top of it consisted of processes designed for individuals at a geographical remove.

▶ VIRTUAL TEAMS

Few organizations are as totally virtual as Verifone. However, an increasing number of organizations have virtual components called virtual teams. **Virtual teams** are defined as "geographically and/or organizationally dispersed coworkers that are assembled using a combination of telecommunications and information technologies to accomplish an organizational task."[6] This definition includes teams whose members seldom meet face-to-face. The members of virtual teams may be in different locations, organizations, time zones, or time shifts. Further, virtual teams may have distinct, relatively permanent membership, or they may be relatively fluid as they evolve to respond to changing task requirements and as members leave and are replaced by new members.

Several reasons explain the growing popularity of virtual teams:

- As information needs mushroom, organizations rely increasingly upon the skills as knowledge of individuals dispersed across different countries, time zones, and organizations.
- The enhanced bandwidths of today's telecommunication technologies promote the use of networks linking individuals, internal and external to the organization.

[6] A. M. Townsend, S. DeMarie, and A.R. Hendrickson, "Virtual Teams: Technology and the workplace of the future," *Academy of Management Executive,* 12, 3 (1998), pp. 17–28.

- Technology in the form of group support systems, groupware, and decision-making support software is available to assist virtual teams in collaborating and making decisions.

- Difficulties in getting relevant stakeholders together physically are relaxed.

Virtual teams clearly offer advantages in terms of expanding the knowledge base through team membership, increasing representation in ad hoc teams, and *following the sun*. In an example of following the sun, London team members of a virtual team of software developers at Tandem Services Corporation initially code the project and transmit their code each evening to U.S. team members for testing. U.S. members forward the code they tested to Tokyo for debugging. London team members start their next day with the code debugged by their Japanese colleagues, and another cycle is initiated.[7] However, time zones can work against virtual team members when they are forced to stay up late or work in the middle of the night in order to communicate with team members in other time zone. A summary of this and other challenges in comparison with more traditional teams can be found in Figure 3.7.

A major communication challenge that virtual teams face stems from their only being able to communicate electronically via e-mail, teleconferences, or messaging systems. Electronic media allow team members to transcend the limitations of space, and even store messages for future references. But, electronic communications may not allow team members to convey the nuances that are possible with face-to-face conversations. In addition, virtual teams differ from traditional teams in terms of technological and diversity challenges. For example, traditional teams, unlike virtual ones, may not have to deal with the hassles of learning new technologies or selecting the technology that is most appropriate for the task at hand. Perhaps the greatest challenges that virtual teams face in comparison to their more traditional counterparts arise from the diversity of the team members. Virtual teams enable members to come from many different cultures and nations. Even though this diversity allows managers to pick team members from a wider selection of experts, global virtual teams are more likely than more traditional teams to be stymied by team members who have different native languages.

Managers cannot manage virtual teams in the same way that they manage more traditional teams. The differences in management control activities are particularly pronounced. Leaders of virtual teams cannot easily observe the behavior of virtual team members. Thus, monitoring of behavior is likely to be more limited than in traditional teams. Performance is more likely to be evaluated in terms of output than on displays of behavior. Because the team members are

[7] Marie-Claude Boudreau, Karen Loch, Daniel Robey, and Detmar Straub, "Going global: Using information technology to advance the competitiveness of the virtual transnational organization," *Academy of Management Executive,* 12, 4 (1998), pp. 120–128.

Challenges	Virtual Teams	Traditional Teams
Communication	• Multiple time zones can lead to greater efficiencies when leveraged, but can also create communication difficulties in terms of scheduling meetings and interactions. • Communication dynamics such as facial expressions, vocal inflections, verbal cues, and gestures are altered.	• Teams are collocated in same time zone. Scheduling is less difficult. • Teams may use richer communication media, including face-to-face discussions.
Technology	• Team members must have proficiency across a wide range of technologies; VT membership may be biased toward individuals skilled at learning new technologies. • Technology offers an electronic repository that may facilitate building an organizational memory. • Work group effectiveness may be more dependent on the ability to align group structure and technology with the task environment.	• Technology is not critical for group processes. Technological collaboration tools, while possibly used, are not essential for communications. Team members may not need to possess these skills. • Electronic repositories are not typically used. • Task technology fit may not be as critical.

Team Diversity	• Members typically come from different organizations and/or cultures. This makes it:
	  • Harder to establish a group identity
	  • Necessary to have better communication skills
	  • More difficult to build trust, norms, and shared meanings about roles, because team members have fewer cues about their teammates' performance
		• Because members are more homogeneous, group identity is easier to form.
		• Because of commonalities, communications are easier to complete successfully.

FIGURE 3.7 Comparison of challenges facing virtual teams and traditional teams.

dispersed, providing feedback is especially important—not just at the end of a team's project, but throughout the team's life. In order to encourage the accomplishment of the team's goal, compensation should be based heavily on the team's performance, rather than just on individual performance. Compensating team

members for individual performance may result in "hot-rodding" or lack of cooperation among team members. Organizational reward systems must be aligned
with the accomplishment of desired team goals. This alignment is especially difficult when virtual team members belong to different organizations, each with
their own unique reward and compensation systems. Each compensation system may affect individual performance in a different way. Managers need to be
aware of differences and attempt to discover ways to provide motivating rewards
to all team members. It is also the manager's responsibility to ensure that virtual team members have the technological support they need to complete the
team's assigned tasks.

▶ FOOD FOR THOUGHT: IMMEDIATELY RESPONSIVE ORGANIZATIONS

A series of ideas are floating around centered on the immediacy of responses that
IS make possible and the organizational forms that result (see, for example, the
popular books *Blur*,[8] *Real Time*,[9] *Corporate Kinetics*,[10] *Adaptive Enterprise*,[11] and
The Horizontal Organization.[12] These ideas suggest that the increased use of IS
in general, and the Internet in particular, make possible the ability to respond
instantly to customer demands, supplier issues, and internal communication needs.
IS are enabling even more advanced organization forms such as the adaptive organization, the horizontal organization, and a relatively new form, the zero time organization.[13] Common to all of these designs is the idea of agile, responsive
organizations that can configure their resources and people quickly and are flexible enough to sense and respond to changing demands.

The zero time organization, for example, describes the concept of instant "cus-
tomerization," or the ability to respond to customers immediately. In order to
accomplish this goal, the organization must master five disciplines:

1. *Instant value alignment:* understanding the customer so well that the company anticipates and is therefore ready to provide exactly what the customer wants.

2. *Instant learning:* building learning directly into the company's tasks and
   processes and making sure that requisite information is readily at hand when
   it is needed.

---

[8] Stan Davis, and Christopher Meyer, *Blur* (Reading, MA: Perseus Books, 1998).

[9] Regis McKenna, *Real Time* (Boston: Harvard Business School Press, 1997).

[10] Michael Fradette and Steve Michaud, *Corporate Kinetics* (New York: Simon and Schuster, 1998).

[11] Stephan H. Haeckel and Adrian J. Slywotzky, *Adaptive Enterprise: Creating and Leading Sense-
and-Respond Organizations* (Boston: Harvard Business School Press, 1999).

[12] Frank Ostroff, *The Horizontal Organization: What the Organization of the Future Actually Looks
Like and How It Delivers Value to Customers* (New York: Oxford University Press, 1999).

[13] R. Yeh, K. Pearlson, and G. Kozmetsky, *ZeroTime: Providing Instant Customer Value Everytime-
All the Time* (New York: Wiley, 2000).

3. *Instant involvement:* using IS to communicate all relevant information to suppliers, customers, and employees and making sure everyone is prepared to deliver their products, services, or information instantly.

4. *Instant adaptation:* creating a culture and structure that enable all workers to act instantly and to make decisions to respond to customers.

5. *Instant execution:* building business processes that involve as few people as possible (no touch), electronically cross organizational boundaries, and result in cycle times so short that they appear to execute instantly when the customer needs their outputs.

Building in the capability to respond instantly means designing the organization so that each of the key structural elements is able to respond instantly. For example, instant learning means building learning into the business processes. It means using IS to deliver small modules of learning directly to the point where the process is being done. For example, at Dell Computers, assembly line workers have access to a terminal directly above their workstations. As an assembly comes to their stations, its bar code tells the information system what type of assembly it is and which instructions to display. When the assembly reaches the table, the instructions are already there. The worker does not have to ask for the instructions, nor go anyplace to find them. IS allows this instant learning to happen.

Few companies qualify as zero time organizations. As IS become ubiquitous and customers increasingly demand instant service, zero time characteristics will become even more common in business.

► SUMMARY

- Incorporating information systems as a fundamental organizational design component is critical to company survival. Organizational strategy includes the organization's design, as well as the manager's choices that define, set up, coordinate, and control its work processes.
- Organizational designers today must have a working knowledge of what information systems can do and how the choice of information system will affect the organization itself.
- Information flows can facilitate or inhibit organizational structures.
- Forms such as flat, hierarchical, and matrix organizations are being enhanced by information technology resulting in networked organizations and virtual organizations that can better respond to dynamic, uncertain organizational environments.
- Information technology affects managerial control mechanisms: monitoring, evaluating, providing feedback, compensating, and rewarding. It is the job of the manager to ensure the proper control mechanisms are in place and the interactions between the organization and the information systems do not undermine the managerial objectives.
- A virtual organization is a structure that makes it possible for individuals to work for an organization and live anywhere. They are made possible through information and communication technologies.

- Virtual teams are defined as "geographically and/or organizationally dispersed coworkers that are assembled using a combination of telecommunications and information technologies to accomplish an organizational task." They are an increasingly common organizational phenomenon and must be managed differently from more traditional teams, especially when team members are from different organizations, cultures, or countries.

▶ KEY TERMS

flat organization
 structure (p. 64)
hierarchical organization
 structure (p. 62)

networked organization
 structure (p. 66)
matrix organization
 structure (p. 65)

organizational strategy
 (p. 60)
virtual organization (p. 71)
virtual team (p. 73)

▶ DISCUSSION QUESTIONS

1. How might IT change a manager's job?

2. Is monitoring an employee's work on a computer a desirable or undesirable activity from a manager's perspective? From the employee's perspective? Defend your position.

3. E-mail makes communications between individuals much easier. Give an example of a type of communication that would be inappropriate if it only took place over e-mail. What is an example of an appropriate communication for e-mail?

4. It is sometimes argued that team members must meet face-to-face in order to accomplish more complex, meaningful tasks? Do you agree? Explain.

5. Consider the brief description of the zero time organization. What is an example of a control system that would be critical to manage for success in the zero time organization? Why?

6. Mary Kay, Inc., sells facial skin care products and cosmetics around the globe. The business model is to provide one-on-one, highly personalized service. More than 500,000 Independent Beauty Consultants (IBCs) sell in 29 markets worldwide. Each IBC runs his or her own business by developing a client base, and then providing services and products for sale to those clients. Recently the IBCs were offered support through an e-commerce system with two major components: mymk.com and Mary Kay InTouch. Mymk.com allows IBCs to create instant online sites where customers can shop anytime directly with their personal IBC. Mary Kay InTouch streamlines the ordering process by automatically calculating discounts, detecting promotion eligibility, allowing the IBCs to access up-to-date product catalogs, and providing a faster way to transact business with the company.[14]

 a. How would the organizational strategy need to change to respond to Mary Kay's new business strategy?

 b. What changes would you suggest Mary Kay, Inc. managers make in their management systems order to realize the intended benefits of the new systems? Specifically, what types of changes would you expect to make in the evaluation systems, the reward systems, and feedback systems?

[14] Adapted from "Mary Kay, Inc.," *Fortune,* Microsoft supplement (November 8, 1999), p. 5.

VIRTUALLY THERE?

Dr. Laura Esserman leans forward and speaks with conviction, making broad gestures with her hands. "Over the past couple of decades, I've watched industries be transformed by the use of information systems and incredible visual displays," she says. "What we could do is to completely change the way we work—just by changing the way we collect and share information."

Sounds familiar, right? But Esserman isn't championing yet another overzealous Silicon Valley start-up—she's envisioning how cancer patients will interact with their doctors. If Esserman, a Stanford-trained surgeon and MBA, has her way, patients won't sit passively on an exam table, listening to impenetrable diagnoses and memorizing treatment instructions. Instead, they'll have access to a multimedia treasure chest of real-time diagnosis, treatment, and success-rate data from thousands of cases like their own. Better still, they won't meet with just one doctor. There will be other doctors on the case—some from the other side of the hospital and some, perhaps, from the other side of the world.

Esserman and her colleagues at the University of California San Francisco's Carol Franc Buck Breast Care Center are pioneers in the new world of virtual teams and virtual tools, a world in which there will be real change in the way highly trained people whose work depends on intense collaboration get things done. Her goal at the Buck Breast Care Center is to use virtual tools to bring more useful information (and more doctors) into the exam room. Why? Because two heads really are better than one. She explains that when patients see their doctors after a breast cancer diagnosis, for example, they are handed a recommended course of treatment that involves serious choices and trade-offs. Of course, most patients don't know enough about the merits of, say, a lumpectomy versus a mastectomy to make an informed choice, so they trust their doctors to tell them what to do.

But a single doctor isn't always equipped to make the best decision, especially since different procedures can have very different long-term physical and emotional impacts—but may not be all that different in their short-term medical outcomes. "Very often," Esserman says, "doctors recommend a particular treatment because they're more familiar with it. But we should be advocates for our patients, rather than our specialties."

Although her full-blown program is a long way off, Esserman has run a pilot project with 24 patients. She worked with both Oracle, the Silicon Valley database giant, and MAYA Viz, a Pittsburgh company that develops "decision community" software, to allow doctors across the country to collaborate virtually. Through Esserman's approach, when a patient arrives at the doctor's office to receive treatment instructions, instead of listening to a physician's monologue, she's handed a printout. On the top left side of the page is the diagnosis, followed by patient-specific data: the size and spread of the tumor, when it was discovered, and the name of the treating doctor. Below that is statistical information generated from clinical-research databases, such as the number of similar cases treated each year and details about survival rates.

A set of arrows point to treatment options. Next, the patient reads the risks and benefits associated with each treatment. She can follow along as the doctor explains the chances that the cancer will recur after each option and the likelihood that a particular treatment will require follow-up procedures, as well as a comparison of survival rates for each one.

At this point, the patient has an opportunity to voice concerns about treatment options, and the physician can explain her experiences with each one. "When you share this kind of information, patients and doctors can make decisions together according to the patient's values," Esserman says. This is where the network tools come into play. Drawing from stored databases of both clinical trials and patient-treatment histories local to the hospital, the physician can compare courses of action and results far beyond her own personal experience. "A medical opinion is really just one physician's synthesis of the information," notes Esserman. "So you need a way to calibrate yourself—a way to continually ask, Are there variations among the group of doctors that I work with? Am I subjecting people to procedures that turn out not to be useful?"

With a real-time, shared-data network, these questions can be answered at the touch of a button instead of after hours, weeks, or months of research. But that's just the beginning. A real-time network also presents the possibility of seeking help from other specialists on puzzling cases, even if those specialists are on the other side of the world.

Discussion Questions

1. Why does this case offer an example of a virtual team? In what ways are the team members on this team dispersed (i.e., location, organization, culture, etc.)?

2. What are the advantages of the virtual team described in this case?

3. What technological support is needed for the virtual team to meet its goals?

4. What suggestions can you offer Dr. Esserman for managing this virtual team?

Source: Excerpted from Alison Overholt, "Virtually There" *FastCompany,* 56 (March 2002), p. 108, available at http://www.fastcompany.com/online/56/virtual.html.

4

INFORMATION TECHNOLOGY AND THE DESIGN OF WORK[1]

In her book, *In the Age of the Smart Machine: The Future of Work and Power,* Shoshana Zuboff studied the effects on data clerks of a new computer system that automated insurance claims processing. Before the implementation, clerks processed claims by hand using paper, pencils, and ledger books. After the information technology (IT) system was implemented, the clerks used only computer keyboards and telephones—and the latter only occasionally, when they needed to call customers for clarifications.

The new IT system created confusion and workers felt distanced from the work process. The clerks did not fully understand where the data on their screens came from, or what the information meant. The sensory satisfaction gained from handling paper forms and writing in ledger books was missing. The information with which the clerks worked became nothing more than streams of data, without apparent meaning or importance. Zuboff found that the clerks were "frustrated by the loss of the concreteness that had provided for them a sense of certainty and control."[2] As one benefits analyst explained, "Now we have numbers without names—no ledgers, no writing, no history, no paper. The only reality we have left is when we get to talk to a customer."

The clerks actually lost skills. A manager described the new system as requiring "less thought, judgment, and manual intervention" than the manual system it had replaced. This sentiment was echoed by a benefits analyst who prided himself on knowing, through memorization and experience, a variety of claims limitations that his job previously required him to know. After the implementation, he noted: "The computer system is supposed to know all the limitations, which is great because I no longer know them. I used to, but now I don't know half the things I used to. I feel that I have lost it—the computer knows more." New clerks, when hired, were chosen for their ability to use the computer, not for their ability to understand the processes of the insurance business.

[1] The author wishes to acknowledge and thank David K. Wolpert MBA, 1999 for his help in researching and writing early drafts of this chapter.

[2] Zuboff, Shoshana, *In the Age of the Smart Machine: The Future of Work and Power* (New York: Basic Books, 1988). All quotes in this section are from pp. 130–135.

The work itself became more routine and mechanical. It was **automated,** which means that technology replaced the human worker, in contrast to work that had been **informed,** which occurs when workers are provided with access to a variety of information that allows them to go beyond the requirements of a job to understand the larger picture and more abstract concepts. One analyst distilled his work description down to "pushing buttons." Other employees observed that they used to work with or for their supervisors, but they now work mainly with machines. The decreased level of human interaction was upsetting to many employees, and some resisted the change imposed upon them.

Although the automation of work may increase productivity and cut costs, it can also lower morale and job satisfaction and cause employees to lose skills. These drawbacks can themselves cause additional problems, such as increased employee turnover or absenteeism, which ultimately may lead to reduced productivity.

The Information Systems Strategy Triangle, discussed in the first and third chapters, suggests that changing information systems (IS) would result in changes in organizational characteristics. The clerical work in the previous example illustrates how it can happen. Even though the deployment of IS was done for business reasons, a number of consequences in the organization were unanticipated. Workers' skills were underutilized in some ways, and workers were not skilled in using the IS. They were unable to do the automated job successfully. Instead, they preferred the manual methods. The managers of this implementation did not make adequate changes in the organizational strategy to support the changes made in the IS.

Chapter 3 explored how IT influences the design of both physical and virtual organizations. This chapter examines how IT affects the human resources aspects of the Information Age. It explores issues related to changing the nature of work, IT's impact on different types of workers, and the rise of new work environments. This chapter looks at how IT enables and facilitates a shift toward work that creates, disseminates, and applies knowledge. It examines how work is changed, where work is done, and how work is managed. The terms *IS* and *IT* are used interchangeably in this chapter, and only basic details are provided on technologies used. The point of this chapter is to look at the impact of IS on the way work is done by individual workers. This chapter should help managers understand the challenges in designing technology-intensive work and develop a sense of how to address these challenges and overcome resistance to IT.

▶ JOB DESIGN FRAMEWORK

A simple framework can be used to assess how emerging technologies may affect work. As suggested by the Information Systems Strategy Triangle (in Chapter 1), this framework links the organizational strategy with IS decisions. This framework is useful in designing key characteristics of jobs by asking key questions and helping identify where IS can affect the performance, effectiveness, and satisfaction of the worker. Consider the following questions:

- *What tasks will be performed?* Understanding what tasks are needed to complete the process being done by the worker requires an assessment of specific outcomes that are needed, inputs, and the transformation needed to turn inputs into outcomes.
- *How will the work be performed?* Some things are best done by people and other things are best done by computer. For example, dealing directly with customers is often best done by people, because the unpredictability of the interaction may require a complex set of tasks that cannot be automated. Further, most people want to deal directly with other people. On the other hand, computers are much better at keeping track of inventory, calculating compensation, and many other repetitive tasks that are opportunities for human error.
- *Who will do the work?* If a person is going to do the work, this assessment is about who that person should be. What skills are needed? What part of the organization will do it and who is in that group? Will the entire group do the work?
- *Where will the work be performed?* With the increasing availability of networks and the Internet, managers can now design work for workers who are not physically near them. Will the work be performed locally? Remotely? By a geographically dispersed work group?
- *How can IS increase performance, satisfaction, and effectiveness of the workers doing the work?* Once the job tasks and the individuals doing the job are identified, the creativity begins. How can IS be used in concert with the person doing the task? How can these two resources help each other? What is the best arrangement for using IS to support the human work? What can be done to increase the acceptance of IT-induced change?

Figure 4.1 shows how these questions can be used in a framework to incorporate IS into the design of jobs. Although it is outside the scope of this chapter to discuss the current research on job design, the reader is encouraged to read the rich literature for models and studies of job design in general.

▶ HOW INFORMATION TECHNOLOGY CHANGES THE NATURE OF WORK

Advances in IT provide an expanding set of tools that make individual workers more productive and broaden their capabilities. They transform the way work is performed—and the nature of the work itself. This section examines three ways in which new IT alters employee life: by creating new types of work, by creating new ways to do traditional work, and by presenting new challenges in human resource management brought about by the use of IT.

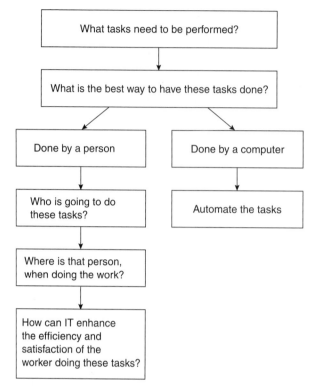

FIGURE 4.1   Framework for job design impacts.

Creating New Types of Work

IT often leads to the creation of new jobs or redefines existing ones. The high-tech field emerged in its entirety over the past 40 years One source estimates that in 1998, more than 3.8 million people around the world were employed in positions directly in the IT sector, such as programmers, analysts, IT managers, hardware assemblers, Web site designers, software sales personnel, and IT consultants. Many of these jobs simply did not exist even a few years before.

More recently, a study by Information Technology Association of America places the number of IT workers in the United States at 9.9 million workers in early 2002.[3] Most of these IT workers work for non-IT companies. Even within traditional non-IT organizations, IS usage creates new types of jobs, such as knowledge managers who manage firms' knowledge systems (see Chapter 9 for more on knowledge management). IS departments also employ individuals who help create and manage the technologies, such as systems analysts and database and network administrators. The Internet has given rise to many other types of jobs, such as Web masters and site designers. Virtually every department in every business has someone who "knows the computer" as part of their job.

---

[3] Information Technology Association of America, "Bouncing Back: Jobs, Skills and the Continuing Demand for Workers," available at http://www.itaa.org/workforce/studies/02execsum.pdf.

New Ways to Do Traditional Work

Changing the Way Work Is Done

IT has changed the way work is done. Many traditional jobs are now done by computers. For example, computers can check spelling of documents, whereas traditionally that was the job of an editor or writer. Jobs once done by art and skill are often greatly changed by the introduction of IT, such as the jobs described at the beginning of this chapter. Workers at one time needed an understanding of not only what to do, but how to do it; now their main task often is to make sure the computer is working because the computer does the task for them. Workers once were familiar with others in their organization because they passed work to them; now they may never know those coworkers because the computer routes the work. In sum, the introduction of IT into an organization can greatly change the day-to-day tasks done by the workers in the organization.

Zuboff describes a paper mill, where paper makers' jobs were radically changed with the introduction of computers.[4] The paper makers mixed big vats of paper and knew when the paper was ready by the smell, consistency, and other subjective attributes of the mixture. For example, one worker could judge the amount of chlorine in the mixture by sniffing and squeezing the pulp. They were masters at their craft, but they were not able to explicitly describe to anyone else exactly what was done to make paper. The company, in an effort to increase productivity in the paper-making process, installed an information and control system. Instead of the workers looking and personally testing the vats of paper, the system continuously tested parameters and displayed the results on a panel located in the control room. The paper makers sat in the control room, reading the numbers, and making decisions on how to make the paper. Many found it much more difficult, if not impossible, to make the same quality paper when watching the control panel instead of personally testing, smelling, and looking at the vats. The introduction of the information system resulted in different skills needed to make paper. Abstracting the entire process and displaying the results on electronic readouts required skills to interpret the measurements, conditions, and data generated by the new computer system.

In another example, salespeople had portable terminals that not only kept track of inventory, but also helped them in the selling function. Prior to the information system, the salespeople used manual processes to keep track of inventory in their trucks. When visiting customers, it was only possible to tell them what was missing from their shelves and to replenish any stock they wanted. With IT, the salespeople became more like marketing and sales consultants, helping the customers with models and data of previous sales, floor layouts, and replenishment as well as forecasting demand based on analysis of the data histories stored in the IS. The skills needed by the salespeople were much more than just a persuasive manner. They needed to be able to do data analysis and floor plan design, in addition to using the computer. The skills needed by the salespeople greatly changed with the introduction of IT.

[4] Zuboff, Shoshana, *In the Age of the Smart Machine: The Future of Work and Power* (New York: Basic Books, 1988) p. 211.

The Internet enables changes in many jobs. For example, within minutes, financial analysts can download an annual report from a corporate Web site and check what others have said about the company's growth prospects. Librarians can check the holdings of other libraries online and request that particular volumes be routed to their own clients, or download the articles from a growing number of databases. Marketing professionals can research competitor's products and services on the Web without alerting these companies of their curiosity. Sales jobs are radically changing to complement online ordering systems. Technical support agents diagnose and resolve problems on client computers using the Internet and software from Motive Communications. The cost and time required to access information has plummeted, increasing personal productivity and giving workers new tools.

Changing Communication Patterns

IT can change the communication patterns of workers. Workers who sit at terminals communicate with a computer for the bulk of the workday. For example, a bank clerk who sits at a terminal processing loan applications has little reason to communicate with coworkers who sit at their terminals doing the same thing. Prior to the computer terminals, the clerks sat at desks from which they could pass paper personally through the process and communicate with coworkers.

Workers who use portable computers while in the field encounter a different experience from their counterparts without portable systems. For example, repair personnel were given portable data terminals, connected by radio to the corporate network. They were able to send and receive short messages, as well as tap into company databases to get current customer information. Before visiting a customer, they could look at the service history and, therefore, were better prepared to fix the current problem.

Changing Organizational Decision Making and Information Processing

IT changes not only organizational decision-making processes, but also the information used in making those decisions. Data processed to create more accurate and timely information are being captured earlier in the process. Consider salespeople who use portable terminals. When they complete their service call, they enter the information into their data terminals, which helps keep the database more current and changes their job from one of simply doing services to one that includes small amounts of data entry. Needless to say, the dozens of data entry personnel, whose jobs were to read the data entry sheets and type the information into the computer, were no longer necessary. The data entry clerk's job was eliminated with the introduction of the field data terminals.

IT can change the amount and type of information available to workers. As previously described, the service force's ability to access company records from their portable terminals. Accessing this information while out in the field gave them much more current information than they previously had. Prior to the data terminals, they only had access to whatever they brought with them. IT gave them real-time access to the entire database. Furthermore, organizations now maintain large historical business databases, called data warehouses, which can be mined by using tools to analyze patterns, trends, and relationships in the data warehouses. For example, Fingerhut, a $2 billion mail-order business, maintains a data warehouse generated from 50 years of sales transactions. Using data mining techniques, Fingerhut's marketing team recently found that customers who change their residence triple their purchasing in the 12 weeks after their move, with the most buying taking place in the first 4 weeks They purchase furniture, telecommunications equipment, and decorations, but abstain from jewelry and home electronics purchase. Marketers at Fingerhut now offer a customized "mover's catalog" to movers, and don't send other catalogs during that 12-week window.[5] Thus, the job of the marketer at Fingerhut changed to reflect the greater information available to them.

IT not only can make critical information more readily accessible to decision makers, but it can also offer them tools such as decision support systems and executive information systems to help improve their decision-making process. For example, Motorola's Semiconductor Products Sector (SPS) implemented an executive information system (EIS) over its intranet, which allows managers to quickly access and analyze data warehouse information from their desktops. In about five minutes, users can determine what customers are buying, their order histories, and the status of their current orders.[6]

In their classic 1958 *Harvard Business Review* article, Leavitt and Whisler boldly predicted that IT would shrink the ranks of middle management by the 1980s.[7] Because of IT, top-level executives would have access to information and decision-making tools and models that would allow them to easily assume tasks previously performed by middle managers. Other tasks clearly in the typical job description of middle managers at the time would become so routinized and programmed because of IT they could be performed by lower-level managers. As Leavitt and Whisler predicted, the 1980s saw a shrinking in the ranks of middle managers. This trend was partly attributable to widespread corporate downsizing. However, it was also attributable to changes in decision making induced by IT. Since the 1980s, IT has become an even more commonly employed tool of executive decision makers. IT has increased the flow of information to these decision makers, and has provided tools for filtering and analyzing the information.

Changing Collaboration

IT helps make work more team-oriented. Workers can more easily send documents over computer networks to others, and they can more easily ask questions using e-mail. The Internet greatly enhances collaboration. Other technologies, such as video teleconferencing and publishing systems, provide collaborative applications. These systems accelerate information exchange in a cost-effective manner. Changes in the

[5] David Pearson, "Marketing for Survival," *CIO Magazine* (April 15, 1998), available from http://www.cio.com/archive/041598/finger_content.html.

[6] Meagan Santosus, "Working Smart: Maximizing the Payoff from IT," *CIO Magazine* (November 15, 1998), available at http://www.cio.com/archive/111598/smart.html.

[7] Harold Leavitt and Thomas Whisler, "Management in the 1980s," *Harvard Business Review* (November–December 1958), pp. 41–48.

job design accompany this technology change, however. Managers often redesign jobs to take advantage of the new group communications. For example, a consulting firm regularly uses Lotus Notes, a groupware program, as the basis for project management and task execution. Consultants use the groupware program to store and analyze data, to compose and edit documents, and to research and transfer knowledge between projects. In short, the entire work process is built around the use of a groupware system, whereas in the past, work was done independently of the information system.

The preceding examples show how IS are a key component in the design of the work done by workers. IT can greatly change the day-to-day tasks, which in turn change the skills needed by workers. The examples show that adding IS to a work environment changes the work done.

New Challenges in Managing People

New working arrangements create new challenges in how workers are supervised, evaluated, compensated, and even hired. When most work was performed individually in a central location, supervision and evaluation were relatively easy. A manager could directly observe the salesperson who spent much of his or her day in an office. It was fairly simple to ascertain whether the employee was present and productive.

Modern organizations, especially virtual organizations, often face the challenge of managing a work force that is spread across the world, working in isolation from direct supervision, and working more in teams. As discussed in the previous chapter, virtual teams use IT to facilitate communications as well as get work done. Rather than working in a central office, many salespeople work remotely and rely on portable computers, cellular phones, and pagers to link them to customers and their office colleagues. The technical complexity of certain products, such as enterprise software, necessitates a team-based sales approach combining the expertise of many individuals; it can be difficult to say which individual closed a sale, making it difficult to apportion individual-based rewards.

One technological solution, electronic employee monitoring (introduced in Chapter 3), replaces direct supervision by automatically tracking certain activities, such as the number of calls processed, e-mail messages sent, or time spent surfing the Web. Direct employee evaluation can be replaced, in part, by pay-for-performance compensation strategies that reward employees for deliverables produced or targets met, as opposed to subjective factors such as "attitude" or "teamwork." These changes are summarized in Figure 4.2.

Hiring is also different because of IT for two reasons. First, in IT-savvy firms workers must either know how to use the technologies that support the work of the firm before they are hired, or they must be trainable in the requisite skills. Hiring procedures incorporate activities that determine the skills of applicants. For example, a company may ask a candidate to sit at a computer in order to answer a basic questionnaire, take a short quiz, or simply browse the Web in order to evaluate the applicant's skill level, or they may only accept applications submitted to a Web site. Second, IT utilization affects the array of nontechnical skills needed in

	Traditional Approach: Subjective Observation	Newer approach: Objective Assessment
Supervision	Personal and informal. Manager is usually present or relies on others to ensure employee is present and productive.	Electronic or assessed by deliverable. As long as the employee is producting value, he does not need formal supervision.
Evaluation	Focus is on process through direct observation. Manager sees how employee performed at work. Subjective (personal) factors are very important.	Focus is on output by deliverable (e.g., produce a report by a certain date) or by target (e.g., meet a sales quota). As long as deliverables are produced and/or targets achieved, the employee is meeting performance expectations adequately. Subjective factors may be less important and are harder to gauge.
Compensation and Rewards	Often individually based.	Often team-based or contractually spelled out.
Hiring	Personal with little reliance on computers. Often more reliance on clerical skills.	Often electronic with recruiting Web sites and electronic testing. More informated work that requires a higher level of IT skills.

FIGURE 4.2   Changes to supervision, evaluations, compensation, and hiring.

the organization. Certain functions—many clerical tasks, for example—can be handled more expeditiously, so fewer workers adept in those skills are required. IT-savvy companies can eliminate clerical capabilities from their hiring practices and focus on more targeted skills.

The design of the work needed by an organization is a function of the skill mix required for the firm's work processes and of the flow of those processes themselves. Thus, an organization that infuses technology effectively and employs a work force with a high level of IT skills will necessarily design the organization differently from an organization that does not. The skill mix required by an IT-savvy firm reflects greater capacity for using the technology itself. It will require less of certain clerical and even managerial skills that are leveraged by technical capacity. It may also deploy skills according to different ratios in central and local units. Consider the cookie company of Mrs. Fields, which uses IT not only for administrative support, but also to alert store managers about the need to bake more cookies based on the day of the week or weather patterns. In Mrs. Fields' case, IT skills are more necessary in the central organization, but much less necessary in the stores—sales skills are now the point of focus for new hires locally. In addition, the very process of job design is likely to be different in an IT-savvy firm, because it must reflect an organization-wide strategy for optimizing the array of skills, as well as the requirements of a process-driven production environment, job design is more likely to be driven centrally but with the participation of process partners across the organization. Thus, Mrs. Fields uses feedback from store managers in designing the job descriptions for branch employees, and store managers use hiring tools rendered strictly consistent from store to store.

New IT also challenges employee skills. Employees who cannot keep pace are increasingly unemployable. As many lower-level service or clerical jobs become partially automated, only those workers able to learn new technologies and adapt to changing work practices can anticipate stability in their long-term employment. Firms institute extensive training programs to ensure their workers possess the skills to use IT effectively.

As summarized in Figure 4.3, IT has drastically changed the landscape of work today. As a result of IT, many new jobs were created. As companies downsize and technology replaces people, however, William Bridges argues that organizations move away from organizational structures built around particular jobs to a setting in which a person's work is defined in terms of "what needed to be done."[8] In many organizations it is no longer appropriate for people to establish their turfs and narrowly define their jobs to only address specific functions. Yet, as jobs "disappear," IT can enable workers to better perform in tomorrow's workplace; that is, IT can help workers function and collaborate in accomplishing work that more broadly encompasses all the tasks that need to be done. In the next section, we examine how IT can change where work is done.

▶ HOW INFORMATION TECHNOLOGY CHANGES WHERE WORK IS DONE

This section examines another important effect of IT on work: the ability of some workers to work anywhere, at any time. The terms *telecommuting* and *mobile*

Work	IT creates millions of new jobs, some in entirely new industries.
Working Arrangements	IT changes the way work is done, communication patterns, decision making, and collaboration. More work is team-oriented, enabled by communications and collaboration technologies. Geographic constraints of some professions are eliminated, enabling telecommuting and virtual teams.
Human Resources	New strategies are needed to hire, supervise, evaluate, and compensate remotely performed, team-oriented work. IT requires new skillsets that many workers lack.

FIGURE 4.3   Summary of IT's effects on employee life.

[8] William Bridges, *JobShift: How to Prosper in a Workplace without Jobs* (New York: Addison-Wesley, 1995).

worker are often used to describe these types of work arrangements. **Telecommuting,** sometimes called teleworking, refers to work arrangements with employers that allow employees to work from home or other convenient locations instead of coming into the corporate office. The term *telecommute* is derived from combining "telecommunications" with "commuting," hence these workers use telecommunications instead of commuting to the office. **Mobile workers** are those who work from wherever they are. They are outfitted with the technology necessary for access to coworkers, company computers, intranets, and other information sources. They possess the ability to be "mobile" and still conduct work.

Telecommuting has been around since the 1970s, but in the late 1990s it gained popularity. Companies found that building telecommuting capabilities can be an important tool for attracting and retaining employees, increasing productivity of workers, providing flexibility to otherwise overworked individuals, reducing office space and associated costs, and complying with the Clean Air Act. For example, at Cisco Systems, two-thirds of the company's employees occasionally work from home. After this change in policy, productivity jumped 25 percent and the company saved $1 million in overhead expenses. Telecommuting was also a boon at a new airline, Jet Blue Airway. Jet Blue's entire force of 550 reservation agents work from their homes, generating savings that helped the airline report its first profit a mere six months after its first flight.[9]

Telecommuting also promises employees potential benefits: schedule flexibility, a better balance between work life and home life, reduced stress, less commuting time and fewer expenses, and greater geographic flexibility. Cisco's employees report that "they love setting their own schedules, skipping rush hour, spending more time with their kids, and working at least part-time in comfortable surroundings."[10] This result goes beyond just Cisco. Nearly 75 percent of telecommuters responding to an AT&T survey said they were more satisfied with their personal and family lives than before they started working at home.[11]

Factors Driving Telecommuting and Mobile Work

IT now allows employees to work from home, at a customer's site, or while traveling. In 2001, according to an annual Telework America study funded by AT&T, more than 28 million Americans telecommuted in some fashion, and this number continues to increase. Some experts predict that in 10 to 15 years, 50 percent of all work will be performed from remote locations. Several factors that drive this trend are shown in Figure 4.4.

First, work is increasingly knowledge-based. The U.S. economy continues to shift from manufacturing to service industries. Equipped with the right IT, an employee can create, assimilate, and distribute knowledge as effectively at home as he or she can at an office. The shift to knowledge-based work thus tends to minimize the need for a particular locus of activity.

[9] Joan Raymond, "Next Frontiers: Moving into the Future," *Newsweek* (April 29, 2002), pp. 40, 42.

[10] Anne Tergesen, "Making Stay-at-Homes Feel Welcome," *Business Week* (October 12, 1998), p. 155.

[11] Amy Dunkin, "Saying Adios to the Office," *Business Week* (October 12, 1998), p. 152.

Driver	Effect
Shift to knowledge-based work	Eliminates requirement that certain work be performed in a specific place.
Changing demographics and lifestyle preferences	Provides workers with geographic and time-shifting flexibility.
New technologies	Makes remotely performed work practical and cost-effective.

FIGURE 4.4   Driving factors of telecommuting.

Second, telecommuters can often time-shift their work to accommodate their lifestyles. For instance, parents can modify their work schedules to allow time to take their children to school and extracurricular activities. Telecommuting provides an attractive alternative for parents who might otherwise decide to take leaves of absence from work for childrearing. Telecommuting also can enable persons housebound by illness, disability, or the lack of access to transportation to join the work force.

Telecommuting also may provide employees with enormous geographic flexibility. The freedom to live where one wishes, even at a remove from one's corporate office, can boost employee morale and job satisfaction. As a workplace policy, it may also lead to improved employee retention. Many employees can be more productive at home, and they actually work more hours than if they commuted to an office. Furthermore, such impediments to productivity as traffic delays, canceled flights, bad weather, and mild illnesses become less significant. Companies enjoy this benefit, too. Those who build in telecommuting as a standard work practice are able to hire workers from a much larger talent pool than those companies who require geographical presence.

The third driving factor of telecommuting is that the new technologies, which make work in remote locations viable, are becoming better and cheaper. For example, prices of personal computers continue to drop, and processing power roughly doubles every 18 months.[12] The drastic increase in capabilities of portable technologies make mobile work more effective and productive. Telecommunication speeds through conventional computer modems or more sophisticated technologies such as ADSL, ISDN, cable modems, and satellite connectivity increase exponentially while costs plummet. The Web offers an easy-to-use "front-end" to sophisticated "back-office" applications used by major corporations, such as those that run on mainframe computers.

New Technologies Supporting Telecommuting and Mobile Work

New software systems are changing the way certain work is performed. For instance, Hewlett-Packard salespeople use laptops equipped with sales force automation software from Trilogy. This software allows them to configure and quote

---

[12] Gordon Moore, head of Intel, observed that the capacity of microprocessors doubled roughly every 12–18 months. Even though this observation was made in 1965, it still holds true. Eventually, it became known in the industry as Moore's Law.

customer orders at the point of sale, ensuring accuracy. This innovation dramatically improved customer satisfaction levels, reduced sales cycle time, and cut costs. The technology rendered the sales force more productive and more mobile. Armed with Trilogy's software, sales representatives no longer have to coordinate the sales process with others who control updated configuration and pricing information.

The product that most enables the mobile work revolution is the laptop computer. The laptop effectively lets workers carry their offices with them. Any work traditionally performed on a desktop computer can now be performed on the road. Recent drops in price and jumps in performance make laptops a realistic alternative for the masses. Earlier laptops lacked processing power, hard drive space, and multimedia capabilities. Users suffered with small screens and poor resolution, which made extended work difficult. They lugged heavy or bulky units. Today's small, lightweight laptops offer screens approaching the size of desktop monitors, powerful microprocessors, wireless connections, ample memory, large hard drives, and extensive multimedia capabilities, all for prices competitive with similarly capable desktop computers. These advances position the laptop as virtual work's primary tool.

Laptops have become indispensable in certain professional fields, such as consulting, where employees frequently travel and need immediate access to their files and means for electronic communication. For example, consultants with PeopleSoft, a vendor of enterprise resource planning software, can plug in their laptops at any company office worldwide and get immediate access to the corporate network without any reconfiguration. The technical constraints of interoffice travel are eliminated.

Laptop computing revolutionizes work in nonprofessional settings as well. For example, university students frequently carry laptops from dormitory to classroom to library. Students can send and receive e-mail, work on group projects, and even take tests from home.

A newer breed of portable computer, the personal digital assistant (PDA), offers a cost-effective alternative for certain functions. PDAs, such as the popular PalmPilot, offer contact management, scheduling, note taking, and e-mail. Because the PalmPilot can be programmed with a simple but robust language, custom applications can be written for it. A PDA typically costs only 10 to 40 percent of the price of a laptop, it fits in a shirt pocket or purse, and is faster and easier to use for certain functions.

Another class of portable computer, the handheld terminal, is typically designed for a single function. Even though its limited use makes it relatively costly, it can be programmed to be optimal for a given task. Handheld terminals are most commonly carried by delivery personnel and repair technicians. For example, United Parcel Service (UPS) delivery personnel carry them to record when and where a package was delivered, whether the intended recipient directly received the merchandise, and how payment was made on COD orders. The units also store recipients' signatures. Additionally, the devices serve as communication tools, sending information between the delivery person and UPS offices via a two-way radio installed in the delivery truck. The terminals put important information at the fingertips of UPS drivers, empowering them to manage their own deliveries by bypassing dispatchers and alleviating the need for check-ins.

Repair mechanics for Otis Elevator use the small, lightweight keyed-data terminal (KDT) to send text messages via radio to individuals and groups. Previously, mechanics were notified of service calls by pager. Because the pagers did not permit two-way communication, and because the mechanics lacked portable phones, they returned service calls to a central dispatch system, often by pay phone. Mechanics lost time finding pay phones—and, more particularly, pay phones that would allow them to accept return calls from central dispatch. In contrast, the KDT sends and receives messages anywhere—even to other mechanics in the field who can help diagnose and resolve mechanical problems. The terminal empowers the mechanic to manage his or her own work more effectively, as well as to access the knowledge of other mechanics.

For a work force in which employees are completely mobile and can work anywhere in the world, a new level of communications technology is necessary. Organizations must ensure that a communications infrastructure, with appropriate security mechanisms, is in place to meet the needs of the mobile work force. To this end, Motorola initiated Project Iridium, an ambitious plan to launch 66 satellites into orbit to provide communications coverage for the entire planet. Equipped with a portable satellite phone, anyone, anywhere, can be reached with a high degree of clarity. It is too early to tell how this innovation may change the way work is performed. We can imagine, for example, how it might affect an engineer for a Texas-based oil drilling equipment manufacturer at work with a client in the middle of the Arabian Desert. If he or she needed to ask another engineer in the company a technical question, he or she could simply dial the satellite phone. That other engineer could be anywhere—on a ship, in a plane, on an oil rig, in another desert, or back in Texas. Key technologies such as portable phones are listed in Figure 4.5.

Disadvantages of Telecommuting and Mobile Work

Telecommuting also has some disadvantages. Remote work challenges managers in addressing performance evaluation and compensation. Managers of telecommuters

Technology	Used By	Impacts
Laptop computers	Professionals, particularly consultants and salespeople	Eliminate constraints of travel. Enable workers to be productive anywhere
PDAs	Mostly professionals, but devices are gaining in mass acceptance	Provides a low-cost, simple way of organizing information and communicating data
Handheld terminals	Service professionals, particularly delivery, technical support, and service and repair technicians	Enhances productivity and adds capabilities and real-time communication
Portable phones	Any worker who travels during his or her work routine	Allows immediate voice (and sometimes data) communication

FIGURE 4.5 Key technologies in redesigning work.

often evaluate employee performance in terms of results or deliverables rather than by the processes used to create those assets. Virtual offices make it more difficult for managers to understand the skills of the people reporting to them, which in turn makes performance evaluation more difficult. For the many telecommuting tasks that do not produce well-defined deliverables or results, or those where managerial controls typically prove inadequate, managers must rely heavily upon the telecommuter's self-discipline. As a result, managers may feel they are losing control over their employees, and some telecommuting employees will, in fact, abuse their privileges. Managers accustomed to traditional work models in which they are able to exert control more easily may strongly resist telecommuting. In fact, managers are often the biggest impediment to implementing telecommuting programs.

Workers who telecommute must be extremely self-disciplined. Workers who go to an office or who must make appearances at customer locations have a structure that gets them up and out of their home. Telecommuters, on the other hand, must exert a level of discipline to ensure they get the work done. Working from home, in particular, is full of distractions such as personal phone calls, visitors, and inconvenient family disruptions. A remote worker must carefully set up a home work environment and develop strategies to enable quality time for the work task.

Telecommuters often opt for the increased flexibility in work hours that remote work offers them. They are lured by the promise of being able work around the schedules of their children or other family members. Paradoxically, because of their flexible work situation, it is often difficult for them to separate work from their home life. Consequently, they may work many more hours than the standard 9-to-5 worker, or experience the stress of trying to separate work from play.

Working remotely can disconnect an employee from his or her company's culture. The casual, face-to-face encounters that take place in offices transmit extensive cultural, political, and other organizational information. These encounters are lost to an employee who seldom, if ever, works at the office. Further, the disconnected employee might feel lonely when working in a solitary environment away from coworkers and other distractions.

Virtual work also raises the specter of **electronic immigration,** or foreign outsourcing of software development and computer services. Once a company establishes an infrastructure for remote work, the work often can be performed abroad as easily as domestically. U.S. immigration laws limit the number of foreigners who may work in the United States. Since the terrorist attacks in New York City and Washington, D.C. on September 11, 2001, these limits have become more restrictive, and legislation is being considered to prohibit foreign nationals, even those contracted through other companies, from working on Department of Defense computer systems. However, no such limitations exist on work performed outside this country by workers who then transmit their work to the United States electronically. Because such work is not subject to minimum wage controls, companies may have a strong economic incentive to outsource work abroad. Popular countries and regions for electronic immigration are India, Russia, Eastern Europe, South Africa, Ireland, and East Asia. Ironically, as India, a major hotbed of electronic immigration, becomes "too expensive," basic jobs such as order entry are being outsourced by the Indians to places like Ghana. Companies find it particularly easy to outsource clerical work related to electronic production, such as data processing and computer programming. For instance, the Russian firm ArgusSof employs 120 programmers contracted to Western firms through the Internet.

The ability to tap human resources where they are least expensive and expertise where it is most available can create a critical strategic asset. Not surprisingly, some labor unions, immigration experts, and politicians, among others, worry that this form of "immigration" may replace U.S. jobs. Firms based in less-developed nations also find economic advantage in retaining employees abroad, rather then competing with U.S. demand and salaries for IT professionals. Benefits and drawbacks of telecommuting are summarized in Figure 4.6.

Managerial Issues in Telecommuting and Mobile Work

Telecommuting requires managers to undertake special planning, staffing, and supervising activities. In terms of planning, business and support tasks must be redesigned to support mobile and remote workers. Everyday business tasks such as submitting employee expense reports in person (as is common when an original signature is needed on the form) and attending daily progress meetings are inappropriate if most of the workers are remote. Support tasks such as fixing computers by dispatching someone from the central IS department may not be feasible if the worker is in a hotel in a remote city. Basic business and support processes must be designed with both the remote worker and the worker remaining in the office in mind. Because telecommuters may not be able to deal with issues requiring face-to-face contact, nontelecommuters may find that they are asked to assume additional tasks. Training should be offered to telecommuters and nontelecommuters alike so that they can anticipate and understand the new work environment.

Not all jobs are suitable for telecommuting. Some jobs may require the worker to be at the work location. Basically only those aspects of jobs that can be performed independently at remote locations are suitable for telecommuting. Further, the employees selected to staff telecommuting jobs must be self-starters. They must

Employee Advantages of Telecommuting	Potential Problems
Reduced stress due to increased ability to meet schedules and less work-related distractions	Increased stress from inability to separate work life from home life
Higher morale; lower absenteeism	Harder to evaluate performance
Geographic flexibility	Employee may become disconnected from company culture
Higher personal productivity	Telecommuters are more easily replaced by electronic immigrants
Housebound individuals can join the workforce	Not suitable for all jobs or employees.

FIGURE 4.6   Advantages and disadvantages of telecommuting.

be responsible for completing work tasks without being in the corporate office. New employees who need to be socialized into the organization's practices and culture are not good candidates for mobile or remote work.

Managers must find new ways to evaluate and supervise those employees without seeing them every day in the office. They must also work to coordinate schedules, ensure adequate communication among all workers, and help their organizations adapt by building business processes to support mobile and remote workers.

▶ INFORMATION SYSTEMS ENABLE MORE GROUP WORK

Collaboration is a key task in many work processes, and IS greatly changes how collaboration is done. Collaboration is central to many types of tasks, particularly those that benefit from exchange of ideas and criticism, such as product design, medical diagnosis, and story development. Groupware tools, such as Lotus Notes and Microsoft Outlook, and technologies, such as video teleconferencing, make it simple and cost-effective for people around the world to create, edit, and share documents and processes in electronic formats.

Product design tasks experience tremendous change with the use of IS. Consider the case of the appliance manufacturer, Whirlpool. The company's product data management (PDM) system unites design teams electronically through a central data repository that stores every element of the design process, from creating CAD drawings to filing change orders.[13] Engineers at Whirlpool facilities in Europe, Brazil, India, Mexico, and the United States collaborate online to create several basic designs for an appliance. Each geographic region then customizes the boilerplate design with the options that its local market demands. PDM cuts the time it takes to design an appliance in half and results in significant cost savings for Whirlpool. Collaboration technologies can also revolutionize product design in the automotive industry. Ford Motor Company now develops cars for world markets by electronically bridging design and engineering centers in the United States and Europe using video teleconferencing and corporate intranets. This faster, more efficient communication allows Ford to move cars from design to production in less time.

Advanced video teleconferencing technologies gave birth to the field known as "telemedicine." Telemedicine enables doctors working on virtual teams to confer with distant colleagues, share data, and examine patients in remote locations, without losing time and money to travel. For example, one manufacturer of electronic imaging equipment helps employees seek medical expertise 2,500 miles away. They can transmit patient X-rays, CAT scans, and other radiological records for analysis by specialists at the UCLA Medical Center. Company executives predict that the program will save $2 million a year in health care costs over seven years while offering patients access to specialty care that is not available locally.[14]

Collaborative technologies can affect creativity tasks as well. At *CIO Magazine*, writers brainstorm topics for articles in a Lotus Notes discussion database. Writers

[13] Carol Hildebrand, "Forging a Global Appliance," *CIO Magazine* (May 1, 1995).

[14] Anne Stuart, "Telecomputing: Going the Distance," *CIO Magazine* (January 1, 1996).

enter their story ideas, then others comment on and debate them and suggest sources. Stories are developed faster because writers do not have to wait for face-to-face meetings to get feedback.

▶ GAINING ACCEPTANCE FOR IT-INDUCED CHANGE

The changes described in this chapter no doubt alter the frames of reference of organizational employees and may be a major source of concern for them. Employees may resist the changes if they view the changes as negatively affecting them. In the case of a new information system that they do not fully understand or are not prepared to operate, they may resist in several ways:

- They may deny that the system is up and running.
- They may sabotage the system by distorting or otherwise altering inputs.
- They may try to convince themselves, and others, that the new system really will not change the status quo.
- They may refuse to use the new system where its usage is voluntary.

To avoid the negative consequences of resistance to change, system implementers and managers must actively manage the change process and gain acceptance for new IS. To help explain how to gain acceptance for a new technology, Professor Fred Davis and his colleagues developed the Technology Acceptance Model (TAM). Many variations of TAM exist, but its most basic form is displayed in Figure 4.7. TAM suggests that managers cannot get employees to use a system until they want to use it. To convince employees to want to use the system, managers may need to change employee attitudes about the system. Employee attitudes may change if employees believe that the system will allow them to do more or better work for the same amount of effort (perceived usefulness), and that it is easy to use. Training, documentation, and user support consultants are external variables that may help explain the usefulness of the system and make it easier to use.

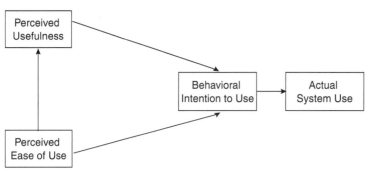

FIGURE 4.7 Technology acceptance model.
Source: Fred Davis, Richard Bagozzi, and Paul Warshaw, "User Acceptance of Computer Technology: A Comparison of Two Theoretical Models," *Management Science,* 35, 8 (1989), p. 985.

TAM assumes that technology will be accepted if people's attitudes and beliefs support its use. One way to make sure that employees' attitudes and beliefs are favorable toward the system is to have them participate in its design and implementation. When future users of the system participate in its design and implementation, they can more easily tell the designers what they need from the system. Being involved in the development also makes them more aware of the trade-offs that inevitably occur during a system implementation. They may be more willing to accept the consequences of the trade-offs. Finally, being involved in the design and development allows users to better understand how the system works, and thus may make it easier for them to use the system.

TAM and its many variants assume that use of the system is under the control of individuals. When employees are mandated to use the system, they may use it in the short-run, but over the long run the negative consequences of resistance may occur. Thus, gaining acceptance of the system is important even in those situations where its use is mandated.

► FOOD FOR THOUGHT: THE PRODUCTIVITY PARADOX

Do information systems make workers more productive? Many researchers argue that worker productivity does not actually increase as a result of IS, despite enormous spending on IS products and services. Others suggest that the evidence indicates employee productivity is finally rising as a result of IS. This issue is debated openly and publicly as the "productivity paradox." The **productivity paradox** is defined as the failure of massive investment in information technology to boost productivity growth.

Why might IT not improve, or even decrease, worker productivity? Some argue that even though IS appear to make workers more productive, the cost of those computers more than offsets any gains in productivity. Others suggest that it is the continual need to upgrade that makes IS less valuable. One researcher compared PCs to the telephone. "PCs may be the telephones of the '90s—standard issue to every information and knowledge worker—but we don't replace our telephones every couple of years. After the first big bite of computerization, the subsequent upgrades, new releases, and added functions are just icing on the economic cake."[15] Still others believe that most of the IT spending goes toward general infrastructure, rather than high-value-added applications.

Another researcher claims the entire increase in total factor productivity outside the computer sector is due to the economic cycle. He argues that after excluding the manufacture of all durable goods as well as of computers, absolutely no increase in labor productivity occurred in the remaining 88 percent of the economy, after adjusting for the cycle.[16]

Still, others who argue for increased productivity claim that returns on computers investments were roughly equivalent to those investments in non-IT equipment.

[15] Ibid.

[16] "Solving the Paradox," *The Economist* (September 2001), available at http://www.economist.com/displayStory.cfm?Story_ID=375522.

One study of 367 large companies from 1988 to 1992 found that IT investments yielded on average a 45 percent return after depreciation in both the manufacturing and nonmanufacturing sectors.[17] Some argue that the way productivity is calculated is flawed. Economists measure productivity as physical output per unit of input. Statistics on productivity, however, are not available for 58 percent of all service workers. Among the remaining 42 percent, for a significant number of industries—notably banking, financial services, education, health care, and government—output is computed solely on the basis of input.[18]

Other proponents of increased productivity argue that lag periods occur before the impact of any technology on productivity can be experienced. Take for example the long lags before both steam power and electricity boosted productivity. Paul David, an economist at Oxford University, suggests that productivity growth did not accelerate until 40 years after the introduction of electric power in the early 1880s when at least half of American industrial machinery became powered by electricity, and when firms had figured out how to reorganize their factories around electric power to reap the efficiency gains. David argues that a technology starts having a significant effect on productivity only when it has reached a 50 percent penetration rate. American computer use reached the 50 percent mark only recently, and other economies are lagging behind. It means that IT is now roughly at the same stage that electricity was in 1920. Predictably, growth in labor productivity in the U.S. business sector is showing an increase.[19]

New metrics may be needed. Our current measures of productivity may measure only the output of employees whose work has been redesigned to incorporate IT. We may not be measuring accurately the labor input needed to generate the output of these workers. In short, our measures may be measuring the work per worker, but not the work per worker per unit of time. "Getting payoff from technology is just not a passive exercise. People aren't yet aware of the navigation measures, because they still view technology as self-harvesting. The next generation of measures will enable organizations to take control of the rate of return."[20]

Yet, results using the current metrics are striking. Labor productivity in the U.S. business sector increased to an annual average of 2.9 percent, beginning in 1996, from an average of 1.4 percent in 1975–1995. In the second quarter of 2000, productivity surged by 5.2 percent. That increase is in part credited to IT-heavy investment and faster productivity growth in the computer industry.[21]

---

[17] Tom Davenport, "Cheap is Beautiful," *CIO Magazine* (March 1, 1998).

[18] See, for example, work done by Erik Brynjolfsson, from MIT Sloan School of Management; or Paul Strassmann, author of *The Squandered Computer*.

[19] "Solving the Paradox," *The Economist* (September 2001), available at http://www.economist.com/displayStory.cfm?Story_ID=375522.

[20] B. E. Baatz, "Altered Stats," *CIO Magazine* (October 15, 1994).

[21] "Solving the Paradox," *The Economist* (September 2001), available at http://www.economist.com/displayStory.cfm?Story_ID=375522.

► SUMMARY

- IT affects clerical and professional workers differently and can result in deskilling or automating. It can also result in informating the work.
- IT affects work by creating new work, creating new working arrangements, and presenting new managerial challenges in employee supervision, evaluation, compensation, and hiring.
- Newer approaches to management reflect greater use of computer and information technology in hiring and supervising employees, a greater focus on output (compared to behavior), and a greater team orientation.
- Companies find that building telecommuting capabilities can be an important tool for attracting and retaining employees, increasing productivity of workers, providing flexibility to otherwise overworked individuals, reducing office space and associated costs, and complying with the Clean Air Act. Telecommuting also promises employees potential benefits: schedule flexibility, better balance between work life and home life, reduced stress, less commuting time and fewer expenses, and greater geographic flexibility.
- Disadvantages of telecommuting include difficulties in evaluating performance, greater feelings of isolation, easier displacement by electronic immigration, and limitations of jobs and workers in its application.
- To gain acceptance of a new technology, potential users must exhibit a favorable attitude toward the technology. In the case of information systems, the users' beliefs about its perceived usefulness and perceived ease of use color their attitudes about the system.
- The shift to knowledge-based work, changing demographics and lifestyle preferences, and new technologies (laptops, PDAs, handheld terminals, and portable phones) all contribute to the growth in remote work.

► KEY TERMS

automated (p. 82)
electronic immigration (p. 95)

informated (p. 82)
mobile worker (p. 91)

productivity paradox (p. 99)
telecommuting (p. 91)

► DISCUSSION QUESTIONS

1. Why might a worker resist the implementation of a new technology? What are some of the possible consequences of asking a worker to use a computer or similar device in his or her job?

2. How can IT alter an individual's work? How can a manager ensure that the impact is positive rather than negative?

3. What current technologies do you predict will show the most impact on the way work is done? Why?

4. Given the growth in telecommuting and other mobile work arrangements, how might offices physically change in the coming years? Will offices as we think of them today exist by 2010? Why or why not?

5. How is working at an online retailer different from working at a brick-and-mortar retailer? What types of jobs are necessary at each? What skills are important?

6. Paul Saffo, director of the Institute for the Future, noted "Telecommuting is a reality for many today, and will continue to be more so in the future. But beware, this doesn't mean we will travel less. In fact, the more one uses electronics, the more they are likely to travel."[22] Do you agree with this statement? Why or why not?

CASE STUDY 4-1

BASEBALL IN THE UNITED STATES

Many cultures have some sort of sport involving a stick and a ball, but none holds the attention of the fans in the United States like baseball. Since the mid-1800s when the first recorded baseball game was played, the game evolved from a contest between amateurs to a professional business. It is no wonder that IS have begun to change the playing field.

In that moment, just before the pitch, the pitcher and batter lock eyes, and each tries to figure out what the other is going to do. Fans revel in it, but baseball managers and players spend careers trying to reduce the uncertainty contained in that moment through an obsession with information to know as much about the opponent as possible. Until 1999, the information was mostly contained in the collective memory of the team players and managers, and decisions were made based on hunches and instincts gleaned from scraps of information compiled through discussions with those who had the information. With the use of IS, however, the old game of intuition is quickly becoming one of research and analysis both on and off the field.

For example, between innings of the 1998 World Series, the championship game that would determine the first place team that year, the New York Yankees' catcher spent much of his time in the dugout thumbing through computerized "spray charts" that show where the San Diego Padres' hitters hit the ball. He also studied graphics highlighting the weak spots in the strike zone so that he could call appropriate pitches the next inning. New York won the series that year, 4 games to 0.

IS are also used to store and sort information about players from the time they appear in their high school teams through their professional careers. Scouts gather information on performance during each game played. They also compile information on contract histories, injuries, psychological makeup, athletic strengths and weaknesses. Some even gather information like personal presence on the field and testimony from their Little League (pre-high school) coach. Players are tracked through all three tiers of the system, from amateur high school and college ball, through professional minor league play, to advanced major league time. Because teams typically have five to six minor league clubs in their network, it can be expensive to gather complete information on each player. Players spend at least two years in the minor league before hitting for the major league, so keeping tabs on everyone helps the team reduce cycle time and expense. Each team considers its scouting applications as its "crown jewels," and its leaders refuse to share specifics with anyone outside the organization.

---

[22] "Online Forum: Companies of the Future," available at http://www.msnbc.com/news/738363.asp (accessed June 11, 2002).

The player's job on the field is still hitting the ball and running the bases, but the jobs off the field are changing rapidly as IS assist in scouting new players, tracking statistics of teams and competition, and assisting in decision making at all levels of the business.

Discussion Questions

1. How is the job of the catcher different as a result of the use of IS?
2. Using the scouting information changes the job of the managers from one of intuition to one of information. Team managers run the team and are responsible for activities such as negotiating deals with new players, trading players with other teams, and pulling together the roster for each game. Describe how you think using IS for scouting changes the manager's job.
3. How do IS for scouting change where work is done for the baseball team?
4. What new jobs help a team use IS successfully?

Source: Adapted from Christopher Koch, "A Whole New Ballgame," *CIO Magazine* (April 15, 1999), pp. 38–47.

CHAPTER 5

INFORMATION TECHNOLOGY AND CHANGING BUSINESS PROCESSES[1]

Executives at CIGNA Corporation faced a challenge: to radically improve operating efficiency. The company's income had fallen nearly 11 percent from the previous year. Benchmarks with other insurance industry leaders suggested that its operating costs exceeded what the market would bear, and, moreover, productivity lagged significantly in some crucial areas. A review of the systems organization revealed that, not only were investments in information technology (IT) failing to support the strategic direction of the company, but in effect, sophisticated new applications were being layered on top of existing organizations and processes, without a full understanding of how they might complement them, let alone improve them.

Accordingly, CIGNA's new chairman initiated a program to radically redesign the company's operating processes in key areas. Beginning with a relatively small volunteer unit—the reinsurance division—CIGNA concentrated on developing an in-house cadre of managers who could become expert in the processes of business transformation and begin to create an experience base that could be useful in successive redesign efforts. The successful efforts of this team in the reinsurance division were subsequently replicated in the information systems (IS) unit, adapted for various overseas groups, and then applied with tremendous success to a core unit that required substantial redirection: the property and casualty group, an 8,000-person business unit facing a $1 billion loss. CIGNA realized savings of more than $100 million from more than 20 reengineering initiatives. Individual units experienced cuts in operating expenses of 42 percent, cycle time improvements of 100 percent, customer satisfaction that increased 50 percent, and quality improvements of 75 percent.[2]

---

[1] The author wishes to acknowledge and thank Jeff Greer, MBA 1999 for his help researching a writing early drafts of this paper.

[2] J. R. Caron, S. Jarvenpaa, and D. Stoddard, "Business Reengineering at CIGNA Corporation: Lesson from the First Five Years," *Management Information Systems Quarterly* 18, 3 (September 1994).

IT can enable or impede business change. The right design coupled with the right technology can result in changes such as CIGNA experienced. The wrong business process design or the wrong technology, however, can force a company into oblivion.

To a manager in the Information Age, an understanding of how IT enables business change is essential. The terms *management* and *change management* are used almost synonymously: To manage effectively means to manage change effectively. As IT becomes ever more prevalent and more powerful, the speed and magnitude of the changes that organizations must address to remain competitive will continue to increase. To be a successful manager, one must understand how IT enables change in a business, one must gain a process perspective of business, and one must understand how to transform business processes effectively. This chapter provides the manager with a view of business process change. It provides tools for analyzing how a company currently does business and for thinking about how to effectively manage the inevitable changes that result from competition and the availability of IT. This chapter also describes an IT-based solution commonly known as enterprise IS.

A brief word to the reader is needed. The term *process* is used extensively in this chapter. In some instances, it is used to refer to the steps taken to change aspects of the business. At other times, it is used to refer to the part of the business to be changed: the business process. The reader should be sensitive to the potentially confusing use of the term *process*.

► SILO PERSPECTIVE VS. BUSINESS PROCESS PERSPECTIVE

Reengineering requires discontinuous thinking—recognizing and shedding outdated rules and fundamental assumptions that underlie operations. "Unless we change these rules, we are merely rearranging the deck chairs on the *Titanic*. We cannot achieve breakthroughs in performance by cutting fat or automating existing processes. Rather, we must challenge old assumptions and shed the old rules that made the business under perform in the first place."[3]

When effectively linked with improvements to business processes, advances in IT enable changes that make it possible to do business in a new way, better and more competitive than before. On the other hand, IT can also inhibit change, which occurs when managers fail to adapt business processes because they rely on inflexible systems to support those processes. Finally, IT can also drive change, for better or for worse. Examples abound of industries that were fundamentally changed by advances in IT, and of companies whose success or failure depended on the ability of their managers to adapt. This chapter considers IT as an enabler of business transformation, a partner in transforming business processes to achieve competitive advantages.

---

[3] Michael Hammer, "Reengineering Work: Don't Automate, Obliterate," *Harvard Business Review* (July–August 1990), p. 4.

Functional (or Silo) Perspective

Many think of business by imagining a hierarchical structure organized around a set of functions. Looking at a traditional organization chart allows an understanding of what the business does in order to achieve its goals. A typical hierarchical structure, organized by function, might look like the one shown in Figure 5.1.

In a hierarchy, each department determines its core competency and then concentrates on what it does best. For example, the operations department focuses on operations, the marketing department focuses on marketing, and so on. Each major function within the organization usually forms a separate department to ensure that work is done by groups of experts in that function. This functional structure is widespread in today's organizations and is reinforced by business education curricula, which generally follow functional structures—students take courses in functions (i.e., marketing, management, accouting, etc.), major in functions, and then are predisposed to think in terms of these same functions.[4]

Even when companies use the perspective of the value chain model (as discussed in Chapter 2), they still focus on functions on delivering their portion of the process and "throwing it over the wall" to the next group on the value chain. These **silos,** or self-contained functional units, are useful for several reasons. First, they allow an organization to optimize expertise. For example, instead of having marketing people in a number of different groups, all the marketing people belong to the same department, which allows them to informally network and learn from each other. Second, the silos allow the organization to avoid redundancy in expertise by hiring one person who can be assigned to projects across functions on an as-needed basis instead of hiring an expert in each function. Third, with a functional organization, it is easier to benchmark with outside organizations, utilize bodies of knowledge created for each function, and easily understand the role of each silo. For example, it is clear that the marketing department produces and executes marketing plans, but it may not be clear what a customer-relationship department does. (It typically has some marketing, some sales, some services. and some accounting processes.)

On the other hand, silo organizations can experience significant suboptimization. First, individual departments often recreate information maintained by other

Typical Hierarchical Organization Structure

FIGURE 5.1   Hierarchical structure.

[4] Thomas Davenport and John Beck, *The Attention Economy* (Boston: Harvard Business School Press, 2001), p. 173.

departments. Second, communication gaps among departments are often wide. Third, as time passes, the structure and culture of a functionally organized business can become ingrained, creating a complex and frustrating bureaucracy. Finally, handoffs between silos are often a source of problems, such as finger-pointing and lost information, in business processes.

A firm's work changes over time. In a functionally organized silo business, each group is primarily concerned with its own set of objectives. The executive officers jointly seek to ensure that these functions work together to create value, but the task of providing the "big picture" to so many functionally oriented personnel can prove extremely challenging. As time passes and business circumstances change, new work is created that relies on more than one of the old functional departments. Departments that took different directions must now work together. They negotiate the terms of any new work processes with their own functional interests in mind, and the "big picture" optimum gets scrapped in favor of suboptimal compromises among the silos. These compromises then become repeated processes; they become standard operating procedures.

Losing the big picture means losing business effectiveness. After all, a business's main objective is to create as much value as possible for its shareholders and other stakeholders by satisfying its customers to the greatest extent possible. When functional groups duplicate work, when they fail to communicate with one another, when they lose the big picture and establish suboptimal processes, the customers and stakeholders are not being well served.

Process Perspective

A manager can avoid such bureaucracy—or begin to "heal" it—by managing from a process perspective. A **process perspective** keeps the big picture in view and allows the manager to concentrate on the work that must be done to ensure the optimal creation of value. A process perspective helps the manager avoid or reduce duplicate work, facilitate cross-functional communication, optimize business processes, and, ultimately, best serve the customers and stakeholders.

In business, a **process** is defined as an interrelated, sequential set of activities and tasks that turns inputs into outputs, and includes the following:

- A beginning and an end
- Inputs and outputs
- A set of tasks (subprocesses) that transform the inputs into outputs
- A set of metrics for measuring effectiveness

Metrics are important because they focus managers on the critical dimensions of the process. Metrics for a business process are things like throughput, which is how many outputs can be produced per unit time; or cycle time, which is how long it takes for the entire process to execute. Some use measures such as number of handoffs in the process or actual work versus total cycle time. Other metrics are based on the outputs themselves, such as customer satisfaction, revenue per output, profit per output, and quality of the output.

Examples of business processes include customer order fulfillment, manufacturing planning and execution, payroll, financial reporting, and procurement. A typical procurement process might look like Figure 5.2. The process has a beginning and an end, inputs (requirements for goods or services) and outputs (receipt of goods, vendor payment), and subprocesses (filling out a purchase order, verifying the invoice). Metrics of the success of the process might include turnaround time and the number of paperwork errors.

The procurement process in Figure 5.2 cuts across the functional lines of a traditionally structured business. For example, the requirements for goods might originate in the operations department based on guidelines from the finance department. Paperwork would likely flow through the administration department, and the accounting department would be responsible for making payment to the vendor.

Focus on the process by its very nature ensures focus on the business's goals (the "big picture"). A process perspective recognizes that processes are often cross-functional. In the diagram in Figure 5.3, the vertical bars represent functional departments within a business. The horizontal bars represent processes that flow across those functional departments. A process perspective requires an understanding that processes properly exist to serve the larger goals of the business, and that functional departments must work together to optimize processes in light of these goals.

This generalization is not to say that managers should focus strictly on processes or fail to consider functional areas or IT strategy. Just as processes exist to serve the larger goals of the business, so too do organizational and IT strategies. The Information Systems Strategy Triangle from Chapter 1 (see Figure 5.4) illustrates that both organizational strategy and information strategy should support overall business strategy. A process focus illuminates suboptimized organizational and information strategies that fail to support the overall business strategy.

For example, Nokia Telecommunications, the telecommunications manufacturing division of the Finnish company Nokia, built its order fulfillment process to include tendering, order delivery, implementation, and after-sales service tasks.[5] The company built cellular systems, switching systems, and transmission systems worldwide to companies offering mobile and fixed telecommunications services. Their order fulfillment process crossed division and product group boundaries, making it a cross-functional business process.

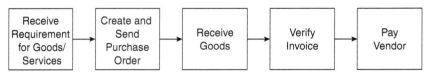

FIGURE 5.2   Sample business process.

[5] For more details about Nokia's efforts see S. Jarvenpaa, and Ilkka Tuomi, "Nokia Telecommunications: Redesign of International Logistics," Harvard Business School case study 9-996-006 (September 1995).

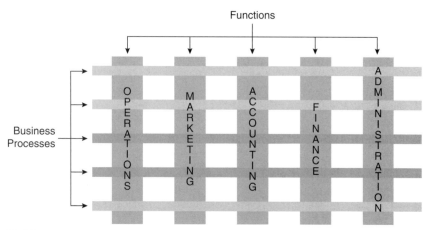

FIGURE 5.3 Cross-functional nature of business processes.

FIGURE 5.4 The information systems strategy triangle.

When managers gain the process perspective, they begin to lead their organizations to change in order to optimize the value that customers and stakeholders receive. These managers begin to question the status quo. They do not accept "because we have always done it that way" as an answer to why business is conducted in a certain way. They concentrate instead on specific objectives and results. They begin to manage processes by:

- Identifying the customers of processes
- Identifying these customers' requirements
- Clarifying the value that each process adds to the overall goals of the organization
- Sharing their perspective with other organizational members until the organization itself becomes more process-focused

The differences between the silo and process perspective are summarized in Figure 5.5. Unlike a silo perspective, a process perspective recognizes that businesses operate as a set of processes that flow across functional departments. It enables a manger to analyze the business's processes in light of its larger goals, as compared to the functional orientation of the silo perspective. Finally, it provides a manager with insights into how those processes might better serve these goals.

	Silo Perspective	Business Process Perspective
Definition	Self-contained functional units such as marketing, operations, finance, and so on	Interrelated, sequential set of activities and tasks that turns inputs into outputs
Focus	Functional	Cross-functional
Goal Accomplishment	Optimizes on functional goals, which might be a suboptimal organizational goal	Optimizes on organizational goals, or "big picture"
Benefits	Highlighting and developing core competencies; functional efficiencies	Avoiding work duplication and cross-functional communication gaps; organizational effectiveness

FIGURE 5.5   Comparison of silo perspective and business process perspective.

▶ THE TOOLS FOR CHANGE

Two techniques are used to transform a business: (1) radical process, which is sometimes called **business process reengineering (BPR)** or simply reengineering, and (2) incremental, continuous process improvement, sometimes referred to using the term **total quality management (TQM).** Although some believe these concepts are passé, most companies either are involved with one or both of these methods of improvement. In the late 1990s, some said that reengineering was dead, but not for many businesses. In fact, some businesses are making radical process reconfiguration a core competency so that they can better serve customers whose demands are constantly changing. Both concepts are important; they continue to be two different tools a manager can use to effect change in the way his or her organization does business. The basis of both approaches is viewing the business as a set of business processes, rather than using a silo perspective.

Total Quality Management (TQM)

At one end of the continuum, managers use TQM to improve business processes through small, incremental changes. This improvement process generally involves the following activities:

- Choosing a business process to improve
- Choosing a metric by which to measure the business process
- Enabling personnel involved with the process to find ways to improve it according to the metric

Personnel often react favorably to TQM because it gives them control and ownership of improvements and, therefore, renders change less threatening. The improvements grow from their grassroots efforts.

Business Process Reengineering (BPR)

TQM approaches work well for tweaking existing processes, but more major changes require a different type of management tool. At the other end of the change continuum, BPR enables the organization to attain aggressive improvement goals (again, as defined by a set of metrics). The goal of BPR is to make a rapid, breakthrough impact on key metrics.

The difference in the TQM and BPR approaches over time is illustrated by the graph in Figure 5.6. The vertical axis measures in one sense, how well a business process meets its goals. Improvements are made either incrementally or radically. The horizontal axis measures time.

Not surprisingly, BPR typically faces greater internal resistance than does TQM. For this reason, managers should use BPR instead of TQM only when they require radical change: for instance, when the company is in trouble, when it imminently faces a major change in the operating environment, or when it must change significantly in order to outpace its competition.

Industry experts Hammer and Champy define **business reengineering** as "[t]he fundamental rethinking and radical redesign of a business process to achieve dramatic improvements in performance."[6] Petrozzo and Stepper define the same term as "[t]he concurrent redesign of processes, organizations, and their supporting information systems to achieve radical improvement in time, cost, quality, and customers' regard for the company's products and services."[7] Both of these definitions require that business processes improve against carefully determined metrics of success. Key aspects of BPR include the following:

- The need for radical change
- Thinking from a cross-functional process perspective (or, as consultants like to say, "thinking outside the box")
- Challenging old assumptions
- Networked (cross-functional) organizing

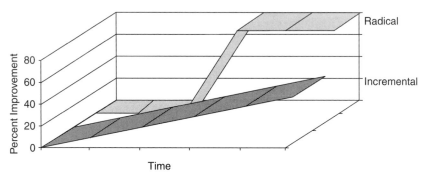

FIGURE 5.6   Comparison of radical and incremental improvement.

[6] Michael Hammer and James Champy, *Reengineering The Corporation* (New York: HarperBusiness, 2001).

[7] Daniel Petrozzo and John Stepper, *Successful Reengineering* (Princeton, NJ: Van Nostrand Reinhold, 1994).

- Empowerment of individuals in the process
- Measurement of success via metrics tied directly to business goals

Radically Redesigning Processes

Many different and effective approaches can be taken to achieve radical process change. Each consultant or academic has a pet method. The methods share three main elements:

1. They begin with a vision of which performance metrics best reflect the success of overall business strategy.
2. They make changes to the existing process.
3. They measure the results using the predetermined metrics.

The diagram in Figure 5.7 illustrates a general view of how radical redesign methods work. A new process is envisioned, the change is designed and implemented, and its impact is measured. A more specific method for changing a business process is illustrated in Figure 5.8. In this process, feedback from each step can affect any of the previous steps

Using a BPR methodology (Figure 5.8), a manager begins by stating a case for action. The manager must understand what it is about current conditions that makes them unfavorable and, in general terms, how business processes must change to address them. Next, the manager must assess the readiness of the organization to undertake change. Only after stating a compelling case for action and addressing organizational readiness should the manager identify those business processes that he or she believes should change to better support the overall business strategy and build a redesign team.

Once the case for action is made, the current process is analyzed. Some BPR experts believe that it is only necessary to do a cursory study of the existing process, just enough to understand the problems, the key metrics, and the basic flow. Others believe a detailed study helps to clearly identify how the process works. Although detail is sometimes helpful, many BPR projects get derailed at this step because of "analysis paralysis," spending an overabundance of time and effort understanding every detail of the process. Such detail is not necessary for BPR, but nevertheless is comforting to the BPR manager.

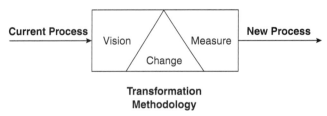

**Transformation
Methodology**

FIGURE 5.7   Conceptual flow of process design.

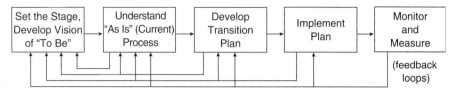

FIGURE 5.8 Method for redesigning a business process.

The tool used to understand a business process is a **workflow diagram,** which shows a picture, or map, of the sequence and detail of each process step. More than 200 products are available for diagramming the workflow. The objective of process mapping is to understand and communicate the dimensions of the current process. Typically, process engineers begin the process mapping procedure by defining the scope, mission, and boundaries of the business process. Next, the engineer develops a high-level overview flowchart of the process and a detailed flow diagram of everything that happens in the process. The diagram uses active verbs to describe activities and identifies all actors, inputs, and outputs of the process. The engineer verifies the detailed diagram for accuracy with the actors in the process and adjusts it accordingly.

Another key task at this stage is to identify metrics of business success that clearly reflect both problems and opportunities in the status quo and that can measure the effectiveness of any new processes. It is vitally important that the metrics chosen relate to the key business drivers in any given situation. Examples include cost of production, cycle time, scrap and rework rates, customer satisfaction, revenues, and quality.

The manager's next step is to develop a transition plan. The plan should include a clearly stated vision, an initial design of the new process that directly addresses the metrics that, in turn, address the goals of the business, and an implementation plan.

CIGNA's Reengineering Efforts

Consider CIGNA and how it managed this process. The company began by building a core reengineering team of 10 specialists, high-performing individuals with 5–10 years of experience in CIGNA. This core team consisted five specialists with strong systems experience, with the remainder possessing operations, business, or business analysis experience. In fact, CIGNA used this group to train future leaders. Each manager had 12–18 months of experience in the reengineering group to help build a culture of acceptance. The project requirements were so great that they brought on extra help, using outside consultants to assist when needed.

The CIGNA Reinsurance division (CIGNA-RE) was the pilot project for the company. Benchmarks set by the reengineering group suggested that CIGNA-RE could be significantly more effective with the same number of employees, that the CIGNA-RE business portfolio needed to change, and that the cost structure of CIGNA-RE was too high for its market. The group was ready to make radical change. The president of the division was even more enthusiastic when she heard a new information system would be part of the process.

The core reengineering team worked with CIGNA-RE managers to build a plan for reengineering its business. The president devoted significant time to this program—50 to 75 percent of her time during the design phase and 30 to 50 percent during the implementation phase. She built an executive committee consisting of her senior staff, which met regularly with the reengineering team.

The redesigned processes mandated a new client-server IS, new individual skills, and new managerial skills. The IS change was particularly difficult because the new client-server platform meant that many of the IS people had to be replaced in order to acquire the right skills in a short amount of time. The administrative and systems staffs were reorganized into teams. Everyone in CIGNA-RE had to apply for a job in this new organization, because none of the original jobs remained. This approach created the much-desired effect of breaking old habits and signaling major change. Much management effort was spent forging a new culture that focused on customer satisfaction and accountability. CIGNA-RE was able to achieve results within about 18 months, while reducing complexity. They reported a 40 percent reduction in operating costs, and notable improvement in process cycle times. The number of different IS applications they used was reduced from 17 applications to 5. And 27 job descriptions were reduced to 5.

CIGNA-RE's president believes that the improvement program at CIGNA will never be done. She wants to promote a climate of adaptability within her division to make sure that better ways to do business are continually embraced by her organization. Further, CIGNA managers realize many similar improvements in their divisions from subsequent reengineering efforts. Today the CIGNA culture includes acceptance for IS-based transformation of business processes.

The Risk of Radical Redesign

The implementation of a radically redesigned process presents any business with a highly complex set of challenges. Strong project management skills are critical (see Chapter 10). Before turning to these matters, however, this chapter discusses a recent development in IS that is currently supporting—and in some cases shaping—large-scale changes in business processes: enterprise systems.

▶ ENTERPRISE SYSTEMS

Computer systems in the 1960s and early 1970s were typically designed around a specific application with each application using its own set of inputs. Databases were not in common use, and a widespread following believed "the notion that a company can and ought to have an expert (or group of experts) create for it a single, completely integrated supersystem—an 'MIS'—to help it govern every aspect of its activity is absurd."[8] These early systems did not interface well with each other and often had their own version of data even though these data were used in other

[8] J. Dearden, "MIS Is a Mirage," *Harvard Business Review* (January–February 1972), p. 109.

systems. Organizational computing groups were faced with the challenge of linking and maintaining the patchwork of loosely overlapping, redundant systems. In the 1980s and 1990s, software companies in a number of countries, including the United States, Germany, and the Netherlands, began developing integrated software packages that used a common database and cut across organizational systems. Some of these packages were developed from administrative systems (e.g., finance and human resources) and others evolved from materials resource planning (MRP) in manufacturing. These comprehensive software packages that incorporate all modules needed to run the operations of a business are called **enterprise systems** or, alternatively, enterprise information systems (EIS). **Enterprise resource planning (ERP)** software packages are the most frequently discussed type of enterprise system. Other enterprise systems may be developed in-house to integrate organizational processes.

Purchased software packages were traditionally more popular with smaller companies than with larger ones, who had resources to build their own. However in the mid-1990s, vendors started pitching ERPs to larger companies that realized the costs of developing in-house integrated systems designed for client-server architectures would be extremely expensive and risky. ERPs were designed to help large companies manage the fragmentation of information stored in hundreds of individual desktop, department, and business unit computers across the organization. They offered the management information system (MIS) department in many large organizations an option for switching from underperforming, obsolete mainframe systems to client-server environments designed to handle the changing business demands of their operational counterparts. The threat of the Year 2000 problem (Y2K), a problem where computers used two digits instead of four digits to represent the year, making it impossible to distinguish between the years such as 2000 and 1900, pushed many senior managers to outside vendors who offered Y2K compliant enterprise systems as the solution for their companies. In some cases, business processes were so untamed that managers thought installing an enterprise system would be a way to standardize processes across their businesses. These managers wanted to transform their business processes by forcing all to conform to a software package. Smaller companies found similar uses for ERPs, especially for sales force automation, supply chain integration, customer relationship management, and product configuration.

By 1998, approximately 40 percent of companies with annual revenues greater than $1 billion had installed ERP software.[9] By far the most widely used enterprise system was offered by a German company, SAP. Their product, R/3, was installed in almost every large global corporation. Many other competitors, including PeopleSoft, Baan, and Oracle, and many other vendors also offered a selection of software systems that, when integrated, formed an enterprise system.

Recently a new type of enterprise system emerged, ERP II systems. Whereas an ERP makes company information immediately available to all departments throughout a company, ERP II makes company information immediately

[9] M. Lynne Markus and Cornelis Tanis, "The Enterprise System Experience—From Adoption to Success," in R. Zmud (ed.), *Framing the Domains of IT Management: Projecting the Future Through the Past* (Cincinnati, OH: Pinaflex Educational Resources, Inc., 2000), p. 175.

available to external stakeholders, such as customers and partners. ERP II enables e-business by integrating business processes between an enterprise and its trading partners.

Characteristics of Enterprise Systems

Enterprise systems have several characteristics:[10]

- *Integration.* Enterprise systems are designed to seamlessly integrate information flows throughout the company. Enterprise systems are configured by installing various modules such as:
  - Manufacturing (materials management, inventory, plant maintenance, production planning, routing, shipping, purchasing, etc.)
  - Accounting (general ledger, accounts payable, accounts receivable, cash management, forecasting, cost accounting, profitability analysis, etc.)
  - Human resources (employee data, position management, skills inventory, time accounting, payroll, travel expenses, etc.)
  - Sales (order entry, order management, delivery support, sales planning, pricing, etc.)

- *Packages.* Enterprise systems are commercial packages purchased from software vendors. Unlike many packages, enterprise systems usually require long-term relationships with software vendors because the complex systems must typically be modified on a continuing basis to meet the organization's needs.

- *Best practices.* Enterprise systems reflect industry best practices for generic business processes. To implement them, business process reengineering is often required.

- *Some assembly required.* The enterprise system is software that needs to be integrated with the organization's hardware, operating systems, databases, and telecommunications. Further, enterprise systems often need to be integrated with proprietary legacy systems. It often requires that **middleware** (software used to connect processes running in one or more computers across a network) or "bolt-on" systems be used to make all of the components operational.

- *Evolving.* Even though enterprise systems were designed first for mainframe systems and then client-server architectures, many systems now are being designed for Web-enabled or object-oriented versions. A major challenge facing many firms is to integrate Internet ERP applications with supply chain management software. One important problem in meeting this challenge is to allow companies to be both more flexible in sourcing from multiple (or alternative) suppliers, while also increasing

---

[10] Ibid., pp. 176–179.

the transparency in tightly coupled supply chains. A second problem is to integrate ERP's transaction-driven focus into a firm's workflow.[11]

Benefits and Disadvantages of Enterprise Systems

The major benefit of an enterprise system is that all modules of the information system easily communicate with each other, offering enormous efficiencies over stand-alone systems. In business, information from one functional area is often needed by another area. For example, an inventory system stores information about vendors who supply specific parts. This same information is required by the accounts payable system, which pays vendors for their goods. It makes sense to integrate these two systems to have a single accurate record of vendors.

Because of the focus on integration, enterprise systems are useful tools for an organization seeking to centralize operations and decision making. One of the benefits of centralization is the effective use of organizational databases. Redundant data entry and duplicate data may be eliminated; standards for numbering, naming, and coding may be enforced; and data and records can be cleaned up through standardization. Further, the enterprise system can reinforce the use of standard procedures across different locations.

The obvious benefits notwithstanding, implementing an enterprise system represents an enormous amount of work. Using the same simple example as previously, if an organization has allowed both the manufacturing and the accounting departments to keep their own records of vendors, then most likely these records are kept in somewhat different forms (one department may keep the vendor name as "IBM," the other as "International Business Machines" or even "IBM Corp," all of which make it difficult to integrate the databases). Such data inconsistencies must be addressed in order for the enterprise system to provide optimal advantage.

Moreover, even though enterprise systems are flexible and customizable to a point, most also require business processes to be redesigned in order to achieve optimal performance of the integrated modules. The flexibility in an enterprise system comes from being able to change parameters in a process, such as the type of part number the company will use. However, all systems make assumptions about how the business processes work, and at some level, customization is not possible. For example, one major *Fortune* 500 company refused to implement a vendor's enterprise system because the company manufactured products in lots of "one" and the vendor's system would not handle the volume this company generated. If they had decided to use the ERP, a complete overhaul of their manufacturing process in a way that executives were unwilling to do would have been necessary.

Organizations are expected to conform to the approach used in the enterprise system, arguably because the enterprise system represents a set of industry best practices. Implementing enterprise systems requires organizations to make changes in their organization structure, and often in the individual tasks done by

---

[11] Amit Basu and Akhil Kumar, "Research Commentary: Workflow Management Issues in e-Business," *Information Systems Research*, 13, 1 (March 2002), pp. 1–14.

workers. Recall in Chapter 1, the Information Systems Strategy Triangle suggests that implementing an information system must be accompanied with appropriate organizational changes to be effective. Implementing an enterprise system is no different. For example, who will now be responsible for entering the vendor information that was formerly kept in two locations? How will that information be entered into the enterprise system? The answer to such simple operational questions often requires managers at a minimum to modify business processes, and more likely to redesign them completely to accommodate the information system.

Furthermore, enterprise systems and the organizational changes they induce tend to come with a hefty price tag. A recent Meta Group survey of 63 small, medium, and large companies found the average total cost of ownership (TCO) of an ERP to be $15 million.[12] The TCOs ranged from $400,000 to $30 million. As discussed in Chapter 9, TCO numbers included hardware, software, professional services, and internal staff costs as well as installing the software and maintaining, upgrading, and optimizing it for two years. Because they are so complex, the cost of professional services and internal staff tend to be quite high. Further, additional hidden costs in the form of technical and business changes are likely to be necessary when implementing an enterprise system.

One of the reasons that enterprise (ERP) systems are so expensive is that they are sold as a suite, such as financials or manufacturing, and not as individual modules. Because buying modules separately is difficult, companies implementing ERP software often find the price of modules they won't use hidden in the cost of the suite.

Enterprise systems are not only expensive, but also risky. The number of enterprise system horror stories demonstrates this risk. For example, Kmart wrote off its $130 million ERP investment. W. L. Gore filed suit against PeopleSoft and Deloitte & Touche for failing to adequately test and debug its $3.5 million payroll and personnel system. The vendor team put fictional names into Gore's database, which they then were not able to remove. So Donald Duck and Mickey Mouse were logged on the payroll. Subsequently debugging the system was estimated to have cost Gore $1 million.[13] Tri Valley Growers, a farm co-op with $8.8 billion in revenues in 1999, wanted a fully integrated ERP to run its entire business. It paid $3.1 million for Oracle's CPG suite. Oracle's initial estimates of $300,000 in November 1996 for consulting to install the software skyrocketed to $2.7 million six months later. Oracle could never get its software to work when loaded onto Tri Valley's hardware, and it continually missed its software deadlines. Though Tri Valley declared Chapter 11 bankruptcy in 2001, it kept active its $20 million suit against Oracle for the savings it was never able to realize from the CPG project.[14]

Oftentimes, installing an enterprise system means the business must reengineer its business processes. Because the enterprise system is an automation of the major

[12] Christopher Koch, "The ABCs of ERP," *CIO Magazine* (February 7, 2002), available at http://www.cio.com/research/erp/edit/erpbasics.html (accessed on February 7, 2002).

[13] Gary Strauss, "When Computers Fail," *USA Today* (December 7, 1999), available at http://www.usatoday.com/life/cyber/tech/ctg838.htm.

[14] Christopher Koch, "Why Your Integration Efforts End Up Looking Like This . . . ," *CIO Magazine* (November 15, 2001), available at http://www.cio.com.

business processes such as financial, manufacturing, and human resource management, and because most enterprise systems are purchased from vendors such as SAP, PeopleSoft, and Oracle, it is rare that an off-the-shelf system is perfectly harmonious with an existing business process. More typical is that either the software requires significant modification or customization to fit with the existing processes, or the processes must change to fit the software. In most installations of enterprise systems, both take place. The system is customized when it is installed in a business by setting a number of parameters, and in the worst case, by modifying the code itself. The business processes are changed, often through a BPR project, as described earlier in this chapter. Many of these projects are massive undertakings, requiring formal, structured project management tools (as discussed in Chapter 10).

The Adoption Decision

When is it appropriate to use the enterprise system to drive business process redesign, and when is it appropriate to redesign the process first, then implement an enterprise system? In several instances, it is appropriate to let the enterprise system drive business process redesign. First, when an organization is just starting out and processes do not yet exist, it is appropriate to begin with an enterprise system as a way to structure operational business processes. After all, most of the processes embedded in the "vanilla" enterprise system from a top vendor are based on the best practices of corporations who have been in business for years. Second, when an organization does not rely on its operational business processes as a source of competitive advantage, then using an enterprise system to redesign these processes is appropriate. Third, it is reasonable for an organization to let the enterprise system drive business process change when the current systems are in crisis and there is not enough time, resources, or knowledge in the firm to fix them. Even though it is not an optimal situation, managers must make tough decisions about how to fix the problems. A business must have working operational processes, therefore using an enterprise system as the basis for process design may be the only workable plan. It was precisely this situation that many companies faced with Y2K.

Likewise, it is sometimes inappropriate to let an enterprise system drive business process change. When an organization derives a strategic advantage through its operational business processes, it is usually not advisable to buy a vendor's enterprise system. Using a standard, publicly available information system that both the company and its competitors can buy from a vendor may mean that any competitive advantage is lost. For example, consider a major computer manufacturer that relied on its ability to process orders faster than its competitors to gain strategic advantage. It would not have been to that organization's benefit to use an enterprise system to drive the redesign of the order fulfillment system because doing so would force the manufacturer to restrict its process to that which is available from enterprise system vendors. More importantly, any other manufacturer could then copy the process, neutralizing any advantages. Furthermore, the manufacturer believed that relying on a third party as the provider of such a strategic system would be a mistake in the long run. Should the system develop a bug or need to be redesigned to accommodate unique aspects of the business, the manufacturer would be forced to negotiate with the enterprise system vendor to get it to modify the enterprise system. With a system designed in-house, the manufacturer was able to ensure complete control over the IS that drive its critical processes.

Another situation in which it would be inappropriate to let an enterprise system drive business process change is when the features of available packages and the needs of the business do not fit. An organization may use specialized processes that cannot be accommodated by the available enterprise systems. For example, many ERPs were developed for discrete part manufacturing and do not support some processes in paper, food or other process industries.[15]

Compaq Computer Corporation found a middle ground in matching its needs with the features of an enterprise system. As described in *Harvard Business Review*, Compaq was changing its business strategy from a build-to-inventory to a build-to-order company.[16] In an effort to quickly transform the company, managers agreed that a new enterprise system would make sense. However, they realized that the key to becoming a build-to-order company was to have a unique order and fulfillment system. Compaq managers decided to build their own module for this business process. To insure compatibility with the vendor's enterprise system, the module was written in the same language as the enterprise system and was designed to be integrated into the other modules. Compaq's installation took longer than a standard enterprise system installation and cost more, but it was able to provide Compaq with the advantages of enterprise systems without costing the company the advantages it sought in its new business strategy.

A third situation would result from lack of top management support, company growth, a desire for strategic flexibility, or decentralized decision making that render the enterprise system inappropriate. For example, Dell Computer stopped the full implementation of SAP R/3 after only the human resources module had been installed because the CIO did not think that the software would be able to keep pace with Dell's extraordinary growth. Enterprise systems were also viewed as culturally inappropriate at the highly decentralized Kraft Foods.

Finally, other alternatives to increasing the level of systems integration are available. One alternative is data warehousing, sometimes described as the "poor man's ERP." A data warehouse cannot completely support, or replace, an ERP. Middleware offers another alternative. Through middleware, companies can integrate software and improve user interfaces. After it terminated its SAP contract, Dell used the middleware approach to integrate its many systems.

▶ FOOD FOR THOUGHT: THE RISKS OF RADICAL REDESIGN ALONE

The original concept of reengineering described a theory of radical change through process design. In his famous *Harvard Business Review* article, reengineering guru

---

[15] M. Lynne Markus and Cornelis Tanis, "The Enterprise System Experience—From Adoption to Success," in R. Zmud (ed.), *Framing the Domains of IT Management: Projecting the Future Through the Past* (Cincinnati, OH: Pinaflex Educational Resources, Inc., 2000).

[16] Thomas H. Davenport "Putting the Enterprise into the Enterprise System." *Harvard Business Review* (July–August 1998), pp. 121–135.

Michael Hammer described the concept of process design as one of starting with a "clean sheet of paper." The idea was not to let the existing process, nor any of the potential constraints in the environment, get in the way of the redesign. Starting with a greenfields approach allowed, in theory, the process designers to create the best possible design. The implementation of these new processes, however, proved more difficult than most organizations were willing to tolerate.

Dozens of stories tell of companies that attempted reengineering, only to fail to realize the advantages they sought. Radically changing a business is not an easy task. Research done to determine why companies failed to reach their goals reveal some of the more common reasons, which are summarized here:

- *Lack of senior management support at the right times and the right places.* Some estimates suggest that 50 percent or more of a senior manager's time is necessary to make radical change successful.

- *Lack of a coherent communications program.* Radical change can scare many employees who are unsure about whether they will have a job when the changes are completed. Companies that fail to communicate regularly, clearly, and honestly experience an increased risk of failure.

- *Introducing unnecessary complexity into the new process design.* For example, some companies try to introduce new IS that are unproven or need extensive customization and training. Such an approach adds a level of complexity to a reengineering project that is often difficult to manage.

- *Underestimating the amount of effort needed to redesign and implement the new processes.* Companies, of course, do not stop operation while they reengineer, and therefore, many companies find themselves spread too thin when trying to reengineer and continue operations. Some compare it to "changing airplanes in midair"—not impossible, but definitely not easy.

- *Combining reengineering with downsizing.* Many organizations really just want to downsize their operations and get rid of some of their labor costs. They call that initiative reengineering rather than downsizing, and think their employees will understand that the new business design just takes fewer people. Employees are smarter than that, and often make the implementation of the radical design impossible.

This chapter described a business as a set of processes and outlined methods for changing these processes. These changes can take the form of either revolution through radical change or evolution through incremental change. In a letter to the editor of *Harvard Business Review*, Gary Hamel argues that radical change is more likely to create large amounts of new wealth than incremental change.[17] However, he then argues that the case for radical change is often distorted in one of five ways:

---

[17] Gary Hamel, "Revolution vs. Evolution: You Need Both," *Harvard Business Review*, 79, 5 (May 2001), pp. 150–156.

1. *A firm must decide to undertake either radical or incremental change.* In reality it may be possible to employ both strategies. Researchers have found that many reengineering projects employ a radical design, but an evolutionary implementation plan.[18] When companies face a crisis, they may have no choice but to implement radical redesign in a revolutionary way. In many cases, however, the objectives of a reengineering project take a minimum of several months to complete. Companies find that too much change too quickly can do more harm than good to their short-term business objectives. Thus, a more common approach is to use reengineering techniques to design a radical new process, but to implement it in smaller, more digestible steps.

2. *Companies should be careful about embracing radical change because it means jettisoning the past.* Rather, firms should leverage brands, assets, and competencies built up over time, even when they are embracing radical change.

3. *Radical change should be avoided because it is too risky.* More immediately, an incremental approach can reduce the short-term risk of failure, ease the adaptation of new processes, and allow individual employees to participate more fully. These gains, however, should not be taken if they raise long-term risks that can only be avoided by adopting a strategy of radical change.

4. *Radical change has no place in the daily running of well-established firms.* Rather, radical change challenges individuals at all levels throughout the firm.

5. *A firm can only tolerate a limited amount of radical change.* Even though incremental change is often linear, radical change is not and one change may force the introduction of a series of radical changes.

The benefits of BPR are seductive, but the risks are high. To mitigate this risk, some propose undertaking a revolutionary design approach but an evolutionary implementation approach, as already described in the first point. Although evolutionary implementation may reduce the risk of rejection, ease the adaptation of the new process, and allow more individuals to participate in the business change, it also means taking longer to realize the benefits of the redesign.

► SUMMARY

- IS can enable or impede business change. IS enables change by providing both the tools to implement the change, and the tools on which the change is based. IS can also impede change, particularly when the desired information is mismatched with the capabilities of the IS.

---

[18] D. Stoddard and S. Jarvenpaa, "Reengineering Design Is Radical, Reengineering Change Is Not!" Harvard Business School case 196–037 (July 1995).

- To understand the role IS play in business transformation, one must take a business process, rather than a functional, perspective. Business processes are a well-defined, ordered set of tasks characterized by a beginning and an end, a set of associated metrics, and cross-functional boundaries. Most businesses operate business processes, even if their organization charts are structured by functions rather than by processes.

- Making changes in business processes is typically done through either TQM or BPR techniques. TQM techniques tend to imply an evolutionary change, where processes are improved incrementally. BPR techniques, on the other hand, imply a more radical objective and improvement. Both techniques can be disruptive to the normal flow of the business; hence strong project management skills are needed.

- Enterprise systems are large information systems that provide the core functionality needed to run a business. These systems are typically implemented in order to help organizations share data between divisions. However, in some cases enterprise systems are used to affect organizational transformation by imposing a set of assumptions on the business processes they manage.

- Information systems are useful as tools to both enable and manage business transformation. The general manager must take care to ensure that consequences of the tools themselves are well understood and well managed.

▶ KEY TERMS

business process reengineering (BPR) (p. 110)
business reengineering (p. 111)
enterprise resource planning (ERP) (p. 115)

enterprise system (p. 115)
middleware (p. 116)
process (p. 107)
process perspective (p. 107)
silos (p. 106)

total quality management (TQM) (p. 110)
workflow diagram (p. 113)

▶ DISCUSSION QUESTIONS

1. Why was radical design of business processes embraced so quickly and so deeply by senior managers of so many companies? In your opinion, and using hindsight, was its popularity a benefit for businesses? Why or why not?

2. Off-the-shelf enterprise IS often force an organization to redesign its business processes. What are the critical success factors to make sure the implementation of an enterprise system is successful?

3. Have you been involved with a company doing a redesign of its business processes? If so, what were the key things that went right? What went wrong? What could have been done better to minimize the risk of failure?

4. What do you think that Jerry Gregoire, former CIO of Dell Computers, meant when he said, "Don't automate broken business processes."[19]

[19] "Technology: How Much? How Fast? How Revolutionary? How Expensive?" *Fast Company*, 56, p. 62, available at http://www.fastcompany.com/online/56/fasttalk.html (accessed on May 30, 2002).

COCA-COLA VENDING MACHINES

Vending machines are often out of their most popular items, waiting for service personnel to replenish them. Coca-Cola Amatil, Ltd., the company that bottles Coca-Cola in Australia and several countries in the Asia-Pacific region, equipped about 35,000 of its vending machines with microprocessors and cellular transmitters that transfer information daily to a database at company headquarters in Sydney, Australia. The system collects sales information that can be used to analyze performance of the vending machines. It also provides a link to the sales and distribution transaction processing system. Sales data are collected and transmitted, enabling service personnel to refill the machines as needed, rather than at predetermined intervals.

The microprocessors also detect faulty machines so repair technicians can be dispatched to fix them more quickly. Each machine is polled every evening to determine usage. This process enables the company to do more efficient delivery routing by knowing which machines need to be filled, what product they need, and how much is needed. The information is also useful to track sales and usage trends.

Discussion Questions

1. What was the business strategy of Coca-Cola Amatil, Ltd. when it made the decision to install this new technology? What would have been the major components of the cost-benefit analysis that justified this project?

2. How does the process of managing sales of sodas through vending machines change with the introduction of this system?

3. How might this system change the process of maintenance and repair of the machines?

Source: Adapted from Bob Violino, "Extended Enterprise," *Information Week* (March 22, 1999), pp. 46–63.

NESTLÉ

In early 1997, Joe Waller, CEO of Nestlé USA a subsidiary of Nestlé SA, decided to transform the company from a hodgepodges of separate brands into *One Nestlé*, an integrated company. To this end, he formed a key stakeholders team to help prepare for the process. Key stakeholders were asked to outline the company's strengths and weaknesses. During the two-hour analysis of each team member, the inefficiencies resulting from the separate, autonomous operations became obvious. The key stakeholders team uncovered 28 points of customer entry and nine general ledgers. It was impossible to determine the volume of sales from any given vendor. A plan, using SAP packages as its cornerstone, was developed to remedy this problem and other redundancies and inefficiencies. The SAP project, BEST (Business Excellence through Systems Technology) was to be implemented under the guidance of the

CIO of Nestlé USA, Jeri Dunn. In assuming responsibility for the BEST project, Dunn warned, "We made it very clear that this would be a business process reorganization and that you couldn't do it without changing the way you did business. There was going to be pain involved, it was going to be a slow process, and this was not a software project."

Dunn had just returned from a stint as assistant vice president of technology and standards for the corporation, Nestlé SA. In this position she developed standards to be implemented throughout the corporation that would allow data sharing across divisions and eliminate redundancies such as paying 29 different prices for vanilla from the same vendor. Unfortunately, when Dunn returned to Nestlé USA, she realized the carefully developed corporate standards were not being implemented within the divisions.

The BEST project started with a team of 50 top business executives and 10 senior IT professionals. The team was charged with developing a set of common work procedures for every Nestlé USA division. A smaller technical team was carefully studying the data in every division to devise a common data structure. By March 1998, the key stakeholders had completed a plan that involved implementing five SAP modules (i.e., purchasing, financials, sales and distribution, accounts payable, and accounts receivables) and a Manugistic's supply chain module that was viewed as less risky than SAP's comparable, but new, supply chain module. Development began in July 1998 with a targeted implementation date for four of the modules to coincide with Y2K.

By late 1999, it became clear that the project's timeline was too ambitious. In their haste, the system implementers failed to include any groups directly affected by the system's use on the key stakeholders team. Massive user resistance and confusion followed when the team tried to roll out BEST. Users did not understand, nor want to learn, how to use the new system. Dunn confessed, "We were always surprising [the heads of sales and the divisions] because we would bring something up to the executive steering committee that they weren't privy to." The forecast demand group demonstrated dismaying resistance when 77 percent of its members chose to resign instead of replacing their old way of forecasting for the complex models in the Manugistics module.

Technical problems besieged the project as well. The BEST project team had overlooked the integration points between modules. Though common names had been achieved, the modules could not interface with one another. For example, a salesperson might give a favored customer a discount rate, but the discount was not transmitted to the accounts receivable personnel. As a result, the accounts receivable personnel considered the account only partially paid.

Dunn realized the need to take drastic measures to save the project. In October 2000, she gathered 19 Nestlé USA key stakeholders and business executives for a three-day off-site self-examination. They concluded that the project needed to retrace its steps and develop business requirements before setting a new project deadline. They also encouraged seeking support for the project from the divisional heads who had been overlooked earlier, and informing employees more fully about the project's purpose and progress.

Dunn placed new emphasis on getting the "big picture" view of how the system components worked together. The team renewed its efforts to implement the domestic sales and distribution and accounts receivable modules. Dunn made the painful decision to halt the rollout of the Manugistics package and replace it with SAP's supply chain module that had since become Nestlé SA's global standard. This last-minute switch resulted in 5 percent of BEST's substantial cost.

When the end-state design was completed by April 2001, relationships with the divisions were still poor. In May, Tom James was appointed director of process change for the BEST project. He and Dunn met more often with the division heads and surveyed the employees to identify problems in dealing with system changes. The results of one survey convinced them to delay the rollout of a manufacturing package by six months.

BEST is projected to cost Nestlé USA $210 million and six years of effort. Its scheduled completion date is the first quarter of 2003. However, Dunn claims that the BEST project has already saved Nestlé USA $325 million. She admits that the project was about change management—not a software implementation: "When you move to SAP, you are changing the way people work. . . .You are challenging their principles, their beliefs, and the way they have done things for many, many years."

Discussion Questions

1. Was it appropriate to implement the BEST project at Nestlé USA? Why or why not?
2. In what ways do you think that Nestlé USA realized savings of $325 million?
3. Why is this story more about change management that software implementation?

Source: Adapted from Ben Worthen, "Nestlé's ERP Odyssey," *CIO Magazine* (May 15, 2002), available at http://www.cio.com/archive/051502/nestle.html.

CHAPTER 6

ARCHITECTURE AND INFRASTRUCTURE[1]

Bridgeport-based People's Bank is Connecticut's largest independent bank. It manages assets of more than $13 billion and a network of 144 branches and more than 200 ATMs. People's Bank provides commercial, consumer, insurance and investment services, and operates a credit card business ranked 16th in the nation. Following its strategy, it offers a wide range of innovative services and delivery channels so that it can stay nimble and customer-friendly. In 1998, People's Bank decided that its highly heterogeneous IT architecture was limiting its flexibility and slowing its speed to market. Instead, it sought an architecture that would allow it to tie together all of its service delivery platforms—Web-based services, branch-based tellers, call center reps, and telephone-based services—back to a common set of business rules. It needed seamless links to its external partners for support of real-time data transfer.

People's Bank new four-tier architecture, implemented in phases, was up and running by October 2000. As shown in Figure 6.1, the first (client) tier has a Web browser front end. The second (server) tier uses an IBM Web application server. The third tier of the architecture, performing transaction processing control, is built around IBM middleware. Linking this tier with the bank's heterogeneous legacy and client/server systems (tier 4) is an IBM message-broker hub designed to simplify the complexity of connections between applications. Seamless linkages to the bank's external data service providers are performed via TCP/IP sockets.

In addition to gaining the ability to develop and introduce new services more rapidly and at lower cost, this architectural solution lowered costs and improved the efficiency of several operational areas including credit card call center operations. In the credit card call center, for example, reps now access data through a single, browser-based interface instead of through the bank's earlier unwieldy combination of interfaces. This approach resulted in cutting customer response times by an estimated 30 percent, producing a comparable increase in customer satisfaction, minimizing the payment of per-transaction charges that it makes to the agencies, and cutting training time in half. Given the high turnover typically prevalent within call

---

[1] The author wishes to acknowledge and thank Vince Cavasin, MBA 1999, for his help in researching and writing early drafts of this chapter.

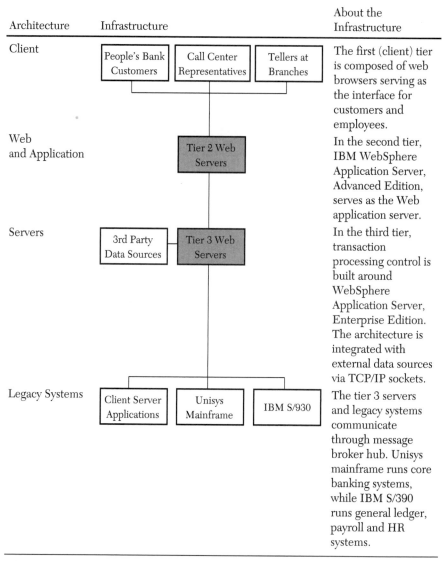

Architecture	Infrastructure			About the Infrastructure
Client	People's Bank Customers	Call Center Representatives	Tellers at Branches	The first (client) tier is composed of web browsers serving as the interface for customers and employees.
Web and Application		Tier 2 Web Servers		In the second tier, IBM WebSphere Application Server, Advanced Edition, serves as the Web application server.
Servers	3rd Party Data Sources	Tier 3 Web Servers		In the third tier, transaction processing control is built around WebSphere Application Server, Enterprise Edition. The architecture is integrated with external data sources via TCP/IP sockets.
Legacy Systems	Client Server Applications	Unisys Mainframe	IBM S/930	The tier 3 servers and legacy systems communicate through message broker hub. Unisys mainframe runs core banking systems, while IBM S/390 runs general ledger, payroll and HR systems.

FIGURE 6.1 Architecture and infrastructure of People's Bank.

Source: An IDC 3-Business Case Study, "People's Bank: Banking on IBM to Build an Integrated e-Infrastructure," available at http://www3.ibm.com/software/success/cssdb.nsf/CS/AWOD-522TWC?Open Document&Site=software (accessed June 23, 2002).

centers, any reductions in training time and costs have a dramatic impact on overall call center costs. Further, moving from thick clients to a browser-based interface lowered the bank's desktop administration costs by more than $100,000 annually.

So far, this text explored the organizational, tactical, and strategic importance of IT. This chapter examines the mechanisms by which business strategy is transformed into tangible IT architecture and infrastructure. The terms *architecture* and *infrastructure* are often used interchangeably in the context of IT. This chapter discusses how the two differ and the role each plays in realizing a business strategy.

▶ FROM VISION TO IMPLEMENTATION

As shown in Figure 6.2, architecture translates strategy into infrastructure. Building a house is similar: the owner has a vision of how the final product should look and function. The owner must decide on strategy about where to live—in an apartment or in a house. The owner's strategy also includes deciding how to live in the house in terms of taking advantage of a beautiful view, having an open floor plan, or planning for special interests by designing such special areas as a game room, study, music room, or other amenities. The architect develops plans based on this vision. These plans, or blueprints, provide a guide—unchangeable in some areas, but subject to interpretation in others—for the carpenters, plumbers, and electricians who actually construct the house. Guided by past experience and by industry standards, these builders select the materials and construction techniques best suited to the plan. The plan helps them determine where to put the plumbing and wiring. When the process works, the completed house fulfills its owner's vision, even though he or she did not participate in the actual construction. As finishing touches, the owner adds window coverings, light fixtures, and furniture to make the new house livable.

An IT **architecture** provides a blueprint for translating business strategy into a plan for IS. An IT **infrastructure** is everything that supports the flow and processing of information in an organization, including hardware, software, data, and network components. It consists of components, chosen and assembled in a manner that best suits the plan and therefore best enables the overarching business strategy.[2] Infrastructure in an organization is similar to the plumbing, wiring, and furnishings in a house.

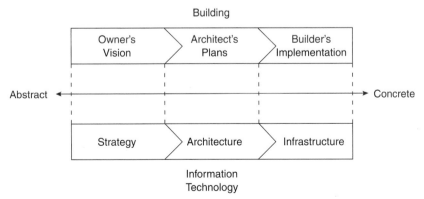

FIGURE 6.2 From the abstract to the concrete—building vs. IT.

[2] Gordon Hay and Rick Muñoz, "Establishing an IT Architecture Strategy," *Information Systems Management* (Summer 1997).

The Manager's Role

Even though he or she is not drawing up plans or pounding nails, the homeowner in this example needs to know what to reasonably expect from the architect and builders. The homeowner must know enough about architecture, specifically about styling and layout, to work effectively with the architect who draws up the plans. Similarly, the homeowner must know enough about construction details such as the benefits of various types of siding, windows, and insulation to set reasonable expectations for the builders.

Like the homeowner, the manager must understand what to expect from IT architecture and infrastructure in order to be able to make full and realistic use of them. The manager must effectively communicate his or her business vision to IT architects and implementers, and, if necessary, modify the plans if IT cannot realistically support them. For without the involvement of the manager, IT architects could inadvertently make decisions that limit the manager's business options in the future.

For example, a sales manager for a large distribution company did not want to partake in discussions about providing sales force automation systems for his group. He felt that each individual salesperson could buy a laptop, if he or she wanted one, and the IT group would be able to provide support. No architecture was designed, and no long-range thought was given to how IT might support or inhibit the sales group. Salespeople did buy laptops, and other personal organizing devices. Soon, the IT group was unable to support all the different systems the salespeople had, so they developed a set of standards for systems they would support, based on the infrastructure they used elsewhere in the company. Again, the manager just blindly accepted that decision, and salespeople with systems outside the standards bought new systems. Then the sales manager wanted to change the way his group managed sales leads. He approached the IT department for help, and in the discussions that ensued, he learned that earlier infrastructure decisions made by the IT group now made it expensive to implement the new capability he wanted. Involvement with earlier decisions and the ability to convey his vision of what the sales group wanted to do might have resulted in an IT infrastructure that provided a platform for the changes the manager now wanted to make. The IT group-built infrastructure lacked an architecture that met the business objectives of the sales and marketing management.

▶ THE LEAP FROM STRATEGY TO ARCHITECTURE TO INFRASTRUCTURE

The huge number of IT choices available, coupled with the incredible speed of technology advances, makes the manager's task of designing an IT infrastructure seem nearly impossible. However in this chapter, the task is broken down into two major steps: first, translating strategy into architecture and, second, translating architecture into infrastructure. This chapter describes a simple framework to help managers sort IT issues. This framework stresses the need to consider business strategy when defining an organization's IT building blocks. Although this framework may not cover every possible architectural issue, it does highlight major issues associated with effectively defining IT architecture and infrastructure.

From Strategy to Architecture

The manager must start out with a strategy, and then use the strategy to develop more specific goals, as shown in Figure 6.3. Then detailed business requirements are derived from each goal.

By outlining the overarching business strategy and then fleshing out the business requirements associated with each goal, the manager can provide the architect with a clear picture of what the IS must accomplish. Of course, the manager's job is not finished here. He or she must now work with the architect to translate these business requirements into a more detailed view of the systems requirements, standards, and processes that shape an IT architecture. This more detailed view includes consideration of such things as data and process demands, as well as security objectives. This process is depicted in Figure 6.4.

From Architecture to Infrastructure

The next step is to translate the architecture into infrastructure. This task entails adding yet more detail to the architectural plan that emerged in the previous phase. Now the detail comprises actual hardware, data, networking, and software. Details extend to location of data and access procedures, location of firewalls, link specifications, interconnection design, and so on. This phase is illustrated in Figure 6.5.

When we speak about infrastructure we are referring to more than the components. Plumbing, electrical wiring, walls, and a roof do not make a house. Rather, these components must be assembled according to the blueprint to create a structure in which people can live. Similarly, hardware, software, data, and networks must be combined in a coherent pattern to have a viable infrastructure. This infrastructure can be considered at several levels. At the most global level infrastructure may focus at the enterprise level and refer to the infrastructure for the entire organization. Infrastructure may also focus on the interorganizational level by laying the foundation for communicating with customers, suppliers, or other stakeholders across organizational boundaries. Sometimes infrastructure

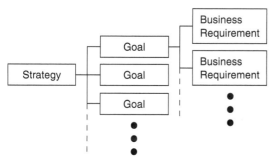

FIGURE 6.3 From strategy to business requirements.

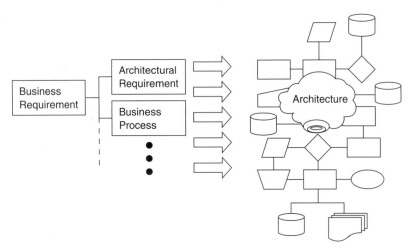

FIGURE 6.4   From business requirements to architecture.

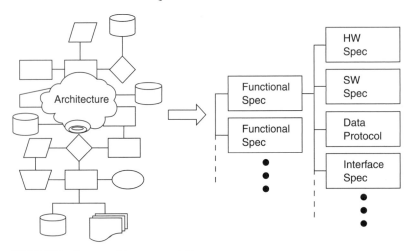

FIGURE 6.5   From architecture to infrastructure.

refers to those components needed for an individual application. When considering the structure of a particular application, it is important to consider databases and program components, as well as the devices and operating environments on which they run. The application-level infrastructure reflects decisions made at the enterprise level. The following discussion relates to infrastructure and architecture at the enterprise level.

A Framework for the Translation

When developing a framework for transforming business strategy into architecture and then into infrastructure these basic components should be considered:

- *Hardware:* The physical components that handle computation, storage, or transmission of data (e.g., personal computers, servers, mainframes, hard drives, RAM, fiber-optic cabling, modems, and telephone lines).
- *Software:* The programs that run on hardware to enable work to be performed (e.g., operating systems, databases, accounting packages, word processors, and enterprise resource planning systems). Some software, such as an operating system like Windows 2000 or XP, or Linux, provides the platform on which other software, the applications, run. Applications, on the other hand, are software that automate tasks such as storing data, transferring files, creating documents, and calculating numbers. Applications include generic software, such as word processors and spreadsheets, and specific software, such as sales force automation systems, human resource management systems, payroll systems, and manufacturing management systems.
- *Network:* Software and hardware components, such as switches, hubs, and routers, that create a path for communication and data sharing according to a common protocol.
- *Data:* The electronic representation of the numbers and text upon which the IT infrastructure must perform work. Here, the main concern is the quantity and format of data, and how often it must be transferred from one piece of hardware to another or translated from one format to another.

The framework that guides the analysis of these components is shown in Figure 6.6a. This framework is simplified to make the point that initially understanding an organization's infrastructure is not difficult. Understanding the technology behind each component of the infrastructure and the technical requirements of the

Component	What	Who	Where
Hardware	What hardware does the organization have?	Who manages it? Who uses it? Who owns it?	Where is it located? Where is it used?
Software	What software does the organization have?	Who manages it? Who uses it? Who owns it?	Where is it located? Where is it used?
Network	What networking does the organization have?	Who manages it? Who uses it? Who owns it?	Where is it located? Where is it used?
Data	What data does the organization have?	Who manages it? Who uses it? Who owns it?	Where is it located? Where is it used?

FIGURE 6.6a Information systems analysis framework.

architecture is a much more complex task. The main point is that the general manager must begin with an overview that is complete and that delivers a big picture.

This framework asks three types of questions that must be answered for each infrastructure component: what, who, and where. The "what" questions are those most commonly asked and that identify the specific type of technology. The "who" questions seek to understand what individuals, groups, and departments are involved. In most cases, the individual user is not the owner of the system nor even the person who maintains it. In many cases, the systems are leased, not owned, by the company, making the owner a party completely outside the organization. In understanding the infrastructure, it is important to get a picture of the people involved. The third set of questions address "where" issues. With the proliferation of networks, many IS are designed and built with components in multiple locations, often even crossing oceans. Learning about infrastructure means understanding where everything is located.

We can expand the use of this framework to also understand architecture. To illustrate the connections between strategy and systems, the table in Figure 6.6b has been populated with questions that typify those asked in addressing architecture and infrastructure issues associated with each component.

Component	What		Who		Where	
	Architecture	Infrastructure	Architecture	Infrastructure	Architecture	Infrastructure
Hardware	Does fulfillment of our strategy require thick or thin clients?	What size hard drives do we equip our thick clients with?	Who knows the most about servers in our organization?	Who will operate the server?	Does our architecture require centralized or distributed servers?	Must we hire a server administrator for the Tokyo office?
Software	Does fulfillment of our strategy require ERP software?	Shall we go with SAP or Oracle Applications?	Who is affected by a move to SAP?	Who will need SAP training?	Does our geographical organization require multiple database instances?	Does Oracle provide the multiple-database functionality we need?
Network	What kind of bandwidth do we need to fulfill our strategy?	Will 10baseT Ethernet suffice?	Who needs a connection to the network?	Who needs an ISDN line to his or her home?	Does our WAN need to span the Atlantic?	Shall we lease a cable or use satellite?
Data	Do our vendors all use the same EDI format?	Which VAN provides all the translation services we need?	Who needs access to sensitive data?	Who needs encryption software?	Will backups be stored on-site or off-site?	Which storage service shall we select?

FIGURE 6.6b Infrastructure and architecture analysis framework with sample questions.

The questions shown in Figure 6.6b are only representative of those to be asked; the specific questions managers would ask about their organizations depend on the business strategy the organizations is following. However, this framework can help managers raise appropriate questions as they seek to translate business strategy into architecture and ultimately into infrastructure in their organizations. The answers derived with IT architects and implementers should provide a robust picture of the IT environment.

An example of architecture popular in many organization is a client/server architecture. **Client/server architecture** is one in which one software program (the **client**) requests and receives data and sometimes instructions from another software program (the **server**) usually running on a separate computer. The hardware, software, networking, and data are arranged in a way that distributes the functionality between multiple small computers. This type of architecture contrasts with another architecture, commonly called a "mainframe architecture." A **mainframe architecture** employs a large central computer that handles all of the functionality of the system. A manager must be aware of the trade-offs when considering architecture decisions. For example, client/server architectures are more modular, allowing additional servers to be added with relative ease, and provide greater flexibility for adding clients with specific functionality for specific users. However, mainframe architectures are easier to manage in some ways, because all functionality is centralized in the main computer, instead of distributed throughout all the clients and servers.

An example of a company making these trade-offs is Air Products and Chemicals.[3] The company's two major data centers are located in the United Kingdom and in Pennsylvania. When the business strategy of Air Products changed from managing growth to managing cost containment and productivity, the managers decided to transfer the processing of mainframe applications from the U.K. center to the United States. While they were making this move, they also changed to a client/server architecture. The move was made to cut costs and, at the same time, encourage sharing of applications to assist the business strategy of global consistency. To accomplish this goal, the architecture was redesigned and included plans to use two large suboceanic communication circuits to continue to support the business needs in Europe. Client/server architecture was a difficult choice for Air Products to implement. As one manager commented, "Running a global system with multiple national platforms and choosing technologies from around the world introduces more problems still. Our old methods of design and implementation for the mainframe just don't apply anymore."

Figure 6.7 summarizes characteristics of mainframe, client/server, peer-to-peer, and wireless (mobile) architectures. Recent technological advances make the peer-to-peer and wireless or mobile architectures possible. These architectures do not necessarily need to be the firm's exclusive architecture. For example, a wireless architecture may operate separately or may be built upon a mainframe or client/server backbone. **Peer-to-peer architecture** allows networked computers to share resources without a central server playing a dominant role. Napster used a

---

[3] Quotes in this section are all from Warren McFarlan, "Air Products and Chemicals: IT Organization and Architecture Considerations," Harvard Business School case study 196-017 (August 22, 1995).

	Mainframe	Client/Server	Peer-to-Peer	Wireless (Mobile)
Definition	A computing environment in which a large, central computer handles all of the functionality of the system. It was popular in Eras I and II when centralized computing with dumb terminal was popular.	Distributed computing environment in which one software program (the client) requests and receives data and sometimes instructions from another software program (the server) usually running on a separate computer. Popular in Era IV (the late 1980s and 1990s) with the advent of networks of personal computers.	Architecture that allows networked computers to share resources without a central server playing a dominant role; Internet-based; became popular in Eras IV and V (the late 1990s).	Environment maintaining a data connection from a remote network using a wireless technology. Relatively new (Era V), with standards still being defined.
Flexibility	Older systems were often proprietary, making change difficult.	Good because of modularity of both clients and servers; open systems.	Good because of modularity at the peer level; open systems; promotes the sharing of spare computational power and files.	Good because of ability to connect from many locations, but service connects not available everywhere; not good for transmitting large amounts of data.
Controls	High in terms of policy and standardization; low user control.	Low policy and standardization controls; moderate user control.	Based on TCP/IP; may use tunneling for communications; good user control.	Multiple standards exist; good user control.

FIGURE 6.7 Characteristics of popular architectures.

	Mainframe	Client/Server	Peer-to-Peer	Wireless (Mobile)
Software	Large set of existing programs; may be a network server.	Software must be loaded onto client; software harder to maintain and more likely to fail than mainframe systems.	Eliminates distinction between roles of client and server; primarily used for sharing files and other resources, distributed computation, and collaboration.	Heavily reliant on middleware; peer-to-peer.
Scalability	Limited to central computer, but increasing in newer mainframes.	Good because of modularity.	Good; well-suited for global systems; peers can be added to network without relying on central directory; may become overloaded and inefficient with large number of nodes that create heavy overhead message traffic.	Very good.
Security	Easiest to maintain due to centralization of the data and programs in the mainframe.	Comparatively easy because servers can be points of centralization that can be protected, but dispersion of them increases risk.	Difficult because of wide distribution.	Difficult because wireless network can be "tapped."

FIGURE 6.7 Characteristics of popular architectures (continued).

peer-to-peer architecture. **Wireless (mobile) architectures** allow communication from remote locations using a variety of wireless technologies (e.g., fixed microwave links, wireless LANs, data over cellular networks, wireless WANs, satellite links, digital dispatch networks, one-way and two-way paging networks, diffuse infrared, laser-based communications, keyless car entry, and global positioning systems).

► OTHER MANAGERIAL CONSIDERATIONS

The framework guides the manager toward the design and implementation of an appropriate infrastructure. Next, this chapter explores managerial issues that arise with regard to both architecture and infrastructure. These issues involve the existing architecture, time-based concerns, financial analysis, and technical concerns.

Understanding Existing Architecture

At the beginning of any project, the first step is to assess the current situation. Understanding existing IT architecture allows the manager to evaluate the IT requirements of an evolving business strategy against current IT capacity. The architecture, rather than the infrastructure, is the basis for this evaluation because the specific technologies used to build the infrastructure are chosen based on the overall plan, or architecture. As previously discussed, it is these architectural plans that support the business strategy. Assuming some overlap is found, the manager can then evaluate the associated infrastructure and the degree to which it can be utilized going forward.

Relevant questions for managers to ask include the following:

- What IT architecture is already in place?
- Is the company developing the IT architecture from scratch?
- Is the company replacing an existing architecture?
- Does the company need to work within the confines of an existing architecture?
- Is the company expanding an existing architecture?

Starting from scratch allows the most flexibility in determining how architecture will enable a new business strategy, and a clean architectural slate generally translates into a clean infrastructure slate. However, it can be a challenge to plan effectively even when starting from scratch. For example, in a resource-starved start-up environment, it is far too easy to let effective IT planning fall by the wayside. Sometimes, the problem is less a shortcoming in IT management and more one of poorly devised business strategy. A strong business strategy is a prerequisite for IT architecture design, which is in turn a prerequisite for infrastructure design.

Of course, managers seldom enjoy the relative luxury of starting with a clean IT slate. More often, they must deal in some way with an existing architecture and infrastructure. In this case, they encounter both opportunity—to leverage the existing architecture and infrastructure and their attendant human resource experience pool—and the challenge of overcoming or working within the old system's shortcomings. By implementing the following steps, managers can derive the most value and suffer the least pain when working with legacy architectures and infrastructures:

1. *Objectively analyze the existing architecture and infrastructure.*
    Remember, architecture and infrastructure are separate entities; managers must assess the capability, capacity, reliability, and expandability of each.

2. *Objectively analyze the strategy served by the existing architecture.* What were the strategic goals it was designed to attain? To what extent do those goals align with current strategic goals?

3. *Objectively analyze the ability of the existing architecture and infrastructure to further the current strategic goals.* In what areas is alignment present? What parts of the existing architecture or infrastructure must be modified? Replaced?

Whether managers are facing a fresh start or an existing architecture, they must ensure that the architecture will satisfy their strategic requirements, and that the associated infrastructure is modern and efficient. The following sections will help managers assess the capabilities most important to their system architectures.

Distinguishing Current vs. Future Requirements

Defining an IT architecture that fulfills an organization's needs today is relatively simple; the problem is, by the time it is installed, those needs change. The primary reason to base an architecture on an organization's strategic goals is to allow for inevitable future changes—changes in the business environment, organization, IT requirements, and technology itself. Considering future impacts should include an analysis of the strategic time frame, technological advances, and financial constraints.

Strategic Time Frame

Understanding the life span of an IT infrastructure and architecture is critical. How far into the future does the strategy extend? How long can the architecture and its associated infrastructure fulfill strategic goals? What issues could arise and change these assumptions?

Answers to these questions vary widely from industry to industry. Strategic time frames depend on industry-wide factors such as level of commitment to fixed resources, maturity of the industry, cyclicality, and barriers to entry. As discussed in Chapter 1, hypercompetition has increased the pace of change to the point that requires any strategic decision be viewed as temporary.

Architectural longevity depends not only on the strategic planning horizon, but on the nature of a manager's reliance on IT, and on the specific rate of advances affecting the information technologies on which he or she depends. Hypercompetition implies that any architecture must be designed with maximum flexibility and scalability to ensure it can handle the imminent business changes. Imagine the planning horizon for a dot-com company in an industry in which Internet technologies and applications are changing daily, if not more often.

Although all industries must address the rapid progress of IT, those facing evolutionary change work with more predictable planning horizons than those facing the potential emergence of a "killer app."[4] The steel industry provides a good example of the former situation. A steel producer can safely design an IT architecture to

[4] Larry Downes and Chunka Mui, *Unleashing the Killer App* (Boston: Harvard Business School Press, 1998).

improve such back-office functions as inventory management, logistics, human resource management, and even production control. The infrastructure components associated with such an architecture are relatively easy to expand over time as business needs change. However, because the product, in this case steel, requires a physical production and delivery infrastructure, it is highly unlikely that IT will radically change the face of competition in this industry over the next several years. The steel producer's strategic planning time frame for IT investments is therefore longer and more predictable than for a business in a more information-intensive industry.

Publishers of reference books provide a good example of an information-intensive industry facing radical IT changes. Consider the case of *Encyclopaedia Britannica*. Until the early 1990s, Britannica's intellectual content, brand, and aggressive sales and marketing efforts yielded the best reputation in the industry and brisk sales. Its IT architecture and infrastructure supported these traditional strengths, but its strategy failed to recognize the threat posed by emerging technologies until Microsoft placed low-end competitor Funk & Wagnalls' product on a CD, added some public domain clip art, called it "Encarta," and virtually started giving it away. Suddenly, a product viewed by Britannica management as more a toy than a serious reference tool began devastating *Encyclopaedia Britannica*'s sales. Rather than rethink its business strategy, Britannica simply modified its IT infrastructure to introduce a CD version as a supplement, and not a replacement, to its printed volumes. Even though a CD version could be reproduced at considerably less expense and in less time than the paper version, Britannica hesitated changing over to CD because of the negative impact it would have on the commissions of the highly skilled sales force who served as the backbone of its previous marketing efforts. Britannica did not consider changing any organizational systems. Nor did it shrink its long planning horizons to respond to a rapidly changing technological environment. The result was a continued decline in sales.[5] Britannica's experience is a lesson for managers in information-related businesses: set shorter planning horizons and prepare to adapt to unexpected changes.

Technological Advances

A manager may think of technological advances as primarily affecting IT infrastructure, but the architecture must be able to support any such advance. Can the architecture adapt to emerging technologies? Can a manager delay the implementation of certain components until he or she can evaluate the potential of new technologies?

At a minimum, the architecture should be able to handle expected technological advances, such as growth rates in storage capacity and computing power. An exceptional architecture also has the capacity to absorb unexpected technological leaps.

The following are guidelines for planning adaptable IT architecture and infrastructure. At this point, these two terms are used together, because in most IT

---

[5] Philip Evans and Thomas Wurster, *Blown to Bits* (Boston: Harvard Business School Press, 2000).

planning they are discussed together. These guidelines are derived from work by Meta Group.[6]

- *Plan for applications and systems that are independent and loosely coupled rather than monolithic.* This approach allows managers to modify or replace only those applications affected by a change in the state of technology.

- *Set clear boundaries between infrastructure components.* If one component changes, others are minimally affected, or if effects are unavoidable, the impact is easily identifiable and quantifiable.

- *When designing a network architecture, provide access to all users when it makes sense to do so (i.e., when security concerns allow it).* A robust and consistent network architecture simplifies training and knowledge sharing, and provides some resource redundancy. An example is an architecture that allows employees to use a different server or printer if their local one goes down.

Note that requirements concerning reliability may mitigate the need for technological adaptability under certain circumstances. If the architecture requires high reliability, a manager seldom is tempted by bleeding-edge technologies. The competitive advantage offered by bleeding-edge technologies is often eroded by downtime and problems resulting from pioneering efforts with the technology. For example, despite Microsoft's virtual monopoly in providing PC operating systems, its Web server runs on only 21 percent of sites; the Linux-based Apache server dominates this reliability-sensitive market with 36 percent of Web sites.[7]

Assessing Financial Issues

Like any business investment, IT infrastructure components should be evaluated based on their expected financial value. Unfortunately, payback from IT investments is often difficult to quantify; it can come in the form of increased productivity, increased interoperability with business partners, improved service for customers, or yet more abstract improvements. For this reason, the Gartner Group suggests focusing on how IT investments enable business objectives rather than on their quantitative returns.[8]

Still, some effort can and should be made to quantify the return on infrastructure investments. This effort can be simplified if a manager works through the following steps with the IT staff.

1. *Quantify costs.* The easy part is costing out the proposed infrastructure components and estimating the total investment necessary. Don't forget to include installation and training costs in the total.

---

[6] Larry R. DeBoever and Richard D. Buchanan, "Three Architectural Sins," *CIO Magazine* (May 1, 1997).

[7] SiteMetrics Corporation, "Internet Server Survey" (February 1998), available at http://www.sitemetrics.com/serversurvey/ssd_98_q1/index.htm.

[8] B. Rosser, "Key Issues in Strategic Planning and Architecture [Gartner Group research note]," *Key Issues* (April 15, 1996).

2. *Determine the anticipated life cycles of system components.* Experienced IT staff or consultants can help establish life cycle trends both for a company and an industry in order to estimate the useful life of various systems.

3. *Quantify benefits.* The hard part is getting input from all affected user groups, as well as the IT group—which presumably knows most about the equipment's capabilities. If possible, form a team with representatives from each of these groups and work together to identify all potential areas in which the new IT system may bring value.

4. *Quantify risks.* Work with the IT staff to identify cost trends in the equipment the company proposes to acquire. Also, assess any risk that might be attributable to delaying acquisition, as opposed to paying more to get the latest technology now.

5. *Consider ongoing dollar costs and benefits.* Examine how the new equipment affects maintenance and upgrade costs associated with the current infrastructure.

Once this analysis is complete, the manager can calculate the company's preferred discounted cash flow (i.e., net present value or internal rate of return computation) and payback horizon. It is unlikely that the manager can fully quantify all costs and benefits associated with new equipment; therefore, the results of this analysis should form only one component of the decision whether to invest. Though he or she may not be able to put a dollar value on it, the manager needs to give significant qualitative weight to any assessment of the company's ability to achieve its strategic goals *without* the proposed IT investment. Approaches to evaluating IT investments are discussed in greater detail in Chapter 9.

Assessing Technical Issues

A large number of technical issues should also be considered when selecting an architecture or infrastructure. A frequently used criterion is scalability. To be **scalable** refers to how well an infrastructure component can adapt to increased, or in some cases decreased, demands. A scalable network system, for instance, could start with just a few nodes but could easily be expanded to include thousands of nodes. Scalability is an important technical feature because it means that an investment can be made in an infrastructure or architecture with confidence that the firm will not outgrow it.

What is the company's projected growth? What must the architecture do to support it? How will it respond if the company greatly exceeds its growth goals? What if the projected growth never materializes? These questions help define scalability needs.

Consider a case in which growth requirements were poorly anticipated: America Online (AOL).[9] In late 1996, AOL management changed its pricing scheme from pay-as-you-surf to a flat fee—an important strategic move in the

---

[9] Christopher Koch, "A Tough Sell," *CIO Magazine* (May 1, 1997).

marketplace. Although AOL thoroughly analyzed the financial reward the change might bring, it failed to consider adequately the impact it could have on its IT infrastructure.

The change vastly overloaded AOL's infrastructure, causing lengthy service interruptions for all customers. It is unlikely that AOL would have had to do any serious systems redesign to respond to the increase in demand; it simply needed to increase its infrastructure capacity. Ultimately, this planning failure cost AOL millions in IT investments and even more in defending its image when customers spoke badly of the service they received from AOL.

AOL's plight underscores the importance of analyzing the impact of strategic business decisions on IT architecture and infrastructure, and at least ensuring a contingency plan exists for potential unexpected effects of a strategy change.

Another important feature deals with commonly used standards. Hardware and software that uses a common standard, as opposed to a proprietary approach, are easier to plug into an existing or future infrastructure or architecture because interfaces often accompany the standard. For example, many companies use Microsoft Office software, making it an almost de facto standard. Therefore a number of additional packages come with translators to the systems in the Office suite to make it easy to move data between systems.

How easy is the infrastructure to maintain? Are replacement parts available? Is service available? Maintainability is a key technical consideration, because the complexity of these systems increases the number of things that can go wrong, need fixing, or simply need replacing. In addition to availability of parts and service people, maintenance considerations include issues such as the length of time the system might be out of commission for maintenance, how expensive and how local the parts are, and obsolescence. Should a technology become obsolete, costs skyrocket for parts and expertise.

A further consideration is whether the IT staff possesses the skills to use the infrastructure components that are selected. If it is important to use an innovative new hardware or software, IT staff can be trained, development may be outsourced, or consultants can be brought in. However each alternative comes with an additional cost. For example, incorporating a wireless network into an otherwise wire-based network would mean additional training costs for the network administration and maintenance staff, whereas growing the network with additional land-based network components would not incur the same training costs.

Differentiating Between Architecture and Infrastructure

Figure 6.8 shows the extent to which current and future requirements, associated financial issues, and technical criteria can be used to evaluate architecture and infrastructure. All seven criteria are important for decisions about architecture. However, issues regarding the infrastructure, the components chosen to implement the architecture, are primarily about technological advances, growth requirements, financial considerations, scalability, standardization, maintainability, and

| | Applicability | |
Criteria	Architecture	Infrastructure
Strategic time frame	Very applicable	Not applicable
Technological advances	Very applicable	Somewhat applicable

Assessing financial issues
    Net present value
    Payback analysis
    Incidental investments
	Somewhat applicable	Very applicable

Growth requirements/scalability	Very applicable	Very applicable
Standardization	Very applicable	Very applicable
Maintainability	Very applicable	Very applicable
Staff experience	Very applicable	Very applicable

FIGURE 6.8 Applicability of evaluation criteria to discussion of architecture and infrastructure.

compatibility with IT staff skills. The strategic time frame is an issue that is decided before the infrastructure discussion begins. The example in the following section demonstrates the steps that must be taken to derive these components.

▶ FROM STRATEGY TO ARCHITECTURE TO INFRASTRUCTURE: AN EXAMPLE

This section considers a simple example to illustrate the application of concepts from preceding sections. The case discussed is BluntCo, a fictitious maker of cigar clippers.

Step 1: Define the Strategic Goals

The managers at BluntCo recognize the increasing popularity of cigars; in fact, they can hardly keep up with demand for their clippers. At the same time, however, BluntCo's president, Tres Smokur, is concerned that cigar mania may end. Smokur wants to ensure that BluntCo can respond to sudden changes in demand for clippers. Along with the board of directors, Smokur sets BluntCo's strategic goals:

- To lower costs by outsourcing clipper manufacturing
- To lower costs by outsourcing clipper distribution
- To improve market responsiveness by outsourcing clipper manufacturing
- To improve market responsiveness by outsourcing clipper distribution

Step 2: Translate Strategic Goals to Business Requirements

To keep things simple, consider more closely only one of BluntCo's strategic goals: To lower costs by outsourcing clipper manufacturing. How can BluntCo's architecture enable this goal? Its business requirements must reflect the following key interfaces to the new manufacturing partners:

- Sales to manufacturing partners: Send forecasts, confirm orders received.
- Manufacturing partner to sales: Send capacity, confirm orders shipped.
- Manufacturing partner to accounting: Confirm orders shipped, electronic invoices, various inventory levels, returns.
- Accounting to manufacturing partner: Transfer funds for orders fulfilled.

Step 3: Apply Strategy-Architecture-Infrastructure Framework

In order to support the business requirements, an architecture needs to be established. One of the major components of the architecture deals with how to obtain, store, and use data to support those business requirements. The database can be designed to provide the sales data to support sales applications such as sending forecasts and confirming orders received. The database can also be designed to support manufacturing applications that confirm orders shipped, manage inventory, and estimate capacity. The database also needs to be designed to support accounting applications for invoicing, handling returns, and transferring funds.

Step 4: Translate Architecture to Infrastructure

With the architecture goals in hand, apply the framework presented in the first section of this chapter to build the infrastructure. Figure 6.9 lists questions raised when applying the framework to BluntCo's architecture goals and related infrastructure. Note that not all questions apply in a given situation. Figure 6.10 lists possible infrastructure components.

Only a few questions that the framework could lead BluntCo to ask are provided; a comprehensive, detailed treatment of this situation would require more information than we can contrive in a simple example.

Step 5: Evaluate Additional Issues

The last task is to weigh the managerial considerations outlined in the second section of this chapter. Weigh them against the same architectural goals outlined in step 2. Figure 6.11 shows how these considerations apply to BluntCo's situation.

Again, note that not every issue in the evaluation criteria was addressed for BluntCo, but this example shows a broad sampling of the kinds of issues that will arise.

▶ FOOD FOR THOUGHT: BUSINESS CONTINUITY PLANNING

The terrorist attacks on New York City and Washington D.C. on 9/11 put a whole new complexion on planning for disaster. Companies realized that their whole company could be brought down by events they could not control. *Disaster* is broadly defined as a sudden, unplanned calamitous event that makes it difficult for the firm to provide critical business functions for some period of time and results in great damage or loss. To counter terrorist attacks, hurricanes, tornadoes, floods, or countless other disasters, firms are realizing more than ever the importance of business continuity planning (BCP). In the face of such manmade and natural disasters, businesses

Component	What		Who		Where	
	Architecture	Infrastructure	Architecture	Infrastructure	Architecture	Infrastructure
Hardware	What kind of supplemental server capacity will the new EDI transactions require?	Will BluntCo's current dual-CPU NT servers handle the capacity, or will the company have to add additional CPUs and/or disks?	NA	Who is responsible for setting up necessary hardware at partner site?	Where does responsibility for owning and maintaining EDI hardware fall within BluntCo?	Which hardware components will need to be replaced or modified to connect to new EDI hardware?
Software	What parts of BluntCo's software architecture will the new architecture affect?	Will BluntCo's current Access database interface adequately with new EDI software?	Who knows the current software architecture well enough to manage the EDI enhancements?	Who will do any new SQL coding required to accommodate new software?	NA	Where will software patches be required to achieve compatibility with changes resulting from new software components?
Network	What is the anticipated volume of transactions between BluntCo and its manufacturing partners?	High volume may require leased lines to carry transaction data; dial-up connections may suffice for low volume.	Who is responsible for additional networking expense incurred by partners due to increased demands of EDI architecture?	NA	Where will security concerns arise in BluntCo's current network architecture?	Where will BluntCo house new networking hardware required for EDI?
Data	Will data formats supporting the new architecture be compatible with BluntCo's existing formats?	Which formats must BluntCo translate?	Who will be responsible for using sales data to project future volumes to report to manufacturing partner?	Who will be responsible for backing up additional data resulting from new architecture?	Where does the current architecture contain potential bottlenecks given changes anticipated in data flows?	Does the new architecture require BluntCo to switch from its current 10Base-T Ethernet to 100Base-T?

FIGURE 6.9 Framework application.

not only must recover, but they must also survive. The chances of surviving can be improved with BCP. Further, BCP allows a company to respond to events that may hurt its business without the company directly experiencing a disaster. For example, the BCP should outline how the company would bill its customers if the U.S. Postal

Hardware	Software	Network	Data
3 servers: • manufacturing • sales • accounting Storage systems	ERP system with modules for: • manufacturing • sales • accounting • inventory Enterprise application integration (EAI) software	Cable modem to ISP Dial-up lines for backup Routers Hubs Switches Firewalls	Database: • sales • manufacturing • accounting

FIGURE 6.10   BluntCo's infrastructure components.

Service were to be shut down, or how the company would respond in a situation where its primary and redundant Internet backbone cables were simultaneously cut because they run together over the same interstate overpass.

A **business continuity plan** is an approved set of preparations and sufficient procedures for responding to a variety of disaster events. It requires careful and thoughtful preparation. The Disaster Recovery Institute International (DRII) defines three major stages of BCP: pre-planning, planning, and post-planning.[10] In the pre-planning phase, management's responsibility is defined, possible risks are evaluated and a business impact analysis is performed.

In the planning stage, alternative business recovery operating strategies are determined. Business recovery operating strategies deal with how to recover business and IT within the recovery time objective while still maintaining the company's critical functions. Off-site storage and alternate recovery sites are prepared or business continuity vendors are selected. An important part of the BCP planning stage is to develop emergency response procedures designed to prevent or limit injury to personnel on site, damage to structures and equipment, and the degradation of vital business functions. These procedures must be kept up-to-date. The final activity in the planning stage is to implement the plan by publishing it and gaining top-management approval for the plan.

The third stage of BCP is to make employees familiar with the plan through awareness and training programs. Regular exercises to test and evaluate the plan should be conducted. Finally, the BCP should be discussed with public authorities, and public relations and crisis communications should be mapped out.

BCP is designed to respond to threats. In preparing a BCP it is important to remember that the biggest threat may come not from terrorist attacks or natural disasters, but from disgruntled or dishonest employees. Companies need to screen their employees carefully, create a culture of loyalty to inhibit the internal threats, and develop systems that help promote security.

[10] "Business Continuity Planning Review," DRI International Professional Development Program, DRP 501.

Criteria	Architecture	Infrastructure
Strategic time frame	Indefinite: Smokur's strategic goal is to be able to respond to fluctuations in market demand.	NA
Technology advances	EDI technology is fairly stable though the impact of Internet-EDI, XML, and VPNs on EdDI transactions needs to be assessed, especially with smaller suppliers and customers.	NA
Financial issues:		
NPV of investment	NA—In this limited case, NPV analysis applies only to infrastructure.	BluntCO will analyze NPV of various hardware and software solutions and ongoing costs before investing.
Payback analysis	BluntCo expects the new architecture to pay for itself within three years.	Various options will be evaluated using conservative sales growth projections to see how they match the three-year goal.
Incidental investments	The new architecture represents a radical shift in the way BluntCo does business and will require extensive training and work force adjustment.	Training costs for each option will be analyzed. Redeployment costs for employees displaced by the outsourcing must also be considered.
Growth requirements/ scalability	Outsourcing should provide more scalability than BluntCo's current model, which is constrained by assembly line capacity. Both primary and secondary vendors will be identified to provide scalability of volume.	The scalability required of various new hardware and software components is not significant, but options will be evaluated based on their ability to meet scalability requirements.
Standardization	NA	BluntCo will adopt the ANSI X12 EDI standard, and make it a requirement of all manufacturing partners.
Maintainability	The new architecture raises some maintenance issues, but also eliminates those associated with in-house manufacturing.	Various options will be evaluated for their maintenance and repair costs.
Staff experience	The new model will displace some current employees. The cost and effect on morale needs to be analyzed.	Current staff is not familiar with EDI. Training and work force adjustment will be needed. Some new staff will be hired.

FIGURE 6.11 BluntCo's managerial considerations.

The tremendous loss of human capital in the collapse of the World Trade Center in New York City on 9/11 highlighted the problem of keeping all of a company's talent in one location. Decentralizing operations, flextime, and telecommuting are ways of dispersing a company's human assets. Similarly, critical technology systems, proprietary computer codes, and other core business assets may need to be distributed.

▶ SUMMARY

- Strategy drives architecture, which drives infrastructure. Strategic business goals dictate IT architecture requirements. These requirements provide an extensible blueprint suggesting which infrastructure components will best facilitate the realization of the strategic goals.
- The manager's role is to understand how to plan IT in order to realize business goals. With this knowledge, he or she can facilitate the process of translating business goals to IT architecture and then modify the selection of infrastructure components as necessary.
- Use a logical framework to guide the translation from business strategy to IS design. This translation can be simplified by categorizing components into broad classes (hardware, software, network, data), which make up both IT architecture and infrastructure.
- While translating strategy into architecture and then infrastructure, it is important to know the state of any existing architecture and infrastructure, to weigh current against future architectural requirements, and to analyze the financial consequences of the various systems options under consideration. Monitor the performance of the systems on an ongoing basis.
- A business continuity plan is an approved set of preparations and sufficient procedures for responding to a disaster event. It is important to carefully step through the development of a plan that is well-communicated throughout the organization and that is frequently tested to ensure that all employees are familiar with it.
- As IT becomes more crucial to creating and sustaining competitive advantage, so does the need for managers to effectively translate business strategy into IT infrastructure. The frameworks and examples presented in this chapter can help facilitate that translation.

▶ KEY TERMS

architecture (p. 129)
business continuity
  planning (p. 147)
client (p. 135)
client/server architecture
  (p. 135)

infrastructure (p. 129)
mainframe architecture
  (p. 135)
peer-to-peer architecture
  (p. 135)
scalable (p. 142)

server (p. 135)
wireless (mobile)
  architecture (p. 137)

► DISCUSSION QUESTIONS

1. Think about a company you know well. What would be an example of IT architecture at that company? An example of the IT infrastructure?

2. What, in your opinion, is the difference between a client/server architecture and a mainframe architecture? What is an example of a business decision that would be affected by the choice of the architecture?

3. How does the Internet affect an organization's architecture?

4. Saab Cars USA, with its network of 212 dealerships and 30 service centers, dedicated itself to providing its customers a level of service reflective of the high quality of its cars. To improve productivity and reduce costs, Saab wanted to facilitate dealer access to corporate information and applications through the Internet using Web browsers. Saab knew it needed to leverage both its legacy hardware and code to make it a cost-effective e-business initiative. It outsourced to IBM Global Services to build its Intranet Retailer Information System (IRIS). IRIS is written in Java, using IBM DB2 Universal Database running on Saab's existing IBM AS/400 server. Lotus Domino is the middleware that leverages the existing infrastructure. Using a standard Web browser, any authorized employee at a Saab dealership or service center in the United States has access to enterprise applications stored on the AS/400 server at the Saab U.S. headquarters. The applications make use of a consolidated repository of vehicle, customer, warranty, sales, and service information stored in DB2 Universal Database. Says Director of IS, Jerry Rode, "DB2 Universal Database has demonstrated incredible scalability and reliability as the data management solution for our IRIS system." Lotus Domino, residing in another logical partition on the AS/400 server, is the middleware that mediates between the back-end applications and the front-end Web interface. For example, if a customer walks in and asks for a black model 9-3 Saab with a tan leather interior, a sales associate logs into the IRIS menu created by Domino and initiates a search. Domino queries DB2 by location, model, and color and puts the results of the query into an HTML form for the dealer. Upon locating the customer's vehicle, that dealer clicks to another vehicle distribution application and orders the car to be brought on site.[11]

a. Use this case to describe how Saab went from vision to infrastructure.

b. What criteria did Saab use in selecting its infrastructure?

CASE STUDY 6-1

BUSH INTERCONTINENTAL AIRPORT IN HOUSTON

Airplane travel is smooth when airports run smoothly, and for an airport to run smoothly, effective IS are critical. A successful operation of the network of IS at an airport is not only a source of personal pride for the airport personnel, but can become a determining factor in an airline's decisions about where to expand its services. It can also directly affect both

---

[11] IBM, "Saab roles out dealer intranet to improve customer service," available at http://www3.ibm.com/software/success/cssdb.nsf/CS/NAVO-4LJQ8N?OpenDocument&Site=software (accessed June 25, 2002).

in which the airport operates. The systems at the Houston Intercontinental Airport (IAH) illustrate this notion. Consider the following scenario:

A Chicago businessperson returns from Mexico City. His plane touches down 20 minutes early for a layover in Houston and is able to taxi directly to a waiting gate. The businessperson deplanes, quickly passes through Immigration, retrieves baggage, and completes Customs with no problems. The passenger checks the video display in the airport to confirm connecting flight information, and learns 45 minutes remain until boarding time, leaving time for him to make a call to the office, have a snack at the food court, visit the restroom, and get to the gate in time to upgrade his seat. The passenger then boards his flight, handing the gate attendant his electronic boarding pass, which is scanned through the computer at the door of the jetway, confirming that the passenger is cleared to board the plane for the next leg of his trip. In this case, various airport systems precleared passengers through Immigration, tracked the early arrival of the plane and made sure personnel were ready to unload the baggage and assist at the baggage carousel, gathered departure information from 20 separate airlines to display for easy viewing, and provided fast, reliable fiber-optic connections to let attendants check records on the spot.

Behind the scene at IAH, the ninth busiest international airport in the United States, is a large, complex information system. Standard airport business applications such as budgeting, records management, rates and charges, warehouse inventory, and purchasing are used by airport personnel. In addition, the airport requires automated systems for managing flight information, security access control, ground transportation, paging/information, airfield lighting, radio and facility maintenance, vehicle maintenance, parking, concession tracking, and a wide range of planning, design, and construction tasks. The parking business alone is a $22 million operation, and in 1999 was outsourced to Amoco Parking. The City of Houston owns and operates the airport through their Department of Aviation (DOA).

The airport consists of four terminals—A, B, C, and IAB, which stands for the Mickey Leland International Airlines Building—for passenger travel. Terminals A and B were built in 1969, C in 1981, and IAB in 1990, resulting in a mix of information technologies to be managed by the Aviation MIS department (AMIS). Even though IAB had the newest technology available, terminals A, B, and C handled the bulk of the traffic and revenue generated by the airport. Terminal C and most of terminal B are leased to Continental Airlines, and they handle 75 percent of all the traffic that passes through the airport. The infrastructure needed to manage this airport must include both old and new technologies. This mixture presents challenges, but it also helps keep innovation in perspective because the airport just needs to make sure things work, rather than be on the leading edge of innovations.

Multiple stand-alone systems used at the airport include a series of LANs and workstations. Four servers support more than 150 terminals or personal computers at IAH. The DOA itself manages eight LANs supporting 455 personal computers and 12 servers. Four Stratus minicomputers also support airport operations. Two of the Stratus systems run IAH's most crucial safety and scheduling systems, and are therefore kept in a secure, air-conditioned room in one of the older terminals. A mainframe computer located in downtown Houston is connected to the DOA network. In addition, each individual airline that leases space from the DOA has installed its own terminals for its own business.

The network at the airport is primarily fiber optic, with T-1 lines connecting the Ethernet-based LANs at each airport to create a citywide WAN. In 1999, a capital improvement program was initiated to install a noncollapsible fiber ring around the city of Houston to connect all the airports to the administration building. It is noncollapsible because the architecture of the network is such that if one link fails, the entire network itself does not collapse. This improvement program will install OC3 service, the equivalent of 100 T-1 lines, as the backbone of the network. And the network itself is leased from the local telephone company, Southwestern Bell Telephone.

Software on the PCs includes standard business applications as well as specialized applications like those previously described. The Microsoft Office suite, including Word, Excel, and Access, is used. All the computers run an e-mail, calendaring, and scheduling program in Microsoft Outlook, which runs on an Exchange server. The system works well for them because everyone throughout the organization uses it to schedule every meeting and appointment. More than 220 custom programs developed by the Applications Development staff are used. Programming is primarily done in the FoxBase development language, which builds applications to run on the database management program. Applications built for diverse situations include emergency preparedness, event tracking, monthly fuel delivery reports, and taxicab trip logs.

Managing flight data at the airport is an interesting task. Airlines provide their own flight information. All airlines, except Continental, use the airport-provided terminals and data for flight arrivals and departures. Continental operates its own systems for displaying that information to passengers. Therefore, terminals A and IAH display multiple airline schedules, while those in B and C only display Continental flights.

Discussion Questions

1. What are the key components of the IS infrastructure at IAH?
2. Consider the software applications in this architecture. Which do you think are running on the local PCs and which are running on the servers or mainframes in the network?
3. What are the advantages and disadvantages to the DOA of leasing the networking from Southwestern Bell?

Source: Some of this material was adapted from "Airport '95," *CIO Magazine* (September 1, 1995), available at www.cio.com/archive/rc_gv_air1_content.html). The rest is from conversations with chief resource officer for the Houston Airport System, Frank Haley (December 2, 1999).

CHAPTER 7

DOING BUSINESS ON THE INTERNET[1]

In 1995, after developing a paper-free check acceptance process, two entrepreneurs decided to market their system, RediCheck, on the Internet. Previous to that point, they targeted their service mainly to telemarketing and mail order companies. Their decision to take the company online and to reposition it as an Internet payment-acceptance company proved to be both astute and well timed. Since that change, the company, now called iTransact Corporation (www.itransact.com), processed many millions of dollars in Internet payments and assisted hundreds of established off-line businesses and online-only start-ups. It is clear to iTransact and many of the companies that use its electronic checking, credit card, and electronic funds transfer (EFT) services that the tide of business has turned toward e-business.

E-business occurs whenever buyers and sellers interact electronically. Engaging in e-business is more than just using a credit card to make purchases. When someone buys a gallon of milk and a box of cereal at the supermarket and pays with a $5 bill, they are engaging in commerce. If, instead, they pay by swiping their MasterCard through the credit card terminal, they are engaging in **electronic commerce (e-commerce),** which is defined as electronic transactions that enable the exchange of goods and services for consideration. Such a transaction represents e-commerce in its simplest form. A considerable amount of paper is still involved: On the customer end alone, the transaction entails a cash register receipt, a credit card receipt, a credit card statement, and a credit card payment (usually via check). At the other end of the spectrum, a transaction such as an electronic funds transfer (EFT)—wherein funds are transferred directly from the buyer's bank account to the seller's—can occur with no "paper trail" whatsoever. If the buyer makes a purchase over the Internet and pays for the items with the same credit card, it is considered e-business. In most environments today, e-commerce is only one of the many forms of electronically enabled business processes that fall under the e-business umbrella. E-business is more than e-commerce because it includes any business activities conducted electronically within or between businesses.

[1] The author wishes to acknowledge and thank Matthew Spafford Sumsion, MBA 1999, for his help in researching and writing early drafts of this chapter.

153

The Internet is the backbone for e-business marketplaces in which transactions occur instantly over the network and involve virtually no paper. The world of e-business in general, and the Internet and World Wide Web in particular, is changing so fast that information in a textbook is surely out of date before the text reaches the students' hands. However, it is such an important topic that this chapter is provided to offer some foundation for managers who will be managing companies in the Internet Age.

To that end, this chapter discusses how the Internet is changing business-to-business (B2B) and business-to-consumer (B2C) commerce. It covers business and professional uses of the Internet, not personal and individual uses. This chapter has most likely left out many current Internet applications, and the authors apologize for that in advance. This chapter attempts to provide a basic understanding and additional interesting ideas that can be used in discussions about current Internet activities.

▶ OVERVIEW OF THE INTERNET

Because the Internet (Net) plays such a great part in e-business, it may be valuable at this point to define and give a short history of the "Internet" and the "World Wide Web." These terms are often used interchangeably, but it is helpful to recognize the distinctions.

Internet

The **Internet** is a global, *inter*connected *net*work (hence the name) of millions of individual computers (called hosts). The history of the Internet begins in 1969 with the U.S. Department of Defense's ARPANET, a network designed to support the communications between cities in the United States in the event of a major disaster. The idea was to build a network based on the concept of openness that would continue to work even if parts of it were destroyed. The network was designed for defense, not commerce. Handling large volumes of communications was not an initial design requirement. In 1985, the National Science Foundation built NSFNET using the ARPANET protocols. NSFNET was essentially the backbone network provided free to universities and research centers, requiring only that these organizations build a connection to it. NSF eventually withdrew as the manager of the network as commercial telecommunications companies and private and public institutions built their own links into the network and started using the Internet for commercial purposes. The often-proprietary demands of businesses and markets, however, are sometimes at odds with the principle of openness upon which the Internet is based. Today, no single "owner" controls the Internet. Instead, it is a collection of networks that all can link to each other, share the same protocols, and support the exchange of packets of information.

The breakthrough technology that allowed this critical interoperability was **TCP/IP,** which stands for *transmission control protocol and Internet protocol.* In the article "How the Internet Works," Richard Wiggins explains that **protocols** "are the specifications for the interface between two computers, and they set standards to define how computers communicate with each other to accomplish specific tasks." TCP/IP protocols define how to divide data into packets in order to transmit them over the Internet. Each TCP/IP packet of information contains three parts: header, data, and trailer. TCP part of the protocol is connection oriented—it establishes a connection between processes on different host computers before data is transmitted. IP "defines a connectionless service through which data is delivered from computer to computer."[2] Each node on the Internet has an IP address, or a 32-bit number assigned to it. When considering addressing, the TCP/IP packet delivers data in a way that can be compared to a standard letter, as diagrammed in Figure 7.1.

Statistics are difficult to acquire because no one well-defined way is available to measure usage. One thing is clear, however; the number of business and individual users continues to grow rapidly. Users from more than 100 countries can link to this computer network for exchanges of news, messages, data, and commerce. The Internet has no governing board or central control; all information available on the Net is simply provided by any individual or organization that chooses to make the information available to the Internet community. Available information can include anything from pictures of someone's cat to Anheuser Busch's current annual report to backwards recordings of Beatles records. This information is available to anyone with access to the Internet. This access is gained, usually by subscription, through an Internet service provider (ISP).

In the United States, it took seven years for at least 30 percent of the population to have access to the Internet. This figure contrasts with the seventeen years it took for television and the forty-six years that it took electricity to have similar penetration rates. In terms of the type of access, ever-increasing numbers of users are connecting to the Internet over broadband channels rather than slower telephone lines.[3] **Broadband** refers to telecommunication such as cable systems and digital subscriber lines (DSLs) in which a wide band of frequencies is available to transmit information. Because a wide band of frequencies is available, more information may be transmitted in a given amount of time.[4] Broadband is much like having more lanes on a highway to allow more cars to travel on it at the same time.

TCP/IP Packet				
Computer address of sender (HEADER)	Computer address of receiver (HEADER)	Packet length (HEADER)	Data	Checksum (TRAILER)
Regular Mail				
Return address	Address		Letter	

FIGURE 7.1 Comparison of regular mail and TCP/IP packet.
Source: This example was provided by Harold Miles.

[2] Richard Wiggins, "How the Internet Works," *Internet World* (October 1996), pp. 59–60.

[3] Available at www.cisco.com.

[4] Definition of broadband from Searchnetworking.com, available at http://searchnetworking.techtarget.com/sDefinition/0,,sid7_gci211706,00.html (accessed January 26, 2003).

World Wide Web

The **World Wide Web (WWW),** also known simply as the Web, is an increasingly popular system for accessing much of the information on the Internet via the use of specially formatted documents. The documents can be formatted in a relatively simple computer language called hypertext markup language (HTML) or any one of a number of more sophisticated languages, such as JAVA or C++. HTML was created by a researcher, Tim Berners-Lee, and his colleagues at CERN in Switzerland in 1989. It is part of an Internet standard called the hypertext transport protocol (the "http" at the beginning of Internet addresses), which enables the access of information stored on other Internet computers, called servers. Hypertext is another name for the usually underlined links (or hyperlinks, hot links, or hot spots), which, by clicking on them, provide access to other documents, graphics, or files located anywhere in the world. In addition to HTML and HTTP, the Swiss researchers created two other WWW building blocks: a Web server and a basic text-based Web browser. **Web browsers** are software programs that enable a large number of users to easily navigate the World Wide Web.

When Marc Andreesen, a University of Illinois graduate student, created MOSAIC, a browser with a graphical user interface, the WWW began to capture widespread interest. Soon MOSAIC was followed by many other browsers including Netscape's Navigator and Microsoft's Internet Explorer.

More Nets: Intranets, Extranets, and Virtual Private Networks

Many derivatives were subsequently developed based on the Internet, including intranets, extranets, and virtual private networks.

An **intranet** looks and acts like the Internet, but it is comprised of information used exclusively within a company and unavailable to the Internet community as a whole. Employees of AT&T, for example, can use company computers to access an employee handbook (containing links to such things as employee data, benefit information, and procedures for dealing with irate callers) via the company's intranet. Using Web browser technology and the TCP/IP protocol, companies build intranets to facilitate information sharing within their business. Because AT&T may not want its customers and competitors to have access to employee information, it may build a security "firewall" between the Internet and the AT&T intranet. Intranets serving as conduits for internal communications are one of the first, and still one of the most popular, Internet applications of many companies.

So what is an extranet? Some sources would argue that it is just another redundant term for the Internet, or that "there is no such thing."[5] It is not quite that simple, however, because a company can utilize an extranet that is distinctly different from its intranet or from the Internet as a whole. Just as a company's intranet contains Internet-style information for exclusive use within the company, the company could also have an **extranet** containing information for use outside the company.

---

[5] Fairdene New Media, available at http://www.fairdene.demon.co.uk/extranet.html (accessed November 8, 1998).

For example, extranet information could be intended for use by a company's sub-contractors or suppliers, or for private use by a specific external subsidiary with a need to know. Dell Computers, for example, created for their key customers Web pages that contain company information and links that are specifically tailored to the interest of that customer. Wal-Mart's extranet provides links to major suppliers such as Proctor & Gamble. As with intranets, extranets are not accessible by the Internet at large and are usually protected by a security firewall.

Often extranets are formed using a virtual private network. A **virtual private network (VPN)** is a private data network that leverages the public telecommunication infrastructure. It maintains privacy through the use of a tunneling protocol and security procedures. Using a client and server approach, a VPN's clients authenticate users, encrypt data, and otherwise manage sessions with VPN servers using a technique called tunneling. Companies realize cost savings by using a public infrastructure like the Internet instead of expensive private leased lines. VPNs are also used to support both remote access to an intranet and connections between multiple intranets within the same organization.

Marketspace vs. Marketplace

Some regard transactions taking place over the Internet as significantly different from those taking place in a physical marketplace. The term *marketspace* was coined by Jeffery Rapport and John Sviokla in 1994.[6] A **marketspace** is a virtual market where the transactions taking place are all based on information exchange, rather than the exchange of goods and services. Take, for example, Internet-based auctions such as those conducted on e-Bay or Amazon.com. At a traditional auction, the goods to be sold are shown to the potential buyers, who then compete in real-time to buy the items. The highest bidder gets the goods and makes payment right then. In a marketspace, like online auctions, the company does not typically own or even hold the inventory it sells to customers. It acts more as a market maker, connecting buyers with suppliers. In marketspace, the goods are not physically available, rather information about the goods is available. Decisions are made about whether to buy an item based on information presented by the auction site and the seller. The interaction takes place over an electronic network involving a wide number of locations, rather than just one physical auction house. Success in a marketspace means identifying what adds value for the customer and then ensuring that level of the transaction is managed appropriately.

Evolution of E-business

Conducting business over electronic channels has been a reality for decades—well before the World Wide Web came into existence. One of the oldest forms of e-business is electronic data interchange. **Electronic data interchange (EDI)** is the direct computer-to-computer transfer of business information, using a standard format, between two businesses. It allows the transfer of business data (such as

[6] J. Rapport and J. Sviokla, "Managing in Marketspace," *Harvard Business Review*, reprint no. 94608 (November–December 1994), pp. 141–153

quote requests, order forms, and invoices) over leased lines with little or no human interaction. EDI uses standards (such as ANSI X12 or EDIFACT) to allow a software program on one company's computer system to relay information back and forth to a software program on another company's computer system, thus permitting organizations to exchange data pertinent to business transactions. Each transmission, or transaction set, comprises one or more data segments framed by header and trailer codes. One transaction set might contain information equivalent to that in a standard business document. Data segments, in turn, comprise strings of data elements, or facts such as prices or product specifications, separated by delimiters.[7]

EDI never lived up to its early growth projections. One reason for this may be that EDI requires substantial setup efforts on the part of the two trading partners. Although virtually all *Fortune* 500 firms were using EDI in the 1990s (and still do so today), smaller companies avoided the technology. Now that Internet EDI is available with the use of browsers and XML is simplifying the standardization process, more companies, especially smaller ones, are conducting their business transactions electronically.

In *Frontiers of Electronic Commerce,* Kalakota and Whinston demonstrate how EDI substantially automates the information flow and facilitates management of a business process.[8] Purchasing, shipping and payment are all accomplished as information flows to and from buyer, seller and transporter companies. The steps are listed in Figure 7.2. Because it allows detailed information to be exchanged electronically with little human interaction and expense, EDI is considered to be e-business.

More typically the term **e-business** refers to business conducted over the Internet. Businesses on the Internet are usually described by a short acronym indicating the basic business model of the organization. Commerce between businesses (B2B) and between businesses and their customers (B2C), are the basic models of e-business. The difference is in who is targeted as the customer. B2B companies primarily focus

Step 1	Customer's computer sends purchase order to supplier's computer.
Step 2	Supplier's computer sends purchase order confirmation to customer's computer.
Step 3	Supplier's computer sends booking request to transport company's computer.
Step 4	Transport company's computer sends booking confirmation to supplier's computer.
Step 5	Supplier's computer sends advance ship notice to customer's computer.
Step 6	Transport company's computer sends status to supplier's computer.
Step 7	Customer's computer sends receipt advice to supplier's computer.
Step 8	Supplier's computer sends invoice to customer's computer.
Step 9	Customer's computer sends payment to supplier's computer.

FIGURE 7.2   EDI transactions for purchase, shipment, and payment.
Source: Adapted from R. Kalakota and A. Whinston, *Frontiers of Electronic Commerce* (Reading, MA: Addison Wesley, 1996), 339-340.

[7] Part of this description is based on information from Whatis.com, available at http://whatis.com/edi.htm (accessed November 8, 1998).

[8] R. Kalakota and A. Whinston, *Frontiers of Electronic Commerce* (Reading, MA: Addison Wesley, 1996), p. 339–340.

on selling and interacting with other businesses, usually as part of the overall value chain (see Chapter 2 for a discussion of the value chain model). Their customers are other businesses who, in turn, either sell goods and services to other businesses or to eventual end-customers. B2C businesses are those that sell directly to consumers. For example, Amazon.com is considered a B2C e-business, selling primarily to consumers. A derivative of the B2C model directly links customers to customers—the C2C model. One of the most successful e-businesses, eBay, pioneered the C2C model. Figure 7.3 summarizes some of the many derivatives of the B2B model.

Despite its short history, business on the Internet has evolved through a number of stages. Commercial Web sites have moved from being content providers to transaction forums, integrated business platforms, and catalysts for industry transformation.

Content Provider: Stage I

The earliest commercial Web sites were viewed as an effective way of providing information to customers, suppliers, and even employees. Reports and printed advertisements were transported to the Web, with attempts to make the Internet version as similar as possible to the printed copy. Businesspeople could see the advantage of the Web in reaching millions of people, but had not yet grown to appreciate what the Web could allow them to do. They took little advantage of the Web's interactive and multimedia capabilities.

Transaction Forum: Stage II

After a few years, many businesses started capitalizing upon the Web's ability to interact with their customers. Though some fears arose about the security of electronic payments, businesses timidly started offering online sales. Their focus was on business-to-consumer (B2C) transactions. The sales were seen to supplement the bread and butter of bricks-and-mortar companies. This "bricks-and-clicks" business model combines an e-business with a physical business. Its Web site is coupled with a traditional, physical business to leverage the best of both the Internet world and the bricks-and-mortar business. The Web business traditionally brings new thinking, new distribution possibilities, and new sales outlets to the table, while the physical business brings some sense of stability and possibly even customers, concepts, brand recognition, and other resources to the Web business. The resulting hybrid is a business

B2B	Business-to-business targets sales and services primarily to other businesses.
B2C	Business-to-consumer targets sales and services primarily to consumers.
B2E	Business-to-employee provides services other companies can use to interface with employees (like retirement funds management, health care management, and other benefits management).
B2G	Business-to-government involves companies who sell the bulk of their goods and services to state, local, and national governments.
C2C	Consumer-to-consumer sites primarily offer goods and services to assist consumers to interact (e.g., auctions).
Hybrid	Combines B2B and B2C models.

FIGURE 7.3 Basic business models for the Internet.

model intended to be the best of both worlds. However, unlike the fledgling dot-coms that started surfacing in the mid-to-late 1990s, the Web site transaction processing of bricks-and-clicks initially was not integrated with the more traditional operations.

Integrator: Stage III

Eventually Web-based business operations were linked smoothly to legacy systems as businesses realized that e-business was in fact part of their business. B2B sites gained in favor as businesses started integrating their online transaction systems with fulfillment, payment, service and support, and personnel systems. Eventually Web sites began integrating the entire chain of sales transactions, order processing, and other such activities with legacy, ERP, and CRM systems.

Catalyst for Industry Restructuring: Stage IV

By the new millennium it became clear that business over the Internet was transforming a number of industries. Some industries were reshaped by compressions and expansions in electronic channels. Other industries were transformed by new information-intensive offerings. For example, E-stamp (stamps.com is attempting to transform postage stamp distribution channels by allowing customers to download computer-generated postage from the Internet. Customers may buy postage online by credit card, electronic funds transfer (EFT), or check. When it is time to place the postage on the envelope, the customer draws the amount from secure hardware called a vault to which stamps.com has already downloaded the purchased postage. A barcode approved by the U.S. Postal Service is printed by a laser printer onto the envelope. The barcode indicates the amount of postage, the ID of the customer and the vault, the address where the mail is going, the date the postage was printed, the postal rate category, and a digital pattern to inhibit counterfeiting. As the number of e-stamp customers grows and as other players enter the field, the face of the postage stamp distribution industry may change dramatically.

E-channel Patterns

An **e-channel** is the chain of electronic "relationships between companies and customers and between companies and their partners/resellers."[9] E-channels can lead to industry restructuring when massive changes are brought about by e-channel compression and channel expansion.

E-channel Compression

E-channel compression means eliminating redundant components in the channel. Often e-channel compression is undertaken to cut costs, improve the efficiency of channel operations, and eliminate unnecessary middlemen, or intermediaries. Shortening a channel results in the **disintermediation,** or the removal of one or more businesses from the e-channel. Targets of disintermediation include travel agents who no longer take part in the sale of Southwest Airlines' tickets over the

---

[9] R. Kalakota and M. Robinson, *e-Business 2.0* (Boston: Addison-Wesley, 2001), p. 76.

Internet, and resellers or retailers whom manufacturers remove from the sales process so that they can establish direct links with their customers over the Internet.

An example of an industry transformed through e-channel compression is the music industry. In the old distribution industry, numerous intermediaries were involved in the production, marketing, and distribution of albums. Each intermediary added its margin to the cost of the album. However, a new digital music industry dramatically compresses the length of the channel and, consequently, the price to the customer. Now the 93 percent of artists who were not represented by major labels can provide their music online through companies like MP3.com. One source of revenue for MP3.com is through the sales of CDs by specific artists and the sales of compilation CDs. Consumers now can purchase specific songs on an album (as opposed to the whole album) directly through companies like MP3.com. As noted in Figure 7.4, this option resulted in the disintermediation of record companies, distributors, and retailers.

Not surprisingly, the record companies are fighting back. They argue that many of their traditional activities such as finding and promoting new talent, producing and recording music, and securing airplay are still needed in the industry. They brought lawsuits against Napster.com, a new intermediary that made possible the free downloading of digital music. Even though the lawsuits bankrupted Napster, other companies soon sprang up to fill in the gap. The record companies are also responding by offering value-added extras for musicians' fans—preference in buying concert tickets, the possibility of climbing on stage, and e-mail exclusives.[10] They are hoping to entice fans to develop an ongoing relationship with the artists whose music they purchase. Each time they buy an album, fans will be given a unique serial number that the record companies will use to maintain and personalize the relationship. The record companies, like other companies faced with massive industry restructuring, cannot afford to stand still.

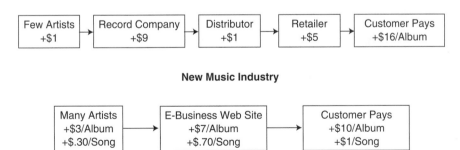

FIGURE 7.4 Example of channel compression.

Source: Adapted from Kalakota and Robinson, *E-Business 2.0* (Boston: Addison-Wesley, 2001).

[10] J. Ordonez and C. Goldsmith, "Music Industry Hopes Exclusives Can Blow Pirates Out of Water," *The Wall Street Journal* (September 16, 2002), p. B8.

E-channel Expansion

E-channel expansion results in lengthening the legacy channel by adding brokering functionality.[11] In e-channel expansion, intermediaries are added to the channel because they offer services or products to improve operations. Some new intermediaries provide additional information, such as CarPoint (www.autos.msn.com) that offers information to people researching a car purchase. Others provide services needed to complete the transaction online. Some major new intermediaries include companies expediting electronic payment or the delivery of goods purchased online.

E-channel expansion is demonstrated in e-marketplaces. E-marketplaces are a special kind of B2B network that bring together different companies. Sometimes called net-markets or exchanges, these networks are typically built by a consortium of key businesses in the marketplace or by a third-party e-business interested in providing the marketplace. Much like the New York Stock Exchange creates a physical marketplace for trading stocks, e-marketplaces create a virtual marketplace for buying, selling, or trading goods and services. E-marketplaces are especially viable in fragmented markets populated by numerous buyers and sellers. Vertical e-marketplaces operate in specific industries, like DirectAg.com, a virtual marketplace for agriculture goods, and Covisint (www.covisint.com), a virtual marketplace for the automobile industry. Horizontal e-marketplaces operate across industries, typically targeting a specific business function or need that occurs in many types of businesses. TradeOut.com is an example of a horizontal e-marketplace site that provides a trading place for surplus equipment.

E-channels affect the relationship of businesses with consumers over time. In the content provider stage, the Internet promoted a one-to-many broadcast mode. The transaction forum and integrator stages made the one-to-many relationship more efficient. Initially little personalization occurred in the message. Over time, the relationship may remain one-to-many, but the technology, especially CRM, creates the impression in the customer's eye that the relationship is one-to-one.

Business relationships also evolve over time. Pre-Web, EDI was seen as a way for a company to conduct business more efficiently with many partners. However, the one-to-many promise of EDI was seldom realized. The proprietary protocols and the difficulty of establishing linkages resulted in a large number of one-to-one relationships. When VANs emerged on the scene, many-to-many relationships became a reality. **Value-added networks (VANs)** are independent third-party companies that provide connection and EDI transaction forwarding services to customer companies using EDI. Many different companies could communicate with one another thanks to the VANs' translation services. Only now, with the advent of Internet EDI, can one-to-many relationships be established by a company directly with its many trading partners without using the services of a VAN. In addition to VANs, e-marketplaces offer many-to-many relationships by linking many buyers to many sellers. Ironically, as firms turn to vertical relationships, they become more

[11] R. Kalakota and M. Robinson, *e-Business 2.0* (Boston: Addison-Wesley, 2001), p. 76.

tied to their trading partners, creating relationships that seem more like one-to-one relationships.

▶ FRAMEWORK OF ELECTRONIC COMMERCE

Kalakota and Whinston offer a generic framework for e-commerce, shown in Figure 7.5. The framework assumes that new applications will continue to be built on existing technology infrastructure—the computers, communications networks, and communication software that comprise the Internet. It uses four key building blocks:

1. Common business services, for facilitating the buying and selling process
2. Messaging and information distribution, as a means of sending and retrieving information
3. Multimedia content and network publishing, for creating a product and a means to communicate about it
4. The Internet, for providing the highway system along which all e-commerce travels

Two pillars supporting all e-commerce are integral to the framework:[12]

- Public policy, to govern such issues as universal access, privacy, and information pricing
- Technical standards, to dictate the nature of information publishing, user interfaces, and transport in the interest of compatibility across the entire network

Common Business Services Infrastructure

The first of the four building blocks is the common business services infrastructure. This building block consists of five main elements: security, electronic payments, directory services and search engines, commerce servers, and personalization.

Security

Security is a major concern for doing business on the Internet. Customers wonder how safe their credit card numbers are if they type them into a Web-based order form. Technologies have come a long way to provide security. Innovative businesspeople use tools that encrypt or otherwise disguise personal information, financial information, and business information. Web sites, called security validators, validate the security level of other sites, and provide a seal of approval when a particular Web site is protected. American Express, MasterCard, and Visa are promoting one-time credit card numbers that only exist for the duration of a single

[12] R. Kalakota and A. Whinston, *Frontiers of Electronic Commerce* (Reading, MA: Addison-Wesley, 1996), p. 314.

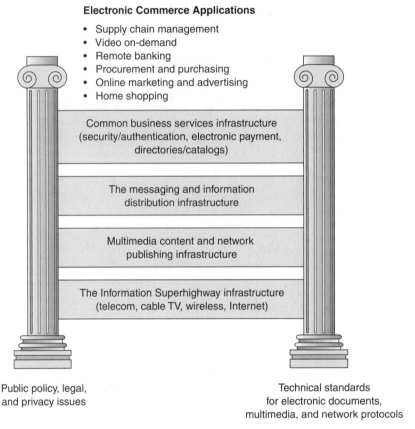

Electronic Commerce Applications

- Supply chain management
- Video on-demand
- Remote banking
- Procurement and purchasing
- Online marketing and advertising
- Home shopping

Common business services infrastructure (security/authentication, electronic payment, directories/catalogs)

The messaging and information distribution infrastructure

Multimedia content and network publishing infrastructure

The Information Superhighway infrastructure (telecom, cable TV, wireless, Internet)

Public policy, legal, and privacy issues

Technical standards for electronic documents, multimedia, and network protocols

FIGURE 7.5 Generic framework for electronic commerce.

Source: R. Kalakota and A. Whinston, *Frontiers of Electronic Commerce* (Reading, MA: Addison Wesley, 1996), p. 314.

transaction. Businesses themselves make security measures more visible through explicit statements, icons, pop-up windows, and other means of communication.

Concerns remain about the safety of e-commerce transactions—what if, for example, someone were to steal all those credit card numbers as they are relayed over the Internet? The risk of the interception of e-commerce data may be no greater than the risks of paper transactions: credit card receipts (and credit cards themselves) are stolen and the numbers used fraudulently. Checkbooks are stolen and signatures are fraudulently forged. Transactions with a paper trail are hardly foolproof and may indeed be riskier than e-commerce transactions. Copy machines can make multiple copies of secure documents just as easily as e-mails can be sent with multiple copies. The difference is in the speed of the communication. A file with secure information can be sent anywhere in the world in a matter of seconds over the Net, whereas the paper-based file takes longer to reach a destination. The security of e-commerce continues to improve. Innovations such as authentication, passwords, digital signatures, encryption, secure servers, and firewalls are already in place, and transactions need no longer be relayed via public forums like e-mail.

Authentication is a security process whereby proof is obtained that the users are truly who they say they are (i.e., their identity is verified as authentic). Authentication can be as simple as verifying the name and password of a user prior to allowing him or her access to an account. Additionally, it can include the use of a digital signature. Authentication can also be used to ensure that data transmissions are delivered to the appropriate receiver, to verify the source (or sender) of the data, and to ensure that the data have not been tampered with en route to their destination.

One simple way to provide authentication is through the use of a password. A **password** is a string of arbitrary characters known only to a select person or group. A computer or software program can be programmed to respond to commands or open messages only after the correct password has been entered; in this way, the system authenticates the identity of the user and prevents unauthorized access. Passwords are most effective when users select characters that would be difficult for others to guess; in practice, however, most people select simple passwords such as birthdates and nicknames, weakening the efficacy of the authentication process. To deal with this security problem, managers must be vigilant is assigning, rotating, and enforcing passwords.

Much like a handwritten signature is used to guarantee that the signer of a paper document is truly the person who composed it, a **digital signature** can be used to prove that the sender of a message (e.g., a file or e-mail message) is truly who he or she claims to be. A digital code is applied to an electronically transmitted message. The recipient of the message can compare this code upon receipt of the message with the sender's digital signature. If the two do not match, either the message originated somewhere other than with the stated sender, or the message has been intercepted and altered. Different forms of encryption can be used to ensure that digital signatures cannot be forged.

Encryption is the translation of data into a format that can only be read by the intended receiver. Here's how it works (Figure 7.6 includes a diagram of the process): the sender composes a message for the recipient in plain text, then uses an encryption key to encode it. The recipient has a **decryption** key and uses it to decode and read the sender's message, once again, as plain text. If an intruder were to observe the sender's message to the recipient, it would be incomprehensible, or **cipher text.**

If both the sender and recipient use the same special "key" to encrypt and decrypt the data, it is called **symmetric encryption.** Another common type of encryption, **asymmetric encryption,** uses differentiated keys, called **public keys** and **private keys.** The sender, for example, has access to the recipient's public key, but so do others. Any of them can compose a message to the recipient and encrypt it with his public key. The message, however, must be decrypted with a private key, and only the recipient has access to it. Two of the most widely used symmetrical encryption types are DES (data encryption standard) and PGP (pretty good privacy). RSA is a popular asymmetric encryption type.

Many companies doing business on the Web use what are called secure servers in order to protect the privacy of the data they send and receive. Normally,

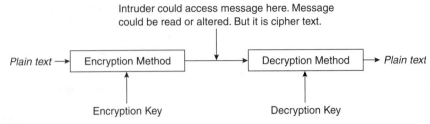

FIGURE 7.6   Encryption.

text transferred from a browser to a Web server is sent as plain text; if anyone were to intercept the transmission, it would be legible. To prevent the interception of plain text, **secure servers** employ encryption technology to convert plain text into encrypted text before it is transmitted. Internet merchants that do not have their own secure servers can partner with an e-commerce provider that will allow the merchant's sensitive transactions to occur on the provider's secure site.

Firewalls are a different type of security measure. **Firewalls** consist of hardware and software that block out undesirable requests for entrance into a Web site, and keep those on the outside from reaching inside. For example, a hacker trying to reach a corporate Web site in order to plant a bug or virus could encounter a firewall, making it much more difficult to get access to the servers.

Of course, even with these innovations, security remains an important concern of any business. All managers should be aware of potential hackers and, more importantly, disgruntled employees. They should be actively involved in the company's technology and maintain audit trails for computer use that will signal possible data corruption. They should regularly back up their data and ensure that any backup capabilities have been put into place by the IT department are actually followed in their departments.

As important as authentication, encryption, and firewalls are to security, companies cannot forget about making all aspects of their systems secure. In addition to the network, the database, operating system, and buildings in which the systems are housed, and the personnel who have any opportunity to access the system must be considered when making a system secure. Managers must develop a comprehensive set of policies and procedures to prevent internal and external threats to the entire system.

Electronic Payments

A number of payment vehicles are available to businesses to make and receive payments on the Internet, including credit cards, electronic checks, EFT, smart cards, and e-cash. Perceptually, these methods are simply the electronic equivalents of everyday, off-line payment methods (e.g., credit cards, checks, and cash).

Because credit card information has been relayed electronically for years, making the switch from current credit card payments to Internet credit card payments does not require a great cognitive or technological leap. Off-line credit card transactions work according to the process outlined in Figure 7.7.

Step 1	Merchant obtains a customer's credit card number and expiration date, either manually (via transcription or a card imprint) or electronically (via a swipe machine).
Step 2	Merchant relays this information and the payment amount to credit card processor, either manually (e.g., mail) or electronically (via a phone line).
Step 3	Processor deposits purchase amounts into merchant's bank account.

FIGURE 7.7 Traditional credit card transactions.

Internet credit card transactions utilize a similar process, but they can eliminate much of the off-line equipment and merchant interface. "Virtual terminals" allow merchants to use the Internet in place of a swipe machine, and "transaction processors" allow merchants to stay out of the transaction entirely.

A **virtual terminal** is the Internet equivalent of the credit card swipe machine. Internet businesses typically cannot obtain actual cards to swipe, so they require a different method for relaying the card information to the processor. They can do it via a virtual terminal as outlined in the process shown in Figure 7.8

Virtual terminal providers generally assess a per-transaction fee. The virtual terminal offers the advantage of allowing a business to accept credit card payments without having to buy or lease more expensive credit card terminals (or "black boxes"). The disadvantage is that the merchant must still manually enter each transaction.

Transaction processors provide the Internet convenience of virtual terminals, but go a step further. They allow the merchant to stay out of the transaction entirely. This service is ideal for merchants who wish to sell products on the Internet and do not want to worry about handling any of the credit card information themselves. Figure 7.9 summarizes the process. Transaction processors such as iTransact (www.itransact.com) generally charge a per-transaction fee. Advantages for a business include not having to obtain credit card equipment and not having to assist in or be present for the actual transactions.

Because many Internet customers do not have credit cards or choose not to use them, **Internet checking** services provide merchants with the ability to accept checks over the Internet. Figure 7.10 summarizes how this process works.

A couple of options as to where the checks are printed are available to the merchant. Some Internet checking providers sell or lease the merchant check-printing software and/or hardware. In this case, the customer's check information is relayed to the merchant, who prints the check in-house. Other providers offer a hands-off

Step 1	Customer visits merchant's website, selects a product or service to purchase, and enters credit card information.
Step 2	This information is relayed to the merchant.
Step 3	When convenient, merchant accesses virtual terminal and inputs or uploads the collected credit card information; this information is relayed to credit card processor.

FIGURE 7.8 Virtual terminals.

| Step 1 | Customer visits merchant's website, selects a product or service to purchase, and enters credit card information. |
| Step 2 | This information is automatically collected by the transaction processor and relayed to the credit card processor. |

FIGURE 7.9   Transaction processors.

Step 1	Customer visits merchant's website, selects a product or service to purchase, and enters check information (specifically, the ABA number printed at the bottom of the check).
Step 2	This information is used to generate an actual paper check, printed with the same information as the other checks in the customer's checkbook. The customer's name is printed on the signature line with a note that the customer has authorized the transaction.
Step 3	The check is then processed exactly like any other check.

FIGURE 7.10   Internet checking.

method, fulfilling a role similar to that of the credit card transaction processor and also handling check printing. Internet checking allows businesses to accept real-time payments from customers who prefer using checks to credit cards. A drawback is that paper is still involved; that is, an actual check must be printed and deposited in the merchant's bank.

Electronic funds transfer (EFT) is similar to Internet checking, but with one distinct difference: no paper check. Funds are simply transferred from the customer's bank account to the merchant's bank account. Figure 7.11 contains a summary of the process. Because no check draft is printed with EFT, a business can potentially receive funds more quickly than with electronic checking. Funds transfers, however, are typically more expensive on a per-transaction basis than electronic checks.

Digital cash, alternatively called *e-cash,* is the nearest equivalent to cash transactions on the Internet. Even though it can be used for purchases of any size, it was designed specifically for small-ticket transactions (several dollars or less), where transaction fees and expenses would make credit card or check purchases impractical. Such micropayments could be used to purchase an item of information or a song, or to play a game. Digital cash also promises anonymity, lower transaction fees, and immediate transaction processing.

Despite the many advantages of digital cash, markets stubbornly fail to adopt the technology. Digicash, the pioneering e-cash company, filed for bankruptcy in 1998. Another major digital cash player, CyberCash, was recently acquired by VeriSign. Merchants other than porn sites may be hesitant about its anonymity feature because digital cash makes it difficult to know their customers or offer them volume discounts and customized products. Law enforcement agencies and the Treasury Department clearly are concerned about digital cash's anonymity in money

Step 1	Customer visits merchant's website, selects a product or service to purchase, and enters check information: specifically, the ABA number printed at the bottom of the check. (Some EFT providers will also allow funds to be transferred from savings accounts.)
Step 2	Merchant relays this information to an EFT provider.
Step 3	EFT provider verifies customer account information against an Automated Clearing House (ACH) database; funds are debited from customer's bank account and credited to merchant's bank account.

FIGURE 7.11 Electronic funds transfer (EFT).

laundering schemes. Digital cash may play a role in Internet transactions in the future, but its current use is rather limited.

Figure 7.12 describes the process. Digital cash providers, such as ECash (www.ecash.com/online/), generally keep a percentage of each transaction.

Digital cash can also be stored on a smart card. A **smart card,** explains Whatis.com, "is a plastic card with an embedded microchip that can be loaded with data, used for telephone calling, electronic cash payments, and other applications, and then periodically 'recharged' for additional use."[13] Smart cards, such as those made available through Mondex (www.mondex.com), currently can be used for such small-ticket items as vending machines, toll booths, bus fares, and phone calls. Keyboards are being designed with smart card swipe capabilities in order to accommodate similar transactions on the Internet.

In deciding on a payment acceptance scheme or schemes, managers must take into account factors such as efficiency, security, price, and ease of customer use.

Directory Services and Search Engines

Additional components of the common business services infrastructure include services used to index the contents of the Internet, such as directory services and search engines. Managers should pay attention to these services for two reasons: first, they provide useful and extensive information about the Internet, and second, they can provide the visibility that becoming listed with them provides in giving potential customers a route of access.

Inter@ctive Week describes a **directory service** as "a collection of industrial-strength databases that store information about the applications, equipment, and

Step 1	Customer signs up with a digital cash provider and purchases a software "purse" of a given amount, which is stored on customer's computer.
Step 2	Customer visits website of merchant who accepts digital cash and agrees to pay via this method.
Step 3	Payment amount is deducted from customer's "purse" and deposited into merchant's account.

FIGURE 7.12 Digital cash.

[13] Whatis.com, available at http://whatis.com/smartcar.htm (accessed November 8, 1998)

users on a network."[14] It provides users with an interface with the applications and equipment on the network in accordance with scripted policies and terms of service. Not only do directory services simplify the utilization of legitimate resources, but they also help maintain a stable degree of security. Microsoft, Novell, Sun, and Netscape continue to develop their directory service applications to provide a shared cross-platform directory.

As briefly mentioned, a **search engine** is a program that searches the Internet (or an intranet or individual site) for specified keywords. A search engine typically contains an interface, allowing a user to enter these keywords. The search engine then sends out a "crawler" or "spider" to collect documents that contain the keywords. It then indexes the collected documents for easy review. Popular search engines on the Internet include Yahoo!, Infoseek, Excite, Google, AskJeeves, and Alta Vista.

Search engines are important because they help potential customers find their way to a company's Web site when hundreds, if not thousands, of competing sites are available. To be listed first on a search list can be crucial for the success, or even survival, of an e-business site. To improve the chances of its Web site being prominently displayed, a company may pay a subscription fee to the search engine, or may program the metatags in the HTML document so that search engines looking at metatags would retrieve the site's address.

Commerce Servers

A core technology used to build B2C e-commerce sites is commerce server software. A **commerce server** is a suite of software components designed to create and manage Web storefronts. It supports a broad range of functions and features including catalog services, storefront design, shopping carts, marketing, and order processing. In addition the commerce server may support affiliate programs and globalization efforts. Affiliate programs pay commissions to third-party sites in exchange for sales referrals. Some commerce servers support globalization efforts by maintaining and displaying product data and site content in multiple languages to suit the preferences of customers around the globe.

Commerce servers usually are tightly integrated with other enterprise applications and databases that are needed to execute marketing, sales, or order fulfillment processes. To achieve this tight integration, enterprise resource planning (ERP) and customer relationship management (CRM) vendors often incorporate commerce server functionality into their products.

Personalization

According to PricewaterhouseCoopers' technology forecast, **personalization** is "the selective delivery of content and services (such as specific product and service offerings, advertising, coupons and other promotions) to customers and

---

[14] Inter@ctive Week, (June 16, 1997), available at http://www.zdnet.com/intweek/print/970616/inwk0028.html (accessed November 8, 1998). Copyright © 1997 Interactive Enterprises, LLC.

prospective customers."[15] Personalization software allows e-businesses to offer customized services to meet the past and current interests of customers based upon data about them that is captured in an electronic format. The data needed for personalization are gathered from many sources: clickstream data, registration data that the customer supplies, past purchases, demographics supplied by third-party vendors, and customer ratings. These data are then processed by a variety of techniques including rule-based systems, neural networks, and artificial intelligence to generate and update customer profiles. In turn, these profiles are used by the firm in many ways, including as a basis for selecting the Web site content that is presented to the customer as a part of marketing, sales, and customer service efforts. For example, by analyzing a customer's current navigation through a site and comparing it to customer profiles, the personalization software can recommend specific products or services to the visitor. Personalization works hand-in-hand with CRMs in catering to customers.

Messaging and Information Distribution Infrastructure

The second building block in the generic framework for electronic commerce is the messaging and information distribution infrastructure. Messaging software facilitates the movement of information through the channels of the Internet. It takes such forms as e-mail, instant messaging, point-to-point file transfers, and groupware.

One of the first uses of the Internet, e-mail, still constitutes a good portion of Internet traffic. Most e-mail messages consist strictly of text, but e-mail can also be used to transfer images, video clips, sound clips, and other types of computer files.

Many e-mail services (e.g., Eudora, Outlook Express) require the user to have an account with a domain or an ISP. An **Internet service provider (ISP)** is a company that sells access to the Internet. Incoming and outgoing e-mail is routed through the domain's or ISP's mail server, and all e-mail a user receives is stored on his or her own computer. However, a growing number of Web-based e-mail providers allow a user to send and receive e-mail from any computer by accessing the provider's Web site and entering a user name and password. Web-based e-mail allows a user to keep the same e-mail address long term (i.e., as long as the provider stays in business), whereas e-mail routed through an ISP usually contains the name of the ISP as part of the e-mail address, and a user must therefore change e-mail addresses each time he or she changes ISPs. Disadvantages of Web-based services include limits on the number of messages that can be stored and on the size of files that can be sent and received. Web-based e-mail is typically offered free; service providers display advertisements on users' pages and collect demographics and other marketing data from users upon enrollment.

Another permutation of e-mail is the mailing list server. Users subscribe to a mailing list; when any user sends a message to the server, a copy of the message is sent

---

[15] PricewaterhouseCoopers, *Technology Forecast: 2002-2004, Volume 1: Navigating the Future of Software* (Menlo Park, CA, 2002), p. 385.

to everyone on the list. This service allows for restricted-access discussion groups; only subscribed members can participate in or view the discussions that are transmitted via e-mail. Popular mailing list providers include ListServ and Majordomo.

Instant messaging (IM) is an Internet protocol (IP)—based application that provides convenient communication between people using a variety of different device types, including computer-to-computer and mobile devices, such as digital cellular phones.[16] It can identify which "buddies" have a "presence" and are able to receive messages at the moment. If a "buddy" is available, the sender's typed message pops up on the receiver's computer screen. Failing to respond quickly to the message typically is perceived to be rude. Although initially a communication tool used exclusively by teenagers, IM now serves as an internal communication systems in large companies, and even allows managers to verify whether their telecommuting employees are logged on to their computer at their homes. With most systems, people need to agree to be on a potential sender's buddy list, and they can set their status to "busy" or "away" if they do not want to be disturbed. Even then, IM is sometimes criticized for being distracting and reducing privacy.

File transfer consists simply of transferring a copy of a file from one computer to another on the Internet. The most common procedure, file transfer protocol (FTP), allows entire files—even large ones—to be transferred within an office or across the globe more quickly and securely than with e-mail.

Groupware is, as its name implies, group software that enables group members to work together on a project, even from remote locations, by allowing them simultaneous access to the same file. Calendars, written documents, e-mail messages, and databases can be shared through such software products as Lotus Notes and Microsoft Exchange. CU-SeeMe and Microsoft NetMeeting actually make electronic "face-to-face" meetings possible.[17] Public groupware sites are increasingly popular, such as groove.net and intranets.com. These sites provide services of interest to geographically dispersed work teams who would like to use the Web, but do not have a server of their own.

Multimedia Content

Multimedia content comprises the third building block in the generic framework for electronic commerce. A wide range of vehicles must travel the **information superhighway,**[18] and not all vehicles can traverse the same routes. Commerce involving the transmission of movies or electronic books, for example, requires routing them according to the technical specifications of their individual components. If movies comprise video and audio components, and electronic books include text, graphics, and photographs, then each may be transmitted quite differently on the Internet.[19]

[16] Available at http://www.iec.org/online/tutorials/instant_msg/ IEC definition of IM (accessed September 9, 2002).

[17] Whatis.com, available at http://whatis.com/groupwar.htm (accessed November 8, 1998).

[18] This term was coined by Al Gore to describe a vision of a communications network that carries high-speed information throughout the world. It is often used as a synonym for the Internet.

[19] R. Kalakota and A. Whinston, *Frontiers of Electronic Commerce* (Reading, MA: Addison Wesley, 1996), pp. 5–6.

After such multimedia content is created, it is stored as electronic documents on servers, which in turn are linked to each other via networks. Customers access them via software and hardware clients. Because multimedia files tend to be substantially larger than text files, accessing them is best done with high-speed broadband connections.

Internet Infrastructure

The fourth and final building block in the generic framework for electronic commerce is the infrastructure of the Internet. How does the Internet actually work? Of what does it consist? To answer these questions, a manager must first understand that information transmitted via the Web is first broken into data "packets." These packets travel independently of each other across the Web, sometimes following entirely different routes. Once the packets arrive at their destination, they are reassembled into a complete message. Rus Shuler of the Revere Group maps the journey of these packets in Figure 7.13 (note that CSU/DSU is channel service unit/data service unit).

An Internet service provider maintains a pool of modems for customers who dial in. A computer manages this pool and controls the flow of data from each modem to a backbone or dedicated line router. The computer usually collects billing and usage information as well. Packets from a customer's computer traverse the phone network and the ISP's local equipment and are routed onto the ISP's backbone. From there the packets may pass through several other routers and backbones, dedicated lines, and other networks until they find their destination, a single computer with a specified address.[20]

Public Policy

This chapter discussed the four building blocks in the generic framework. Just as important are two pillars supporting that framework: public policy and technical standards.

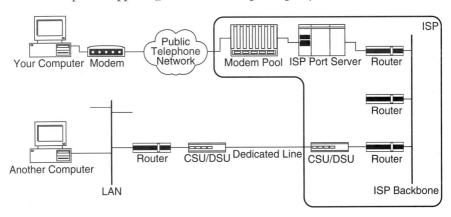

FIGURE 7.13 A sample journey of information from one Internet computer to another.
Source: Rus Shuler, Ballantyne Consulting Group. Used with permission.

[20] Available at http://rus1.home.mindspring.com/whitepapers/internet_whitepaper.html (accessed December 13, 1998). Copyright © 1998 Rus Shuler/The Revere Group.

In the rapidly developing world of e-commerce, basic policy and legal questions are emerging. Because of the tremendous potential impact of the Internet on their economies, governments around the world have started to politicize the Web. The United States is contemplating policies, regulations, and laws over a broad range of issues including the cost of accessing information, taxation of online sales, regulation to protect consumers from fraud and to protect their right to privacy, and the policing of information traffic to detect terrorism, pirating, or pornography.[21] For example, the Justice Department's Anti-Terrorism Act of 2001 would expand the federal government's authority to conduct electronic surveillance and otherwise collect information about U.S. citizens. Many claim that this act weakens privacy protection without increasing security.

In April 1998, the U.S. Department of Commerce released "The Emerging Digital Economy," a detailed report about the evolution of e-commerce. Privacy issues figured prominently. The report cited three common e-commerce practices as causing privacy concerns: requesting personal information from new visitors to a site, creating customer profiles based on personal information gathered in order to deliver purchased goods, and leaving electronic "footprints" of visits to different Web sites and of purchases made, without the knowledge of the customer. The report argued that consumers should be given the opportunity to block the gathering of information or, when they freely give it, to indicate how they would like it to be used.[22]

When it comes to regulation, two approaches are possible: self-regulation and imposed regulation. For the time being, at least, the U.S. government relies on industry self-regulation to address these privacy issues. For example, the private sector is encouraged to establish rules of conduct, which would be disclosed to consumers, as well as mechanisms for tracking compliance and offering recourse to consumers in situations of noncompliance. Consumers should know the identity of any collector of personal information and the intended uses of the information. In addition, they should have the right to access information about themselves that a company holds and to correct or amend it as necessary.[23] In contrast the governments of China and the United Arab Emirates are adopting a policy of imposed regulation when they use firewall systems that control the access of their citizens to certain types of Internet sites—those that contain nudity, sexual content, or religious information. China even restricts access of its citizens to the popular Google search engine.[24]

Because of its global reach, it is impossible for any one nation to regulate the Internet. Consider the attempts of the U.S. government to ban pornography when it only has jurisdiction over sites in the United States. Sites of companies based in Denmark are not subject to this legislation. When the U.S. government attempted

---

[21] R. Kalakota and A. Whinston, *Frontiers of Electronic Commerce* (Reading, MA: Addison Wesley, 1996), p. 6.

[22] Available at http://www.ecommerce.gov/emerging.htm, Chapter 5 (accessed November 8, 1998).

[23] *Ibid.*

[24] Y. Dreazen, "Computer Whiz Tois to Save Internet's Soul," *The Wall Street Journal* (September 16, 2002), p. B1.

to ban online gambling, companies with gambling sites merely moved to locations outside of the United States.

Technical Standards

The second pillar upon which the e-commerce framework rests is technical standards for electronic documents, multimedia, and network protocols. Such standards are essential to e-commerce because they ensure seamless integration across the data transportation network, as well as access for consumers on any device they choose—laser disc, PC, handheld devices—and on all operating systems.[25]

All Internet-connected computers, regardless of manufacturer or operating system, must speak the TCP/IP language in order to communicate with each other. Therefore, before investing in computers and networking systems, managers should ascertain that the systems conform to these standards.

Perhaps one of the most heavily promoted payment standards is secure electronic transaction (SET) for secure payments for online credit card transactions. MasterCard, Visa International, IBM, Microsoft, and Netscape began developing SET in 1997, but ran into cultural and technical difficulties that limited its adoption. In 2001, most online credit card transactions still used secure sockets layer (SSL), a protocol for encrypting Web transactions that is easier for merchants to implement.[26] Unlike SSL, SET offers a nonrepudiation feature. SSL only authenticates the merchant's identity. On the other hand, SET uses public key infrastructure and digital certificates to mutually verify that the merchant and the customer are who they claim to be, and to ensure that the buyer will not later deny the purchase. SET offers this feature to ensure that customer credit card numbers cannot be used fraudulently by unscrupulous merchants.

A considerable number of application protocols are also basically transparent to the Internet user, but are used in conducting business on the Internet. They include file transfer protocol (FTP), hypertext transfer protocol (HTTP), simple network management protocol (SNMP), post office protocol (POP), and multimedia Internet mail extensions (MIME). Further, institutions such as ISO, IEEE, and ANSI define standards for hardware configurations and software.

Because the Internet is relatively new, at least from a commercial perspective, it is often hard to predict future standards. Managers who bet on the wrong standard often put their companies at a distinct competitive disadvantage. A classic case is when managers chose to use what they considered to be the better Beta standard instead of VHS, which ultimately dominated the market. In today's multimedia environment, Real, Windows Media, and QuickTime are all competing for users and distributors. Microsoft and Sun are both jockeying to create a Java standard that best suits their own company. Unfortunately, picking the wrong standard can make a company uncompetitive down the road.

[25] R. Kalakota and A. Whinston, *Frontiers of Electronic Commerce* (Reading, MA: Addison Wesley, 1996), p. 7.

[26] PricewaterhouseCoopers, *Technology Forecast: 2002-2004, Volume 1: Navigating the Future of Software* (Menlo Park, CA, 2002), p. 385.

▶ FOOD FOR THOUGHT I: E-LEARNING

E-learning is using the Internet to enable learning. The Internet provides a basis for radically changing the way learning is done. Traditional learning takes place in a classroom, typically with an instructor and a room full of students. Regardless of whether the students are graduates, undergraduates, executives, or even those attending a corporate training session, the traditional model is the default model for most learning situations. The Internet is beginning to change that.

Today, businesses do not want their employees to ever stop learning. In the fast-paced environment of today's business world, having current knowledge is a strategic advantage. Further, relatively little within an organization is static. That was not the case a short while ago. In the past, someone wanting to go to work received training by apprenticing with an expert whom the student modeled, studied, and imitated in order to learn a trade. When the apprenticeship ended, the worker was considered fully trained and ready to earn a living practicing the trade. But that is not the case any longer. A business that does not encourage employees to continually learn and adapt, and that does not build in the ability to learn and adapt, is setting itself up for failure.

Consider Cisco, the maker of routers and other devices used to create networks that become roadways for the Internet. John Chambers, CEO, believes e-learning is a critical success factor for Cisco. "There are two fundamental equalizers in life— the Internet and education. E-learning eliminates the barriers of time and distance creating universal, learning-on-demand opportunities for people, companies, and countries."[27] Cisco managers believe that e-learning helps them increase productivity as well as build loyalty. How do they and others investing in e-learning participate?

Many different types of e-learning exist. Figure 7.14 summarizes some of them, including computer-based training, distance learning, online learning, and on-demand learning. In today's environment, the terms are often used interchangeably, but several distinct concepts are embedded within the alternatives. Distance learning, for example, is when students are geographically spread out, but use technology to engage in a collective learning session such as a class. This learning experience is different from online learning, where the learner uses a computer as the primary teaching vehicle. It is somewhat different from on-demand learning, where information is broken up into small chunks, or nuggets, and pushed out to learners within the context of their work processes.

If learning can be embedded within the business processes executed by workers, then organizations can make major changes in their business strategy and their organization strategy. Embedding learning within a business process means that when the individual executing the process requires assistance, the process is smart enough to detect it and push information out to the learner to assist him or her in completing the task. It might operate somewhat like an electronic "on-the-job training" opportunity. The advantage is that if it is done right, the skills needed to complete the job change. It may mean hiring different types of individuals for the job.

[27] John Chambers as quoted on the Cisco Web site (May 25, 2000), available at www.cisco.com.

Type of E-learning	Definition
Computer-based training	Any course or lesson presented on a computer, typically not connected to a network.
Distance learning	Any type of educational situation in which the instructor and students are separated by location.
Online learning	Courses presented on a computer that is hooked up to a network
Technology-based instruction	Training through media other than the classroom. That includes computers, but also refers to television, audiotape, videotape, and print.
Web-based instruction	Courses available on the Internet which typically have embedded links to other Web-based resources.
On-demand learning	Learning broken up into knowledge chunks and delivered as demanded within a business process.

FIGURE 7.14 Types of e-learning.
Source: Adapted from Carliner, S. "An Overview of Online Learning," a white paper published by Lakewood conferences, on website http://www.lakewoodconferences.com/wp, May 25, 2000.

Further, if the information pushed out to the learner must be updated, the computer system can do it instantly. It provides a distinct advantage over traditional courses, where materials must be prepared weeks in advance in order to be ready for the classroom.

E-learning is a relatively new concept. The features of the Internet are enabling innovative organizations to rethink how they disseminate knowledge, information, and training to their employees. And the effects this technology will have on universities and traditional schools is one of the most debated topics of e-business.

▶ FOOD FOR THOUGHT II: IS THERE REALLY A "NEW ECONOMY"?

In his article, "Strategy and the Internet," Michael Porter suggests what people call the "new economy" is really nothing other than the old economy that has access to new technology.[28] He is concerned that the term *e-business* encourages managers to view their Internet operations separately from the rest of their business. By focusing on e-business as a separate entity and failing to integrate the Internet into their proven strategies, well-established businesses are unable to leverage the Internet's capabilities.

Porter views the Internet as the latest stage in the ongoing IT evolution. He argues that the Internet alone can rarely be used by businesses to create competitive advantage. Rather, companies can compete successfully only when they use the Internet to complement traditional ways of competing. To gain and sustain competitive advantage, Internet initiatives must be integrated with their firm's current operations and must be judged using traditional measures of profitability (and not

[28] Michael Porter, "Strategy and the Internet," *Harvard Business Review* (March 2001), pp. 63–78.

the number of eyeballs viewing a site or click-through rates). Even though a new set of rules appeared to emerge during the dot-com boom, the subsequent bust suggests that in fact the traditional rules and fundamental business practices underlie success in the current Information Age.

Porter also dispels the myths of the "first mover" and partnering as a "win-win" situation. The myth of the first mover assumes that the Internet increases switching costs, making customers hesitant to switch to other Web sites, thus giving the advantage to the first entrant in a market. Porter counters that the Internet in fact lowers switching costs. Customers can easily click from one Web site to another. A switchover to another business is made easier by companies like PayPal that automate electronic payment online. Further, the Internet's openness removes barriers to entry, and Internet businesses have not been able to eliminate the brand recognition of well-established companies.

The myth of partnering as a win-win situation does not always hold either according to Porter. Partnering may speed industry growth and reduce narrowminded competition, but it can also prove detrimental for firms across an industry. For example, standardizing an industry's product offerings can increase rivalry and reduce profitability for all firms in the industry.

Porter concludes that well-established firms can use the Internet to achieve a sustainable competitive advantage either through operational effectiveness or by strategically positioning themselves so that they provide a unique type of value to their customers. They need to create value throughout their industry chains and leverage their own cross-activity integration within their own firm.

▶ SUMMARY

- The Internet has the distinction of being an entirely new marketplace, a previously nonexistent place to conduct business on a global scale. Internet-based e-commerce is becoming less mysterious and more commonplace; soon it will be second nature to consumers. Quite simply, the Internet provides a popular method for conducting business, whether it is B2B transactions or B2C transactions. Its rules, however, are still in the formative stages, so innovative and forward-thinking business people have the potential to shape them in lucrative and otherwise rewarding ways.

- Derivatives of the Internet include intranets (networks used within a business to communicate between individuals and departments) and extranets (networks that connect a business with individuals, customers, suppliers, and other stakeholders outside the organization's boundaries). Virtual private networks (VPNs) are a form of extranets that make use of public telecommunication infrastructures, maintaining privacy through the use of a tunneling protocol and security procedures.

- Web sites continue to go through a number of stages ranging from content provider to transaction forum, integrator and catalyst for industry restructuring.

- If managers are to use e-commerce for maximum effectiveness and efficiency, they must understand the elements that comprise it. Kalakota and Whinston place the key elements in a generic framework for electronic commerce, which consists of four building blocks and two pillars. (The framework is depicted in Figure 7.5.)

- The first building block is the common business services infrastructure, and it includes security and authentication (various methods a manager can use to protect electronic information), electronic payment (ways in which a business can accept payments via the Internet), directory services and search engines (services a manager can use both to locate important business information and to increase market awareness of his or her business offering), commerce servers (a core technology used to build business-to-consumer e-commerce sites), and personalization (the selective delivery of content and services).

- The second building block is the messaging and information distribution infrastructure, which includes electronic methods whereby a business can increase the efficiency of its internal and external communications.

- The third building block iås multimedia content to disseminate business offerings.

- The final building block is the information superhighway infrastructure, which a manager should understand in order to know how information gets from point A to point B on the Internet.

- The first pillar is composed of public policy and legal and privacy issues. Managers must stay abreast of these issues because they are still being formulated and fundamentally affect how business is conducted on the Internet. The second pillar consists of technical standards and protocols. TCP/IP is a protocol critical for Internet operations. Standards for payments over the Internet include SET and SSL. Managers must ascertain that their systems, as well as their electronic products and services, speak the Internet's language.

- Business managers can expect a future in which the Internet becomes larger, faster, more powerful, and more commonplace. In the near future, Internet connections may even become portable. Therefore, it could be argued that consideration of the Internet and its role in the exploding world of e-commerce should figure into all important business decisions. Managers must ask themselves these questions: Which elements of our business can be made available online? If elements of our business can be electronically automated but are not yet, how long can we afford to perform them manually? If we offer a product or service that potentially can be delivered online, even in part, are we prepared to offer it online? If we are not yet prepared to do so, will we be prepared before our competitors are or before an online substitute becomes available? Is Porter right or do first movers, in fact, have a distinct advantage? In addressing these questions, managers can gain efficiencies, improve products, and open markets.

▶ KEY TERMS

asymmetric encryption (p. 165)
authentication (p. 165)
broadband (p. 155)
cipher text (p. 165)
commerce server (p. 170)
decryption (p. 165)
digital cash (p. 168)

digital signatures (p. 165)
directory service (p. 169)
electronic data interchange (EDI) (p. 157)
electronic funds transfer (EFT) (p. 168)
e-business (p. 153)
e-channel (p. 160)

e-learning (p. 176)
electronic commerce (e-commerce) (p. 153)
encryption (p. 165)
extranet (p. 156)
file transferring (p. 172)
firewalls (p. 166)
groupware (p. 172)

information
  superhighway (p. 172)
instant message (p. 172)
Internet (p. 154)
Internet checking
  (p. 167)
Internet service provider
  (ISP) (p. 171)
intranet (p. 156)
marketspace (p. 157)

password (p. 165)
personalization (p. 170)
private key (p. 165)
public key (p. 165)
search engine (p. 170)
secure server (p. 166)
smart card (p. 169)
symmetric encryption
  (p. 165)
TCP/IP (p. 154)

transaction processors
  (p. 167)
value-added network
  (VAN) (p. 162)
virtual private network
  (VPN) (p. 157)
virtual terminal (p. 167)
Web browser (p. 156)
World Wide Web
  (WWW) (p. 156)

▶ DISCUSSION QUESTIONS

1. What is the difference in B2B and B2C applications on the Internet? What features of the Internet are more relevant to B2B transactions? To B2C transactions? Give examples of each type of transaction. What might be the next business model?

2. What are current uses of the Internet for organizations with which you have worked? How might they use the Internet to improve their organizational strategy? Their business strategy?

3. When an organization implements a Web site, what changes in its organizational strategy should it anticipate? Why?

4. What is your prediction of the next big breakthrough for the Internet? Support your forecast with points drawn from this chapter and from your experience with the Internet.

5. How will e-learning change the business strategy of an organization? The organizational strategy? Support your claims with examples, either hypothetical or from real companies.

6. Melinda Mason is contemplating entering cyberspace. Her flower shop in Manhattan's Upper West Side has been in the family for three generations. Over the years the business carefully cultivated a large number of regular customers. Lately many of these customers asked her when Mason's Flower Shop will have a Web site. They told her they would like the ease of ordering online along with the option of ordering and paying for flowers online. Many of her customers order elaborate arrangements on a periodic basis. One, like Mr. Schliermann, likes to buy a single red rose for his wife each Tuesday.

In addition to these customers, Melinda also realizes that a web site for ordering and paying for flowers would be appealing to the increasingly large number of customers who winter in South Florida, but who send flowers to their friends and family in New York City. Plus she read that being a brick-and-click can open your business to customers around the globe. Naturally this prospect is appealing to her.

Melinda hired you to explore the options for online payment. In particular, she heard about Mondex from her friends and wonders whether she should make it a payment option. She is not sure how Mondex compares to such electronic payment options as PayPal. Finally, she heard about iTransact from the shopkeeper next door and wonders whether this payment option might be best for her.

Melinda would like you to evaluate these options and make a recommendation to her about the online payment option(s) that she should adopt. She wants an approach that is easy for her and her customers to use, but that is a good value in terms of cost. Her steady customers in Florida must be able to pay online, and it would be nice if the payment approach also could appeal to customers around the globe. Most of the online orders will be over $25, though she would also like to have an option that purchasers of a single rose could use.

CASE STUDY 7-1

AMAZON.COM

No company exemplifies the new business era of the Internet more than Amazon.com. What started out as a book company emerged as a serious competitor to dozens of industries. If founder and CEO Jeff Bezos achieves his vision, "Amazon.com will be a place where you can find anything." Given the activities, expansions, and successes to date, Amazon is making significant headway on its ambitious plans to take over the entire e-commerce e-tailing world.

Amazon.com started in 1996 selling books over the Internet. Since that time, the company pioneered many of the innovations that define electronic shopping, such as one-click shopping, customer reviews, affiliation programs, and online gift-wrapping. It was the first site for customers to actually buy anything over the Internet. It is the largest seller of online books, music, and videos, with 25 million customers in 2001. Second quarter revenues in 2002 surged 21 percent to $806 million in a weak market. It went public in 1997, and the stock price eventually rose from $1.50 a share into the heady triple digits.

To increase the number of customers to its site, Amazon.com established an affiliation program that awards other sites a percentage of the sale when customers are linked from their site to Amazon.com to make a recommended purchase. A customer visiting the Amazon.com site is greeted with a busy Web page showing key specials that day, and giving opportunity to navigate to the type of product the customer wants to buy. If books are the purchase to be made that day, the customer can click on the books link, and search for a book by title, author, or subject. So far, the scenario is not much to get excited about, but the power behind the Amazon.com business model is not yet shown. If a customer searches for a particular book, not only does Amazon.com's site give the details of the book, but potential buyers can read the table of contents, look at comments written by other readers of the book, link to other books of a related topic or by the same author. Comments give a sense of community to the Amazon.com site where customers can contribute or read comments easily. Further, the Amazon.com systems track purchases of the book at hand, and can tell the new customer of other books purchased by those who purchased the current book. Their "suggestions" are based on real data culled from an extensive database of transactions, making the suggestions that much more relevant to the current customer.

The purchasing transaction is innovative, too. The standard process lets customers add a selection to their shopping cart and either continue shopping or finish out the transaction. Shipping options are presented and purchases are paid for with credit cards. If the customer is a repeat customer, the system already has payment and shipping information, and the purchase can be quickly made with a single "click" of the mouse. E-mail is sent to the purchaser at several points along the process, including a confirmation that the order was received and a notice of the shipping of the order. E-mail is also automatically generated to alert customers of specials related to purchases they made, such as a new book by a favorite author. By combining a transaction system with real time information, customer connections and dissemination systems make retailing on the Web, or e-tailing, a different experience from traditional buying at the local bookstore or mall.

Bezo's vision is for Amazon.com to be the center of the e-commerce world. That goal means selling or at least locating books, videos, CDs, electronics, pet food, housewares, garden supplies, games, or whatever a shopper on the Internet wants to buy. The company also offers an online auction. In mid-1999, Amazon.com announced two more e-tailing options. All Product Search is a product browser that helps customers locate items at Amazon.com, its partners, or anywhere on the net. Amazon.com hosts Z-shops, an online mall, where anyone or any company can set up a store, by paying a small monthly fee and commission. In return, these stores gain potential access to the 25 million customers of Amazon.com. It now also hosts online operations and fulfillment for more established retail rivals like Toys "R" Us, Target, and Circuit City in return for a percentage of sales, per-unit payments, or periodic fixed payments. For example, in their partnership with Toy "R" Us, the toy company provides the product while Amazon.com sells and delivers it. This partnership suggests that Amazon realizes it can't compete outside its core markets without significant help and Toys "R" Us acknowledges that it needs to build upon its core competency.

What is next for Amazon.com? Bezos is quoted as saying, "The idea is to let people find anything they might want to buy online. Amazon is a 'Katrina Store' or a 'Jeff Store.' The notion is that you take the customers and put them at the center of their own universe."

Discussion Questions

1. How has Amazon.com and their use of the Internet changed the retailing industry? Give some specific examples.

2. Comparisons have been made between giant bookstore retailer Barnes & Noble and Amazon.com. Barnes & Noble operates dozens of bookstores in many local communities. Yet Amazon.com's reach goes anywhere and everywhere with the Web. What, in your opinion, should Barnes & Noble do to compete with Amazon.com?

3. In order to more quickly realize and sustain its profitability should Amazon.com have remained a solely clicks-based e-business (without warehouses) selling only books? Why or why not?

4. How can Amazon.com complete Bezos's vision? What do they need to do to individualize their services to 25 million customers?

Source: Adapted from Katrina Brooke, "Amazon vs. Everybody," *Fortune* (November 8, 1999), pp. 120–128; and Chip Bayers, "The Last Laugh," *Business 2.0* (September 2002), pp. 86–93.

CHAPTER 8

THE MANAGEMENT INFORMATION SYSTEMS ORGANIZATION[1]

Until January 1993, Cisco Systems maintained a traditional information systems (IS) department. Considered a cost center, it reported through the finance department. However, in an effort to increase information technology's (IT's) contribution to the bottom line, Cisco made three organizational changes: (1) IS began reporting to Customer Advocacy; (2) it introduced client funding, charging project costs to the client department and reducing the portion charged to general and administrative expenses; and (3) IT investment decisions that had been made by an IS steering committee were now made by line organizations. Cisco's new budgeting method made each business executive think seriously about IT expenses and how they should be allocated.[2]

Cisco still manages IT centrally, and even client-funded projects are managed by the central IT organization. The **chief information officer (CIO)** has authority over all IT staff and contractors. Cisco management believes that its organizational strategy helped stabilize the company during a period of fast growth.

IS organizations come in all shapes and sizes. Each is built around processes that it performs or supports. These processes fulfill specific needs of internal customers. For instance, a telecommunications company with a large technology infrastructure may require distributed processing capabilities, whereas a regional manufacturing plant may require only back-office support.

Although each IS organization is unique in many ways, all have elements in common. The focus of this chapter is to introduce managers to the typical activities of an IS organization in order to facilitate interaction with management information systems (MIS) professionals. Managers will be a more effective consumer of services from MIS professionals in their organization if they understand, in general, what they do. This chapter examines the roles and tasks of the IS organization. In addition, it addresses recent issues about organizing and controlling information resources—in particular, outsourcing, structuring, and globalization.

---

[1] The authors wish to acknowledge and thank David M. Zahn, MBA 1999 for his help in researching and writing early drafts of this chapter.

[2] R. Nolan and K. Porter, "Cisco Systems, Inc.," Harvard Business School case 398–127 (April 2000).

183

▶ UNDERSTANDING THE MIS ORGANIZATION

Consider an analogy of a ship in a regatta to help explain the purpose of an IS organization and how it functions. A ship transports people and cargo to a particular destination in much the same way that an IS organization directs itself toward the strategic goals set by the larger enterprise. Sometimes the IS organization must navigate perilous waters or storms to win a regatta. For both the IS organization and the ship, the key is to perform more capably than any competitors. It means employing the right resources to propel the enterprise through the rough waters of business. Each of these resources is discussed in the following sections.

Chief Information Officer

If an IS organization is like a ship, then the CIO is at the helm. The CIO is an executive who manages IT resources in order to implement enterprise strategy. The Gartner Group defines a **CIO** as one who "provides technology vision and leadership for developing and implementing IT initiatives that create and maintain leadership for the enterprise in a constantly changing and intensely competitive marketplace."[3]

This definition may seem clear, but to understand what the CIO does, we should explore the historical origins of this position. The CIO function is a relatively new position when compared to the more established chief executive officer (CEO) or chief financial officer (CFO), which have existed in the corporate structure for decades. In fact, the CIO position did not really emerge until the early 1980s, when top management perceived a need for an executive-level manager to focus on cutting the ever-increasing costs of IT. Cost-cutting measures typically took the form of outsourcing arrangements, which are addressed later in this chapter.

The evolution of the CIO's role closely follows the evolution of technology in business. Throughout the late 1980s and into the 1990s, technology grew from an expensive necessity to a strategic enabler. As technology's role increased in importance, so did that of the CIO. In fact, many organizations include the CIO as an integral member of the executive-level decision-making team.

CIOs are a unique breed. They have a strong understanding of the business and of the technology. In many organizations they take on roles that span both of these areas. More often than not, CIOs are asked to play strategic roles at some part of their day, and operations roles at other times, rather than spending all of their time on one or the other. It appears that the scope and depth of the CIO are expanding. Now, twelve main responsibilities often define the CIO role:

1. *Championing the organization.* Promoting IT within the enterprise as a strategic tool for growth

2. *Architecture management.* Setting organizational direction and priorities

3. *Business strategy consultant.* Participating in executive-level decision making

4. *Business technology planning.* Bridging business and technology groups for purposes of collaborating in planning and execution

---

[3] Available at http://www.cio.com/forums/executive/gartner_description.html.

5. *Applications development.* Overseeing legacy and emerging enterprise initiatives, as well as broader strategic business unit (SBU) and divisional initiatives

6. *IT infrastructure management (e.g., computers, printers, and networks).* Maintaining current technologies and investing in future technologies

7. *Sourcing.* Developing and implementing a strategy for outsourcing (versus retaining in-house) IT services and/or people

8. *Partnership developer.* Negotiating relationships with key suppliers of IT expertise and services

9. *Technology transfer agent.* Providing technologies that enable the enterprise to work better with suppliers and customers—both internal and external—and consequently, increase shareholder value

10. Customer satisfaction management. Understanding and communicating with both internal and external customers to ensure that customer satisfaction goals are met

11. Training. Providing training to IT users, as well as senior executives who must understand how IT fits with enterprise strategy

12. Business discontinuity/disaster recovery planning. Planning and implementing strategies to limit the impact of natural and human-made disasters on information technology and, consequently, the conduct of business

A CIO must work effectively not only within the technical arena, but also in overall business management. This unique skill set demands a specialized background. The following nine skills are considered essential for success as a CIO:[4]

1. A strong orientation toward business in the enterprise, industry, or through related activities, such as consulting

2. Ability to realize the benefits and manage the cost and risks associated with IT

3. Ability to bridge any gaps between available technologies and business needs

4. Familiarity with the needs of nontechnical internal clients

5. Strong organizational skills to manage localized IS resources and applications as well as broader SBU and divisional resources and initiatives

6. Ability to conceive, build, and implement multiple IT projects on time and within budget

7. Ability to articulate and advocate for a management vision of IT

8. Ability to mesh well with the existing management structure

9. A strategic vision for the enterprise that extends beyond IT

Where the CIO fits within an enterprise is often a source of controversy. In the early days of the CIO position, when the CIO was predominantly responsible

---

[4] Some of these skills are adapted from "CIO Position Description," cio.com, available at http://www.cio.com/ forums/executive/gartner_description.html.

for controlling costs, the CIO reported to the chief financial officer (CFO). Because the CIO was rarely involved in enterprise governance, this reporting structure worked. However, as IT burgeoned into a source for competitive advantage in the marketplace, reporting to the CFO proved too limiting. Conflicts arose because the CFO misunderstood the vision for IT or saw only the costs of technology, or because management still saw the CIO's primary responsibility as controlling costs. More recently, CIOs report directly to the CEO, president, or other executive manager.

Confusion often occurs regarding whether the CIO is more of a strategist or operational manager. He or she is often asked to be both. Because the CIO is the top IS professional in the hierarchy, it is imperative that this person also be a strategist. The title CIO signals to both the organization and to outside observers that this executive is a strategic IS thinker, and is responsible for linking IS strategy with the business strategy. With the increasing importance of the Internet to every business, the CIO is increasingly asked to assist, advise, and participate in discussions where business strategy is set. However, just as the CFO is somewhat involved in operational management of the financial activities of the organization, the CIO is involved with operational issues related to IS. These include activities such as identifying and managing the introduction of new technologies into the firm, setting purchasing and vendor policies, and managing the overall IT budget. Actual day-to-day management of the data center, the vendor portfolio, and other operational issues is typically not handled directly by the CIO, but by one of the managers in the IS organization.

Some organizations choose not to have a CIO. These organizations typically hire an individual to be responsible for running the computer systems and possibly to manage many of the activities described later in this chapter. But they signal that this person is not a strategist by giving them the title of data processing manager or director of information systems or some other reference that clearly differentiates this person from other top officers in the company. Using the words *chief* and *officer* usually implies a strategic focus, and some organizations do not see the value of having an IS person on their executive team.

What, then, does a CIO do? Although there is no such thing as an average day in the life of a CIO, the following example provides a reference point. In 1996, Levi Strauss & Company sought a new CIO.[5] Although Levi Strauss's IT was in acceptable shape, problems existed. First, the IS organization was viewed by many as a stepchild, a necessary component of the enterprise, but one that did not contribute materially to its success. Second, Levi Strauss was working to recover from a massive reorganization earlier in the decade, which had cost millions of dollars and hundreds of jobs, as well as waning morale, lingering resentment, and general ill will. Finally, the role of IT was poorly matched to the strategic goals of the company. The new CIO faced a daunting job: solve Levi Strauss's Y2K problem, deliver new IT tools—such as those that could produce the new custom-fit jeans called Personal Pair to retail outlets—develop new metrics for tracking IT's value, and forge new relationships with external and internal business leaders.[6]

[5] Tom Field, "Great Expectations: Growing Companies and Changing Times Make Tomorrow a Challenge for Today's New CIOs," *CIO Magazine* (September 15, 1997), p. 245.

[6] Ibid.

The new CIO, Linda Glick, was a 21-year veteran of Levi Strauss known for her practicality, partnering capabilities, and ability to get the job done. Peter Jacobi, the president of Levi Strauss, described her as fearless. In her job as CIO, Glick tackled the Y2K problem, brought a new attitude to the much-maligned IS department, and began to form the executive-level partnerships necessary to become an advocate for IT within the Levi Strauss organization. She led Levi Strauss, in late 1998, to enter the world of electronic commerce with an online store. No one could tackle all of Levi Strauss's problems overnight, but Glick's situation typifies the challenges CIOs face.

Chief Technology Officer, Chief Knowledge Officer, and Other Similar Roles

Although the CIO's role is to guide the enterprise toward the future, this responsibility is frequently too great to accomplish alone. Many organizations recognized that certain strategic areas of the IS organization require more focused guidance. This recognition led to the creation of new positions, such as the chief knowledge officer (CKO), chief technology officer (CTO), chief telecommunications officer (also CTO), chief network officer (CNO), chief information security officer (CISO), chief privacy officer (CPO), and chief resource officer (CRO). See Figure 8.1 for a list of their different responsibilities. Each of these positions typically subordinates to the CIO, with the occasional exception of the chief technology officer.

The **chief technology officer (CTO)** often works alongside the CIO. The CTO must have enough business savvy and communication skills to create an

Title	Responsibility
Chief technology officer (CTO)	Track emerging technologies Advise on technology adoption Design and manage IT architecture to ensure consistency and compliance
Chief knowledge officer (CKO)	Create knowledge management infrastructure Build a knowledge culture Make corporate knowledge pay off
Chief telecommunications officer (CTO)	Manage phones, networks, and other communications technology across entire enterprise
Chief network officer (CNO)	Build and maintain internal and external networks
Chief resource officer (CRO)	Manage outsourcing relationships
Chief information security officer (CISO)	Ensure information management practices are consistent with security requirements
Chief privacy officer (CPO)	Responsible for processes and practices that ensure privacy concerns of customers, employees, and vendors are met

FIGURE 8.1 The CIO's lieutenants.

organizational vision for new technologies, as well as to oversee and manage the firm's technological operations and infrastructure. The new position is often created because one person isn't qualified to fill the broadly defined CIO role.

New "chief" roles spring up almost daily as enterprises try to share the complex and growing responsibilities of managing IT. Giving someone the title of "chief" is one way to signal that this individual is ultimately responsible for decisions in their area, even though he or she does not report directly to the CEO of the enterprise. This individual is recognized to be the most senior person in the organization charged with responsibility for that functional area. For example, Earthlink, one of the largest U.S. information service providers (ISPs), created the office of chief privacy officer (CPO) to interface with the FBI and privacy advocates about the mandated use of Carnivore, a controversial e-mail surveillance tool. The CPOs at AllAdvantage.com, AT&T, and Excite@home represent customers' privacy interests in negotiations with business developers, top management, and technology executives.[7] General Motors established divisional CIO positions that report to the corporate CIO.[8] Other firms eliminated the CIO altogether in favor of some configuration of the typically subordinate positions. These enterprises hope that flatter organizations will prove more effective.

Other Information Systems Organizational Roles

In addition to the CIO role, MIS organizations are home to many different types of professionals. Figure 8.2 describes some of the most common roles such as IS manager, system developer, business analysts, database administrator (DBA), operations personnel, support personnel, developer, and Web-based roles. Some of the many other roles within an IS organization include networking specialists, implementation consultants, and vendor relationship specialists. The simplified IS organization chart shown in Figure 8.3 gives a view of the reporting relationships that can exist.

▶ INFORMATION SYSTEMS ORGANIZATION PROCESSES

The general manager needs to understand the processes internal to the IS group in order to interact effectively with that group to accomplish business goals. Several processes that typify most organizations' IS, as well as the personnel responsible for performing them, are discussed next.

Systems Development

The primary processes performed by most IS organizations are that of building and developing systems. Systems development itself is discussed in more detail in

---

[7] Steve Ulfleder, "ohNo, Not Another O," *CIO Magazine* (January 15, 2001), available at http://www.cio.com/archive/011501/ohno_content.html (accessed June 21, 2002).

[8] Lauren Gibbons Paul, "A Separate Piece," *CIO Magazine* (October 15, 1998).

Job Title	Job Description	Needed Skills
IS Manager	Implement strategy; lead systems implementation projects; counterpart to general manager	Understand both business and technology; can see "big picture" and details of operations
System Developer	Write new software applications; upgrade and maintain existing systems. Some systems developers (i.e., Web developers) code and implement Web-based systems that are seen by both internal employees and external stakeholders.	Programming abilities, familiarity with systems development and related life cycle methodologies, creative problem-solving talents, cross-technology knowledge
Business Analyst	Translate business requirements into implementable IT solutions	Understand core business requirements; technical and communication skills
Database Administrator (DBA)	Implement and maintain the software and hardware needed for corporate data	Knowledge of technology: database management systems, multiple operating systems, hardware products and services, programming languages, telecommunications, and other technologies that use databases
Operations Personnel	Run, monitor, and maintain the production hardware and software applications within an IS organization; often found in data centers where mainframes and servers are housed	Specialized knowledge to monitor and maintain hardware and software
Support Personnel	Fill support roles such as help desk, project management, and desktop services	Skills vary depending upon role
Developer	Develop new processes, methodologies, products and services; may serve on cross-functional teams	Multidisciplinary skills to develop or identify next generation products
Webmaster	Bear responsibility for all Web activities (Web sites viewed internally and externally)	Extensive knowledge of coding, design, hyper-linking, and Web trends
Web Designer	Design the interface for each Web page	Knowledge of user interface design, graphic arts or other visual expertise

FIGURE 8.2 IS organization roles.

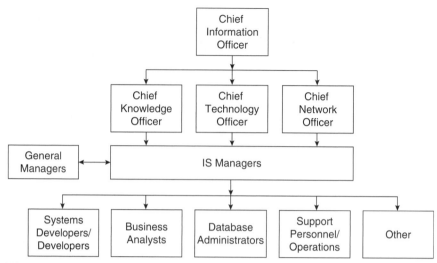

FIGURE 8.3   Sample IS organization chart.

Chapter 10, the chapter on project management. In this core IS organization process, business analysts and systems developers work together in analyzing needs, designing the software, writing or coding the software, and testing to make sure the software works and meets the business objectives. However, with the proliferation of software companies offering a wide range of packages off the shelf, the trend is toward buying, rather than making, systems. In that case, systems development processes identify and acquire outside software packages to fill a need for individuals in the organizations. This process also includes installing the package and setting any necessary options and parameters to ensure the system runs properly.

One special case of systems development is Web-based systems development. Applications that run on the Web require expertise that differs from that required to develop traditional systems. Most IS organizations follow one set of processes for developing systems that run on their internal computers and service internal employees, and a second set of processes (and often languages) to develop Web-based systems.

Systems Maintenance

Once installed, systems do not function entirely on their own. Many people work toward their continued maintenance. For instance, once a general ledger system is installed, support personnel or DBAs monitor the daily processing of transactions and reports. Developers and business personnel address post-implementation needs, such as writing additional reports or reconciling system errors. Systems developers provide upgrades as they become available. General business managers interact with IS managers and developers to arrange access to new reports, or to report problems they experience with systems functioning.

Data Center Operations

Data centers are common among enterprises that take a more centralized approach to IS organization. The data center typically houses large mainframe computers or rows of servers. Most of the company's data and business applications reside somewhere in the data center alongside remote-access technologies that connect the enterprise to the outside world.

Data center personnel vary in skill, but most maintain familiarity with the nuts and bolts of the installed hardware and software. Operations personnel run, monitor, and maintain a company's production hardware and software applications. Often, the most technical of the support personnel can be found in data centers due to the mission-critical nature of the technologies that reside there.

General managers rarely have direct contact with data center personnel unless they experience processing problems. Such problems are usually reported to IS managers during processing meetings attended by business and IS representatives. Although these reports are sometimes made electronically, larger problems often require direct contact. A typical report looks similar to Figure 8.4.

Information Management and Database Administration

Managing the information in the enterprise is of particular concern to the MIS organization. This text devotes an entire chapter to knowledge management (Chapter 11), however the management of the data itself is a process unique to the MIS group. This process includes the activities of collecting and storing the actual data created, developed, or discovered by the enterprise. For example, deciding on the format of the stored data, the location of the stored data, and the indexing system are tasks typically done by database administration processes.

Internet Services

Such technologies as intranets, extranets, Web pages, and e-mail are becoming essential in most business environments. General managers must interact with the Web master, Web designers, and Web developers who develop and maintain

Problem Ticket #	Description of Problem	Resolution of Problem	Contact	Status	Cost of Non-Conformance
PR-17390	Job # 182 ended abnormally due to a disk failure	*2200 hours—* Problem detected *2300 hours—* Bad disk replaced *2310 hours—* Job restarted	Sally Operator	Closed	Delay did not affect processing window

FIGURE 8.4 Morning problem report example.

Internet capabilities. Because levels of these services vary greatly with each organization, working with the right person is essential. Often Internet business needs remain ambiguous unless the general manager and IS staff can collaborate to develop a strong vision for the enterprise.

To implement a successful Web site, the IS manager and the general manager must agree on a team to support a variety of activities. At a minimum, processes needed by an organization to run a robust Web page include the site design process and the site maintenance process. Increasingly, companies are considering outsourcing many of their Web-based activities, which means that someone must manage and coordinate these services in order to ensure that the right services are provided. For example, should managers decide to use a Web-based ERP system, someone in either the IS organization or the business itself must be charged with managing the vendor and with ensuring that the appropriate level of service is obtained.

Networking Services

Since the early 1980s, networks have grown tremendously, resulting in a growth of networking groups as well. When problems connecting to the local area network (LAN) arise or when a new user needs to set up new PCs for a department, the networking group eventually processes the request. This side of the IS organization is visible to most end users.

Networking groups design network architecture. They also build and maintain the network infrastructure, keeping abreast of the latest technology and anticipating future needs. Upgrading networks is often expensive and slow, so anticipating future needs is an important concern. Networking people tend to be in high demand. The wide range of technologies on the market and the variable nature of networks require personnel who can stay abreast of new technologies and understand how to use them within a given network architecture.

Often the set of processes that manage the physical telephone network is called telecommunications. Although some may not realize that telecommunications falls under the purview of IS, it constitutes a vitally important strategic concern. Telephone systems, certain networking systems, and access to the Internet all may fall under the rubric of telecommunications. As new wireless technologies become popular, they are also managed by these processes. General managers should concern themselves with telecommunications because the quality of service provided affects the daily operations of the business. Telephones that do not work or voice mail systems that lose messages can affect the bottom line. Moreover, telecommunications costs are typically charged back to the business area cost center.

New Technology Introduction

Staying abreast of new technology is one of the most important functions an IS organization can perform, yet it is sometimes neglected. Missing technology trends gives the competition the chance to capitalize on new cost savings or sources of revenue. IT assumes such strategic importance in the enterprise that new technology deserves a particular focus within IS.

The chief technology officer (CTO) or new technology groups assess the costs and benefits of new technologies for the enterprise. They are the way many innovations formally enter an organization. The CTO or new technology group works closely with business groups to determine which technologies can provide the greatest benefit and how the technologies might impact the organization. Technology personnel and developers stay abreast of trends through online newsletters, periodicals, trade shows, product testing, and close relationships with user groups and vendors.

Resource Management

Business projects often require support from personnel with specific IS skills. On occasions when these skills are not to be found within the IS organization, business managers must still rely on IS colleagues to aid in the search outside the organization. Sometimes, IS personnel directly manage all hiring or contracting for the required services because they can leverage specialized knowledge of contract labor houses, offshore outsourcing shops, or negotiated outsourcing relationships.

General Support

Processes in place to support day-to-day business operations vary depending on the size of the enterprise and the levels of support required. Typically, support requests are centralized so they can be tracked for quality control purposes. This centralization simplifies the interaction between business and IS. Often, a central support desk dispatches support personnel to address the problem at hand.

Often IS organizations maintain first client contact through a centralized help desk even for such diverse services as networking and telecommunications. The help desk serves as the primary point of contact for technical questions and problem reporting. Centralizing help desk activities allows IS managers to track performance and results more efficiently. It also gives businesspeople a single phone number or e-mail address to remember in times of need.

Help desks are not usually manned by people who solve the problem. Help desk personnel collect pertinent information, record it, determine its priority, contact the appropriate support personnel, and follow up with the business contacts with updates or resolution information. For help beyond daily support, most organizations also maintain a customer service request (CSR) process. A paper or electronic form is used to allow a businessperson to describe the nature of the request, its priority, the contact point, and the appropriate cost center. CSRs initiate much of the work in IS organizations.

► WHAT A MANAGER CAN EXPECT FROM THE IS DEPARTMENT

This chapter explored the roles and processes done by a typical MIS organization. In particular, we looked at the MIS department from an organizational perspective. We now turn to the customer of the MIS organization, the general manager or "user" of the systems. What can a manager expect from the IS department?

Managers must learn what to expect from the IS organization so they can plan and implement business strategy accordingly. A manager can expect seven core activities: (1) anticipating new technologies, (2) participating in setting and implementing strategic goals, (3) innovating current processes, (4) managing supplier relationships, (5) establishing architecture platforms and standards, (6) planning for business discontinuities, and (7) managing human resources.[9]

Anticipating New Technologies

Given the breakneck speeds at which technology moves, IT must keep an eye toward the horizon in order for an enterprise to leverage state-of-the art tools. Doing so is not as simple as saying, "We need the latest version of WareSoft Version 2.1." IT must weigh the risks and potential benefits of early adoption of technology. IT must understand technology trends so that the enterprise does not invest heavily in new technologies that quickly become obsolete or incompatible with other enterprise standards. This situation is not unlike the situation many experienced after investing in the Beta format for VCRs, only to find themselves with useless equipment and tapes when the VHS format became the de facto standard. To correctly assess the enterprise's needs, business and IS staff must work closely to evaluate which technologies can best advance the business strategy. It is the job of the IS department to scout new technology trends and help the business integrate them into planning and operations.

Strategic Direction

Ideally, IS staff enable business managers to achieve strategic goals by acting as consultants or by teaching them about developing technologies. As consultants, IS can advise managers on best practices within IT and work with them to develop IT-enhanced solutions to business problems. For example, Jim Dowling, the director of corporate information systems at Bose Corporation, designated more than 100 of his IT personnel as internal IT consultants.[10] He asked them to fulfill a role similar to that of external consultants in that they understand and address both technical and business issues. As consultants, they act with a degree of autonomy from the current IT organization; their status provides them unusual flexibility in order to move quickly and, ultimately, save money.

IS personnel also educate managers about current technologies as well as IT trends. Sharing business and technical knowledge between groups encourages better, more informed decisions across the enterprise. No longer anonymous techies, IS staff are partners in moving the enterprise forward. IS staff must seek to initiate, foster, and grow strong partnerships with their business colleagues. Greg Walton, vice president and CIO at Carilion Health System in Roanoke, Virginia, for instance, stations his internal consultants within the enterprise

[9] John F. Rockart, Michael J. Earl, and Jeanne W. Ross, "Eight Imperatives for the New IT Organization," *Sloan Management Review* (Fall 1996), pp. 52–53.

[10] Alan S. Horowitz, "IS Ambassadors," *Computerworld* (April 20, 1998), available at http://www.computerworld.com/home/features.nsf/all/980420mgt.

business units.[11] Thus, Carilion's IT professionals represent both business concerns to the IS organization and IS concerns to the business leaders. This tighter relationship improves integration between systems and business and helps in using IT to the company's strategic advantage.

Process Innovation

IT staff, especially IS managers, business analysts and developers, work with managers to innovate processes that can benefit from technological solutions. Such solutions can range from installing voice mail to networking personal computers or automating general ledger transactions. Business process reviews usually begin with a survey of best practices. IT becomes an integral component of new processes designed for the enterprise. Thus, IS personnel can play a crucial role by designing systems that facilitate these new ways of doing business.

When systems are incorrectly designed, or when IS processes do not function correctly, IS can become a "disabler" of innovation. In some cases, the lack of flexibility in existing systems, and the reluctance to discard technology before the investment return is realized, block business managers from implementing decisions they would otherwise choose to make.

Supplier Management

As more companies adopt outsourcing as a means of controlling IT costs and acquiring "best of breed" capabilities, managing these supplier relationships becomes increasingly important. IS must maximize the benefit of these relationships to the enterprise and preempt problems that might occur. Failure in this regard could result in deteriorating quality of service, loss of competitive advantage, costly contract disputes, low morale, and loss of key personnel.

One of the most famous illustrations of supplier management derives from the experience of an originator of the concept: the Eastman Kodak Company. In 1989, Kodak outsourced its data center operations to IBM, its network to Digital Equipment Company, and its desktop supply and support operations to Businessland.[12] Kodak managed these relationships through strategic alliances.[13] Kodak retained IS staff to act on behalf of its business personnel with outsource vendors. Vendor contracts created incentives for new investment in technology and provided enough flexibility to encourage quick problem resolution. Vendors made fair profits and received additional business if they performed well. Within a couple of years, Kodak's capital expenditures attributable to computing dropped by 90 percent.[14] Its approach to supplier management became a model

[11] *Ibid.*

[12] L. Applegate and R. Montealegre, "Eastman Kodak Co: Managing Information Systems Through Strategic Alliances," Harvard Business School case 192030 (September 1995).

[13] Anthony DiRomualdo and Vijay Gurbaxani, "Strategic Intent for IT Outsourcing," *Sloan Management Review* (June 22, 1998).

[14] Steven L. Alter, *Information Systems: A Manager's Perspective* (San Francisco: Benjamin Cummings, 1996).

emulated by Continental Bank, General Dynamics, Continental Airlines, and National Car Rental.[15]

Architecture and Standards

Given the complex nature of IT in the enterprise, the role of IS in developing, maintaining, and communicating standards is critical. Failure could mean increased maintenance costs due to incompatibilities between platforms, redundant or incorrect data, and slow processing. For example, precise naming standards are crucial in implementing a new data warehouse or accounts payable system. Even small variations in invoice entries—the difference between showing a payment to "IBM," "I.B.M.," or "International Business Machines"—could yield incomplete information when business managers query the data warehouse to understand how much was paid to the vendor in a given period. Inconsistent data undermines the integrity of a data warehouse.

Business Continuity Planning

The events of September 11, 2001, presented disaster impacts that few organizations ever face. Yet, it is important for companies to anticipate this and other human-made disasters, as well as natural disasters created by hurricanes, tornadoes, floods, or other forces of nature. Business continuity planning by the MIS organization ensures that the company is not put out of business by failing information systems. We explored this topic in Chapter 6, but we reiterate it here because of its critical role in MIS organizations.

Because of its business continuity planning, the Nasdaq was back up and trading within six days of the World Trade Center catastrophe. Nasdaq used extensive Y2K and decimalization plans to help rehearse for disasters that might force it to discontinue trading. Its plan included an established 24/7 emergency "crisis line" teleconference call; several site-specific hotlines to inform staff of site closures, redirections, and status; a Website with real-time situation updates; three separate contact phone groups; and psychological and emotional counseling availability to employees within a day.[16] Because the information resources are so integral to business operations, the IS organization is typically in charge of planning for possible scenarios leading to business discontinuity. This planning may include establishing "cold sites" or "hot sites" where computing can be brought back up if the main site is put out of commission. It also means preparing, distributing, and rehearsing responses to situations that would cause a company to stop its operations for any reason.

Human Resource Management

IS must manage its own resources. Doing so means providing sufficient business and technical training so that staff can perform effectively and retain their value to

[15] Mary C. Lacity, Leslie P. Willcocks, and David F. Feeny, "The Value of Selective IT Sourcing," *Sloan Management Review* (March 22, 1996).
[16] Gregor Bailar, "Nasdaq Lessons Learned from Sept. 11," *CIO Magazine* (October 24, 2001), available at http://www.cio.com/online/102401_nasdaq.html.

the enterprise. Additional human resource activities include hiring and firing, training, tracking time, and managing budgets, operations, and projects. These activities often affect one another. For example, some companies seek to fill positions that require "hot" skills, or technology skills that are in high demand, by hiring IS staff who have acquired and used the needed skills at other organizations. Other companies turn to electronic immigration for immediate fulfillment of hot skills needs. Still other companies adopt a policy of growing their own. They attempt to hire and retain their employees for the employees' entire work careers. To make sure that these employees have hot skills when needed, they maintain a skills inventory and train employees according to a plan that reflects anticipated technical needs. Because most IS organizations lack their own human resource (HR) departments, individual managers bear these responsibilities. It is often wise for them to work with company HR personnel, who may be familiar with interviewing approaches, personnel laws, regulations, and trends. For example, HR personnel may be aware of professional issues related to the retirement of baby boomers that IS managers may not tend to consider.

Most IS activities fall within the categories described in this section. In addition, however, business managers can expect the user management activities shown in Figure 8.5.

► WHAT THE IS ORGANIZATION DOES NOT DO

This chapter presented typical roles and processes for IS organizations. Although most IS professionals are asked to perform a wide range of tasks for their organization, in reality the IS organization should not do a number of specific tasks. Clearly, the IS organization does not directly do other core business functions such as selling, manufacturing, and accounting. Sometimes, however, managers of these functions

Traditional IT Activities (often supplied through alliances with vendors)	The New IT Activities (often supplied by MIS organization)	User's Activities (Supplied by IS person on payroll in end user department)
• Data Center Management • Network Management • Application Design, Development and Maintenance • Desktop Hardware Procurement, Installation, and Maintenance	• Architecture, Standards and Technology Planning • IT Strategic Planning • Process Innovation • Vendor Management • Training and Internal Consulting	• Technology scanning and development • Applications Strategy • Choose and maintain Desktop, Laptop, Personal Digital Assistant or other Personal Devices • Implementation

FIGURE 8.5 User management activities.
Source: Adapted from J. Ownes, "Transforming the Informations Systems Organization," CISR Endicott House XXIX presentation (December 2–3, 1993)

inadvertently delegate key operational decisions to the IS organization. When general managers ask the IS professional to build an information system for their organization and do not become active partners in the design of that system, they are in effect turning over control of their business operations. Likewise, asking an IS professional to implement a software package without partnering with that professional to ensure the package not only meets current needs, but future needs as well, is ceding control. The IS organization does not design business processes.

As discussed in Chapter 2, when using IS for strategic advantage, the general manager, not the IS professional, sets business strategy. However, in many organizations, the general manager delegates critical technology decisions to the CIO, which in turn may limit the strategic options available to the firm. The role for the IS professional in the discussion of strategy centers on suggesting technologies and applications that enable strategy, identifying limits to the technologies and applications under consideration, and consulting with all those involved with setting strategic direction to make sure they properly consider the role and impact of IS on the decisions they make. The IS organization does not set business strategy.

▶ ORGANIZING AND CONTROLLING IS PROCESSES

IS managers confront many of the same challenges other managers face in today's business environment. How IS managers address them directly affects the work of the general managers. The earlier example concerning naming standards illustrates this point. Because small decisions, such as a standard spelling for "IBM" on vendor payments, can have far-reaching effects, larger decisions, especially strategic ones, may reach even further. This section discusses three key issues related to organizing and managing IS processes: outsourcing, structuring, and globalization.

Outsourcing

Beginning in the 1970s, some IT managers turned to outsourcing as an important weapon in the battle to control costs. **Outsourcing** means the purchase of a good or service that was previously provided internally. With IT outsourcing an outside vendor provides IT services traditionally provided by the internal MIS department. Over the years, however, certain motives for outsourcing changed. This section examines outsourcing's drivers and disadvantages, models for outsourcing, and ways of avoiding pitfalls.

Outsourcing Drivers

What factors drive companies to outsource? One of the most common is the need to reduce costs. Outsourcing suppliers derive savings from economies of scale. They realize these economies through centralized data centers, preferential contracts with suppliers, and large pools of technical expertise. Most often, enterprises lack such resources on a sufficient scale within their own IS departments. A single company may need only 5,000 PCs, but an outsourcer can negotiate a contract for 50,000 and achieve a much lower unit cost.

A second common factor driving companies to outsource is to help a company transition to new technologies. Outsourcers generally provide access to larger pools of talent and more current knowledge of advancing technologies. For example, many outsourcers gained vast experience solving Y2K problems, whereas IS staff within a single company only had limited experience. The vendor's experienced consultants were more readily available to the marketplace than any comparably trained and experienced IT professionals who might be recruitable for in-house employment. Many companies turned to outsourcers to help them implement Web sites, EPR, and client/server systems.

Third, by bringing in outside expertise, management often can focus less attention on IS operations and more on information itself. MIS department personnel manage the relationships with outsourcers and are ultimately still responsible for IS services. Using outsourcers, which are separate businesses rather than internal departments, frees up managers to devote their energies to areas that reflect core competencies for the business.

Fourth, to the extent that outsourcers specialize in IS services, they are likely to understand how to hire, manage, and retain IS staff effectively. An outsourcer often can offer IS personnel a professional environment that a typical company cannot afford to build. For example, a Web designer would have responsibility for one Web site within a company, but for multiple sites at an outsourcer. It becomes the outsourcer's responsibility to find, train, and retain highly marketable IT talent. An outsourcing vendor often can provide greater opportunity for training and advancement in IT than can a single MIS organization. Outsourcing relieves an employer of costly investments in continuous training so that IT staff can keep current with marketplace technologies, and the headaches of hiring and retaining a staff that easily can change jobs with more pay or other lures.

Fifth, as long as contract terms effectively address contingencies, the larger resources of an outsourcer provide greater capacity on demand. For instance, at year-end, outsourcers potentially can allocate additional mainframe capacity to ensure timely completion of nightly processing in a manner that would be impossible for an enterprise running its own bare-bones data center.

Finally, an outsourcer may help a company overcome inertia to consolidate data centers that could not be consolidated by an internal group, or following a merger or acquisition. Outsourcing may also offer an infusion of cash as a company sells its equipment to the outsourcing vendor. These drivers are summarized in Figure 8.6.

Outsourcing Disadvantages

Opponents of outsourcing cite a number of disadvantages (see Figure 8.6). A manager should consider each of these before making a decision about outsourcing. Each can be mitigated with effective planning and ongoing management.

First, outsourcing requires that a company surrender a degree of control over critical aspects of the enterprise. The potential loss of control could extend to several areas: control of the project, scope creep, the technologies, the costs, and their company's IT direction. By turning over data center operations, for example, a

Drivers	Disadvantages
Offer cost savings	Abdication of control
Ease transition to new technologies	High switching costs
Offer better strategic focus	Lack of technological innovation
Provide better management of IS staff	Loss of strategic advantage
Handle peaks	Reliance on outsourcer
Consolidate data centers	Problems with security/confidentiality
Infuse cash	Evaporization of cost savings

FIGURE 8.6   Drivers and disadvantages of outsourcing.

company puts itself at the mercy of an outsourcer's ability to manage this function effectively. A manager must choose an outsourcer carefully and negotiate terms that will support an effective working relationship.

Second, outsourcing decisions can be difficult and expensive to reverse. Unless experienced IT staff can contribute elsewhere in the firm, outsourcing major IT functions means staff will be lost either to the outsourcers or to other companies. When IT staff get news that their company is considering outsourcing, they often seek work elsewhere. Even when staff are hired by the outsourcer to handle the account, they may be transferred to other accounts, taking with them critical knowledge. If an outsourcing relationship becomes difficult to manage, or if anticipated cost savings are not realized, **backsourcing,** or returning to an "in-sourced" status, requires the enterprise to acquire the necessary infrastructure and staff.

Third, outsourcing contracts may not adequately anticipate new technological capabilities. Outsourcers may not recommend so-called bleeding edge technologies for fear of losing money in the process of implementation and support, even if implementation would best serve the client. Thus, poorly planned outsourcing risks a loss in IT flexibility. For example, some outsourcers were slow to adopt Internet technologies for their clients because they feared the benefits would not be as tangible as the costs of entering the market. This reluctance impinged on clients' ability to realize business strategies involving e-business.

Fourth, by surrendering IT functions, a company gives up any real potential to develop them for competitive advantage—unless, of course, the outsourcing agreement is sophisticated enough to comprehend developing such advantage in tandem with the outsourcing company. However, even these partnerships potentially compromise the advantage when ownership is shared with the outsourcer, and the advantage may become available to the outsourcer's other clients. Under many circumstances, the outsourcer becomes the primary owner of any technological solutions developed, which allows the outsourcer to leverage the knowledge to benefit other clients, possibly even competitors of the initial client.

Fifth, contract terms may leave clients highly dependent on their vendor, with little recourse in terms of terminating troublesome vendor relationships. Outsourcers avoid entering relationships in which they might face summary dismissal. Clients must ensure that contract terms allow them the flexibility they require to manage and, if necessary, sever supplier relationships. The 10-year contracts that were so popular in the early 1990s are being replaced with shorter duration contracts lasting 3–5 years. The contracts are being tightened by adding clauses describing actions to be taken in the event of a deterioration in quality of service or noncompliance to service-level agreements. Service levels, baseline period measurements, growth rates, and service volume fluctuations are specified to reduce opportunistic behavior on the part of the outsourcing vendor. Research demonstrates that tighter contracts tend to lead to more successful outsourcing arrangements.[17] Unfortunately, a tight contract does not provide much solace to an outsourcing company when a vendor goes out of business.

Sixth, when a company turns to an outsourcer, it must realize that its competitive secrets are harder to keep. Its databases are no longer kept in-house, and the outsourcer's other customers may have easier access to sensitive information.

Finally, although many companies turn to outsourcing because of perceived cost savings, these savings may never be realized. Typically, the cost savings are premised upon activities that were performed by the company. However, implementation of new technologies may fail to generate any savings because the old processes upon which they were premised are no longer performed. Further, the outsourcing company is, to some extent, at the mercy of the outsourcer. Increased volumes due to unspecified growth, software upgrades, or new technologies not anticipated in the contract may end up costing a firm considerably more than it anticipated when it signed the contract. Finally, some savings, while real, may be hard to measure.

Outsourcing Models

The classic outsourcing model dictates that an enterprise should outsource only those functions that do not give it competitive advantage. For instance, mainframe computer maintenance and monitoring are not often considered core competencies of an enterprise and therefore are often farmed to vendors such as Computer Sciences Corporation or Electronic Data Systems. In the early days of outsourcing, such contracts ran long term—often for 10 years or more. Frequently, outsourcers took over entire IS departments, including people, equipment, and management responsibility. This classic approach prevailed through most of the 1970s and 1980s, but then experienced a decline in popularity.

In 1989, Kodak's multivendor approach to meeting its IS needs created the "Kodak effect." Kodak's watershed outsourcing arrangement ushered in changes to outsourcing practices in the 1990s that put all IS activities up for grabs, including aspects that provide competitive advantage. As relationships with outsourcers become more sophisticated, companies realize that even such essential functions as customer service are sometimes better managed by experts on the outside. In addition, the ubiquity of the Internet spawns a series of new application service providers (ASPs) who perform similar services using Web-based applications.

[17] See, for example, C. Saunders, M. Gebelt, and Q. Hu, "Achieving Success in Information Systems Outsourcing," *California Management Review*, 39, 2 (1997), pp. 63–79; and M. Lacity and R. Hirschheim, *Information Systems Outsourcing: Myths, Metaphors and Realities* (New York: John Wiley & Sons, 1995).

Application Service Provider Model   An **application service provider (ASP)** is a company that "rents" the use of an application to the customer. In return, the ASP provides not only the software, but also the infrastructure, people, and maintenance to run it. It is different from the traditional outsourcing relationship in which an entire IS shop is run by an outside organization. With an ASP, the outsourcing occurs application by application. The goal is to provide trouble-free operation for the customer. This model is particularly useful for the IS that are necessary, but not core, to the business. Companies use ASPs to free up IT staff, combine data resources, rapidly deploy new applications, control a widely distributed user base, develop a non-IT-based application, implement new technologies, and in many other ways. For example, Agillion.com offers a site for the small businessperson. The site offers tools for managing customers, interacting with customers, and supporting the marketing, sales, and communications functions throughout the business. When a customer uses Agillion.com, all information processing is done at Agillion.com's computer center, not at the customer's computer. Agillion.com, in essence, proposes to be the information systems (IS) team for its customers. A large number of ASPs are available; WebHarbor.com offers a search engine to help locate the ASP that offers exactly the services needed.

First among the many benefits to using ASPs, in this age of the IS professional shortage, is that ASPs relieve their customers of the burden of finding and hiring IS staff. Second, the ASP is typically responsible for security and maintenance of the systems, which makes it easier to scale and manage systems. Third, ASPs deploy and install new applications, making it possible to manage the uneven requirements typically associated with these activities. By relying on ASPs, IS organizations can focus their resources on core business applications that are not only critical to the business, but provide strategic or operational advantages. Finally, companies turn to ASPs to provide the infrastructure and applications necessary to get the business up and running. The CEO of Barnesandnoble.com commented that his company plans to outsource nearly its entire Web infrastructure. "We're not going to be in the server business. I want to run the interface, the content, and the user experience. But I don't want to have to power it myself," he said.[18]

Full vs. Selective Outsourcing Models   Once a company decides to outsource, despite possible disadvantages, it must decide whether to pursue it fully or selectively. As the term **full outsourcing** implies, an enterprise can outsource all its IT functions from desktop services to software development. An enterprise would outsource everything if it does not view IT as a strategic advantage that it needs to cultivate internally. Full outsourcing can free resources to be employed in areas that add greater value. It can also reduce overall cost per transaction due to size and economies of scale.[19] Many companies outsource IT simply to allow their managers to focus attention on other business issues. Others outsource to accommodate growth and respond to their business environment. Palm Inc. had

[18] Carol Sliwa, "Internet Outsourcing Increasingly Popular," *ComputerWorld* (October 11, 1999), available at http://www.cnn.com/TECH/computing/9910/11/outsource.idg/ (accessed February 18, 2003)

[19] Tom Field, "An Outsourcing Buyer's Guide: Caveat Emptor," *CIO Magazine* (April 1, 1997).

no choice but to outsource when it split off from parent 3Com Corp. It was a $3 billion company with a 100 percent annual growth rate that had to build its internal capabilities quickly.[20]

With **selective outsourcing,** an enterprise chooses which IT capabilities to retain in-house and which to give to an outsider. A "best-of-breed" approach is taken in which suppliers are chosen for their expertise in specific technology areas. Areas include Web site hosting, business process application development, help desk support, networking and communications, and data center operations. Although an enterprise can acquire top-level skills and experience through such relationships, the effort required to manage them grows tremendously with each new supplier. Still, selective outsourcing gives greater flexibility and often better service due to the competitive market.[21] To illustrate, an enterprise might retain a Web development firm to handle electronic commerce and at the same time select a large outsourcer, such as Perot Systems, to assume mainframe maintenance. Such firms as GM and Southland Corporation have adopted this approach, also called "strategic sourcing."

To illustrate the ins and outs of selective and full outsourcing, consider the case of a company that pursued both approaches. British Petroleum (BP) selected only a few outsourcers with short-term contracts to meet its IT needs.[22] BP awarded Sema Group management of its data center, Science Applications International Corporation, its European IT facility management and company-wide applications support, and Syncordia, its telecommunications and telex networks. This arrangement was selective in that BP chose each company for its particular expertise, but full in that BP turned over a significant percentage of its IT to outsourcers. Thus, it gained the benefits of best of breed and competitive pricing along with fewer contract management worries and the ability to develop long-term relationships. BP encouraged the outsourcers to work together to provide high-quality services.

What were the results of BP's approach? The company saw its IT costs fall from $360 million in 1989 to $132 million in 1994. At the same time, it gained more flexible IT systems and higher-quality service. BP saw its IT staff shrink by 80 percent. The remaining staff became internal consultants throughout the company. In fact, BP is considering outsourcing its internal consultants to other companies. Not all outsourcing arrangements are so successful, but BP illustrates the best-case scenario.

Avoiding Outsourcing Pitfalls

Outsourcing decisions must be made with adequate care and deliberation. The steps outlined in Figure 8.7 are recommended when considering this option.

What is the future of outsourcing? Every enterprise faces different competitive pressures. These factors shape how it will view IT and how it will decide to leverage IT for the future. Most will need to outsource at least some IT functions. How each enterprise chooses to manage its outsourced functions will be crucial to its success.

[20] Lorraine Cosgrove Ware, "Adventures in Outsourcing," *CIO Magazine* (May 3, 2002), available at http://www2.cio.com/research/surveyreport.cfm?id=78 (accessed June 22, 2002).

[21] Tom Field, "An Outsourcing Buyer's Guide: Caveat Emptor," *CIO Magazine* (April 1, 1997).

[22] J. Cross, "IT Outsourcing: British Petroleum," *Harvard Business Review* (May–June 1995), pp. 94–102.

- Do not focus negotiation solely on price.
- Craft full life-cycle service contracts that occur in stages.
- Establish short-term supplier contracts.
- Use multiple, best-of-breed suppliers.
- Develop skills in contract management.
- Carefully evaluate your company's own capabilities.
- Thoroughly evaluate outsourcers' capabilities.
- Choose an outsourcer whose capabilities complement yours.
- Base a choice on cultural fit as well as technical expertise.
- Determine whether a particular outsourcing relationship produces a net benefit for your company.

FIGURE 8.7   Steps to avoid pitfalls.

▶ CENTRALIZED VS. DECENTRALIZED ORGANIZATIONAL STRUCTURES

Organizational approaches to IS evolved in a cyclic manner. At one end of the spectrum, **centralized IS organizations** bring together all staff, hardware, software, data, and processing into a single location. **Decentralized IS organizations** scatter these components in different locations to address local business needs. Companies' organizational strategies exist along a continuum from centralization to decentralization, with a combination of the two, called federalism, found in the middle (see Figure 8.8). Enterprises of all shapes and sizes can be found at any point along the continuum. Over time, however, each enterprise tends to gravitate toward one end of the continuum or the other, and often a reorganization is in reality a change from one end to the other.

   To illustrate these tendencies, consider the different approaches taken to organize IS in the five eras of information usage. (See Figure 8.9.) In the 1960s, mainframes dictated a centralized approach to IS because the mainframe resided in one physical location. Centralized decision making, purchasing, maintenance, and staff kept these early computing behemoths running.[23] The 1970s remained centralized due in part to the constraints of mainframe computing, although the minicomputer

FIGURE 8.8   Organizational continuum.

[23] Bill Laberis, "Recentralization: Breaking the News," *Computerworld* (June 29, 1998), p. 1.

	Era I 1960s	Era II 1970s	Era III 1980s	Era IV 1990s	Era V 2000+
Primary Role of IT	Efficiency / Automate existing paper-based processes	Effectivenes / Solve problems and create opportunities	Strategic / Increase individual and group effectiveness	Strategic / Transform industry/organization	Value creation / Create collaborative partnerships
Justify IT Expenditures	ROI	Increasing productivity and better decision quality	Competitive position	Competitive position	Adding value
Target of Systems	Organization	Organization/group	Individual manager/group	Business processes	Customer, supplier, ecosystem
Information Models	Application specific	Data-driven	User-driven	Business-driven	Knowledge-driven
Dominant Technology	Mainframe "centralized intelligence"	Minicomputer, mostly "centralized intelligence"	Networked, microcomputers "decentralized intelligence"	Client/Server, global "distributed intelligence"	Internet, global "ubiquitous intelligence"
Basis of Value	Scarcity	Scarcity	Scarcity	Plentitude	Plentitude
Underlying Economics	Economics of information bundled with economics of things	Economics of information bundled with economics of things	Economics of information bundled with economics of things	Economics of information separated from economics of things	Economics of information separated from economics of things

FIGURE 8.9 Eras of information usage in organizations.

began to create a rationale to decentralize. The 1980s saw the advent of the personal computer (PC). PCs allowed computing power to spread beyond the raised-floor, super-cooled rooms of mainframes. This phenomenon gave rise to decentralization, a trend that exploded with the advent of LANs and client/server technology. The Web, with its ubiquitous presence and fast network speeds, shifted some back to a more centralized approach. However, the increasingly global nature of many businesses makes complete centralization impossible. What are the most important considerations in deciding how much to centralize or decentralize? Figure 8.10 shows some of the advantages and disadvantages of each approach.

Approach	Advantages	Disadvantages	Companies Adopting
Centralized	• Global standards and common data • "One voice" when negotiating supplier contracts • Greater leverage in deploying strategic IT initiatives • Economies of scale and a shared cost structure • Access to large capacity • Better recruitment and training of IT professionals • Consistent with centralized enterprise structure	• Technology may not meet local needs • Slow support for strategic initiatives • Schism between business and IT organization • Us versus them mentality when technology problems occur • Lack of business unit control over overhead costs	Alcoa Levi-Strauss Mobil
Decentralized	• Technology customized to local business needs • Closer partnership between IT and business units • Greater flexibility • Reduced telecommunication costs • Consistency with decentralized enterprise structure • Business unit control over overhead costs	• Difficulty maintaining global standards and consistent data • Higher infrastructure costs • Difficulty negotiating preferential supplier agreements • Loss of control • Duplication of staff and data	Bethlehem Steel VeriFone

FIGURE 8.10   Advantages and disadvantages of organizational approaches.

The two approaches amalgamated in the 1990s. Companies began to adopt a strategy based on lessons learned from earlier years of centralization and decentralization. Most companies would like to achieve the advantages derived from both organizational paradigms. This desire leads to federalism.[24] **Federalism** is a structuring approach that distributes power, hardware, software, data, and personnel between a central IS group and IS in business units. Many companies adopt a form of federal IT, yet still count themselves as either decentralized or centralized, depending on their position on the continuum. Other companies, such as Home Depot, recognize this hybrid approach and actively seek to take advantage of its benefits. Figure 8.11 shows how these approaches interrelate.

Bethlehem Steel adopted a decentralized approach, which mirrors their decentralized business strategy. A global company that traces its roots to 1857 when it was called Saucona Iron Company, Bethlehem Steel has grown its revenues to roughly $4.4 billion and ships 8.6 million tons of steel annually.[25] Bethlehem produces high-quality steel products including hot and cold rolled sheet, carbon and alloy plates, coke, standard rails, forging blooms, billets, flatbars, and large-diameter pipe. The business

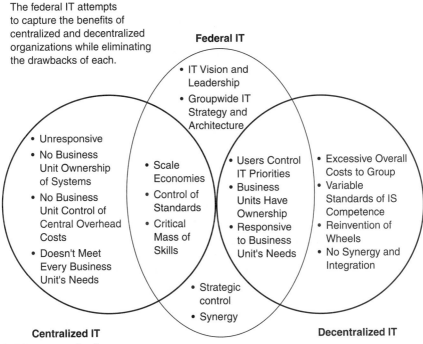

FIGURE 8.11 Federal IT.

Source: John F. Rockart, Michael J. Earl, Jeanne W. Ross, *Eight Imperatives for the New IT Organization, Sloan Management Review* (Fall 1996), pp. 52–53.

[24] John F. Rockart, Michael J. Earl, Jeanne W. Ross, "Eight Imperatives for the New IT Organization," *Sloan Management Review,* (Fall, 1996), pp. 52-53

[25] Information available from http://www.bethsteel.com (accessed February 12, 2003).

units themselves are decentralized, with major plants in Steelton, Pennsylvania; Sparrows Point, Maryland; Burns Harbor, Indiana; and Lackawanna, New York.

The challenge to Bethlehem is to develop new products that respond to alternatives to steel, to implement a capital-intensive facilities plan, to improve quality and cost-effectiveness, and to acquire and maintain human resource competencies.[26] Given these circumstances, Bethlehem and its sole IT provider, Electronic Data Systems, chose a decentralized approach to IT. Bethlehem managers believed that computing power and decision making should be located within local business units. Bethlehem found this approach effective and continues to explore its advantages.

On the other hand, a company that took a different approach is Levi Strauss, the company discussed earlier in this chapter. Under the guidance of new CIO Linda Glick, Levi Strauss adopted a centralized strategy. Levi Strauss management wanted to gain better control over strategic IT resources, minimize duplication of resources across its business, and maximize sharing of scarce resources. The managers decided that a centralized approach would achieve this goal.

Managing the Global Considerations

How does the management of IT differ when the scope of the organization is global, rather than just within one country? Typically, large global MIS organizations face many of the same organizational issues as any other global department. Managers must figure out how to manage when employees are in different time zones, speak different languages, have different customs and holidays, and come from different cultures. In the case of information management, various issues arise that put the business at risk beyond the typical global considerations. Figure 8.12 summarizes how a global IT perspective affects six information management issues.

▶ FOOD FOR THOUGHT: GOING OFFSHORE FOR IS DEVELOPMENT

Managing a global network from within a single enterprise is a challenge. Managing a global network, however, when different parts of it are owned by different enterprises greatly changes the management issues. Countries such as India, the Philippines, Israel, Ireland, and Canada offer MIS organizations an alternative to in-house systems development using a practice called offshoring. When the MIS organization uses contractor services, or even builds its own data center in a distant land, in effect it is engaged in **offshoring,** or **outsourcing offshore.**

Forrester Research found that 44 percent of the 45 surveyed companies with annual revenues exceeding $1 billion currently outsource offshore, and the remaining two-thirds of them expect to go offshore by 2003.[27] Because communications are made difficult by differences in culture, time zones, and, sometimes, language, outsourced tasks are usually those that can be well-specified.

[26] Thomas Conarty, Jr., "Redefining IS: We Are The Business," *Information Week*, p. 1.
[27] Tom Field, "Offshore Outsourcing Primer," *CIO.com* (April 1, 2002), available at http://www.cio.com/archive/040102/middle_sidebar_3.html (accessed June 25, 2002).

Issue	Global IT Perspective	Example
Political Stability	Investments in IT in a country with an unstable government should be carefully considered: How much do you invest? How risky is the investment?	Much offshoring is done with companies in India, a country that is facing an atomic war in its conflict with Pakistan.
Transparency	Domestically, an IT network can be end-to-end with little effort compared to global networks, which makes it difficult for these two types of systems to have the same look and feel, or, sometimes, to get to the data.	SAP-R3 is used to support production processes. When it is not installed in one country, managers cannot monitor the processes in that country the same way.
Business Continuity Planning	When crossing borders, it is important to make sure that contingency plans are in place and working.	After 9/11, many businesses are considering placing backup data centers in remote locations, but the concern when crossing borders is whether that data center will be available when/if needed.
Cultural Differences	Different countries have different cultures; some things are acceptable one place but not another. IT systems must not offend or insult those of a different culture	Using images or artifacts from one culture may be insulting to another culture. For example, DitchWitch could not use its logo globally because a witch is offensive in some countries.
Sourcing	Getting the IT hardware within every country of operation may be difficult. Some technologies cannot be exported from the United States, and other technologies cannot be imported into specific countries. Vendors do not always have the same technologies available in every country.	Some technology is considered a potential threat to national security, such as encryption technologies, so exporting it to some countries, especially those that are not political allies of the United States, is not possible.
Data Flow Across Borders	Data, especially private or personal data, are not allowed to cross some borders.	Brazil refused to let data come across its borders from other countries, making it difficult for businesses to integrate their Brazilian operations into the corporate operations.

FIGURE 8.12 Global considerations for the MIS organization.

Typically offshoring is an attractive business proposition because the labor rates in the distant country are much more favorable than in the home country of the enterprise. Programmer salaries can be a fraction of those in the home country in part because the cost of living and the standard of living in the distant country is much lower.

Some countries are more attractive than others as hosts of offshoring business. With English as the predominate language of MIS, countries with a high English proficiency are more attractive than those where different languages prevail. Geopolitical risk is another factor that affects the use of offshore firms in a country. Countries on the verge of war, countries with high rates of crime, and countries without friendly relationships with the home country are typically not suitable candidates for this business. The level of technical infrastructure available in some countries also affects the attractiveness of a country. For example, some countries, such as Singapore, invested significantly in their IT infrastructure, in part to help build up the technical capabilities of their society.

Some countries make an entire industry of offshoring. India, for example, took an early mover advantage in this industry. With a large, low-cost, English-speaking labor pool, many entrepreneurs set up programming factories that produce high-quality software to meet even the toughest standards. One measure of the level of proficiency of the development processes within an MIS organization is the Software Engineering Institute's Capability Maturity Model (CMM). Level 1 means that the software development processes are immature, bordering on chaotic. Few processes are formally defined, and output is highly inconsistent. At the other end of the model is level 5, where processes are predictable, repeatable, highly refined, and consistently innovating, growing and incorporating feedback. Domestic MIS organizations strive for level 5, and measure their processes using this scale. The software factories in many of the Indian enterprises are well known for their CMM level 5 software development processes, making them extremely reliable, and ultimately desirable as vendors.

Risks come with offshoring, however. The Indian offshore outsourcing industry was hardest hit of all Pacific Rim industries in the month and a half following the 9/11 catastrophe. U.S.-based firms were reluctant to send their employees to India to discuss software needs or to enter into new outsourcing agreements, and Indian software developers had difficulty traveling to the United States to further project efforts. Offshore outsourcing in India has since regained its momentum, especially for larger companies. After 9/11, the attention paid to security and business continuity planning has grown fivefold.[28]

Offshoring raises the fundamental question of what do you send offshore, and what do you keep within your enterprise MIS organization. Will a CIO be losing some important learning opportunities if they outsource, and ultimately offshore, basic programming processes? What will the growth of the offshore industry mean for the information services vendors who traditionally offer a complete outsourcing service, from strategy definition to systems design to operations?

---

[28] "The Supply Side," News—Archives, available at http://www.tataelxsi.com/news/News42.htm (accessed June 25, 2002).

▶ SUMMARY

- The chief information officer (CIO) is a high-level IS officer who performs many important organizational functions including championing the organization, managing the IT architecture and infrastructure, participating in the development of business and IT strategy, planning for technology, overseeing application development, sourcing, overseeing training, advising on emerging technologies, interfacing with internal and external customers, and planning for business discontinuities.

- Key job titles found in traditional IS organizations include IS manager, system developer, business analyst, database administrator, operations personnel, support personnel, developer, and Web-based roles.

- Typical processes and tasks done by IS organizations include system development, system maintenance, data center operations, Internet and networking services, information management and data administration, new technology introduction, resource management, and general support.

- IS organizations can be expected to anticipate new technologies, set strategic direction, implement innovative uses of technology, work with supplier management, establish architecture and standards, plan for business continuity, and manage IS staff. It does not perform core business functions or independently develop business strategy.

- Because each organization differs depending on the nature of the enterprise, a business manager must know the particular needs of his or her organization—just as the IS manager must educate him or her on the IT available. If neither seeks the other out, then a schism can develop between business and IS. The enterprise will suffer due to missed opportunities and expensive mistakes

- In addition to understanding the structure of an IS organization, a manager should work with IT leaders to develop a lean, competitive enterprise in which IT acts as a strategic enabler. Working as a team, business and IS managers can fruitfully address crucial organizational issues such as outsourcing, centralization, and globalization. Such collaboration is essential if the enterprise is to remain afloat amid the difficult waters of business competition.

- Full or selective outsourcing allows an organization alternative top-performing IS services in-house. Cost savings or filling the gaps in the organization's IT skills are powerful drivers for outsourcing. The numerous risks involved in outsourcing arrangements must also be carefully assessed by IS and general managers alike.

- Alternative structuring approaches are possible. Centralized IS organizations place IT staff, hardware, software, and data in one location to promote control and efficiency. At the other end of the continuum, decentralized IS organizations with distributed resources can best meet the needs of local users. Federalism is in the middle of the centralized/decentralized continuum.

- Global MIS organizations face a host of issues that domestic departments avoid. Geopolitical risk, language and cultural barriers, business continuity planning, and transborder data flow issues must be reexamined in a global organization, and each country's laws and policies considered in the architectural design.

▶ KEY TERMS

application service
provider (ASP) (p. 202)
backsourcing (p. 200)
centralized IS organiza-
tion (p. 204)
chief information officer
(CIO) (p. 183)
chief information security
officer (CISO) (p. 187)

chief knowledge officer
(CKO) (p. 187)
chief technology officer
(CTO) (p. 187)
decentralized IS organi-
zation (p. 204)
federalism (p. 207)
full outsourcing (p. 202)
offshoring (p. 208)

outsourcing (p. 198)
selective outsourcing
(p. 203)

▶ DISCUSSION QUESTIONS

1. Using an organization with which you are familiar, describe the role of the most senior IS professional. Is that person a strategist or an operationalist?

2. What advantages does a CIO bring to a business? What might be the disadvantages of having a CIO?

3. The debate about centralization and decentralization is heating up again with the advent of network computing and the increasing use of the Internet. Why does the Internet make this debate topical?

4. The make-versus-buy decision is important every time a new application is requested of the IS group. What, in your opinion, are the key reasons an MIS organization should make its own systems? What are the key reasons it should buy an application?

5. When does using an ASP make sense for a large corporation that already has an IS organization? Give an example of when an ASP might make sense for a start-up company?

6. Premiere Technologies, Inc., a fast-growing supplier of communication services in more than 30 countries, provides an example of successful use of an ASP. Premiere began to implement an enterprise resource planning (ERP) system, and found that whenever there was a problem or call to work on a "revenue producing" information system, all resources were diverted from the implementation of the ERP.

   In fall of 1998, Premiere decided to outsource the ERP applications. The ASP came in not only to help plan how to best make the ERP system successful, but it bought and maintained the servers on which the ERP runs, installed and configured the ERP software, and staffed the help desk to make the deployment smooth. When Premiere acquires a new company, something they do regularly, the ASP takes care of incorporating the new acquisition into the ERP. By one estimate, Premiere saved about $3 million over five years by using the ASP instead of doing it themselves.[29]

   a. Discuss the advantages an ASP offers Premiere Technologies, Inc.?

   b. What possible risks are associated with Premiere's use of an ASP?

   c. What would determine which application(s) to give to an ASP versus the ones to keep in-house?

[29] Adapted from Cynthia Morgan, "ASPs Speak the Corporate Language," *Computerworld* (October 25, 1999), pp. 74–77.

HOSTILE IS OUTSOURCING: THE STORY OF MANUFACT

In February 1998, John Smith, 52 years old, hair graying but with a deep suntan, leaned back in his spacious deck chair and reread a letter from Jim Lawler, his former boss. In the letter, Lawler asked him to come back to his old company, to help sort out a tricky situation.

IS Outsourcing in ManuFact

Until March 1997, Smith had been IS director in ManuFact, a mid-sized European company in the kitchenware industry. He had the job for eight years, leading a centralized IT department of 39 people, with a budget of about US$4 million and a largely mainframe-based technology portfolio. Including three subsidiaries, ManuFact had a total of 3,500 employees, mainly in production and distribution. The financial situation was stable and good. Smith reorganized the IS capability from a marginally successful semi-independent subsidiary to an internal department, and received good feedback about his ability to keep the IT costs down and maintain a satisfactory service level.

In May 1996, Lawler took over as Smith's boss. Lawler, with a background as chief counsel for ManuFact, was part of a three-person top management committee with responsibility for administration, personnel, and legal issues as well as IS. Lawler was also a member of the board. He had little IT experience, but had read about "downsizing" and "facilities management" and wanted to know what these terms meant and whether they could apply in ManuFact. Lawler also wondered whether IS was running their operations as efficiently as they could. Smith thought so, but suggested looking into facilities management as an option. Lawler also asked about outsourcing the development side, but Smith did not think outsourcing was a good idea, given the high degree of company-specific knowledge needed there. In agreement with Lawler, Smith contacted the three main vendors of facilities management in the country, one of which was ISCorp, the local subsidiary of a large, international technology corporation. After some research and talks with the companies, Smith wrote a report to Lawler indicating that ManuFact, by employing facilities management, would save about $275,000 per year over a five-year period. However, the transition costs—personnel and to a certain extent the costs of getting out of some equipment contracts—would make it a break-even proposition at best.

When Smith went to discuss the report with Lawler, he was in for a shock: Lawler had been approached by ISCorp directly, and had entered an agreement with the local ISCorp office to outsource the entire IS department. ISCorp, which was keen to move into outsourcing as a new line of business, indicated that this move would save ManuFact $6 million over five years. The contract meant that all IS employees would be made redundant on November 15, but each would be offered work elsewhere within ISCorp. Lawler asked Smith to stay on to negotiate the contract with ISCorp and manage the transition.

Smith thought that, given the situation, the best he could do was to try and make the transition as smooth as possible. He soon found that the savings were nowhere close to what was promised, chiefly because ISCorp had underestimated the complexity of the systems, particularly in manufacturing. Eventually, ISCorp came back with an "extra bill" of $1.5 million to cover work not specified in the contract. Furthermore, Smith discovered that the number of system development hours specified by ISCorp was only half of what the IS department currently was putting in—but each hour was billed considerably higher. The IS department would have been less expensive than ISCorp if they had calculated with the same number of hours. However, Smith was not successful in communicating this point to Lawler.

ISCorp had expected 10 to15 of the system developers to continue with their current work for ManuFact as employees of ISCorp. However, when the outsourcing agreement was announced to the department, and ISCorp representatives showed up to negotiate, the employees refused to talk to them. Within two months, the whole department, save two developers, had quit and found new jobs—several of them on better terms than ManuFact had offered. ISCorp had to recruit and train new people, meaning that no development was done for nine months while the new employees and consultants from ISCorp tried to understand the systems. During this period, the corporate data center was closed, and the technology moved to ISCorp's premises.

Smith had not been successful in finding a new job. His severance terms included full salary payments for one year. Lawler had given Smith excellent recommendations, describing his handling of the transition as conscientious, competent, and professional.

The Situation in February 1998

In February 1998, the systems were finally running reliably, but substantial new systems development still had not started. Complaints from the line organization about ISCorp's lack of customer service were increasing. The subsidiary companies, which had not been consulted about the outsourcing, complained about an aging technology infrastructure. The outsourcing contract did not contain any provisions for upgrading the technology, effectively locking the company in at the same technology generation for the next five years.

Recently, Smith had heard that some of the subsidiaries were trying to break out of the outsourcing contract altogether, wanting to move on to new technology. Now, here he was, looking at the letter from Lawler, where he was asked to come back to help ManuFact sort out the situation.

Discussion Questions

1. Discuss advantages of outsourcing illustrated in the case.
2. Discuss the disadvantages of outsourcing that are exemplified in this case.
3. Discuss the outsourcing pitfalls that ManuFact fell into.
4. If Smith were to accept Lawler's offer and return to work for ManuFact, what do you suggest that he do?

Source: Excerpted from Espen Andersen, available at http://www.bi.no/dep2/infomgt/cases/manufact.html.

CHAPTER 9

FUNDING IT

The CIO of Avon Products, Inc., in New York relies heavily on hard-dollar metrics such as net present value (NPV) and internal rate of return (IRR) to demonstrate the business value resulting from IT investments. Although these are not the typical IT metrics, they are the language of business. Funding IT becomes a matter of speaking the language of business. "We apply all of the analytical rigor and financial ROI tools against each of our IT projects as well as other business projects," the CIO of Avon Products remarked. Avon uses payback, NPV, IRR, and risk analyses for every investment. Further, each IT project is monitored using a green/yellow/red-coded dashboard to convey the status as "on target," "warning," or "having serious problems." Monthly reports to the senior management team inform them about the status of major projects. Other business tools, such as investment-tracking databases, and monitors on capital spending, assist the CIO's office in managing the funds allocated to the IT group.[1]

The business side of IT is similar to the business itself. Projects are funded through budget allocations or a multitude of other sources, and managing those funds is done with prudent business practices. As the Avon's CIO comments indicate, the basic tools of finance and accounting are the basic tools for the financial management of IT, and further, for determining and communicating the value received from IT investments.

In this chapter we explore issues related to the financial side of IT. We begin by looking at ways of funding the IT department, then continue with an exploration of several ways to calculate the cost of IT investments, including total cost of ownership and activity based costing, and ways of monitoring IT investments once they are made. These topics are critical for the IT manager to understand, but a general manager must understand how the business of IT works in order to successfully propose, plan, manage, and use IT systems.

▶ FUNDING THE IT DEPARTMENT

Who pays for IT? The users? The IT department? The corporate function? Certain costs are associated with designing, developing, delivering, and maintaining the IT systems. How are these costs recovered? The three main funding methods are

[1] Adapted from Thomas Hoffman, "How Will You Prove IT Value?" *Computerworld* (January 6, 2003).

chargeback, allocation, and corporate budget. Both chargeback and allocation methods distribute the costs back to the businesses, departments, or individuals within the company. This distribution of costs is used for management reasons, so that managers can understand the costs associated with running their organization, or for tax reasons, where the costs associated with each business must be paid for by the appropriate business unit. Corporate budgeting, on the other hand, is a completely different funding method in which IT costs are not linked directly with any specific user or business unit; costs are recovered using corporate coffers.

Chargeback

With a **chargeback funding method,** IT costs are recovered by charging individuals, departments, or business units based on actual usage and cost. The IT department collects usage data on each system it runs. Rates for usage are calculated based on the actual cost to the IT group to run the system and billed out on a regular basis. For example, a desktop PC might be billed out at $100/month, which includes the cost of maintaining the system, any software license fees for the standard desktop configuration, e-mail, network access, a usage fee for the help desk, and other related services. Each department receives a bill showing them the number of desktops they have and the charge per desktop, the number of printers they have and the charge per printer, the number of servers they have and the charge per server, the amount of mainframe time they have used and the cost per second of that time, and so on. When the IT department wants to recover administrative and overhead costs using a chargeback system, these costs are built into rates charged for each of the services.

Chargeback systems are popular because they are viewed as the most equitable way to recover IT costs. Costs are distributed based on usage or consumption of resources, ensuring that the largest portion of the costs is paid for by the group or individual who consumes the most. Chargeback systems can also provide managers with the most options for managing and controlling their IT costs. For example, a manager may decide to use desktop systems rather than laptop systems because the unit charge is more advantageous financially. The chargeback system gives managers the details they need to understand both what IT resources they use and how to account for IT consumption in the cost of their products and services. Because the departments get a regular bill, they know exactly what their costs are.

Creating and managing a chargeback system, however, is a costly endeavor itself. IT departments must build systems to collect details that might not be needed for anything other than the bills they generate. For example, if PCs are the basis for charging for network time, then the network connect time per PC must be collected, stored, and analyzed each billing cycle. The data collection quickly becomes large and complex, which often results in complicated, difficult-to-understand bills. In addition, picking the charging criteria is more of an art than a science. For example, it is relatively easy to count the number of PCs located in a particular business unit, but is that number a good measure of the network resources used? It might be more accurate to charge based on units of network time used, but how would that be captured and calculated?

Allocation

To simplify the cost recovery process compared to the chargeback method, an allocation system can be used. An **allocation funding method** recovers costs based on something other than usage, such as revenues, login accounts, or number of employees. For example, suppose the total spending for IT for a year is $1 million for a company with 10,000 employees. A business unit with 1,000 employees would be responsible for 10 percent, or $100,000, of the total IT costs. Of course, with this type of allocation system, it does not matter whether these employees even use the IT; the department is still charged the same amount.

The allocation mechanism is simpler to implement and apply each month. Actual usage does not need to be captured. The rate charged is often fixed at the beginning of the year. It offers two main advantages. First, the level of detail required to calculate the allocations is much less, and for many organizations that aspect saves expense. Second, the charges from the IT department are constant, or at least expected, each period. Some organizations allocate the same amount each month to ensure predictability of the IT bill. Unlike the chargeback mechanism, where each bill opens up an opportunity for discussion about the charges incurred, the allocation mechanism seems to generate far less frequent arguments from the business units. Often, quite a bit of discussion takes place at the beginning of the year, when rates and allocation bases are set, but less discussion occurs each month, because the managers are not surprised by the amount billed.

Two major complaints are made about allocation systems. First is the free rider problem: a large user of IT services pays the same amount as a small user when the charges are not based on usage. Second, deciding the basis for charging out the costs is an issue. Choosing the number of employees over the number of desktops or other basis is a management decision, and whichever basis is chosen, someone will pay more than their actual usage would imply. Allocation mechanisms work well when a corporate directive requires use of this method and when the units agree on the basis for dividing up the costs.

Often when an allocation process is used, a true-up process occurs at the end of the year, in which total IT expenses are compared to total IT recovered from the business units and funds are given back or additional funds are needed. IT managers want to avoid asking for additional funds to make up for shortfalls in their budget. In addition, the cost/unit often changes during the year, as hardware, software, or support costs fluctuate. Also, because IT managers are constantly looking for ways to improve efficiency and productivity, changes may occur in the actual costs of doing the IT tasks. The rate charged to the business units is fixed for the year, however. In many allocation systems, therefore, at the end of the year when the IT department determines its actual costs for the year, IT may use a process to reconcile its intake with its costs. Managers who use a true-up process find that their business counterparts prefer the predictability of their monthly IT bills, and appreciate any funds returned to them at the end of the fiscal year, over the relative unpredictability of being charged actual costs each month.

Corporate Budget

An entirely different way to pay for IT costs is to simply consider them all to be corporate overhead and pay for them directly out of the corporate budget. With the **corporate budget funding method,** the costs fall to the corporate bottom line, rather than levying charges on specific users or business units.

Corporate budgeting is a relatively simple method for funding IT costs. It requires no calculation of prices of the IT systems. And because bills are not generated on a regular cycle to the businesses, concerns are raised less often by the business managers. IT managers control the entire budget giving them control of the use of those funds, and ultimately more input into what systems are created, how they are managed, and when they are retired. This funding method also encourages the use of new technologies because learners are not charged for exploration and inefficient system use.

As with the other methods, certain drawbacks come with using the corporate budget. First, all IT expenditures are subjected to the same process as all other corporate expenditures, namely the budgeting process. In many companies, this process is one of the most stressful events of the year: everyone has projects to be done, and everyone is competing for scarce funds. If the business units do not get billed in some way for their usage, many companies find that they do not control their usage. Getting a bill for services motivates the individual business manager to reconsider his or her usage of those services. Finally, if the business units are not footing the bill, the IT group may feel less accountable to them, which may result in an IT department that is less end-user or customer-oriented.

Figure 9.1 summarizes the advantages and disadvantages of these methods.

▶ HOW MUCH DOES IT COST?

The three major IT funding approaches in the preceding discussion are designed to recover the costs of building and maintaining the information systems in an enterprise. The goal is to simply cover the costs, not to generate a profit (although some MIS organizations are actually profit centers for their corporation). The most basic method for calculating the costs of a system is to add up the costs of all the components including hardware, software, network, and the people involved. Many MIS organizations calculate the initial costs and ongoing maintenance costs in just this way.

Activity-Based Costing

Another method for calculating costs is known as **activity-based costing (ABC).** Traditional accounting methods account for direct and indirect costs. Direct costs are those costs that can be clearly linked to a particular process or product, such as the components used to manufacture the product and the assembler's wages for time spent building the product. Indirect costs are the overhead costs, which

Funding Method	Description	Why Do It?	Why Not Do It?
Chargeback	Charges are calculated based on actual usage.	Fairest method for recovering costs because it is based on actual usage. IT users can see exactly what their usage costs.	IT department must collect details on usage, which can be expensive and difficult. IT must be prepared to defend the charges, which takes time and resources.
Allocation	Total expected IT expenditures are divided by nonusage basis such as number of login IDs, employees, or desktops.	Less bookkeeping for IT because rate is set once per fiscal year, and basis is well understood.	IT department must defend allocation rates; may charge low-usage department more than their usage would indicate is fair.
Corporate Budget	Corporate allocates funds to IT at annual budget session.	No billing to the businesses. IT exercises more control over what projects are done. Good for encouraging use of new technologies.	Competes with all other budgeted items for funds.

FIGURE 9.1 Comparison of IT funding methods.

include everything from the electric bill, the salary of administrative managers, and the expenses of administrative function, to the wages of the supervisor overseeing the assembler, the cost of running the factory, and the maintenance of machinery used for multiple products. Further, depending on the funding method used by the organization, indirect costs are allocated or absorbed elsewhere in the pricing model. The allocation process can be cumbersome and complex, and often is a source of trouble for many organizations. The alternative is ABC.

Activity-based costing (ABC) counts the actual activities that go into making a specific product or delivering a specific service. *Activities* are processes, functions, or tasks that occur over time and produce recognized results. They consume assigned resources to produce products and services. Activities are useful in costing because they are the common denominator between business process improvement and information improvement across departments.

Rather than allocate the total indirect cost of a system across a range of services according to an allocation formula, ABC calculates the amount of time that system was spent supporting a particular activity and allocates only that cost to that activity. For example, an accountant would look at the ERP (enterprise resource planning system) and divide its cost over the activities it supports by calculating how much of the system is used by each activity. Product A might take up 1/12 of an ERP system's capacity to control the manufacturing activities needed to make it, so it would be allocated 1/12 of the system's costs. The help desk might take up a whole server, so the entire server's cost would be allocated to that activity. In the end, the costs are put in buckets that reflect the products and services of the business, rather than the organization structure or the processes of any given department. In effect, ABC is the process of charging all costs to "profit centers" instead of to "cost centers."

Total Cost of Ownership

When a system is proposed and a business case is created to justify the investment, summing up the initial outlay and the maintenance cost does not provide an entirely accurate total system cost. Other costs are involved, and a time value of money affects the total cost. One technique used to calculate a more accurate cost is **total cost of ownership (TCO).** It is fast becoming the industry standard. Gartner Group introduced TCO in the late 1980s when PC-based IT infrastructures began gaining popularity.[2] Other IT experts have since modified the concept, and this section synthesizes the latest and best thinking about TCO.

TCO looks beyond initial capital investments to include costs associated with technical support, administration, and training. This technique estimates annual costs per user for each potential infrastructure choice; these costs are then totaled. Careful estimates of TCO provide the best investment numbers to compare with financial return numbers when analyzing the net returns on various IT options.

A major IT investment is for infrastructure. Figure 9.2 uses the hardware, software, network, and data categories to organize the TCO components the manager needs to evaluate for each infrastructure option. This table allows the manager to assess infrastructure components at a medium level of detail, and categorically to allocate "softer" costs like administration and support. More or less detail can be used. It sometimes helps to separate soft costs into a separate category when a single department provides them. The manager can adapt this framework for use with varying IT infrastructures.

TCO Component Breakdown

To clarify how the TCO framework is used, this section examines the hardware category in greater detail. As used in Figure 9.2, hardware means computing platforms and peripherals. The components listed are somewhat arbitrary, and an organization in which every user possesses every component would be highly unusual. For shared components, such as servers and printers, TCO estimates should be computed per component and then divided among all users who access them.

---

[2] Gartenberg, M. "Beyond the Numbers: Common TCO Myths Revealed." GartnerGroup Research Note: Technology, March 2, 1998.

Category	Infrastructure component	Option 1 per end user cost	Option 2 per end user cost
Hardware	Desktops Servers Mobile platforms Printers Archival storage Technical support Administration Training Informal support Total Hardware Cost		
Software	OS Office Suite Database Proprietary Technical support Administration Training Informal support Total Software Cost		
Network	LAN WAN Dial-in lines/modems Technical support Administration Total Network Cost		
Data	Removable media Onsite backup storage Offsite backup storage Total Data Cost Total Cost of Ownership		

FIGURE 9.2 TCO component evaluation.

For more complex situations, such as when only certain groups of users possess certain components, it is wise to segment the hardware analysis by platform. For example, in an organization where every employee possesses a desktop that accesses a server and half the employees also possess stand-alone laptops that do not access a server, one TCO table could be built for desktop and server hardware, and another for laptop hardware. Each table would include software, network, and data costs associated only with its specific platforms.

Soft costs, such as technical support, administration, and training are easier to estimate than they may first appear. To simplify, these calculations can be broken down further using a table such as Figure 9.3.

Category	Component	Responsible party	Annual hours	Cost/ hour	Total cost
Technical support	Hardware phone support	Call center			
	In-person hardware troubleshooting	IT operations			
	Hardware hot swaps	IT operations			
	Physical hardware repair	IT operations			
	Total cost of technical support				
Administration	Hardware setup	System administrator			
	Hardware upgrades/ modifications	System administrator			
	New hardware evaluation	IT operations			
	Total cost of administration				
Training	New employee training	IT operations			
	Ongoing administrator training	Hardware vendor			
	Total cost of training				
	Total soft costs for hardware				

FIGURE 9.3 Soft costs considerations.

The final soft cost, informal support, may be harder to pin down, but it is important nonetheless. Informal support comprises the sometimes highly complex networks that develop among coworkers through which many problems are fixed and much training takes place without the involvement of any official support staff. In many circumstances, these activities can prove more efficient and effective than working through official channels. Still, managers want to analyze the costs of informal support for two reasons:

1. The costs—both in salary and in opportunity—of a nonsupport employee providing informal support may prove significantly higher than analogous costs for a formal support employee. For example, it costs much more in both dollars per hour and foregone management activity for a mid-level manager to help a line employee troubleshoot an e-mail problem than it would for a formal support employee to provide the same service.

2. The quantity of informal support activity in an organization provides an indirect measure of the efficiency of its IT support organization.

The formal support organization should respond with sufficient promptness and thoroughness to discourage all but the briefest informal support transactions.

Various IT infrastructure options affect informal support activities differently. For example, a more user-friendly systems interface may alleviate the need for much informal support, justifying a slightly higher software expenditure. Similarly, an investment in support management software may be justified if it reduces the need for informal support.

Although putting dollar values on informal support may be a challenge, managers want to gauge the relative potential of each component option to affect the need for informal support.

TCO As a Management Tool

This discussion focused on TCO as a tool for evaluating which infrastructure components to choose, but TCO also can help managers understand how infrastructure costs break down. Gartner Group research consistently shows that the labor costs associated with an IT infrastructure far outweigh the actual capital investment costs.[3] TCO provides the fullest picture of where managers spend their IT dollars. Like other benchmarks, TCO results can be evaluated over time against industry standards (much TCO target data for various IT infrastructure choices are available from industry research firms). Even without comparison data, the numbers that emerge from TCO studies assist in decisions about budgeting, resource allocation, and organizational structure.

▶ VALUING IT INVESTMENTS

Monetary costs and benefits are important but not the only considerations in making IT investments. Soft benefits, such as the ability to make future decisions, are often part of the business case for IT investments, making it difficult to measure the payback of the investment.

Several unique factors of the IT function increase the difficulty of assessing value from IT investments. First, in many enterprises, IT is a significant part of the annual budget. Hence it comes under close scrutiny. Second, the systems themselves are complex, and as already discussed, calculating the costs is an art, not a science. Third, because many IT investments are for infrastructure, the payback period is much longer than other types of capital investments. Fourth, many times the payback cannot be calculated because the investment is a necessity rather than a choice, without any tangible payback. For example, upgrading to a newer version of software or buying a new design of hardware may be required because the older models are broken or simply not supported any longer. Many managers do not want to be placed in the position of having to upgrade simply because the vendor thinks an upgrade is necessary. Instead managers may resist IT spending on

[3] Kirwin, W. "TCO: The Emerging Manageable Desktop." GartnerGroup Top VIEW, September 24, 1996.

the grounds that the investment adds no incremental value. These factors and more fuel a long-running debate about the value of IT investments.

For example, because of the large expense of preparing for the year 2000, the Y2K crisis strained IT budgets.[4] Y2K compliance was a business necessity addressed only by implementing new systems or upgrading existing ones. Limited financial resources caused management executives to examine more closely the expected return on other IT investments. A 1998 survey by *InformationWeek* found that "more than 80% of the 150 IS executives at U.S. companies surveyed say their organizations require them to demonstrate the potential revenue, payback, or budget impact of their IT projects."[5]

Thus, a clear need exists to understand the true return on an IT project. Measuring this return is difficult, however. To illustrate, consider the relative ease with which a manager might analyze whether the enterprise should build a new plant. The first step would be to estimate the costs of construction. The plant capacity dictates project production levels. Demand varies and construction costs frequently overrun, but the manager can find sufficient information to make a decision about whether to build.

Most of the time, the benefits of investing in IT are less tangible than those of building a plant. Such benefits might include tighter systems integration, faster response time, more accurate data, better leverage to adopt future technologies, among others. How can a manager quantify these intangibles? He or she should also consider many indirect, or downstream, benefits and costs, such as changes in how people behave, where staff report, and how tasks are assigned. In fact, it may be impossible to pinpoint who will benefit from an IT investment when making the decision.[6]

Despite the difficulty, the task of evaluating IT investments is necessary. Knowing which approaches to use and when to use them are important first steps. A number of approaches are summarized in Figure 9.4. Managers should choose based on the attributes of the project. For example, **return on investment (ROI)** or payback analysis can be used when detailed analysis is not required, such as when a project is short lived and its costs and benefits are clear. When the project lasts long enough that the time value of money becomes a factor, **net present value (NPV)** and **economic value added (EVA)** are better approaches. EVA is particularly appropriate for capital-intensive projects.

---

[4] The Y2K crisis, otherwise known as the Millennium Bug, refers to software that was unable to distinguish between years beginning with the "20" from years beginning with "19". Some programs were not set up to distinguish between "1919" and "2019" for example. The fear was that programs would crash, or act in abnormal ways, when the century turned over. The amount of systems affected by this problem was enormous. Most government and corporations were busy in the latter half of the 1990's addressing this problem. In reality, however, most of the problems were fixed before the century started, and very few entities experienced the anticipated problems.

[5] Bob Violino, "ROI In the Real World," *Information Week* (April 27, 1998), p. 2.

[6] John C. Ford, "Evaluating Investment in IT," *Australian Accountant* (December 1994), p. 3.

Valuation Method	Description
Return on investment (ROI)	Percentage rate that measures the relationship between the amount the business gets back from an investment and the amount invested using the formula: ROI = (Estimated lifetime benefits – Estimated lifetime costs)/Estimated lifetime costs. Although popular and easy to use and understand, ROI lacks sophistication in assessing intangible benefits and costs.
Net present value (NPV)	Finance departments typically use NPV because it accounts for the time value of money. After discounting and then adding the dollar inflows and outflows, a positive NPV indicates a project should be undertaken, as long as other IT investments do not have higher values. It is calculated by discounting the costs and benefits for each year of the system's lifetime using the present value factor calculated each year as 1/(1+ discount rate) year.
Economic value added (EVA)	EVA accounts for opportunity costs of capital to measure true economic profit and revalues historical costs to give an accurate picture of the true market value of assets.[a] EVA is sufficiently complex that consultants typically are required to implement it. It provides no hard and fast rules for intangibles. Calculating EVA is simple: EVA = Net operating profit after taxes – [(Capital)(Cost of capital)].[a]
Payback analysis	Simple, popular method that determines the payback period, or how much time will lapse before accrued benefits overtake accrued and continuing costs.
Internal rate of return (IRR)	Calculation is made to determine the return that the IT investment would have, and then it is compared to the corporate policy on rate of return. If IT investment's rate of return is higher than the corporate policy, the project is considered a good investment.
Weighted scoring methods	Costs and revenues/savings are weighted based on their strategic importance, level of accuracy or confidence, and comparable investment opportunities.
Prototyping	A scaled-down version of a system is tested for its costs and benefits. This approach is useful when the impact of the IT investment seems unclear.
Game theory or role-playing	These approaches may reveal behavioral changes or new tasks attributable to a new system. They are less expensive than prototyping.
Simulation	A model is used to test the impact of a new system or series of tasks. This low-cost method surfaces problems and allows system sensitivities to be analyzed.

[a] http://www.sternstewart.com.

FIGURE 9.4 Valuation methods.

An IT manager may encounter a number of pitfalls when analyzing return on investment. First, not every situation calls for in-depth analysis. Some decisions— such as whether to invest in a new operating system to become compatible with a client operating system—are easy to make. The costs are unlikely to be prohibitively high, and the benefits are clear.

Second, not every evaluation method works in every case. Depending on the assets employed, the duration of the project, and any uncertainty about implementation, one method may work better than another.

Third, circumstances may alter the way a particular valuation method is best employed. For instance, in a software implementation, estimates of labor hours required often fall short of actual hours spent. Accordingly, some managers use an "adjusting" factor in their estimates.

Fourth, managers can fall into "analysis paralysis." Reaching a precise valuation may take longer than is reasonable to make an investment decision. Because a single right valuation may not exist, "close enough" usually suffices. Experience and an eye to the risks of an incorrect valuation help decide when to stop analyzing.

Finally, even when the numbers say a project is not worthwhile, the investment may be necessary to remain competitive. For example, UPS faced little choice but to invest heavily in IT. At the time, FedEx made IT a competitive advantage and was winning the overnight delivery war.

▶ MONITORING IT INVESTMENTS

An old adage says: "If you can't measure it, you can't manage it." Management's role is to ensure that the money spent on IT results in benefits for the organization. Therefore, an agreed-upon set of metrics must be created, and those metrics must be monitored and communicated to senior management and customers of the IT department, typically the users or their managers. These financial metrics are but one category of measures used to manage IT investments. In this section, other methods for monitoring investments, and the effectiveness of the MIS organization as a whole, are discussed.

In a three-round Delphi study, CIOs and business planners identified and ranked the dimensions they thought were most important in determining whether the IT department was performing well. The top 10 dimensions and the associated measures being used in their firms are reported in Figure 9.5.

Not surprisingly, many metrics for IT department performance focus on its stewardship of IT investments. The metrics that relate primarily to IT investments and the department's management of them are highlighted in Figure 9.5. One important category is IT's financial contribution to the performance of the firm. In measuring IT investment, however, managers are also concerned that the investments deliver high-quality information output, work well (i.e., show operational efficiency), keep their users satisfied, and were developed on time, within budget, and do what they are supposed to do (i.e., were developed using good systems development practices).

The dimensions that were ranked in this study reflect the Era IV issues prevalent when this 1992 study was performed. A survey conducted today would

Rank	Dimension	Description°	Associated Measures°
1	IT impact on strategic direction	The extent to which the IT department enhances the firm's competitive position by developing new systems that support overall organizational goals	• Market share increases attributable to IT department • Profit increases attributable to IT department • Organization would be out of business without IT
2	Integration of IT planning with corporate planning	The extent to which IT planning is tied to the corporate strategic plan and must allow inputs from top executives	• IT-documented plan supports the corporate strategic plan • Forecasts of IT capabilities exist • Corporate and IT plans developed jointly
3	Quality of information outputs	The accuracy, usefulness, and timeliness of the information that IT departments produce; also indirect responsibility for the quality of user-generated output	• End-user surveys (in-house) • Customer/client surveys (individuals not in organization) • Log of errors encountered by users
4	IT contribution to the firm's financial performance	Financial measures to gauge their performance and the financial health of IT investments	• Return on investment • Return on assets • Cost allocation • Value added by information technology (return on management) • Industry average comparison of IT budgets as a percentage of revenue • Budget performance (ability to meet IT budgets) • Cost of maintaining systems
5	IT department operational efficiency	The extent to which the IT department ensures high quality and close to zero defects based on technical metrics that measure system availability, reliability, and responsiveness of hardware and software	• Log of system availability • Users' perceptions surveys • User turnaround time • Log of computer and communication up/down time • System response time

° Highlighting indicates dimensions and measures with a major focus on IT investments.

FIGURE 9.5 Dimensions and measures of IT department performance (continues).

Source: Adapted from C. Saunders and J. Jones, "Measuring the Performance of the Information Systems Function," *Journal of Management Information Systems,* 8, 4 (1992), pp. 63–82.

Rank	Dimension	Description°	Associated Measures°
6	User/management attitudes about IT department	Users' satisfaction and perceptions of IT responsiveness, service level, and quality of IT investments	•Management and user perceptions of IT performance •User surveys of user participation in systems development and IT responsiveness to user needs •Time for IT department to respond to user complaints •Complaint logs
7	IT staff competence	Ability to recruit and maintain a technically and managerially competent staff that is able to interface successfully with users and management throughout the firm	•Number of managerial and technical education programs for IT staff •Career ladder(s) for IT staff •Formal performance appraisal system •Level of education of IT staff: degrees and professional certifications
8	Integration with related technologies across other units in the firm	The extent to which IT interacts across all business functions and facilitates a smooth, cost-effective flow of information across the firm	•User/IT development of user/IT budget
9	Adequacy of systems development practices	The extent to which the IT department promotes an organized approach to system design, development and documentation throughout the firm; (Development projects should be on time, within the budget and should deliver the right product.)	•Percentage of projects completed on time and /or within budget •Standard methodology for system analysis and design exists •Evaluation of user and IT department documentation •Estimates of number of labor-hours in backlog of systems development requests
10	Ability of the IT department to identify and assimilate new technology	The extent to which the IT department promotes an innovative climate that encourages its staff and organizational users to capitalize on new technologies	•Formal reward system for innovative thinking and suggestions for using IT •Number of technical breakthroughs

° Highlighting indicates dimensions and measures with a major focus on IT investments.

FIGURE 9.5   Dimensions and measures of IT department performance (continued).

probably uncover a greater need to measure Era V issues such as the ability to facilitate communications between suppliers and customers and to support better ways of doing business.

One metric that would no doubt be added to the list is the ABC metric discussed earlier in this chapter. A major objective of the ABC process is to determine a better way of doing business. Because of ABC's ability to place costs on activities and their outputs, it provides a clear metric for setting long-term priorities for improvement or for measuring near-term success. With ABC, functional users can characterize the value of, or need for, improving each activity, and can get rid of the waste before automating (or re-automating) activities.

The Balanced Scorecard

Deciding upon appropriate measures is half of the equation for effective MIS organizations. The other half of the equation is ensuring that those measures are accurately communicated to the business. Two methods for communicating these metrics are the scorecards and dashboards.

Financial measures may be the language of stockholders, but managers understand that they can be misleading if used as the sole means of making management decisions. One methodology used to solve this problem, created by Robert Kaplan and David Norton, and first described in the *Harvard Business Review* in 1992, is the **balanced scorecard,** which focuses attention on the organization's value drivers (which include, but are not limited to, financial performance).[7] Companies use it to assess the full impact of their corporate strategies on their customers and work force, as well as their financial performance.

This methodology allows managers to look at the business from four perspectives: customer, internal business, innovation/learning, and financial. For each perspective, the goals and measures are designed to answer these basic questions:

- How do customers see us? (Customer perspective)
- At what must we excel? (Internal business perspective)
- Can we continue to improve and create value? (Innovation and learning perspective)
- How do we look to shareholders? (Financial perspective)

Figure 9.6 graphically shows the relationship of these perspectives.

Since the introduction of the Balanced Scorecard, many have modified it or adapted it to apply to their particular organization. Managers of information technology found the concept of a scorecard useful in managing and communicating the value of the IT department. For example, US West used this methodology when it undertook an e-commerce project. The manager of this project described its use:

[7] R. Kaplan and D. Norton, "The Balanced Scorecard-Measures That Drive Performance," *Harvard Business Review* (January–February 1992).

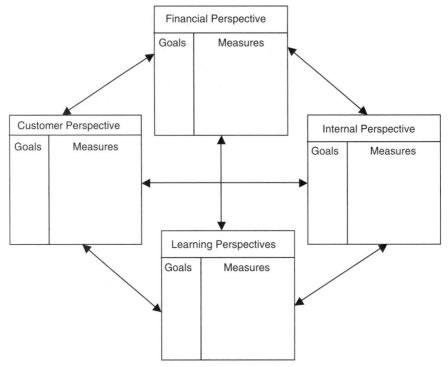

FIGURE 9.6 The Balanced Scorecard perspectives.
Source: Adapted from Kaplan and Norton, "The Balanced Scorecard—Measures That Drive Performance," *Harvard Business Review* (January–February 1992), p. 72.

> The Balanced Scorecard approach defined goals in areas beyond the technical, e-commerce platform. It helped us look at internal processes, employee impact and finances. It meant getting the associated computer systems Y2K compliant in the internal processes category, implementing an IT career structure in the employee learning category and meeting overall budget commitments in the financial category. The Balanced Scorecard helped us organize our thoughts, and it was then used for all of our IT planning.[8]

Applying the categories of the balanced scorecard to IT might mean interpreting them more broadly than originally conceived by Kaplan and Norton. For example, the original scorecard speaks of the customer perspective, but for the MIS scorecard, the customer is a user within the company, not the external customer of the company. The questions asked when using this methodology within the IT department are summarized in Figure 9.7.

David Norton commented, "[D]on't start with an emphasis on metrics—start with your strategy and use metrics to make it understandable and measurable (that

[8] Robin Robinson, "Balanced Scorecard," *Computerworld* (January 24, 2000).

Dimension	Description	Example IT Measures
Customer perspective	*How do customers see us?* Measures that reflect factors that really matter to customers	Impact of IT projects on users, impact of IT's reputation among users, and user-defined operational metrics
Internal business perspective	*What must we excel at?* Measures of what the company must do internally to meet customer expectations	IT process metrics, project completion rates, and system operational performance metrics
Innovating and learning perspective	*Can we continue to improve and create value?* Measures of the company's ability to innovate, improve, and learn	IT R&D, new technology introduction success rate, training metrics
Financial perspective	*How do we look to shareholders?* Measures to indicate contribution of activities to the bottom line	IT project ROI, NPV, IRR, cost/benefit, TCO, ABC

FIGURE 9.7   Balanced Scorecard applied to IT departments.

is, to communicate it to those expected to make it happen and to manage it)."[9] He found the balanced scorecard to be the most effective management framework for achieving organizational alignment and strategic success.

FirstEnergy, a multibillion-dollar utility company, provides a good example of how the MIS scorecard can be used. The company set a strategic goal of creating "raving fans" among its customers. In addition, they identified three other business value drivers: reliability, finance, and winning culture. The MIS group interpreted "raving fans" to mean satisfied internal customers. They used three metrics to measure their performance along this dimension:[10]

- Percentage of projects completed on time and on budget
- Percentage of projects released to the customer by agreed-upon delivery date
- Client satisfaction recorded on customer surveys done at the end of a project

[9] "Ask the Source: Interview with David Norton, *CIO Magazine* (July 25, 2002) www.cio.com on February 22, 2003.

[10] Adapted from Eric Berkman, "How to Use the Balanced Scorecard," *CIO Magazine* (May 15, 2002).

A scorecard used within the IT department helps senior IS managers understand their organization's performance and measure it in a way that supports its business strategy. The IT scorecard is linked to the corporate scorecard and ensures that the measures used by IT are those that support the corporate goals. At DuPont Engineering, the balanced scorecard methodology forces every action to be linked to a corporate goal, which helps promote alignment and eliminate projects with little potential impact. The conversations between IT and the business focus on strategic goals and impact rather than on technology and capabilities.[11]

IT Dashboards

Scorecards provide summary information gathered over a period of time. Another common MIS management monitoring tool is the IT **dashboard,** which provides a snapshot of metrics at any given point in time. Much like the dashboard of an automobile or airplane, the IT dashboard summarizes key metrics for senior managers in a manner that provides quick identification of the status of the organization. Like scorecards, dashboards are useful outside the IT department, and are often found in executive offices as a tool for keeping current on critical measures of the organization. For this section, we focus on the use of these tools within the IT department.

Dashboards provide frequently updated information on areas of interest within the IT department. Depending on who is actually using the dashboard, the data tend to focus on project status or operational systems status. For example, a dashboard used by GM North America's IT leadership team contains a metric designed to monitor project status.[12] Because senior managers question the overall health of a project rather than the details, the dashboard they designed provides red, yellow, or green highlights for rapid comprehension. A green highlight means that the project is progressing as planned. A yellow highlight means at least one key target has been missed. A red highlight means the project is significantly behind and needs some attention or resources to get back on track.

At GM, each project is tracked and rated monthly. GM uses four dashboard criteria: (1) performance to budget, (2) performance to schedule, (3) delivery of business results, and (4) risk. At the beginning of a project, these metrics are defined and acceptable levels set. The project manager assigns a color status monthly, based on the defined criteria, and the results are reported in a spreadsheet. When managers look at the dashboard, they can immediately tell whether projects are on schedule based on the amount of green, yellow, or red on the dashboard. They can then drill into yellow or red metrics to get the projects back on track. The dashboard provides an easy way to identify where their attention should be focused. The director of IT operations explains, "Red means I need more money, people or better business buy-in. ...The dashboard provides an early warning system that allows

IT managers to identify and correct problems before they become big enough to derail a project."[13]

Dashboards are useful for projects, but they have additional applications within the IT department. A number of organizations also use a similar dashboard to track operations to measure network performance, system availability, help desk satisfaction, and a number of other key performance data. Green means the metric is within acceptable limits; yellow means the metric has slipped once or twice; and red means the metric is consistently outside the acceptable range.

At Intel, the MIS department uses a "CIO dashboard" that condenses about 100 separate pieces of paper into one unified set of indicators in a matrix format.[14] Each key topic area is represented by a trend indicator as well as a status indicator. The Intel dashboard also uses green-yellow-red, as well as an arrow to indicate up, down, or sideways movement of a trend. All Intel employees, including IT staff, can scan the dashboard, which is electronically stored and updated, on the Intel intranet. In this way, issues can be identified and handled without waiting for the monthly CIO meeting, and dashboard statistics are monitored frequently to enable proactive behavior. In Intel's case, the dashboard improved both the reporting process, as well as team communication, because it made information available in real time in an easy-to-read manner.

▶ FOOD FOR THOUGHT: OPTIONS PRICING

Options pricing has long been used on financial assets as a method of locking in a price to be paid in the future. For example, you may have been able to purchase an option to buy 500 shares of Cisco stock at $50 per share on January 1, 2003, for a price (i.e., $600). The concept of options can be extended to evaluating IT investments. In this case, an IT project is viewed as an option to exchange the cost of the project for its benefits down the road. In particular, investing in one phase of an IT project may result in an option to invest in the next phase, as long as the project is not terminated before then.

The reason that options pricing is so appealing is that it offers management the opportunity to take some future action (such as abandoning, deferring, or expanding the scale of a project) in response to uncertainty about changes in the business and its environment. **Options pricing** offers a risk-hedging strategy to minimize the negative impact of risk when uncertainty can be resolved by waiting to see what happens. To be applied, managers need to have a project that can be divided into investment stages, and be armed with estimates of costs of the project at each stage, the projected revenues or savings, and the probability of these costs and revenues/savings being realized.

Figure 9.8 offers a simple example of how options pricing would work for a new CRM system that has two major components: a customer identification

---

[13] Ibid.

[14] Adapted from Johanna Ambrosio, "Walking the Walls No More," *Computerworld* (July 6, 2001).

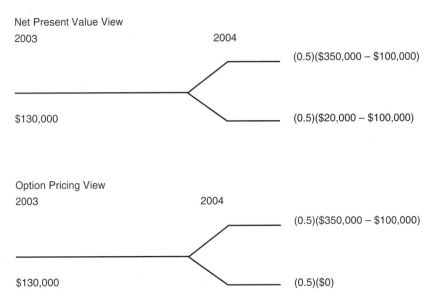

FIGURE 9.8 NPV vs. option pricing view.
Source: Adapted from Ram Kumar, "Managing Risks in IT Projects: An Options Perspective," *Information & Management,* 40 (2002), pp. 63–74.

module and a customer tracking module. (*Note:* In this model all costs and revenues reflect discounting.) The customer identification module is projected to cost $130,000 in 2003, and the customer tracking module, which is built upon the customer identification module, is estimated to cost $100,000 in 2004. The customer identification module has a 50 percent chance of generating $350,000 in additional revenues in 2004 if conditions are favorable. If they are unfavorable, revenues are projected to be only $20,000. The net present value (NPV) view would assume a 50 percent chance of positive net revenue of $250,000 (i.e., $350,000 – $100,000) in 2004, and a 50 percent chance of loss of $80,000 (i.e., $20,000 – $100,000) in 2004. Options pricing views this investment opportunity a little differently. With options pricing there is a 50 percent chance of net revenue of $250,000 and a 50 percent chance of net revenue of $0 a year later, because the option to invest $100,000 in the customer tracking module need not be exercised if conditions are unfavorable.

Conceptualizing risk hedging in terms of options can help managers better understand and manage IT investment decisions. It offers an analysis approach that matches the way many senior managers think about the risk in making investments. Sometimes it may result in investment decisions that would be rejected based on NPV or cost-benefit analysis. For example, IT infrastructure investments often fare poorly on NPV analysis because the immediate expectation of payback is limited. However, from an options pricing perspective these investments provide the business with opportunities that would not be possible without the IT investment. Ideally, the investment yields applications with measurable revenue.

Option pricing is especially applicable in the following situations:[15]

- *When an investment decision can be deferred.* When considerable uncertainty surrounds a major project, dividing it into "chunks" allows managers to monitor their investment over time.

- *In helping managers strike a balance between waiting to obtain valuable information and forgoing revenues or strategic benefits from an implemented project.* For example, Yankee 24 could have used options pricing when deciding to offer a POS debit card network to its member institutions. Yankee 24 was established in 1984 to provide electronic banking network services, such as ATMs, to more than 200 member institutions. As early as 1987, Yankee's president, Richard Yanak, realized the potential for a POS network. If customer acceptance were as slow as it had been in California a decade earlier, revenues would be low and could not offset the heavy investment required for network infrastructure. The question that options pricing could have resolved was how long should Yankee wait before investing in this infrastructure and POS technology without giving its competitor, the New York Cash Exchange, a first mover advantage.

- *For emerging technology investments.* For example, IBM OS/2-based computing infrastructures became less attractive as Microsoft Windows NT gained a large installed base in the world of client/server computing. Thus, the use of IT projects with a phased rollout of an OS/2 platform, or of applications depending on OS/2 for critical support, would have been negatively affected over time using an options pricing model.

- *For prototyping investments.* When managers are uncertain about whether an application can "do the job," a prototype provides value in the options that it offers the firm for future actions.

- *For technology-as-product investments.* When the technology is at the core of a product, issues of level of commitment, timing, rollout, deferment, and abandonment can be considered more fully.

Like all of the evaluation approaches, options pricing has a downside.[16] Option value calculations are sensitive to certain parameters, especially volatility. Having multiple stakeholders involved in estimation and calculating for a range of parameter values are two strategies that can help lessen this sensitivity. Options pricing

[15] M. Benaroch, and R. J. Kauffman, "A Case for Using Real Options Pricing Analysis to Evaluate Information Technology Project Investments," *Information Systems Research*, 10, 1 (1999), pp. 70–86.

[16] Ram Kumar," Managing Risks in IT Projects: An Options Perspective," *Information & Management*, 40 (2002), pp. 63–74.

may be attractive for infrastructure investments that open the door to possible applications in the future, but a number of assumptions must be made about those opportunities in order for the options model to work. However, the probability of all the assumptions coming true is small.

▶ SUMMARY

- IT is funded using one of three methods: chargeback, allocation, or corporate budget.
- Chargeback systems are viewed as the most equitable method of IT cost recovery because costs are distributed based on usage. Creating an accounting system to record the information necessary to do a chargeback system can be expensive and time consuming, and usually has no other useful application.
- Allocation systems provide a simpler method to recover costs, because they do not involve recording system usage in order to allocate costs. However, allocation systems can sometimes penalize groups with low usage.
- Corporate budgeting systems do not allocate costs at all. Instead, the CIO seeks and receives a budget from the corporate overhead account. This method of funding IT does not require any usage recordkeeping, but is also most likely to be abused if the users perceive "it is free."
- Total cost of ownership is a technique to understand all the costs, beyond the initial investment costs, associated with owning and operating an information system. It is most useful as a tool to help evaluate which infrastructure components to choose, and to help understand how infrastructure costs occur.
- Activity-based costing is another technique to group costs into a meaningful bucket. Costs are accounted for based on the activity, or product or service, they support. ABC is useful for allocating large overhead expenses.
- ROI is difficult, at best, to calculate for IT investments because the benefits are often not tangible. The benefits might be difficult to quantify, difficult to observe, or long range in scope.
- Popular metrics for IT investments measure quality of information outputs, IT contributions to a firm's financial performance, operational efficiency, management/user attitudes, and the adequacy of systems development practices.
- Monitoring and communicating the status and benefits of IT is often done through the use of balanced scorecards and IT dashboards.
- Options pricing offers a risk-hedging strategy to minimize the negative impact of risk when resolving uncertainty by waiting to see what happens.

▶ KEY TERMS

activity-based costing (ABC) (p. 219)
allocation funding method (p. 218)
balanced scorecard (p. 230)
chargeback funding method (p. 217)
corporate budget funding method (p. 219)
dashboard (p. 233)
economic value added (EVA) (p. 225)
net present value (NPV) (p. 225)
options pricing (p. 234)
return on investment (ROI) (p. 225)
total cost of ownership (TCO) (p. 221)

▶ DISCUSSION QUESTIONS

1. Under what conditions would you recommend using each of these funding methods: allocation, chargeback, and corporate budgeting?

2. Describe the conditions under which ROI, payback period, NPV, and EVA are most appropriately applied.

3. A new inventory management system for ABC Company could be developed at a cost of $250,000. The estimated net operating costs and estimated net benefits over six years of operation would be:

Year	Estimated Net Operating Costs	Estimated Net Benefits
0	$250,000	$ 0
1	7,000	52,000
2	9,400	68,000
3	11,000	82,000
4	14,000	115,000
5	15,000	120,000
6	16,000	120,000

    a. What would the payback period be for this investment? Would it be a good or bad investment? Why?

    b. What is the ROI for this investment?

    c. Assuming a 15 percent discount rate, what is this investment's NPV?

4. Would you suggest using options pricing on the investment described in Question 3? Why or why not?

5. Compare and contrast the IT scorecard and dashboard approaches.

6. TCO is one way to account for costs associated with a specific infrastructure. This method does not include additional costs such as disposal costs—the cost to get rid of the system when it is no longer of use. What other additional costs might be of importance in making total cost calculations?

CASE STUDY 9-1

DAIMLERCHRYSLER

DaimlerChrysler, the large global automaker, implemented an enterprise-wide material cost management system to help the 54 component teams collaborate on streamlining the number of common parts used on each of the production lines. The system was built on Lotus Notes and took less than one month to develop and roll out. It cost less than $1 million and has been wildly successful, generating more than 500 weekly ideas to improve vehicles.

    For example, the system helped DaimlerChrysler cut the number of fog lamps used in the different vehicles. That idea alone saved the company $7 million. In another example, the number of seat structure components was reduced, leading to another $40 million in savings during the next two years. They also reduced the number of powertrain controllers used over the product lines, saving $20 million per year. "The ROI for the project has been unbelievable," according to the CIO.

The biggest benefit comes from the perception of the value of IT. While the CIO was away at a meeting, her team's IT budget was presented to senior management. The result was complete buy-in for her budget; the department heads all agreed that they could not afford to cut the IT budget because of the business value IT creates.

Discussion Questions

1. Why is the ROI of the cost management system "unbelievable," according to the CIO?

2. Why, in your opinion, is this system so popular and generates so many ideas?

3. What additional information would you need on this system to calculate the TCO?

4. What has the CIO done to foster the impression that IT creates business value?

Source: Adapted from Kaplan and Norton, "The Balanced Scorecard-Measures That Drive Performance," *Harvard Business Review* (January–February 1992), p. 72.

10

PROJECT MANAGEMENT[1]

In 1993, Oxford Health Plans Inc. began a project to replace its existing database management system with one by Oracle Corporation. The database was finally completed in September 1996 only to collapse under the load of transactions required by its users. This failure led to serious delays in payment of claims for HMO members and temporarily halted the issuance of thousands of monthly statements. Oxford cited this crucial system failure as a factor in its 1997 third quarter loss of $78 million and in the additional $45 million loss in 1998 first quarter earnings.

This example highlights the possible financial consequences of a failed information systems (IS) project. Such failures occur at an astonishing rate. The Standish Group, a technology research firm, found that 73 percent of all software projects are delivered late or over budget or simply fail to meet their performance criteria. Business projects increasingly rely on IS to attain their objectives, especially with the increased focus to do business on the Internet. Thus, a crucial IS project raises the risk in many business projects. To succeed, a general manager must also be a project manager, and must learn how to manage this type of risk.

In the current environment, businesses face competition from companies equipped to copy existing products and services and then distribute them at lower prices. Often, the quality that differentiates firms in the marketplace—and destines them for success or failure—is the ability to adapt existing business processes and systems faster than the competition. The process of continual adaptation to the changing marketplace drives the need for business change and thus for successful project management. Typical adaptation projects include the following elements:

- Rightsizing the organization
- Reengineering business processes
- Adopting more comprehensive, integrative processes

Projects comprise a set of one-time activities that can transform the current situation into the desired new one. Firms seek to compete through new products and processes, but the work of initially building or radically changing these outcomes falls outside the scope of normal business operations. That is where projects come in. When work can only be accomplished through methods that

[1] The author wishes to acknowledge and thank W. Thomas Cannon, MBA 1999 for his help in researching and writing early drafts of this chapter.

fundamentally differ from those employed to run daily operations, the skilled project manager plays a crucial role.

Successful business strategy requires executive management to decide which objectives can be met through normal daily operations and which require specialized project management. Virtually all projects involve an information technology (IT) component, including both a computer system and an information flow. Rapidly changing business situations make it difficult to keep both of these IT elements aligned with business strategy. Furthermore, the amount of resources required to complete IT-intensive projects has increased over the years due to their growing complexity—magnifying the risk that the finished product or process will no longer satisfy the needs of the business. Thus, on most projects the critical element to manage is the IT portion. Executive management no longer has an option but to consider skilled IT project management as fundamental to business success.

This chapter provides an overview of what a project is and how to manage one. It discusses the aspects of IT-intensive projects that make them uniquely challenging. Finally, it identifies the issues that shape the role of the general manager in such projects and help them to manage risk.

▶ WHAT DEFINES A PROJECT?

In varying degrees, organizations combine two types of work—projects and operations—to transform resources into profits. Both types require people and a flow of resources. The flight of an airplane from its point of departure to its destination is an operation that requires a pilot and crew, the use of an airplane, and fuel. The operation is repetitive: After the plane is refueled, it takes new passengers to another destination. The continuous operation of the plane creates a transportation service. However, the development of the design for such a plane is a project that may require years of work by many people. When the design is completed, the work ends. Figure 10.1 compares characteristics of both project and operational work. The last two characteristics are distinctive and form the basis for the following formal definition:

> [A] **project** is a temporary endeavor undertaken to create a unique product or service. Temporary means that every project has a definite beginning and a definite end. Unique means that the product or service is different in some distinguishing way from all similar products or services.[2]

To organize the work facing a project team, the project manager may break a project into subprojects. He or she then organizes these subprojects around distinct activities, such as quality control testing. This organizing method allows the project manager to contract certain kinds of work externally in order to limit costs or other drains on crucial project resources. At the macro level, a general manager may choose to organize various projects as elements of a larger program, if doing so creates efficiencies. Such programs then provide a framework from which to manage competing resource requirements and shifting priorities among a set of projects.

[2] Project Management Institute Standards Committee, *A Guide to the Project Management Body of Knowledge* (Project Management Institute, 1996).

Characteristics	Operations	Projects
Labor skills	Low	High
Training time	Low	High
Worker autonomy	Low	High
Compensation system	Hourly or weekly wage	Lump sum for project
Material input requirements	High degree of certainty	Uncertain
Supplier ties	Longer duration More formal	Shorter duration Less formal
Raw materials inventory	Large	Small
Scheduling complexity	Lower	Higher
Quality control	Formal	Informal
Information flows	Less important	Very important
Worker-mgmt communication	Less important	Very important
Duration	On-going	Temporary
Product or service	Repetitive	Unique

FIGURE 10.1 Characteristics of operational and project work.

► WHAT IS PROJECT MANAGEMENT?

Project management is the "application of knowledge, skills, tools, and techniques to project activities in order to meet or exceed stakeholder needs and expectation from a project."[3] Project management always involves continual trade-offs and it is the manager's job to manage them.

These trade-offs can be subsumed in the project triangle (see Figure 10.2), which highlights the importance of balancing scope, time, and cost. **Scope** may be divided into product scope (the detailed description of the product's quality, features, and functions), and project scope (the work required to deliver a product or service with the intended product scope). **Time** refers to the time required to complete the project, while **cost** encompasses all the resources required to carry out the project. A successful balance of scope, time, and cost yields a high-quality project—one in which the needs and expectations of the users are met. The tricky part of project management is successfully juggling these three elements while on a high wire, which amounts to shifting the triangle's base to keep it in balance. Changes in any one of the sides of the triangle effects one or both of the other sides. For example, if the project scope increases, more time and/or more resources (cost) are needed to do the additional work. This increase in scope after a project has begun is aptly called *scope creep*. In most projects only two of these elements can be optimized, and the third must be adjusted to maintain balance. It is important that the project stakeholders decide on the overriding "key success factor" (i.e., time, cost, or scope), though the project manager has the important responsibility of demonstrating to the stakeholders the impact on the project of selecting any of these.

[3] Ibid.

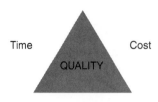

Time

Cost

QUALITY

Scope

FIGURE 10.2 Project triangle.

The project manager's role is to develop a system to effectively and efficiently manage these competing demands. Typical activities include the following:

- Ensuring progress of the project according to defined metrics
- Identifying risks and assessing their probability of occurrence
- Ensuring progress toward deliverables within constraints of time and resources
- Running coordination meetings of the project team
- Negotiating for resources on behalf of the project in light of its scope

A general manager often oversees more than one project, and his or her role can vary. The manager may be the customer for any given project, as well as the source of its resources. These dual roles can make it easier for the general manager to ensure attention to both a project's risks and its business value.

▶ PROJECT MEASUREMENT

Some metrics used for IS projects are the same as those used for all business projects: on-time, on-budget, and met specifications. Projects are measured against budgets of cost, schedules of deliverables, and the amount of functionality in the system scope.

IT projects are difficult to estimate, despite the increasing amount of attention given to mastering this task. Most software projects fail to meet their schedules and budgets. Managers attribute that failure to poor estimating techniques, poorly monitored progress protocols, and the idea that schedule slippage can be solved by simply adding additional people.[4] Not only does this assume that people and months are interchangeable, but if the project is off schedule, it may be that the project was incorrectly designed in the first place, and putting additional people on the project just hastens the process to an inappropriate end.

Many projects are measured in "man-months," the most common unit for discussing the size of a project. For example, a project that takes 100 man-months means that it will take one person 100 months to do the work, or 100 people can

[4] Frederick Brooks, *The Mythical Man-Month: Essays on Software Engineering* (Reading, MA: Addison-Wesley, 1982).

do it in a month. Some problems accompany this metric. For example, some projects cannot be sped up with additional people. An analogy is that of pregnancy. It takes one woman nine months to make a baby, and putting nine people on the job for one month cannot speed up the process. Software systems often involve highly interactive, complex sets of tasks that rely on each other to make a completed system. In some cases additional people can speed up the process, but most projects cannot be made more efficient simply by adding labor. Often, adding resources to a late project only makes the project later.[5]

Measuring how well the system meets specifications and business requirements laid out in the project scope is more complex. Metrics for functionality are typically divided along lines of business functionality and system functionality. The first set of measures are those derived specifically from the requirements and business needs that generated the project, such as automating the order entry process or building a knowledge management system for product design. In examples such as these, a set of metrics can be derived to measure whether the system meets expectations. However, other aspects of functionality, related to the system itself, are also important to measure. An example is usability, or how well the individual using the system can and does use it. Sample measures might be the number of users who use the system, the satisfaction of the users for the system, the time it takes to learn the system, the speed of performance, and the rate of errors made by users. Another common metric is system reliability. For example, one might measure the amount of time the system was up (or running), and the amount of time the system was down (or not running).

▶ PROJECT ELEMENTS

Project work requires in-depth situational analyses and the organization of complex activities into often coincident sequences of discrete tasks. The outcomes of each activity must be tested and integrated into the larger process to produce the desired result. The number of variables affecting the performance of such work is potentially enormous.

Four elements essential for any project include a (1) common project vocabulary, (2) teamwork, (3) a project cycle plan, and (4) project management. A common project vocabulary allows all those involved with the project to understand the project and communicate effectively. Teamwork ensures that all parts of the project come together correctly and efficiently. The plan represents the methodology and schedule to be used by the team to execute the project. Finally, management is necessary to make sure the entire project is executed appropriately and coordinated properly. As a result of good project management, the project scope can be realistically defined and the project can be completed on time and within budget.

It is essential to understand the interrelationships among these elements and with the project itself. Both a commitment to teamwork and a common project vocabulary must permeate the management of a project throughout its life. The

[5] Ibid.

project plan consists of the sequential steps of organizing and tracking the work of the team. Finally, project management itself comprises a set of tools to balance competing demands for resources and ensure the completion of work at each step and as situational elements evolve through the project plan.

Common Project Vocabulary

The typical project teams combine consultants who are new to the organization, a growing number of technical specialists, and business members. The different expertise and technical vocabulary that each member brings to the team creates a challenging environment in which to carry on conversations, meetings, and memos. For example, a market research analyst and a software analyst each have many words unique to their specialty; they may also attach different meanings to the same word. Clear thinking requires effective communication and thus a common project vocabulary. Each project team should develop its own glossary of terms, and team members should commit to its consistent use.

The common project vocabulary helps reduce misunderstandings in a couple of ways. First, many terms have multiple meanings. Sorting out, and recording, the exact meaning for the project is done with the common project vocabulary. Second, as with most specialties, a large number of cryptic words is common to a software project. The common project vocabulary is a place where these words are recorded and explained. The common project vocabulary includes the many terms and meanings that may be unfamiliar to the general manager. To improve their communications with general managers, users, and other nontechnical people, technical people should limit their use of acronyms and cryptic words, and only sparingly place them in the common project vocabulary.

Teamwork

Business teams often fail because members don't understand the nature of the work required to make them effective. Teamwork begins by clearly defining the objective of the team and each person's role to help obtain the objective. It is especially important to identify the mutual dependency of the roles on the team. Teams require a common standard of conduct, shared rewards, and team spirit.

Project teams organize people around specific activities. Their staffing can be flexible to allow the assignment of human resources on an as-needed basis. Team members often bring specific experiences, such as technical, process, or organizational skills, that can be applied as needed. Team members who represent larger functional units within the organization also serve to transmit information across the boundary of the group. A marketing or research and development (R&D) manager can share departmental information in project meetings. Such information sharing may constitute the first step toward building consensus on critical project issues that will affect the entire organization. Thus, effective project managers use teamwork both to organize and apply human resources and to collect and share information throughout the organization.

Project Cycle Plan

The project cycle plan organizes discrete project activities and sequences them in steps along a timeline so that the project delivers according to the requirements of customers and stakeholders. It identifies critical beginning and end dates and breaks the work spanning these dates into phases. Using the plan, the time and resources needed to complete the work based on the project's scope are identified, and tasks are assigned to team members. The general manager tracks the phases in order to coordinate the eventual transition from project to operational status, a process that culminates on the "go live" date. The project manager uses the phases to control the progress of work. He or she may establish control gates at various points along the way in order to verify that project work to date has met key requirements regarding cost, quality, and features. If it has not met these requirements, he or she can make corrections to the project plan and adjust the cycle as necessary.

The project cycle plan can be developed using various approaches and software tools. The three most common approaches are the project evaluation and review technique (PERT), critical path method (CPM), and Gantt chart. PERT identifies the tasks within the project, orders the tasks in a time sequence, identifies their interdependencies, and estimates the time required to complete the task. Tasks that must be performed individually and that, together, account for the total elapsed time of the project are considered to be critical tasks. Noncritical tasks are those for which some slack time can be built into the schedules without affecting the duration of the entire project. A PERT chart is shown in Figure 10.3.

CPM is a project planning and scheduling tool that is similar to PERT. Unlike PERT, CPM incorporates a capability for identifying relationships between costs and the completion date of a project, as well as the amount and value of resources that must be applied in alternative situations. The two approaches differ in terms of time estimates. PERT builds upon broad estimates about the time needed to complete project tasks. It calculates the optimistic, most probable, and pessimistic time estimates for each task. In contrast, CPM assumes that all time requirements for completion of individual tasks are relatively predictable. Because of these differences, CPM tends to be used on projects for which direct relationships can be established between time and resources (costs).

Gantt charts are a commonly used visual tool for displaying time relationships of project tasks and for monitoring the progress toward project completion. A Gantt chart is displayed in Figure 10.4.

Software tools, such as Microsoft Project, Primavera Project Planner, and Timeline, can help manage scheduling and other aspects of planning. These applications enable the definition of tasks at various levels of detail, the delineation of relationships among tasks, the allocation of resources to tasks, and the calculation of the project's critical path. They can also generate charts such as PERT and Gantt charts.

FIGURE 10.3 PERT chart.

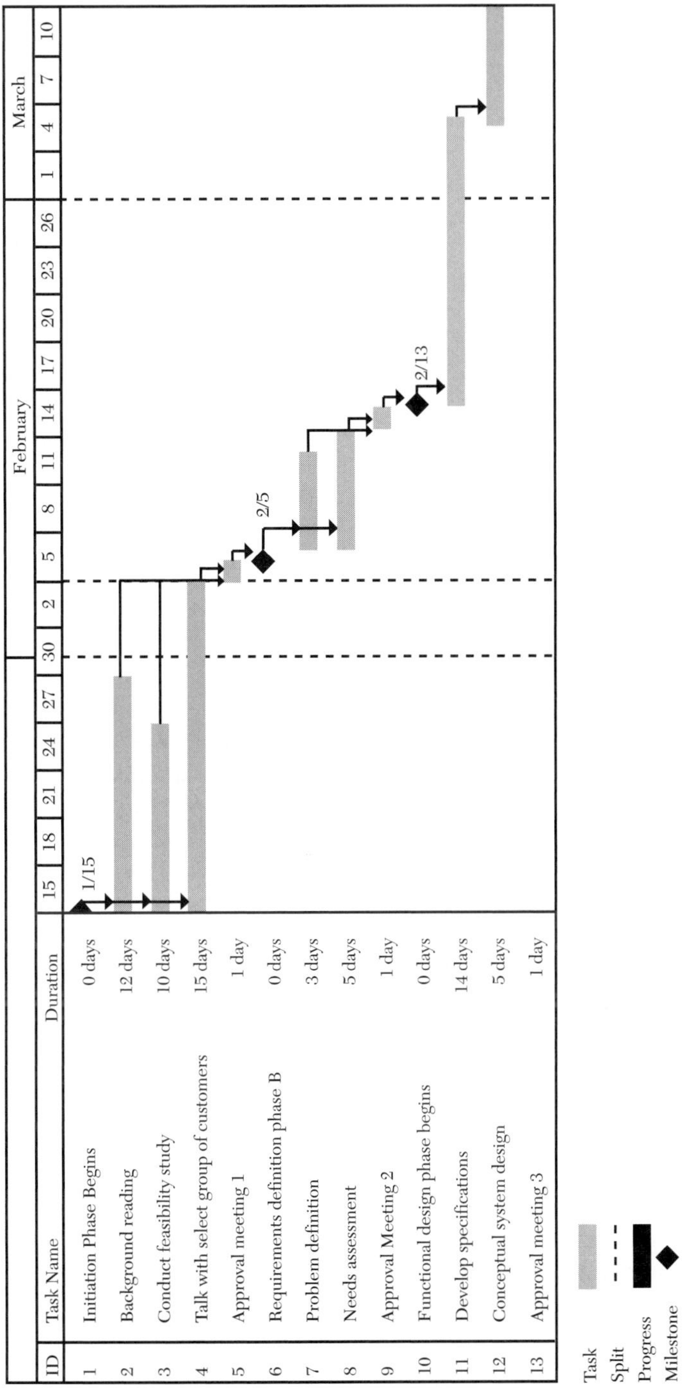

ID	Task Name	Duration
1	Initiation Phase Begins	0 days
2	Background reading	12 days
3	Conduct feasibility study	10 days
4	Talk with select group of customers	15 days
5	Approval meeting 1	1 day
6	Requirements definition phase B	0 days
7	Problem definition	3 days
8	Needs assessment	5 days
9	Approval Meeting 2	1 day
10	Functional design phase begins	0 days
11	Develop specifications	14 days
12	Conceptual system design	5 days
13	Approval meeting 3	1 day

Task
Split
Progress
Milestone

FIGURE 10.4 Gantt chart.

Requirements Definition Period				Production Period					Deployment/ Dissemination Period	
Investigation Task Force										
User requirement definition	Research concept definition	Information use specification	Collection planning phase	Collection and analysis phase	Draft report phase				Publication phase	Distribution phase
Typical High Tech Commercial Business										
Product requirements phase	Product definition phase	Product proposal phase	Product develop- ment phase	Engineer model phase	Internal test phase	External test phase		Production phase	Manufac- turing sales & support phase	
Generic Project Cycle Template										
User require- ment definition phase	Concept definition phase	System specifi- cation phase	Acqui- sition planning phase	Source selection phase	Development phase		Verifica- tion phase	Deploy- ment or produc- tion phase	Operations/ maintenance or sales/ support phase	Deacti- vate phase

FIGURE 10.5   Project cycle template.

Source: Adapted from K. Forsberg, H. Mooz, and H. Cotterman, *Visualizing Project Management* (New York: Wiley & Sons, 1996). Used with permission.

Figure 10.5 compares a generic project cycle plan with one for a typical high-tech commercial business and with one for an investigative task force. Notice that while each of these plans has unique phases, all can loosely be described by three periods (shown at the top of the diagram): requirements period, development period, and production/distribution period.

The manager must attend to the following aspects of the work throughout the project cycle:[6]

- The technical aspect includes all activities related to satisfying the technical and quality requirements.
- The budget aspect describes all activities related to the appropriation of project funds by executive management and the securing and accounting of funds by the project manager.
- The business aspect encompasses all activities related to the management of the project and any associated contracts.

These aspects of a project interrelate as they develop through the cycle. They reflect the project triangle to the extent that a change in the quality requirements for the project will normally alter the cost, scope, and time involved. The elements of project management presented next provide tools to use in balancing the varying aspects of a project.

[6] Kevin Forsberg, Hal Mooz, and Howard Cotterman, *Visualizing Project Management* (New York: Wiley & Sons, 1996).

Elements of Project Management

The nine elements described in this section represent management skills that can be organized into a toolbox of sorts. Each element addresses a specific factor that affects a project's chances of success. The challenge facing a project manager is to learn and apply the techniques properly in the situations that require them. The elements include (1) identification of requirements, (2) organizational integration, (3) team management, (4) risk and opportunity management, (5) project control, (6) project visibility, (7) project status, (8) corrective action, and (9) project leadership. Figure 10.6 summarizes these elements.

Identification of Requirements

The project manager must determine what the project needs to deliver, and he or she must manage against these project requirements as they change over time. The

Elements of Management	Rationale	Major Focus
Requirements	Failure to manage requirements which initiate and drive projects is the major cause of failure.	Formulate
Organizing	Putting structure around the key activities, people, and resources is critical to successful management.	
Project Team	Teams are newly formed for each project and include subcontractors and outsourcing.	
Planning	Needed to provide roadmap of tasks to be done including schedule, budget, and deliverables.	Proactive
Risk and Opportunity Management	Significant cause of project failures if not specifically managed.	
Project Control	When properly implemented, controls identify whether project is proceeding appropriately.	
Visibility	Needed to keep all stakeholders informed.	
Status	Need hard metrics, measures, and variances to supplement activity reports.	Variance Control
Corrective Action	Innovative actions needed to get back on track with plan.	Reactive
Leadership	Creation of team energy to succeed with plan.	Motivate

FIGURE 10.6 Elements of management.
Source: K. Forsberg, H. Mooz, and H. Cotterman, *Visualizing Project Management* (New York: Wiley & Sons, 1996). Used with permission.

process of identifying project requirements involves determining the project scope, which comprises numerous tasks. Some of them are selection in concept, decomposition or analysis, definition, documentation, definitive identification, integration into the project plan, specification, substantiation, validation, and verification. Managing this process may entail systems analysis and design, establishing the traceability of requirements identified, assigning accountability, and modeling to specification.

Organizational Integration

Ideally, the project manager should start with a structure similar to the organization in support of the project. Doing so might mean revising organizational reporting relationships and reward systems for members of the project team so they can spend time on the project. The following models are helpful to structure simple projects:[7]

- *Pure functional structure* (Figure 10.7) works best for a single project that operates with relative independence in terms of organizational interface or technology. This model falls short when an organization must manage multiple projects.

- *Pure purpose (project) structure* (Figure 10.8) works best when performance according to scheduling, geographic, or product cost considerations is paramount and the cost of development is relatively unimportant.

- *Conventional matrix structure* (Figure 10.9) works well when the project manager truly controls the project funds and enjoys clearly defined relationships with supporting managers, including formal commitments and their participation in project planning. This model fails when the project manager is seen as a mere coordinator of activity and the supporting managers perform only on a "best effort" basis.

- *Co-located matrix structure* (Figure 10.10) should be considered for high-priority projects that depend on key resources and/or technologies and when ongoing involvement with operating strategy is secondary.

In many organizations the project must simply fit itself into existing structures. Even in this instance, it remains important to understand the trade-offs made by adapting the project to the organizational context.

Team Management

The project manager must acquire and manage the required human resources. Tools commonly available in human resource departments assess professional competencies and skills, as well as personal traits and behaviors. Such assessments can help the project manager select team members with specific roles in mind. As a project progresses through its life cycle, the number of people assigned typically increases, at least periodically. Such growth adds to the need for ongoing management by the project manager.

---

[7] Ibid.

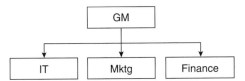

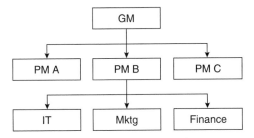

FIGURE 10.7 Pure functional structure.

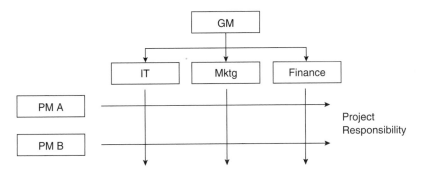

FIGURE 10.8 Pure purpose (project) structure.

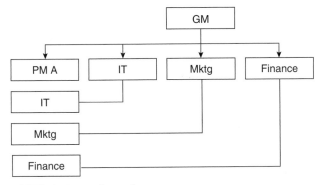

FIGURE 10.9 Conventional matrix structure.

FIGURE 10.10 Co-located matrix structure.

Risk and Opportunity Management

Managing risks and opportunities throughout the project life cycle is a critical task of the team. The first step is to identify risks and opportunities, and assess the probability, potential impact on the project, and any anticipated outcomes. Then it is helpful to compare the outcomes that can be predicted as particular risks and opportunities arise and prioritize them in terms of the magnitude of their effects. Once those tasks are done, strategies can be developed to maximize opportunities and minimize risks, and cost estimates of all alternatives can be made. By comparing costs and benefits of various courses of action, the team can select which sequence of actions to take and obtain agreement from necessary parties. As a precaution, all decisions, and the rationales leading to those decisions, should be documented. Then, when questions arise, the documentation provides a way to analyze the effectiveness of the action and why it was chosen. Managing project risk is discussed in greater detail later in this chapter.

Project Control

Effective project management requires the exercise of control sufficient to minimize risks and maximize the likelihood of meeting or exceeding requirements. The following variables affect the quality of project control:

- *The nature and number of entities that require control.* Examples include changes in process or project requirements, the roles or performance of key team members, and the schedule for various phases of the work.
- *Control standards.* Which criteria provide the most telling measures of success in any phase of the project?
- *Control authority.* The team must identify those groups or individuals whose requirements define the performance criteria.
- *Control mechanisms.* The project plan must include devices, structures, or events that can track progress or performance against the identified standards.
- *Variance detection.* The team must understand at what point its process has veered substantially from the critical path or where performance has fallen significantly short of identified standards, so that it can make needed corrections.

To illustrate, if the management issue is control of the project schedule, the control standard might be the agreed-upon master schedule, and the business manager the control authority. Status review modules in Microsoft Project software might provide the control mechanism, as well as opportunities to detect intolerable variances from the standard. Missing or easily bypassed controls can prevent the successful completion of a project.

Project Visibility

It is essential to manage communication among team members and between the team and any project stakeholders. Techniques can usefully range from the old-fashioned approach sometimes called "managing by walking around" to the more technological approaches of video conferencing, e-mail, and voice mail. One effective technique to raise visibility uses a project information center comprised of physical displays in a central location.

Project Status

Status checks measure the project's performance against the plan to alert everyone to any adjustments needed to the budget, schedule, or other business or technical aspects of the project. The status of these elements should be evaluated in a combined format, because of their interrelationship.

Corrective Action

Corrective techniques can place the project back on track after a variation from the plan is detected. Examples of these reactive techniques include adding work shifts, lengthening work hours, and changing leadership.

Project Leadership

Project leadership is the management quality that binds the other eight elements together. Lack of leadership can result in unmotivated people doing the wrong things and ultimately derailing the project. Strong project leaders skillfully manage team composition, reward systems, and other techniques to focus, align, and motivate team members. Figure 10.11 reflects the inverse relationship between the magnitude of the project leader's role and the experience and commitment of the team. In organizations with strong processes for project management and professionals trained for this activity, the need for aggressive project leadership is reduced. However, strong project leaders are needed to help the organization develop project competency to begin with.

▶ IT PROJECT DEVELOPMENT METHODOLOGIES

One of the sayings in the industry is that there is no such thing as an IT project; all projects are really business projects involving varying degrees of IT. Sometimes, managing the IT component of a project is referred to separately as an IT project, not only for simplicity, but because the business world perceives that managing an IT project is somehow different from managing any other type of project. However, projects done by the IT department typically include an associated business case; and even though the project owner may be an IT person, mounting evidence indicates that IT projects are just business projects involving significant amounts of technology. The more complex the IT aspect of the project, the higher is the risk of failure of the project

The choice of development methodologies and managerial influences also distinguish IT projects from other projects. The general manager needs to understand the issues specific to the IT aspects of projects in order to select the right management tools for the particular challenges presented in such projects. IT professionals use four main methodologies to manage the technology projects. Of

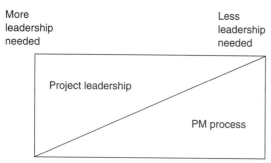

More leadership needed

Less leadership needed

Project leadership

PM process

No PM process exists
Team is new to PM process
Team does not value process

PM process exists
Team is fully trained in process
Team values process

FIGURE 10.11   Project leadership vs. project management process.

those methods, **systems development life cycle (SDLC)** is a popular method for developing information systems. Other methods are prototyping, rapid applications development (RAD), and joint applications development (JAD).

Systems Development Life Cycle

Systems development is the set of activities used to create an IS. The SDLC typically refers to the process of designing and delivering the entire system. Although the system includes the hardware, software, networking, and data (as discussed in Chapter 6), the SDLC generally is used in one of two distinct ways. On the one hand, SDLC is the general project plan of all the activities that must take place for the entire system to be put into operation, including the analysis and feasibility study, the development or acquisition of components, the implementation activities, the maintenance activities, and the retirement activities. In the context of an information system, however, SDLC can refer to a highly structured, disciplined, and formal process for design and development of the software of the system. In either view, the SDLC is grounded upon the systems approach and allows the developer to focus on system goals and trade-offs.

SDLC refers to a process in which the phases of the project are well documented, milestones are clearly identified, and all individuals involved in the project fully understand what exactly the project consists of and when deliverables are to be made. This approach is much more structured than other development approaches, such as prototyping, RAD, or JAD. However, despite being a highly structured approach, no single well-accepted SDLC process exists.

For any specific organization, and for a specific project, the actual tasks under each phase may vary. In addition, the checkpoints, metrics, and documentation may vary somewhat. SDLC typically consists of seven phases (see Figure 10.12). Each phase is carefully planned and documented. The first phase is the initiation of the

Phase	Description	Sample Activities
Initiation and feasibility	Project is begun with a formal initiation and overall project is understood by IS and user/customers.	Document project objectives, scope, benefits, assumptions, constraints, estimated costs and schedule, and user commitment mechanisms.
Requirements definition	The system specifications are identified and documented.	Define business functionality; review existing systems; identify current problems and issues; identify and prioritize user requirements; identify potential solutions; develop user acceptance plan, user documentation needs, and user training strategy.
Functional design	The system is designed.	Complete a detailed analysis of new system including entity-relationship diagrams, data-flow diagrams, and functional design diagrams; define security needs; revise system architecture; identify standards, define systems acceptance criteria; define test scenarios; revise implementation strategy; freeze design.
Technical design and construction	The system is built.	Finalize architecture, technical issues, standards and data needs; complete technical definition of data access, programming flows, interfaces, special needs, inter-system processing, conversion strategy, and test plans; construct system; revise schedule, plan, and costs, as necessary.
Verification	The system is reviewed to make sure it meets specifications and requirements.	Finalize verification testing, stress testing user testing, security testing, error handling procedures designed, end-user training, documentation and support.
Implementation	The system is brought up for use.	Put system into production environment; establish security procedures; deliver user documentation; execute training and complete monitoring of system.
Maintenance and review	The system is maintained and repaired as needed throughout its lifetime.	Conduct user review and evaluation, and internal review and evaluation; check metrics to ensure usability, reliability, utility, cost, satisfaction, business value, etc.

FIGURE 10.12 Systems development life cycle (SDLC) phases.

project, where it is initially discussed and scoped. Approval is acquired before proceeding to the second phase, after it is determined that the project is technically, operationally, and financially feasible. The second phase is the requirements definition phase, where the problem is defined and needs and prerequisites are assessed and documented. Often the requirements are determined by studying the existing systems. Again, approval is obtained before proceeding. The third phase involves the functional design, at which point the specifications are discussed and documented.

The system is designed in conceptual terms. Approval is obtained on the functional specifications before technical design is begun. At phase four, functional specifications are translated into a technical design, and construction takes place. Here the system is actually built. If the system is acquired, it is at this point customized as needed for the business environment. Following construction is the verification phase, where the system is tested to ensure usability, security, operability, and that it meets the specifications for which it is designed. Multiple levels of testing are performed in this phase: unit testing, pairs testing, system testing, and acceptance testing.

After acceptance testing, project sign-off and approval signal that the system is acceptable to the users, and implementation, the sixth phase, begins. This phase is the "cutover" where the new system is put in operation and all links are established. Cutover may be performed in several ways: the old system may run alongside the new system (parallel conversion), the old system may stop running as soon as the new system is installed (direct cutover), or the new system may be installed in stages across locations, or in phases. Finally, the system enters the maintenance and review phase, where metrics are taken to ensure the system continues to meet the needs for which it was designed. Maintenance and enhancements are conducted on the system until it is decided that a new system should be developed and the SDLC begins anew. The maintenance and review phase is typically the longest phase of the life cycle.

Prototyping

Several problems arise with using traditional SDLC methodology for current IT projects. First, many systems projects fail to meet objectives, even with the structure of SDLC. The primary reason is often because the skills needed to estimate costs and schedules are difficult to obtain, and each project is often so unique that previous experience may not provide the skills needed for the current project. Second, even though objectives that were specified for the system were met, those objectives may reflect a scope that is too broad or too narrow. Thus, the problem the system was designed to solve may still exist, or the opportunity that it was to capitalize upon may not be appropriately leveraged. Third, organizations need to respond quickly because of the dynamic nature of the business environment. Not enough time is available to adequately do each step of the SDLC for each IT project. Therefore, three other methodologies have become popular: prototyping, RAD, and JAD. These methodologies all use an iterative approach, as shown in Figure 10.13.

Prototyping is a type of evolutionary development, the method of building systems where developers get the general idea of what is needed by the users, and

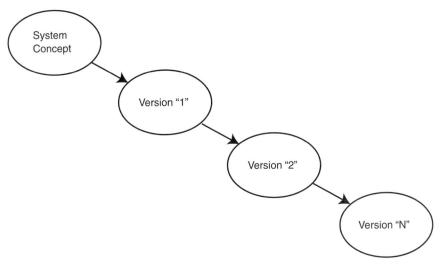

FIGURE 10.13 Iterative approach to systems development.

then build a fast, high-level version of the system as the beginning of the project. The idea of prototyping is to quickly get a version of the software in the hands of the users, and to jointly evolve the system through a series of iterative cycles of design. In this way, the system is done either when the users are happy with the design, or when the system is proven impossible, too costly, or too complex. Some IS groups use prototyping as a methodology by itself because users are involved in the development much more closely than is possible with the traditional SDLC process. Users see the day-to-day growth of the system and contribute frequently to the development process. Through this iterative process, the system requirements usually are made clear.

The drawbacks to this methodology are, first, documentation may be more difficult to write. Because the system evolves, it takes much more discipline to ensure the documentation is adequate. Second, because users see the prototype develop, they often do not understand that a final prototype may not be scalable to an operational version of the system without additional costs and organizational commitments. Once users see a working model, they assume the work is also almost done, which is not usually the case. An operational version of the system needs to be developed. However, an operational version may be difficult to complete because the user is unwilling to give up a system that is up and running, and they often have unrealistic expectations about the amount of work involved in creating an operational version. This reluctance leads to the fourth drawback. Because it may be nearly impossible to definitively say when the prototype is done, the prototyping development process may be difficult to manage. Fifth, this approach is not suitable for all systems. It is difficult to integrate across a broad range of requirements, which makes this approach suited for "quick and dirty" types of systems. Developers should rely on a more structured approach such as the SDLC for extremely large and complex systems. Finally, because of the speed of development, system design flaws may be more prevalent in this approach and the system may be harder to maintain than when the system is developed using the SDLC.

Rapid Applications Development and Joint Applications Development

Rapid applications development (RAD) is similar to prototyping in that it is an interactive process, where tools are used to drastically speed up the development process. RAD systems typically have tools for developing the user interface—called the graphical user interface (GUI)—reusable code, code generation, and programming language testing and debugging. These tools make it easy for the developer to build a library of standard sets of code (sometimes called objects) that can easily be used (and reused) in multiple applications. Similarly, RAD systems typically have the ability to allow the developer to simply "drag and drop" objects into the design, and the RAD system automatically writes the code necessary to include that functionality. Finally, the system includes a set of tools to create, test, and debug the programs written in the pure programming language. RAD is commonly used for developing user interfaces and rewriting legacy applications. It may incorporate prototyping to involve users early and actively in the design process. Although RAD is an approach that works well in the increasingly dynamic environment of systems developers, it does have some drawbacks. Sometimes basics principles of software development (e.g., programming standards, documentation, data-naming standards, backup and recovery, etc.) are overlooked in the race to finish the project. Also, the process may be so speedy that requirements are frozen too early.[8]

Joint applications development (JAD) is a version of RAD or prototyping in which users are more integrally involved, as a group, with the entire development process up to and, in some cases, including coding. JAD uses a group approach to elicit requirements in a complete manner. Interviewing groups of users saves interviewing and data collection time, but it can be expensive in terms of the travel and living expenses needed to get the participants together. A summary of the advantages and disadvantages of the SDLC, prototyping, RAD, and JAD are found in Figure 10.14.

A general manager may run into other development methodologies in the course of managing a project. One methodology that is gaining in popularity is based on a different type of programming environment, an object-oriented environment. Object-oriented development utilizes a different view of information systems components. Each is viewed as a set of objects. Object-oriented development (like object-oriented analysis, design, and programming) is based on a totally different paradigm than more traditional methodologies. Object orientation combines

---

[8] Joey F. George, "The Origins of Software: Acquiring Systems at the End of the Century," in R. Zmud (ed.), *Framing the Domains of IT Management* (Cincinnati, OH: Pinnaflex Education Resources, 2000).

Methodology	Advantages	Disadvantages
SDLC	• Structured approach with milestones and approvals for each phase • Uses system approach • Focuses on goals and trade-offs • Emphasizes documentation	• Systems often fail to meet objectives • Needed skills are often difficult to obtain • Scope may be defined too broadly or too narrowly • Very time consuming
Prototyping	• Improved user communications • Users like it • Speeds up development process • Good for eliciting system requirements • Provides a tangible model to serve as basis for production version	• Often underdocumented • Not designed to be an operational version • Often creates unrealistic expectations • Difficult-to-manage development process • Integration often difficult • Design flaws more prevalent than in SDLC • Often hard to maintain
RAD	• Speed of development • Heavy user participation • Use of GUI and other development tools	• Requirements frozen too early • Basic standards often overlooked
JAD	• Saves interviewing and data collection time • Structured process • Highly collaborative withbusiness	• Expensive • Low use of technology

FIGURE 10.14 Comparison of IT project development methodologies.

data stored about an entity with the functions the program performs that uses these entity data. It allows easy reuse of previous written software modules. Many good references are available for systems development, but further detail is beyond the scope of this text. The interested general manager is referred to a more detailed systems development text for a deeper understanding of this critical IS process.

▶ MANAGERIAL INFLUENCES

General managers face a broad range of influences during the development of projects. Many of these technical, organizational, and socioeconomic influences are relatively unique to IT projects.

Technical Influences

Complex technical issues potentially command attention that might be better focused on business and budget issues. General managers who are uncomfortable with technology often either ignore the issues, delegating entirely to the IS organization, or focus inappropriate attention on managing the technology to counter their fear. The technical aspects of IT projects do require special attention, but no more than the people, financial, or other resources of the project.

Many IT projects are built using *computer-aided software engineering* (CASE) tools. This suite of tools helps minimize the complexity and risk associated with the IS development process. CASE tools can be used to summarize system requirements, develop flow and entity relationship diagrams, schedule development tasks, prepare documentation, control software versions, and even develop program code. Three additional software tools used to aid in managing the technical issues are the software development library, an automated audit trail, and software metrics.

The *software development library* is a controlled collection of software, documentation, test data, and associated tools. Programs, utilities, and other software modules are kept here for several reasons. First is integrity. With multiple copies of a piece of software floating around an organization, it is difficult to know which copy is the actual one for the project. The software library keeps the copy that other modules can use to ensure that the correct version is available. Second is reuse. A software library is useful for programmers who need code, but do not know where to find it. The library is the storage area where programmers would look for code they want to reuse in their module. Third is control. Not only does the library ensure that the software is the right one, but it can make sure that only those authorized to work on the code have access to it.

Another tool, an *automated audit trail,* allows the team to track each change made to the code. Each step is recorded in such a way as to capture exactly what was done, making it possible to undo if necessary. The ability to trace each step is important should a problem be found. It allows the troubleshooter to retrace and in some cases to regenerate old code to identify where the problem originates. Further, some quality assurance processes require analysis of the generation process, and the audit trail provides that information.

Software metrics are another tool used to manage the technical aspects of the project. The following list serves to identify some of the key terms that a general manager is likely to encounter.

- *Source lines of code (SLOC):* The number of lines of code in the source file of the software product
- *Source statement:* The number of statements in the source file
- *Function points:* The functional requirements of the software product, which can be estimated earlier than total lines of code
- *Inheritance depth:* The number of levels through which values must be remembered in a software object
- *Schedule slip:* The current scheduled time divided by the original scheduled time
- *Percentage complete:* The progress of a software product measured in terms of days or effort

Taken together, these tools can help the team to manage technical aspects of a project in such a way as to maintain a balance with other business aspects.

Managing Organizational and Socioeconomic Influences

The general manager must understand three major organizational influences (see Chapter 1 for a discussion of these factors): organizational systems, organizational culture, and organizational structure. The control systems used for non-project-based operations usually do not support project management in an efficient manner. For example, financial reporting systems designed for daily transaction-based operations do not fit well with the reporting needs of a project. Knowing daily profit and loss may not be the best metric for managing a project. A better system would link financial and other metrics with the goals of project stakeholders such as project cost or completion progress. A consultant who bills monthly based on the percentage of the project that is complete should be monitored with a financial system that tracks resource costs based on percentage complete. The general manager should strive to align the organizational systems with the goals of the project.

The organizational culture influences the leadership style of the project manager and the communication between team members. When selecting a project manager, cultural factors should be evaluated. For example, a culture that rewards individual achievement over team participation may hinder a project team. Members might hoard information instead of sharing it. A leader who sets the example for the team has the opportunity to eliminate or reinforce these barriers. Project time and leadership might also be allocated to help the project teamwork through these barriers.

Socioeconomic influences on projects include government and industry standards, globalization, and cultural issues. Trends external to the organization, such as changes in industry standards and regulations, usually affect all projects in varying degrees. An example is the growth of Java as an operating standard for Web-developed applications. This factor greatly affected projects written in other languages. Programmers were increasingly difficult to find and many of the best and brightest only wanted jobs in the newest language. In certain cases the standards or regulations may not be known, and managing them means including possible scenarios in the risk management program. Globalization trends create the need for projects that span time zones, oceans, and national boundaries, adding to already complex conditions. Cultural influences, such as economic, ethical, and religious factors, affect the relationship between people and between organizations. All of these factors need to be considered in the project decisions made by the general manager. These influences should not be underestimated—every management text considers them important enough to warrant extensive coverage.

▶ MANAGING PROJECT RISK

IT projects are often distinguished from many non-IT projects on the basis of their high levels of risk. Consider this case example: A general manager is given six months and $500,000 to install a corporate Web site from which customers can order the company's product directly. What should the manager be thinking about as he or she begins organizing a project to accomplish this objective? Certainly project risk is an important factor to be managed. We consider risk to be a function of complexity, clarity, and size.

Complexity

What determines risk on IT projects? The first determinant is the complexity level, or the extent of difficulty and interdependent components, of the project. Several factors contribute to greater complexity in IT projects. The first is the sheer pace of technological change. The increasing numbers of products and technologies affecting the marketplace cause rapidly changing views of any firm's future business situation. For example, introducing a new programming language such as Java creates significantly different ideas in people's minds about the future direction of Web development. Such uncertainty can make it difficult for project team members to identify and agree on common goals. This fast rate of change also creates new vocabularies to learn as technologies are implemented, which can undermine effective communication.

The development of more complex technologies accelerates the trend toward increased specialization among members of a project team and multiplies the number of interdependencies that must be tracked in project management. Team members must be trained to work on the new technologies. More subprojects must be managed, which, in turn, means developing a corresponding number of interfaces to integrate the pieces (i.e., subprojects) back into a whole.

High complexity played a part in the failure of BAE Automated Systems to provide the City of Denver Airport with a single automated baggage handling system as described in the press and documented in a Harvard Business School case.[9] The original baggage system was scheduled to be completed in June 1993 and was planned to service the concourse of a single carrier: United Airlines. However, during the course of the project the City of Denver asked BAE to expand the system to encompass baggage handling for the entire airport. This project proved to be too complex to be accomplished in the time available. The technology and software systems could not be scaled up to meet the demands of the whole airport, and after long delays, court battles, and millions of dollars lost, the airport installed two additional baggage systems that had been developed by other firms.

Complexity can be determined once the context of the project has been established. Questions that might be used to build this context include the following:

- How many products will this Web site sell?
- Will this site support global, national, regional, or local sales?

[9] For more detail, see L. Applegate, R. Montealegre, H. J. Nelson, and C. Knoop, "BAE Automated Systems (A): Denver International Airport Baggage-Handling System," Harvard Business School case 396311 (November 1996), pp. 1–15.

- How will this sales process interface with the existing customer fulfill-ment process?
- Does the company possess the technical expertise in-house to build the site?
- What other corporate systems and processes will this project affect?
- How and when will these other systems be coordinated?

Clarity

A project is more risky if it is hard to define. Clarity is concerned with the ability to define the requirements of the system. A project has low clarity if the users cannot eas-ily state their needs or define what they want from the system. The project also has low clarity if user demands for the system or regulations that guide the structure of the sys-tem change considerably over the life of a project. A project with high clarity is one in which the systems requirements do not change and can be easily documented. Purchasing a scheduling software package that applies scheduling rules across a broad range of organizations would be an example of a high-clarity project for most firms.

Size

Size also plays a big role in project risk. All other things being equal, big projects are riskier than smaller ones. A project can be considered big if it has the follow-ing characteristics:

- Large budget relative to other budgets in the organization
- Large number of team members (and hence reflecting a large number of man-months)
- Large number of organizational units involved in the project
- Large number of programs/components
- Large number of function points or lines of code

It is important to consider the relative size.[10] At a small company with an aver-age project budget of $30,000, $90,000 would be a large project. However, to a major corporation that just spent $2 million implementing an ERP, a $90,000 budget would be peanuts.

High Risk Level

The IS project management literature usually views risk management as a two-stage process: first the risk is assessed and then actions are taken to control it.[11] The pro-ject's complexity, clarity, and size determine its risk. Varying levels of these three determinants differentially affect the amount of project risk. At one extreme, large, highly complex projects that are low in clarity are extremely risky. In contrast, small

[10] L. Applegate, F. W. McFarlan, and J. L. McKenney, *Corporate Information Systems Management: Text and Cases,* 5th ed. (Boston: Irwin McGraw-Hill, 1999).

[11] R. Schmidt, K. Lyytinen, M. Keil, and P. Cule, "Identifying Software Project Risks: An International Delphi Study," *Journal of Management Information Systems,* 17, 4 (Spring 2001), pp. 5–36.

projects that are low in complexity and high in clarity are low risk. Everything else is somewhere in between.

The level of risk determines how formal the project management system and detailed the planning should be. When it is difficult to estimate how long or how much a project will cost because it is so complex or what should be done because its clarity is so low, formal management practices or planning is inappropriate. A high level of planning is not only almost impossible in these circumstances because of the uncertainty surrounding the project, but it also makes it difficult to adapt to external changes that are bound to occur. On the other hand, formal planning tools may be useful in low-risk projects because they can help structure the sequence of tasks as well as provide realistic cost and time targets.[12]

Managing the Complexity Aspects of Project Risk

The more complex the project, the greater is the risk. The increasing dependence on IT in all aspects of business means that managing the risk level of an IT project is critical to a general manager's job. Organizations increasingly embed IT deeper into their business processes, raising efficiency but also increasing risk. Many companies now rely entirely on IT for their revenue-generating processes, whether the process uses the Internet or not. For example, airlines are dependent on IT for generating reservations and ultimately sales. If the reservation system goes down, that is, if it fails, agents simply cannot sell tickets. In addition, even though the airplanes technically can fly if the reservation system fails, the airline cannot manage seat assignments, baggage, or passenger loads without the reservation system. In short, the airline would have to stop doing business should its reservation system fail. That type of dependence on IT raises the risk levels associated with adding or changing the system. The manager may adopt several strategies in dealing with complexity including leveraging the technical skills of the team, relying on consultants to help deal with project complexity, and other internal integration strategies.

Leveraging the Technical Skills of the Team   When a project is complex, it is helpful to have a leader with experience in similar situations, or who can translate experiences in many different situations to this new complex one. For projects high in complexity, it also helps to have team members with significant work experience, especially if it is related.

Relying on Consultants and Vendors   Few organizations develop or maintain the in-house capabilities they need to complete complex IT projects. Risk-averse managers want people who possess crucial IT knowledge and skills. Often that skill set can be attained only from previous experience on similar IT projects. Such people are easier to find at consulting firms because consultants' work is primarily project based. Consulting firms rely on processes that develop the knowledge and experience of their professionals. Thus, managers often choose to "lease" effective IT team skills rather than try to build them within their own people. However, the project manager must balance the benefits achieved from bringing in outsiders with the costs of not developing that skill set in-house. When the project is over and the consultants leave, will the organization be able to manage without them? Having too many outsiders on a team also makes alignment more difficult. Outsiders may have different objectives, such as selling more business, or learning new skills, which might conflict with the project manager's goal of completing the project.

Integrating Within the Organization   Highly complex projects require good communication among the team members, which helps them to operate as an integrated unit. Ways of increasing internal integration include holding frequent team meetings, documenting critical project decisions, and conducting regular technical status reviews.[13] These approaches ensure that all team members are "on the same page" and are aware of project requirements and milestones.

Managing Clarity Aspects of Project Risk

When a project has low clarity, project managers need to rely more heavily upon the users to define system requirements. It means managing project stakeholders and sustaining commitment to projects.

Managing Project Stakeholders   A project's low clarity may be the result of its multiple stakeholders' conflicting needs and expectations for the system. Stakeholders are individuals and organizations that are actively involved in the project, or whose interests may be positively or negatively affected as a result of project execution or successful project completion.[14] The project manager must balance the goals of the various project stakeholders to achieve desired project outcomes. The project manager may also need to specifically manage stakeholders. It is not always a simple task to identify project stakeholders. They may be employees, managers, users, other departments, or even customers. However, failure to manage these stakeholders can lead to costly mistakes later in the project if a particular group is not supportive of the project.

Key stakeholders on every project include the following:[15]

- *Project manager:* This individual is responsible for managing the project.
- *Customer:* This individual or organization uses the project product. Multiple layers of customers may be involved. For example, the customers for a new pharmaceutical product may include the doctors who prescribe it, the patients who take it, and the insurers who pay for it.
- *Performing organization:* This enterprise provides the employees who are most directly involved in doing the work of the project.
- *Sponsor:* This individual or group within the performing organization provides the financial resources, in cash or in kind, for the project.

[13] Barki et al.,"An Integrative Contingency Model of Software Project Risk Management"; and Applegate et al., *Corporate Information Systems Management.*

[14] Project Management Institute Standards Committee, *A Guide to the Project Management Body of Knowledge* (Project Management Institute, 1996), p. 15.

[15] Ibid.

Managing the expectations and needs of these people often involves both the project manager and the general manager. Project sponsors are especially critical for IT projects with organizational change components. Sponsors use their power and influence to remove project barriers by gathering support from various social and political groups both inside and outside the organization. They often prove to be valuable when participating in communication efforts to build the visibility of the project.

Sustaining Commitment to Projects

A key job of the project management team is to gain commitment from stakeholders and to sustain that commitment throughout the life of the project. Research indicates four primary types of determinants of commitment to projects (see Figure 10.15).[16] They include project determinants, psychological determinants, social determinants, and organizational determinants. Project teams often focus on only the project factors, ignoring the other three types because of their complexity. By identifying how these factors are manifested in an organization, however, project managers can use tactics to ensure a sustained commitment. For example, to maintain commitment, a project team might continually remind stakeholders of the benefits to gain from completion of this project. Likewise, assigning the right project champion the task of selling the project to all levels of the organization can maintain commitment. Other strategies to encourage stakeholder, especially user, buy-in so that they can help clarify project requirements are making a user the project team leader; placing key stakeholders on the project team; placing key stakeholders in charge of the change process, training or installing the system; and formally involving stakeholders in the specification approval process.

Pulling the Plug

These various risk management strategies are designed to turn potentially troubled projects into successful ones. Often, projects in trouble persist long after they should be abandoned. Research shows that the amount of money already spent on a project biases managers toward continuing to fund the project even if its prospects for success are questionable.[17] Other factors can also enter in the decision to keep projects too long. For example, when the penalties for failure within an organization are high, project teams are often willing to go to great lengths to ensure that their project persists, even if it means extending resources. Also, a propensity for taking risks or an emotional attachment to the project by powerful individuals within the organization can contribute to a troubled project continuing well beyond reasonable time limits.

---

[16] See, for example, Mark Keil, "Pulling the Plug: Software Project Management and the Problem of Project Escalation," *MIS Quarterly*, 19, 4 (December 1995), pp. 421–447; and Michael Newman and Rajiv Sabherwal, "Determinants of Commitment to Information Systems Development: A Longitudinal Investigation," *MIS Quarterly*, 20, 1 (March 1996), pp. 23–54.

[17] M. Keil, et al, "A Cross-Cultural Study on Escalation of Commitment Behavior in Software Projects," *MIS Quarterly*, 24, 2 (2000), pp. 299–325.

Determinant	Description	Example
Project	Objective attributes of the project such as cost, benefits, expected difficulty, and duration	Projects are more likely to have higher commitment if they involve a large potential payoff.
Psychological	Factors managers use to convince themselves things are not so bad, such as previous experience, personal responsibility for outcome, and biases	Projects are more likely to have higher commitment when there is a previous history of success.
Social	Elements of the various groups involved in the process, such as rivalry, norms for consistency, and need for external validation	Projects are more likely to have higher commitment when external stakeholders have been publicly led to believe the project will be successful.
Organizational	Structural attributes of the organization, such as political support, and alignment with values and goals	Projects are more likely to have higher commitment when there is strong political support from executive levels.

FIGURE 10.15 Determinants of commitment for IT projects.

Source: Adapted from Mark Keil, "Pulling the Plug: Software Project Management and the Problem of Project Escalation," *MIS Quarterly* (December 1995); and Michael Newman and Rajiv Sabherwal, "Determinants of Commitment to Information Systems Development: A Longitudinal Investigation," *MIS Quarterly* (March 1996).

Measuring Success

How does a manager know when a project has been a success? At the start of the project, the general manager should consider several aspects based on achieving the business goals. Care is needed to prevent forming a set of goals that is too narrow or too broad. It is important that the goals be measurable so that they can be used throughout the project to provide the project manager with feedback.

Four dimensions of success are shown in Figure 10.16. The dimensions are defined as follows:

- *Resource constraints:* Does the project meet the established time and budget criteria? Most projects set some measure of success along this dimension, which is a short-term success metric that is easy to measure.

- *Impact on customers:* How much benefit does the customer receive from this project? Although some IT projects are transparent to the organization's end customer, every project can be measured on the benefit to the immediate customer of the IS. This dimension includes performance and technical specification measurements.

Success	Low Tech	Medium Tech	High Tech
Dimension	*Existing technologies with new features*	*Most technologies are new but available before the project*	*New, untested technologies*
Resource Constraint	Important	Overruns acceptable	Overruns most likely
Impact on Customers	Added value	Significantly improved capabilities	Quantum leap in effectiveness
Business Success	Profit; Return on Investment	High profits; Market share	High, but may come much later; Market leader
Prepare the Future	Gain additional capabilities	New market; New service	Leadership-core and future technologies

FIGURE 10.16   Success dimensions for various project types.

Source: Adapted from Aaron Shenhar, Dov Dvir, and Ofer Levy, "Project Success: A Multidimensional Strategic Approach," Technology and Innovation Management Division (1998).

- *Business success:* How high are the profits and how long do they last? Did the project meet its return on investment goals? This dimension must be aligned with the business strategy of the organization.

- *Prepare the future:* Has the project altered the infrastructure of the organization so that in the future business success and customer impact are more likely? Today many companies are building Internet infrastructures in anticipation of future business and customer benefits. Overall success of this strategy will only be measurable in the future, although projects underway now can be evaluated on how well they prepare the business for future opportunities.

What other considerations should be made when defining success? Is it enough just to complete a project? Is it necessary to finish on time and on budget? What other dimensions are important? The type of project can greatly influence how critical each of these dimensions is in determining the overall success of the project. It is the responsibility of the general manager to coordinate the overall business strategy of the company with the project type and the project success measurements. In this way, the necessary organizational changes can be coordinated to support the new information system.

▶ FOOD FOR THOUGHT: OPEN SOURCING

Linux, the brainchild of Linus Torvalds, is a world-class operating system created out of part-time hacking by several thousand developers scattered all over the planet, and connected only by the Internet. This system was built using a development approach called **open sourcing,** or the process of building and improving "free" software by an Internet community. Torvalds managed the development process by releasing early and often, delegating as much as possible, being open to new ideas, and archiving and managing the various versions of the software.

Eric Raymond, the author of *The Cathedral and the Bazaar,* suggests that the Linux community resembles a great bazaar of differing agendas and approaches (with submissions from *anyone*) out of which a coherent and stable system emerged. This development approach is in contrast to cathedrals, in which software is carefully crafted by company employees working in isolation. The most frequently cited example of a cathedral is Microsoft, a company known, if not ridiculed, for espousing a proprietary approach to software development.[18]

Open sourcing is premised upon the concept of free software. *Free software* offers the following freedoms for the software users:

- The freedom to run the program, for any purpose.
- The freedom to study how the program works, and adapt it to your needs. Access to the source code is a precondition for this.
- The freedom to distribute copies so that you can help your neighbor.
- The freedom to improve and release your improvements to the public, so that the whole community benefits. Access to source code is a precondition for this.[19]

A user who modifies the software must observe the rule of *copyleft*, which stipulates that the user cannot add restrictions to deny other people their central freedoms regarding the free software.

Open sourcing is a movement that offers a speedy way to develop software. Further, because it is made available to a whole community, testing is widespread. Finally, its price is always right—it is free. However, a number of managerial issues are associated with its use in a business organization.

- *Preservation of intellectual property.* The software is open to the whole community. It cannot be sold, and its use cannot be restricted. So the community is the "owner" of the code. Yet, how are the contributions of individuals recognized?
- *Updating and maintaining open source code.* A strength of the open-source movement is that it is open to the manipulation of members of an entire community. That very strength makes it difficult to channel the updating and maintenance of code.

---

[18] Eric S. Raymond, "The Cathedral and the Bazaar," available at http://www.tuxedo.org/~esr/writings/cathedral-bazaar/ (accessed June 27, 2002).

[19] GNU Project—Free Software Foundation, "The Free Software Definition," available at http://www.gnu.org/philosophy/free-sw.html (accessed April 3, 2002).

- *Competitive advantage.* Because the code is available to all, a company would not want to open-source a system that it hopes can give it a competitive advantage.
- *Tech support.* The code may be free, but technical support usually isn't. Users of a system that was open-sourced must still be trained and supported.
- *Standards.* Standards are open. Yet in a technical world that is filled with incompatible standards, open sourcing may be unable to charter a viable strategy for selecting and using standards.

▶ SUMMARY

- A general manager fulfills an important role in project management. As a participant, the general manager may be called upon to select the project manager, to provide resources to the project manager, and to provide direction to the project.
- Project management involves continual trade-offs. The project triangle highlights the need to delicately balance cost, time, and scope in order to achieve quality in a project.
- Four important project elements are common project vocabulary, teamwork, project cycle plan, and project management.
- Understanding the complexity of the project, the environment in which it is developed, and the dimensions used to measure project success allows the general manager to balance the trade-offs necessary for using resources effectively and to keep the project's direction aligned with the company's business strategy.
- Four popular information technology project development methodologies are the SDLC, prototyping, JAD, and RAD. Each of these methodologies offers both advantages and drawbacks.
- In increasingly dynamic environments, it is important to manage project risk. Project risk is a function of project size, clarity, and level of complexity. For low-clarity projects, it is important to interface with users and gain their commitment in the project. Projects that are highly complex require leveraging the technical skills of the team members, bringing in consultants when necessary, and using other strategies to promote internal integration.
- Projects are here to stay, and every general manager must be a project manager at some point in his or her career. As a project manager, the general manager is expected to lead the daily activities of the project. This chapter offers insight into the necessary skills, processes, and roles that project management requires.

▶ KEY TERMS

cost (p. 241)
joint applications development (JAD) (p. 258)
open sourcing (p. 269)
project (p. 240)

project management (p. 241)
prototyping (p. 256)
rapid applications development (RAD) (p. 258)

scope (p. 241)
systems development life cycle (SDLC) (p. 254)
time (p. 241)

► DISCUSSION QUESTIONS

1. What are the trade-offs between cost, quality, and time when designing a project plan? What criteria should managers use to manage this trade-off?

2. Why does it often take a long time before troubled projects are abandoned or brought under control?

3. What are the critical success factors for a project manager? What skills should managers look for when hiring someone who would be successful in this job?

4. What determines the level of technical risk associated with a project? What determines the level of organizational risk? How can a general manager assist in minimizing these risk components?

5. Lego's Mindstorms Robotics Invention System was designed for 12-year-olds. But after more than a decade of development at the MIT Media Lab using the latest advances in artificial intelligence, the toy created an enormous buzz among grown-up hackers. Despite its stiff $199 price tag, Mindstorms sold so quickly that store shelves were emptied two weeks before its first Christmas in 1998. In its first year, a staggering 100,000 kits were sold, far beyond the 12,000 units the company had projected. Seventy percent of Mindstorms' early customers were old enough to vote. These customers bought the software with the intention of hacking it. They wanted to make the software more flexible and powerful. They deciphered Mindstorms' proprietary code, posted it on the Internet, began writing new advanced software, and even wrote a new operating system for their robots. To date Lego has done nothing to stop this open-source movement, even though thousands of Lego's customers now operate their robots with software the company didn't produce or endorse, and can't support. The software may end up damaging the robot's expensive infrared sensors and motors.[20]

   a. What are the advantages of Lego's approach to open sourcing?

   b. What are the disadvantages of Lego's approach to open sourcing?

   c. How should Lego manage the open-source movement?

CASE STUDY 10-1

AVON PRODUCTS, INC., FINANCIAL SYSTEMS

Avon Products, Inc., founded in 1886, has grown from door-to-door sales in the Northeast United States to a global sales force calling on customers in more than 120 nations. Expansion into emerging markets is growing faster than sales in established economies such as the United States, Canada, and Western Europe. The door-to-door sales strategy is especially well suited to nations with underdeveloped retail infrastructures since unreliable transportation, inadequate storage facilities, and limited advertising opportunities make traditional types of retailing near impossible.

---

[20] Excerpted from Paul Keegan, "Lego: Intellectual Property Is Not a Toy," *Business 2.0* (October 2001), available at http://www.business2.com/articles/mag/0,1640,16981,FF.html (accessed June 27, 2002).

operational management tools. And they must be flexible enough to adapt to local market requirements. For example, Brazil has over 200 different district and regional taxing organizations, and each has its own requirements. So Avon must customize its financial statements to address all the laws in each area.

The rollout of the global system required detail planning. This began with a corporate task force made up of financial mangers from several countries, and corporate financial and IS staff. Systems requirements were developed from a detailed study of regulations, taxes, and so on for each country and region. A corporate implementation team of less than 20 people managed 35 divisional teams lead by local personnel. The corporate team developed a single prototype plan as the basic structure for each location. The hardware was standardized on the AS/400 instead of the latest client/server hardware because many regions did not have technical expertise to support the newest technologies. The implementation plans were developed to deploy the system in 40 countries, and documents were translated into local languages.

Implementation at each site took about nine months—the first three months were used to plan and install equipment, and the last six months were used for software installation and training. The Global Finance Director assigned his financial accounting manager and two others to work on the implementation full time. The finance department formed an Avon Users Group to provide a mechanism for communication and support. It offered a company-wide bulletin board for sharing tips to make the implementation go smoothly. It was especially useful for sites in Asia, which needed information outside the normal U.S. business hours.

Local acceptance was critical to the systems success. Local financial directors were in charge of the implementation in their locations to encourage acceptance and to avoid a "top-down" mandate that might have been resisted. The local teams reported weekly on their progress to the corporate team. Problems and potential bottlenecks were identified as quickly as possible and plans made to eliminate them. Problems in one location were used as red flags for other areas. For example, departments in different countries used different formulas for allocating expenses. In response, a common database containing all of these formulas was made so all sites could access them.

The implementation was a success. Locations with antiquated systems have automated tedious manual tasks, such as the Mexico office, which used to type checks by hand. The new system can use electronic funds transfer to pay bills. Best practices were identified from around the world and expanded to include the whole corporation. And unexpected savings came from a variety of sources, such as the Canadian office saving $21,000 per year on computer paper since eliminating the batch processing on their mainframe. Planning and execution minimized culture shock. For example, accountants needed to be convinced that they could accurately keep the books with the new, automated system. But once implemented, the tools that streamlined Avon's financial systems gave them the platform for further expansion into even more remote locations and villages around the world.

Discussion Questions

1. What were the sources of risk for Avon's global rollout of its new system? What do you think the corporate team planned to do to minimize this risk?
2. What were the key roles used to manage this project? What role did the local financial managers play in this project? What might have been used as an incentive to get local managers to align with corporate objectives?
3. How might the corporate team ensure that local best practices from around the world be preserved, and possibly transferred to others in the company?

Source: Condensed from Peter Fabris, "Financial Systems: Global Market Scents," *CIO Magazine* (September 1, 1995).

KNOWLEDGE
MANAGEMENT[1]

The accounting and consulting firm Ernst & Young (E&Y) implemented a state-of-the-art knowledge management system through which 84,000 people in its global organization can share leading practices and intelligence. This intranet allows access to more than 1,200 internal knowledge bases and external sources supplying business knowledge and global news and information. In addition, E&Y developed software tools that rate information in the knowledge bases according to its reliability and that respond to search requests with unsought information that may be relevant to the situation at hand. The firm created a Center for Business Knowledge, a network of subject-matter professionals at 14 strategic locations around the world. The center packages knowledge—from client reports and other forms of internal documentation—for easy assimilation, develops proprietary insight into business situations, and monitors and updates E&Y's knowledge bases. The firm's Center for Business Innovation also fosters strategic thinking on business process, information technology (IT), change management, and knowledge management to develop practical solutions.

In 2002, E&Y was ranked as one of the top 10 Most Admired Knowledge Enterprises in North America, according to a study conducted by Teleos and The KNOW Network, and was named to the Hall of Fame for Most Admired Organizations for Knowledge Management because of its knowledge leadership, collaborative enterprise knowledge sharing, and value creation through customer knowledge. Its knowledge management efforts contributed to the firm's success: E&Y sustained steady revenue growth even in sluggish economies, and often led the "Big Five" in revenue growth. E&Y exemplifies a comprehensive strategic approach to knowledge management. Knowledge management, one of the most popular business solutions, seeks to collect, organize, and distribute knowledge to leverage its value collectively across the organization. Many companies concentrate their efforts on gathering and storing information that may provide continuing value, but they fail to follow through on helping their employees to use it effectively. E&Y

[1] The authors wish to acknowledge and thank Ben Ballengee, MBA 1993, PhD 2001 for his help in researching and writing early drafts of this chapter.

emphasizes strategies for organizing information and providing it to employees when it is most useful to them.[2]

This chapter provides an overview of knowledge management; describes its infrastructure and key elements, functions, and strategies; and briefly examines the role played by technology in managing knowledge. This chapter defines **knowledge management** as the processes necessary to generate, capture, codify, and transfer knowledge across the organization to achieve competitive advantage. Individuals are the ultimate source of organizational knowledge. The organization gains only limited benefit from knowledge isolated within individuals or among workgroups; to obtain the full value of knowledge, it must be captured and transferred across the organization. In this chapter, we focus on knowledge management as infrastructure for business applications, not as an application itself.

Knowledge management is related to information systems (IS) in three ways. First, information technologies make up the infrastructure for knowledge management systems. Second, knowledge management systems make up the data infrastructure for many IS and applications. The knowledge management system provides the source for information needed to run the business. Third, knowledge management is often referred to as an application of IS, much like e-mail, word processing, and spreadsheets. It is increasingly being used as a business application itself in such forms as document management, information retrieval, product document management, data mining, and data visualization.

Two other terms frequently encountered in discussions of knowledge are *intellectual capital* and *intellectual property*. **Intellectual capital** is defined as knowledge that has been identified, captured, and leveraged to produce higher-value goods or services or some other competitive advantage for the firm. Both knowledge management and intellectual capital are often used imprecisely and interchangeably to describe similar concepts. IT provides an infrastructure for capturing and transferring knowledge, but does not create knowledge and cannot guarantee its sharing or use.

Intellectual property allows individuals to own their creativity and innovation in the same way that they can own physical property. Owners can be rewarded for the use of their ideas and can have a say in how their ideas are used. To protect their ideas, owners typically apply for and are granted intellectual property rights, though some protection such as copyright arises automatically, without any registration, as soon as a record is made in some form of what has been created. The four main types of intellectual property are patents for inventions, trademarks for brand identity, designs for product appearance, and copyrights for literary and artistic material, music, films, sound recordings, broadcasts and software.[3] Furthermore, the Digital Tech Corps Act of 2002, recently passed in the U.S. House of Representatives, seeks to protect intellectual property by placing a lifetime ban

---

[2] Mark Klimek and Nate Hardcastle, "How Winners Do It," *Forbes* (August 24, 1998).

[3] "What Is Intellectual Property or IP?" available at http://www.intellectual-property.gov.uk/std/faq/question1.htm (accessed June 25, 2002).

on employees from revealing trade secrets, and imposing a criminal penalty of up to five years in prison and a $50,000 fine.[4]

▶ DATA, INFORMATION, AND KNOWLEDGE

The terms *data*, *information*, and *knowledge* are often used interchangeably, but have significant and discrete meanings within the knowledge management domain. The differences are shown in Figure 11.1. **Data** are specific, objective facts or observations, such as "inventory contains 45 units." Standing alone, such facts have no intrinsic meaning, but can be easily captured, transmitted, and stored electronically.

Information is defined by Peter Drucker as "data endowed with relevance and purpose."[5] People turn data into information by organizing them into some unit of analysis (e.g., dollars, dates, or customers). Deciding on the appropriate unit of analysis involves interpreting the context of the data and summarizing them into a more condensed form. Consensus must be reached on the unit of analysis.

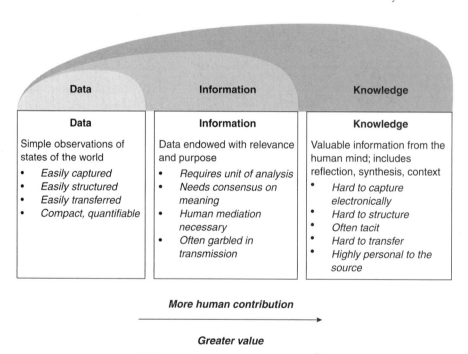

FIGURE 11.1   The relationships between data, information, and knowledge.

Source: Adapted from Thomas H. Davenport, *Information Ecology* (New York: Oxford University Press, 1997), p. 9.

[4] Jason Miller, "House Passes IT Employee Exchange Program," *Government Computer News*, available at http://www.gcn.com/vol1_no1/regulation/18347-1.html (accessed June 25, 2002).

[5] Peter F. Drucker, "The Coming of the New Organization," *Harvard Business Review* (January–February 1988), pp. 45–53.

Knowledge is a mix of contextual information, experiences, rules, and values. It is richer and deeper than information, and more valuable because someone has thought deeply about that information and added his or her own unique experience, judgment, and wisdom. One way of thinking about knowledge is to consider the different types of knowing.[6] *Knowing what* often is based upon assembling information and eventually applying it. It requires the ability to recognize, describe, and classify concepts and things. The process of applying knowledge helps generate *knowing how* to do something. This kind of knowing requires an understanding of an appropriate sequence of events or the ability to perform a particular set of actions. Sometimes the first inkling of knowing how to do something stems from an understanding of procedures, routines, and rules. Knowing how to do something is fully learned by actually experiencing a situation. Finally knowing how and knowing what can be synthesized through a reasoning process that results in *knowing why*. Knowing why is the causal knowledge of why something occurs. These types of knowing are modeled in Figure 11.2.

Values and beliefs are also a component of knowledge; they determine the interpretation and the organization of knowledge. Tom Davenport and Larry Prusak, experts who have written about this relationship, say, "The power of knowledge to organize, select, learn, and judge comes from values and beliefs as much as and probably more than, from information and logic."[7] Knowledge also involves the synthesis of multiple sources of information over time.[8] The amount of human contribution increases along the continuum from data to information to knowledge. Computers work well for managing data, but are less efficient at managing information. The more complex and ill-defined elements of knowledge (for example, "tacit" knowledge, described next) are difficult if not impossible to capture electronically. Figure 11.1 summarized these three concepts.

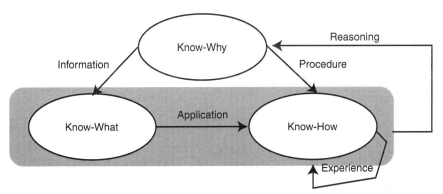

FIGURE 11.2 Taxonomy of knowledge.
Source: H-W Kim and S. M. Kwak, "Linkage of Knowledge Management to Decision Support: A System Dynamics Approach," presented at the National University of Singapore, July, 2002.

[6] M. H. Zack, "Managing Codified Knowledge," *Sloan Management Review,* 40, 4 (1999), pp. 45–58.

[7] Thomas H. Davenport and Laurence Prusak, *Working Knowledge* (Boston: Harvard Business School Press, 1998), p. 12.

[8] Thomas H. Davenport, *Information Ecology* (New York: Oxford University Press, 1997), pp. 9–10.

Tacit vs. Explicit Knowledge

Knowledge can be further classified into two types: tacit and explicit. Tacit knowledge was first described by philosopher Michael Polyani in his book, *The Tacit Dimension*, with the classic assertion that "We can know more than we can tell."[9] For example, try writing a memorandum, or even explaining verbally, how to swim or ride a bicycle. **Tacit knowledge** is personal, context-specific, and hard to formalize and communicate. It consists of experiences, beliefs, and skills. Tacit knowledge is entirely subjective and is often acquired through physically practicing a skill or activity.

IT has traditionally focused on **explicit knowledge,** that is, knowledge that can be easily collected, organized, and transferred through digital means, such as a memorandum or financial report. Individuals, however, possess both tacit and explicit knowledge. Explicit knowledge, such as the knowledge gained from reading this textbook, is objective, theoretical, and codified for transmission in a formal, systematic method using grammar, syntax, and the printed word.

The distinction between the two kinds of knowledge is important to keep in mind when considering later in the chapter how to capture and transfer knowledge. Figure 11.3 summarizes these differences. Although some experts in the field of artificial intelligence argue to the contrary, most tacit knowledge cannot be captured effectively outside the human mind. Collin's four classes of knowledge are helpful in distinguishing what knowledge can easily be captured and transferred.[10] In particular, symbol-type knowledge can be captured and transferred. However, embodied knowledge (i.e., knowledge contained in a person's body), embrained knowledge (i.e., knowledge associated with the physical setup of the brain), and encultured knowledge (i.e., knowledge associated with a society) cannot be.

Consider this example of embodied knowledge: The baseball legend Mark McGwire, with 70 home runs in 1998, broke the record for number of home runs hit in a single season. Even if it were possible to verbally describe Mark McGwire's home-run swing and put that description into writing, the process would be extremely difficult and ultimately futile. McGwire's swing incorporates so much of

Tacit Knowledge	Explicit Knowledge
• Knowing how to identify the key issues necessary to solve a problem • Applying similar experiences from past situations • Estimating work required based on intuition and experience • Deciding on an appropriate course of action	• Procedures listed in a manual • Books and articles • News reports and financial statements • Information left over from past projects

FIGURE 11.3 Examples of explicit and tacit knowledge.

[9] Michael Polanyi, *The Tacit Dimension*, 1966 ed. (Magnolia, MA: Peter Smith, 1983), p. 4.

[10] Harry M. Collins, "Humans, Machines, and the Structure of Knowledge," *Stanford Humanities Review*, 4, 2 (July 20, 1995), pp. 67-83, available at www.stanford.edu/group/SHR/4-2 /text/collins.html (accessed January 10, 2003).

his own personal experience and kinesthetic memory that it is impossible to separate that knowledge from the hitter himself. His bone structure, muscular development, and the nerves between his arm and his brain all make it possible for him to really whack the ball.

▶ AN EVOLVING CONCEPT

Managing knowledge is not a new concept,[11] but it has been invigorated and enabled by new technologies for collaborative systems and the emergence of the Internet and intranets, which in themselves act as a large, geographically distributed knowledge repository. The discipline draws from many established sources, including anthropology, cognitive psychology, management, sociology, artificial intelligence, IT, and library science. Knowledge management remains, however, an emerging discipline, with few generally accepted standards or definitions of key concepts. It will take time for new capabilities to evolve and for their opportunities to be fully understood. As industry experience is gained, and academics continue to research knowledge management, greater understanding and consensus will emerge. Persons involved with knowledge management projects should remain flexible, open to new ideas, and willing to view knowledge management as a journey rather than an end.

The most profound aspect of knowledge management is that, ultimately, an organization's only sustainable competitive advantage lies in what its employees know and how they apply that knowledge to business problems. Exaggerated promises and heightened expectations, couched in the hyperbole of technology vendors and consultants, may create unrealistic expectations. Knowledge management is not a magic bullet, an appropriate solution for all business problems. While reading this chapter, managers should consider the implications of managing knowledge, but should not believe that knowledge management by itself is the sole answer for managerial success. Knowledge must serve the broader goals of the organization, and managing knowledge must be balanced with other management tasks and the day-to-day issues of running a business.

▶ WHY MANAGE KNOWLEDGE?

Although knowledge has always been important to the success of organizations, it was presumed that the natural, informal flow of knowledge was sufficient to meet organizational needs and that no explicit effort had to be made to manage that knowledge. The value chain,[12] discussed in earlier chapters of this text, illustrates the need for knowledge in such diverse areas as raw materials handling, operations, manufacturing, sales and marketing, product distribution, customer service, firm infrastructure, human resources, research and development (R&D), and purchasing.

---

[11] The cuneiform texts found at the ancient city Ebla (Tall Mardikh) in Syria are, at more than 4,000 years old, some of the earliest known attempts to record and organize information.

[12] Michael E. Porter, *Competitive Advantage: Creating and Sustaining Superior Performance* (New York: Free Press, 1985), pp. 39–43.

Each element of the chain, for example R&D, also becomes knowledge intensive: technological developments, market trends, product design, and customer requirements must all be known and managed. In short, information and knowledge are now the fields on which businesses compete. Several trends highlight the need for businesses to manage knowledge for competitive advantage.

Sharing Best Practices

As the workplace becomes more complex and chaotic, workers and managers seek ways to share knowledge. The familiar scenario is that of an experienced guru within a business, sought by others within the organization who want to learn from the guru's experience. Sharing best practices is the concept of leveraging knowledge gained by a subset of an organization. It is increasingly important for organizations whose livelihood depends on applying expertise, such as accounting firms, consulting firms, training firms, architectural firms, and engineering firms. In these types of environments, it is inefficient to have everyone "reinvent the wheel" themselves. Rather, managers set up knowledge management systems to capture best practices and to disseminate that experience throughout the firm.

Problems commonly arise with sharing best practices, including protecting gurus and changing assumptions of institutionalized "best practices." Gurus who are rewarded for having specialized knowledge may be reluctant to share it with a knowledge management system, as was the case when KPMG Peat Marwick designed the Shadow Partner, an early knowledge management system to capture and disseminate best practices learned on client engagements. Consultants were hesitant to share their knowledge because in doing so, they were giving away something that was of value. Peers could just tap into the knowledge management system rather than contact the consultants, which decreased the power and rewards the consultants got from their work environment. KPMG Peat Marwick had to carefully manage the diffusion of the Shadow Partner to ensure that the threats of sharing information were minimized in its organization.[13]

Institutionalizing best practices by embedding them in IT makes it more efficient for an organization to handle routine, linear, and predictable situations in stable environments. When major, discontinuous change is involved, the basic premises of the best practices stored in organizational knowledge bases must be constantly reevaluated.[14]

Globalization

Products can be made and sold anywhere around the world. Designing, testing, and manufacturing can occur in parallel at different locations and the results exchanged electronically. The entire supply chain, when organized effectively, can function

[13] For more information on this case, see R. Eccles and J. Gladstone, "KPMG Peat Marwick: The Shadow Partner," Harvard Business School case 492002 (October 1995).

[14] Yogesh Malhotra,"Knowledge Management in Inquiring Organizations," in the Proceedings of 3rd Americas Conference on Information Systems (Philosophy of Information Systems Mini-track), Indianapolis, IN (August 15–17, 1997), pp. 293–295; available at http://www.brint.com/km/km.htm.

globally at a lower cost than required to operate in a single domestic economy subject to the vagaries of local supply and demand. New computing and telecommunications technologies allow data, information, and knowledge, albeit explicit knowledge, to flow instantly around the world, resulting in the emergence of an interconnected global economy. Developing countries are rapidly adapting to technological advances and building competitive production infrastructures capable of manufacturing high-quality goods at lower labor costs than developed nations. Pricing pressures resulting from these new sources of competition preclude inefficient production processes.

In the past, land, labor, and capital gave nation-states their comparative economic advantage. As a greater percentage of economic growth arises from the knowledge sector, comparative advantage derives instead from the collective ability to leverage what people know. Knowledge-based businesses seem to grow according to previously unforeseen patterns, creating new markets, and attracting and producing innovations with little need for the traditional requirements of land, labor, and capital. Figure 11.4, adapted from a similar model at IBM, summarized these forces.

Peter Drucker described this trend as follows:

> Another implication [of the emerging knowledge society] is that how well an individual, an organization, an industry, a country, does in acquiring and applying knowledge will become the key competitive factor. The knowledge society will inevitably become far more competitive than any society we have yet known—for the simple reason that with knowledge being universally accessible, there will be no excuses for nonperformance...
>
> Knowledge has become the key resource for a nation's military strength as well as for its economic strength... It is not tied to any country. It is portable. It can be created everywhere, fast and cheaply. Finally, it is by definition changing. Knowledge as the key resource is fundamentally different from the traditional key resources of the economist—land, labor, and even capital.[15]

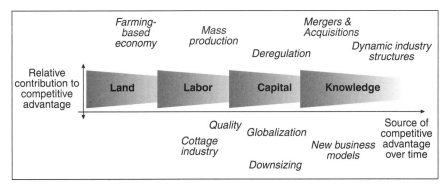

FIGURE 11.4   Forces driving knowledge as the key source of competitive advantage.
Source: © IBM Global Services. Used with permission.

[15] Peter F. Drucker, "The Age of Social Transformation," *The Atlantic Monthly* (November 1994).

Rapid Change

Rapid change means that existing knowledge becomes obsolete faster and that employees must learn new skills in less time. New technologies and unexpected forms of competition are announced daily. To keep up, new tools, processes, and strategies must be introduced. Knowledge management provides a way to optimize the use of existing knowledge and streamline the transfer and absorption of new knowledge across the firm. Rather than "reinventing the wheel," firms can customize preexisting solutions for unique customer needs. The combination of knowledge-intensive businesses, highly skilled knowledge workers, and new and relatively inexpensive computing and telecommunications technologies creates the need to organize and transfer information and knowledge in new ways. Firms must be able to sense and respond to changing trends and markets, encourage creativity and innovation, and help knowledge workers to continuously learn and improve their productivity.

Downsizing

Downsizing initiatives tend to eliminate employees and remove knowledge, in the form of experience, from the organization. By firing experienced workers and driving away the talented, important knowledge captured in the heads of former employees is lost. A change in corporate direction can result in the wholesale firing (sometimes incorrectly called a "restructuring") of an entire class of employees with specialized knowledge. As a result, veteran employees with extensive knowledge about an organization and its processes become increasingly rare. New employees, even if educated in the subject matter, need time and experience to develop specialized knowledge unique to the firm.

Downsizing also changes the traditional contract between firms and their employees, creating a more mobile work force than in the past. The changing contract results in an organizational knowledge base that becomes more volatile with employee transience. As workers change jobs more frequently, retaining knowledge within the organization, rather than in the heads of individuals, becomes more important.

By reducing the number of employees, firms increase the pressure on those remaining to accomplish more with less. Fewer employees are available to maintain and update the organization's knowledge, and less slack time is available for acquiring new knowledge. Concurrently, the speed of innovation is increasing so that knowledge evolves and must be assimilated at a more rapid rate.

Managing Information and Communication Overload

The growth of information resources along with the accelerating rate of technological change produces a mass of information that often exceed the ability of managers and employees to assimilate and use it productively. Individuals complain of receiving hundreds of e-mail messages, in addition to voice mail messages, faxes, regular telephone calls, and paper mail. As one manager put it, "If I am to keep up with my job I have to spend all of my time, both on and supposedly off the job, communicating. I don't have a life anymore."[16] According to a recent report, this flood of communication translates into white-collar workers spending a total of two hours

[16] Thomas H. Davenport, *Information Ecology* (New York: Oxford University Press, 1997), p. 48.

each day on e-mail alone, and as many as 10 billion non-spam e-mail messages per day.[17] No wonder managers complain of being stressed and overwhelmed as a result.

Even push technology, with its promise of individualized delivery of information, does not address the issues of limited time and attention, and how to store and manage the information once it is received. Data must be categorized in some manner if they are to be accessed, reused, organized, or synthesized to build a picture of the company's competitive environment or solve a specific business problem.

Knowledge Embedded in Products

Products and services are becoming increasingly complex, giving them a significant information component. Consulting firms, software manufacturers, and research laboratories all sell knowledge. Managing that knowledge is as important to them as managing inventory is to a manufacturing firm. However, other firms not traditionally viewed as knowledge-based are beginning to realize that much of the value in their products lies in the knowledge embedded in those products. Traditional manufacturing firms differentiate themselves from competitors by offering products that embed specialized knowledge. One classic example is the development of an automatic bread-baking machine by the Japanese firm Matsushita. To design the machine, Matsushita sought out a master baker, observed his techniques, and incorporated those techniques into the machine's functionality.[18] The intangibles that add the most value to goods and services are becoming increasingly knowledge-based, such as creativity, engineering, design, marketing, customer knowledge, and innovation.

Sustainable Competitive Advantage

Perhaps the best reason for knowledge management is that it can be a source of lasting and sustainable competitive advantage. It has become increasingly difficult to prevent competitors from copying and improving on new products and processes. The mobility of workers, the availability of powerful and relatively inexpensive technology, and reverse engineering make the advantages of new products and efficient processes more difficult to maintain. The life cycle of innovation is growing shorter. Competitors can usually meet or exceed the standards of price and quality developed by the market leader in a short period of time. Before that happens, however, the company managing its knowledge can move to new levels of efficiency, quality, and creativity. Unlike raw material, knowledge is not depleted through use. Shared knowledge enriches the recipient while still remaining with the original source. Knowledge is not governed by the law of diminishing returns; on the contrary, the more knowledge that is shared and used, the more new knowledge that is generated. In an age of increasing competition and unprecedented change, only one sustainable competitive advantage remains: the capacity to learn. Figure 11.5 summarizes the sustainable competitive advantages.

[17] T. Davenport and J. C. Beck, *The Attention Economy* (Boston: Harvard Business School Press, 2001), pp. 190–191.

[18] Ikujiro Nonaka and Hirotaka Takeuchi, *The Knowledge-Creating Company* (New York: Oxford University Press, 1995), p. 100.

▶ KNOWLEDGE MANAGEMENT PROCESSES

Knowledge management involves four main processes: the generation, capture, codification, and transfer of knowledge. **Knowledge generation** includes all activities that discover "new" knowledge, whether such knowledge is new to the individual, the firm, or to the entire discipline. **Knowledge capture** involves continuous processes of scanning, organizing, and packaging knowledge after it has been generated. **Knowledge codification** is the representation of knowledge in a manner that can be easily accessed and transferred. **Knowledge transfer** involves transmitting knowledge from one person or group to another, and the absorption of that knowledge. Without absorption, a transfer of knowledge does not occur. Generation, codification, and transfer all take place constantly without management intervention. Knowledge management seeks to enhance the efficiency and effectiveness of these activities and leverage their value for the firm as well as the individual. Knowledge management is a dynamic and continuously evolving process.

Knowledge Generation

Knowledge generation concerns the intentional activities of an organization to acquire or create new knowledge. In this context, knowledge does not have to be newly created, only new to the organization. The two primary ways of generating

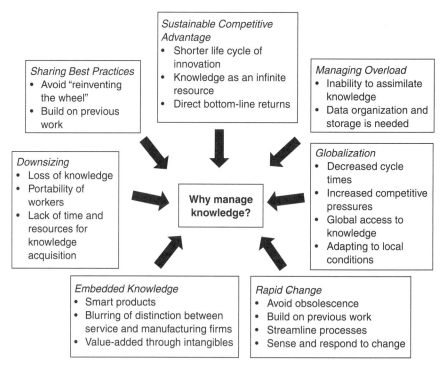

FIGURE 11.5   Reasons for managing knowledge.
Source: Adapted from IBM Global Services. Used with permission.

knowledge are knowledge creation (exploration) and knowledge sharing (exploitation).[19] Knowledge creation (exploration) involves experimenting, seeking, and discovering knowledge about alternatives. It generates new knowledge. Knowledge sharing (exploitation) uses and develops available knowledge. It tends to be faster than knowledge creation. Techniques for knowledge generation are summarized in Figure 11.6. Exploration techniques include creation and adaptation to changing circumstances. Exploitation techniques include purchase or rental, shared problem solving, and development through informal networks. Facilitating knowledge generation promotes continuous innovation and growth of knowledge in the firm.

Research and Development

True creation of knowledge is the rarest form of knowledge generation. Besides funding outside research, another way to create knowledge is through use of a dedicated R&D unit. Financial returns on research often take years to develop. Focusing on short-term profitability makes R&D, in addition to payroll, an attractive target for budget cuts. Such a short-term view may lead to long-term deficits in knowledge and competitiveness. Realizing value from R&D depends largely, however, on how effectively the new knowledge is communicated and applied across the rest of the firm.

Knowledge generated by R&D efforts, or by individuals, frequently arises from synthesis. Most new inventions are not based on entirely new ideas, but combine knowledge from different sources in unique ways so that new ideas emerge. For example, the first airplane was an innovative synthesis of three preexisting ideas: the bicycle, the motor, and the airfoil.[20] Synthesis brings disparate pieces of knowledge together, often from extremely diverse sources, then seeks interesting and useful relationships among them.

Adaptation

Firms must often generate knowledge in response to external threats; new products or competitors, changes in economic or social conditions, and government

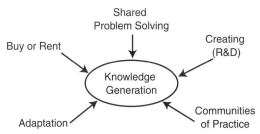

FIGURE 11.6 Knowledge generation strategies.

[19] D. A. Levinthal and J. G. March, "The Myopia of Learning," *Strategic Management Journal*, 14 (Winter 1993), p. 95-112.

[20] Rudy Ruggles, "Knowledge Tools: Using Technology to Manage Knowledge Better," working paper, Ernst & Young Center for Business Innovation (July 28 1997), available at http://www.businessinnovation.ey.com/mko/pdf/TOOLS.PDF.

regulation are examples. These outside threats force knowledge generation because if the firm does not change, it will cease to exist.[21] Adaptation is the ability to apply existing resources in new ways when external changes make old ways of doing business prohibitive. A firm's ability to adapt is based on two factors: having sufficient internal resources to accomplish change and being open and willing to change. A firm's *core capabilities*—competitive advantages built up over time that cannot be easily duplicated—can simultaneously be core rigidities, or the unwillingness to modify tried-and-true business practices. Put another way, past successes can sow the seeds of failure by inculcating managers and employees with an unwillingness to do things differently. For example, Sears failed to even list Wal-Mart as a competitor well into the 1980s.[22] Sears managers thought of Wal-Mart as a discount mass merchandiser and did not think things would change.

Buy or Rent

Knowledge may be acquired by purchasing it or by hiring individuals, either as employees or consultants, who possess the desired knowledge. Another technique is to support outside research in exchange for rights to the first commercial use of the results.

One motivation for placing a value on intellectual capital (or the knowledge of an organization), discussed later in this chapter, is to determine a fair purchase price. Organizations possessing significant knowledge may be difficult to acquire while keeping the knowledge intact. Uncertainties surrounding corporate takeovers, changes in work environment, relocation, and disruption of internal work processes may cause employees with key knowledge to leave the firm. The acquiring company may also fail to integrate new knowledge effectively. Differences in culture and internal politics may lead to resistance among new employees to share their knowledge, and among old employees to use it. Successful purchase of knowledge requires efforts to protect and integrate newly acquired employees and their knowledge into the acquiring firm.

One example of a successful purchase is IBM's acquisition of Tivoli Systems in 1996. The merger gave Tivoli new resources and global reach, while IBM allowed the firm to continue to operate autonomously without disrupting the firm's internal culture. Since the acquisition, Tivoli emerged as a leader in the enterprise management software market, and IBM increased software sales through the success of Tivoli's products.

Shared Problem Solving

Also called "fusion," shared problem solving brings together people with different backgrounds and cognitive styles to work on the same problem. Although this practice can cause divisiveness, it also provides opportunities for creative solutions. Even the most intelligent individuals can be bound by prior experience and personal style when attacking a problem.

[21] Although theoretically related, a discussion of self-organizing, complex adaptive systems is beyond the scope of this chapter. See, generally, Stuart A. Kauffman, *At Home in the Universe: The Search for the Laws of Self-Organization and Complexity* (New York: Oxford University Press, 1995).

[22] Dorothy Leonard, *Wellsprings of Knowledge* (Boston: Harvard Business School Press, 1995), pp. 30–31.

The creative energy generated by problem-solving groups with diverse backgrounds has been termed *creative abrasion*.[23] The term *diversity*, as used to describe the backgrounds of individuals in the group, should not be equated with race- or gender-based diversity as popularly conceived; rather, the key element of diversity for shared problem solving is a difference in cognitive styles. Creative abrasion does, however, require some common ground among group members, namely, a common vocabulary or shared elements of knowledge about the problem and the organization.

This overlapping knowledge is sometimes referred to as "knowledge redundancy" and provides a basis for group members to communicate about the problem.[24] Some cultural ideas that can help fusion work more effectively include (1) fostering awareness of the value of the knowledge sought and a willingness to invest in it; (2) emphasizing the creative potential inherent in different styles of thinking and viewing the differences as positive, and (3) clearly specifying the parameters of the problem to focus the group on a common goal.[25]

Communities of Practice

Informal, self-organizing networks within firms are another source of knowledge generation. Known as **communities of practice,** these groups are composed of workers who share common interests and objectives, but who are not necessarily employed in the same department or physical location, and who occupy different roles on the organization chart. The workers communicate in person, by telephone, and e-mail to solve problems together. Communities of practice are held together by a common sense of purpose and a need to know what other members of the network know. Members' effective collaboration can generate new knowledge.

Managers can nurture knowledge generation by providing sufficient time and incentives for employees to collaborate and exchange ideas. They can also recognize that knowledge generation is an important activity for the firm and encourage employees to engage in knowledge-generating activities. "[Since] it is axiomatic that a firm's greatest asset is its knowledge, then the firm that fails to generate new knowledge will probably cease to exist."[26]

Knowledge Codification

Generating knowledge by itself is a pointless task. Aside from concerns about intellectual property and proprietary knowledge, once knowledge has been generated, it must be used or shared to be of value. Codification puts the knowledge in a form that makes it possible to easily find and use. One challenge to knowledge codification is that it is difficult to measure knowledge in discrete units. Although data can be compared to a record, and information to a message, knowledge resembles an inventory. It accumulates and changes over time. Like inventory, knowledge has

[23] Ibid., p. 63.
[24] Ikujiro Nonaka and Hirotaka Takeuchi, *The Knowledge-Creating Company* (New York: Oxford University Press, 1995), p. 86.
[25] Thomas H. Davenport and Laurence Prusak, *Working Knowledge* (Boston: Harvard Business School Press, 1998), p. 62.
[26] Ibid., p. 67.

a "shelf life" to the extent that it may only add value for a period of time, depending upon its purpose and use.

The boundaries of knowledge are difficult to identify because of context sensitivity; one person's crucial fact is another person's irrelevant trivia. Consider, for example, when an instructor imparts his or her knowledge to a class. Each student in the class hears the same information, but acquires different knowledge. The instructor's personal knowledge exists in the world that he or she knows. When that instructor imparts it, it leaves that world and its associated context. The students receive that which was imparted and then map it against that which they know in order to make it their own knowledge. Because each student's base of knowing is different, each will map the information differently and, thus, will have different knowledge.[27]

In one respect, knowledge capture and codification embody the same idea: although knowledge may be technically "captured" when it resides in a database or on a sheet of paper, that knowledge is unavailable across the firm until it has been codified in a manner that will allow those who need it to find it. Davenport and Prusak identify four basic principles of knowledge codification:[28]

1. Decide what business goals the codified knowledge will serve (define strategic intent).
2. Identify existing knowledge necessary to achieve strategic intent.
3. Evaluate existing knowledge for usefulness and the ability to be codified.
4. Determine the appropriate medium for codification and distribution.

Defining Strategic Intent

Successful capture and codification require clear identification of the business problem to be solved and alignment of the knowledge to be captured with business objectives. The vague idea of making "knowledge" available to employees is not sufficiently specific. Codification is not an all or nothing proposition, and relevance is more important than completeness. Through whatever means knowledge is captured, inevitably, more knowledge will be available than can be maintained. By implementing capture and codification on a small scale in a narrow, specific problem domain, the techniques can be improved and refined before being applied to other business problems across the organization.

Identifying and Evaluating Existing Knowledge

Determining knowledge requirements can be a difficult problem because it involves understanding how persons make sense of their environment and is an extremely subjective process. At one company, a team created to define information requirements initially asked three questions: (1) What constitutes key information? (2) How should boundaries be placed around that information? and (3) From what sources should the information be obtained? These questions raised significant political,

---

[27] We are indebted to a reviewer for this example.
[28] Thomas H. Davenport and Laurence Prusak, *Working Knowledge* (Boston: Harvard Business School Press, 1998), p. 69.

psychological, cultural, and strategic issues within the firm. Potential users disagreed vehemently with content suggestions made by managers. To resolve the problem, the original team was supplemented by consultants, systems analysts, and users, all of whom were required to reach consensus on content. Throughout the process, the team maintained a tightly coupled connection between content and users' needs. The result combined "hard" information—reports, memoranda, and accounting data traditionally developed internally—with "soft" information such as ideas, gossip, and opinion. By combining both kinds of information, the team developed a knowledge requirements design that offered a rich picture of the competitive environment and was capable of dealing with imprecise and ad hoc queries.[29]

The problem with evaluating knowledge is that we cannot always know what will be, or even is, useful. Without a problem, it is difficult to define what we can use. Knowledge that is actually useful may be judged irrelevant if the problem has not been articulated. This issue certainly was the experience of the FBI and CIA with their terrorist intelligence in the months just preceding 9/11.[30]

Determining Appropriate Media

The appropriate means for codification and transmission will vary with the richness and complexity of the knowledge captured. To contort McLuhan's well-worn phrase, "The message determines the medium."

Knowledge Capture

Knowledge capture takes into account the media to be used in the codification process. Three major knowledge capture activities are scanning, organizing, and designing knowledge maps.

Scanning

Scanning typically combines electronic and human approaches as a first step in capturing knowledge after strategic knowledge has been identified. Electronic scanning can capture relevant information from a particular source (provided the information is available electronically), then filter out redundant or duplicative information. Human analysts, however, can add the most value to the scanning process by using their own knowledge of what is important to the company to provide context, interpretation, comparison, and condensation. Humans are also needed to scan and filter the soft, unstructured information available from experts and through rumor. Organizations usually have no formal or centralized scanning process and leave the scanning up to individual employees. Such individual scanning can be effective, provided the information is shared with others in the organization. The Japanese electronics firm Toshiba maintains a central team that continuously scans news wires, broadcasts, and business and industry publications for information relevant to the firm. The team synthesizes a daily

---

[29] Thomas H. Davenport, *Information Ecology* (New York: Oxford University Press, 1997), pp. 139–140.

[30] We are indebted to a reviewer for this example.

report distributed to selected users, then indexes the source data by subject and archives them to laser disc for later retrieval.[31]

Organizing

This process attempts to take the mass of knowledge accumulated through scanning and structure it into an accessible form. Some structure is necessary to permit rapid access; however, too much structure can effectively hide knowledge from employees whose mental models do not fit those of the organizer. One example would be the index of the Yellow Pages (the real ones, not the knowledge management variety to be discussed later). One person might look under "car sales" and find no entries, while another might look under "auto dealers" and discover a large number of listings. Categorization schemes are always arbitrary and never value-neutral. They necessarily reflect the views of the person creating the taxonomy. To make appropriate decisions about how to categorize knowledge, the following questions should be considered: (1) What business function will be served by the proposed categorization scheme? (2) What individual knowledge behaviors will be optimized by the proposed scheme? (3) Does the information to be categorized have any structure that lends itself to natural categorization? (4) Can an existing standardized scheme be applied without doing harm to knowledge management objectives? (5) How will the scheme be maintained and updated?[32]

One scheme for categorizing knowledge uses four broad classifications:[33]

- *Process knowledge.* Sometimes referred to as "best practices," this kind of knowledge is useful for increasing efficiency.

- *Factual knowledge.* Basic information about people and things that has been synthesized and placed in context; easy to document.

- *Catalog knowledge.* Individuals who possess catalog knowledge know where things are. These people are like directories of expertise, and while such knowledge can often be codified into a sort of Yellow Pages, the dynamics within organizations change so quickly, some individuals will always be more valuable because they know where to go for the right knowledge.

- *Cultural knowledge.* Knowing how things actually get done in an organization, culturally and politically. The absence of cultural knowledge can reduce efficiency when employees must learn or relearn invisible norms and behaviors.

An organizational thesaurus is another term for a categorization scheme. An excellent example of a standardized thesaurus can be found in the American

---

[31] Thomas H. Davenport, *Information Ecology* (New York: Oxford University Press, 1997), p. 143.

[32] Ibid., p. 146.

[33] Rudy Ruggles, "Knowledge Tools: Using Technology to Manage Knowledge Better," working paper, Ernst & Young Center for Business Innovation (July 28 1997); available at http://www.businessinnovation.ey.com/mko/pdf/TOOLS.PDF.

Productivity & Quality Center's (APQC) Process Classification Framework.[34] The framework—originally developed for benchmarking best practices among firms—allows organizations to communicate across industry boundaries and overcome proprietary vocabularies. It defines generic business processes found in multiple industries and sectors, including manufacturing, service, health care, government, education, not-for-profit, and others. The framework provides a common language for organizations to identify their processes. A number of organizations used the framework to categorize internal and external knowledge. The framework is a living document, regularly updated and maintained at the APQC Web site.

Another interesting example of a categorization scheme is *Encyclopædia Britannica*'s "Propædia," or "Outline of Knowledge." The Propædia was originally developed as a framework to classify all knowledge for inclusion in the printed encyclopedia. The designers of the search and retrieval system for *Encyclopædia Britannica*'s CD-ROM edition and Web site used the Propædia as a benchmark to measure the effectiveness of their system. The written Propædia structure told them which articles, from various parts of the encyclopedia, should be retrieved by a given query. The developers used the results to optimize their search algorithms.[35] The search engine developed from the Propædia is now being used at a Web site developed by Britannica called eBLAST.[36] A team of editors and indexers scans and identifies high-quality knowledge resources, which are then concisely described, rated according to consistent standards, and indexed for retrieval using the organizational hierarchy taken from the Propædia. The eBLAST Web navigator uses the Propædia categorization scheme to classify Web sites indexed in the system.

Designing Knowledge Maps

A **knowledge map** (see Figure 11.7) serves as both a guide to where knowledge exists in an organization and an inventory of the knowledge assets available. Although it may be graphically represented, a knowledge map can consist of nothing more than a list of people, documents, and databases telling employees where to go when they need help. A good knowledge map gives access to resources that would otherwise be difficult or impossible to find. Maps may also identify knowledge networks or communities of practice within the organization.

Some think a knowledge map is a type of organization chart. However, an organization chart is not necessarily a substitute for a knowledge map; job titles can be misleading and an employee's job description or place on the chart may not represent the expertise held by that employee. Moreover, organization charts do not reflect accessibility. Knowledge workers identified on a knowledge map must not only have the requisite knowledge, but must have the time and inclination to share it with colleagues. A knowledge map should focus on a clearly defined need or type of information rather than attempting to list all possible kinds of knowledge held by the firm. Once again, relevance is more important to mapping knowledge than completeness.

[34] American Productivity & Quality Center, Process Classification Framework (APQC International Benchmarking Clearinghouse, 1997), available at http://www.apqc.org/download/framewrk.pdf.

[35] James Fallows, "The Java Theory," *The Atlantic Monthly* (March 1996), pp. 113–117.

[36] Available at http://www.eblast.com/.

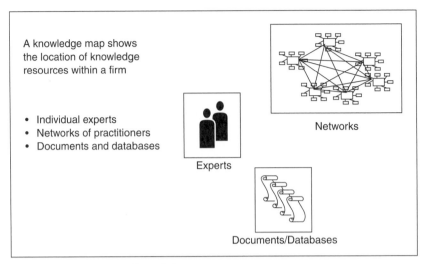

FIGURE 11.7 Contents of knowledge maps.
Source: © IBM Global Services. Used with permission.

Several different schemes may be used to map knowledge. A common, but fairly ineffective, way to map knowledge is by its physical location within the firm's IS, identifying the databases, file servers, document management systems, and groupware locations where it resides. This categorization scheme can help technically astute employees find information quickly because it shows them exactly where to find it. However, *physical mapping* is primarily of use only to those who are interested in learning the IT architecture of the organization.

Qualitative mapping points to information by topic rather than location. Qualitative mapping can be organized around processes, functions, or concepts. *Process mapping* uses a generalized model of how a business functions—such as the APQC framework previously discussed—and maps it to the knowledge contained in the organization. *Functional mapping* is based loosely on the organizational chart and is usually not effective for sharing knowledge across functions, because most workers do not have time to browse through the knowledge assets of other functional areas in hopes of finding something useful. *Conceptual mapping* is the most useful of these methods for organizing knowledge, but harder to design, build, and maintain. Conceptual maps organize information around objects, such as proposals, customers, or employees. These objects or topical areas contain information originally produced in different functional areas, which leads to transfer of knowledge across the organization.[37]

The most useful mapping technique in a given situation depends on the individual user's personal preferences, the information required, and pieces of information

---

[37] Tom Davenport, David DeLong, and Mike Beers, "Building Successful Knowledge Management Projects," working paper, Ernst & Young Center for Business Innovation (June 6, 1997); available at http://www.businessinnovation.ey.com/mko/pdf/KPROJE.PDF.

with which they begin the search. Harkening back to the political dilemmas that arose when management tried to define knowledge content without user input, companies find that the best method is to reach consensus among users, analysts, and developers before finalizing and implementing any knowledge map design.

Codifying Tacit Knowledge with Narratives

Mapping the identities of experts in an organization does not guarantee access to those experts' knowledge. An expert must have both the time and the willingness to share the knowledge. If the expert is unavailable or leaves the firm, the value of his or her knowledge is lost. A partial answer to this problem is to transfer as much knowledge as possible through mentoring or apprenticeship programs so that important tacit knowledge is not entirely concentrated in one person. Capturing tacit knowledge through narratives provides another answer.

Research shows that knowledge is communicated most effectively through a good story that, told with feeling, resonates with other people. "War stories" can convey a rich and complex understanding of an event or situation in human context, making them one of the most effective ways to capture tacit knowledge without losing much of its value. Knowledge is most likely to be absorbed if shared in a context that is understood by the listeners. More firms are beginning to circulate videotapes that tell the story, for example, about how an important sale was closed. These narratives "codify" the expert's tacit knowledge of how to close a sale in a way that conveys much of its underlying meaning.[38] The very act of telling the story shapes the firm's meaning about how expert salespeople should act.

At IDEO, a leading design firm, knowledge is spread through stories and not databases. Typically half the weekly Monday morning meetings are dedicated to sharing stories about projects or best business practices. "People hold stories in their heads better than other forms of inform," says IDEO president Tim Brown.[39]

In theory, at least, tacit knowledge can also be codified when it is embedded in a product or service. As with the Matsushita bread-baking machine discussed previously, the knower uses his or her expertise to include some of what he or she knows in the product or process. This codification can be problematic, however. If the knower departs or is "restructured," deciphering the codified knowledge may require an almost complete reverse-engineering of the product.

Knowledge Transfer

In their book *The Knowledge Creating Company*, Ikujiro Nonaka and Hirotaka Takeuchi describe four different modes of *knowledge conversion*, their term for knowledge transfer (see Figure 11.8). The modes are (1) from tacit knowledge to tacit knowledge, called **socialization**, (2) from tacit knowledge to explicit knowledge, called **externalization**, (3) from explicit knowledge to explicit knowledge, called **combination**, and (4) from explicit knowledge to tacit knowledge, called **internalization**.[40]

[38] Thomas H. Davenport and Laurence Prusak, *Working Knowledge* (Boston: Harvard Business School Press, 1998), p. 82.

[39] Catherine Fredman, "The IDEO Difference," *Hemispheres* (August 2002), pp. 52–57.

[40] Ikujiro Nonaka and Hirotaka Takeuchi, *The Knowledge-Creating Company* (New York: Oxford University Press, 1995), pp. 62–70.

TO

	Tacit Knowledge	Explicit Knowledge
FROM Tacit Knowledge	SOCIALIZATION Transfering tacit knowledge through shared experiences, apprenticeships, mentoring relationships, on-the-job training, "talking at the water cooler"	EXTERNALIZATION Articulating and thereby capturing tacit knowledge through use of metaphors, analogies, and models
Explicit Knowledge	INTERNALIZATION Converting explicit knowledge into tacit knowledge; learning by doing; studying previously captured explicit knowledge (manuals, documentation) to gain technical know-how	COMBINATION Combining existing explicit knowledge through exchange and synthesis into new explicit knowledge

FIGURE 11.8   The four modes of knowledge conversion.

Source: Ikujiro Nonaka and Hirotaka Takeuchi, *The Knowledge-Creating Company* (New York: Oxford University Press, 1995) p. 62.

Socialization is the process of sharing experiences; it occurs through observation, imitation, and practice. Common examples of socialization are apprenticeships, conferences, and casual, unstructured discussions in the office or "at the water cooler." Capturing tacit knowledge requires articulating it in explicit form (i.e., externalization), such as videotaping a story about closing a big sale to a customer. Copying and distributing the tape converts the knowledge from one explicit form to another (i.e., combination), and transferring it to members of the sales force disseminates it so others can benefit from the experience. Internalization is the process of experiencing knowledge through an explicit source. For example, after viewing the videotape and combining the new knowledge conveyed by the narrative with prior experiences, a salesperson might close a sale he or she would have otherwise lost.

▶ TYPES OF KNOWLEDGE MANAGEMENT PROJECTS

Although knowledge management projects involve a technology infrastructure, they differ radically from pure IT projects. As Davenport and Prusak point out in their "33⅓% rule," if more than one-third of the time and money spent on a project is spent on technology, the project becomes an IT project rather than a knowledge management project.[41] Figure 11.9 summarizes the contrast between knowledge management and IT projects.

[41] Thomas H. Davenport and Laurence Prusak, *Working Knowledge* (Boston: Harvard Business School Press, 1998), p. 78.

Knowledge Management Project	Information Technology Project
• Emphasizes valued-added information for users	• Emphasizes accessibility of information for users
• Supports organizational improvement and innovation	• Supports existing operations
• Adds value to content by filtering, interpretation, and synthesis	• Delivers content only
• Requires on-going user contributions	• Emphasizes one-way transfer of information
• Balanced focus on both technology and culture	• Primary focus on technology
• Variety of inputs often precludes automated capture of knowledge	• Assumes capture of all information inputs can be automated

FIGURE 11.9 Knowledge management vs. information technology projects.

Source: David DeLong, Tom Davenport, and Mike Beers, *What is a Knowledge Management Project?* Working paper, Ernst & Young Center for Business Innovation, February 17, 1997, http://www.businessinnovation.ey.com/mko/pdf/KMPRES.PDF.

Knowledge management initiatives can have either an internal or external focus, and have thus far been built around the following four themes: (1) developing knowledge repositories, (2) providing knowledge access, (3) improving the knowledge environment, and (4) evaluating knowledge assets.[42]

Knowledge Repositories

The idea of knowledge repositories is to take documents with knowledge embedded in them, such as memos, reports, or news articles, and store them so they can be easily retrieved. Another less-structured form of repository is the discussion database, in which participants record their own experiences on an issue and react to others' comments. Three fundamental types of repositories have been identified: (1) externally focused knowledge, sometimes called competitive intelligence; (2) structured internal knowledge, such as research reports, marketing materials, and production processes; and (3) informal internal knowledge, such as discussion databases for "lessons learned" and internal best practices. **Data warehouses,** or collections of data designed to support management decision making, sometimes serve as repositories of organizational knowledge. Data warehouses contain a wide variety of data used to create a coherent picture of business conditions at a single point in time.

Perhaps the greatest repository of knowledge is the Web. The problem here is not that everything on the Web is correct, at least to us. That which we *know* is the truth to us. Unfortunately, we too often discover that what we know is not really true. Knowledge repositories are riddled with both the unknown and the untrue. An example would be the established computer companies such as DEC knowing

---

[42] This taxonomy is derived from Tom Davenport, David DeLong, and Mike Beers, "Building Successful Knowledge Management Projects," working paper, Ernst & Young Center for Business Innovation (June 6, 1997), available at http://www.businessinnovation.ey.com/mko/pdf/KPROJE.PDF.

that the personal computer (PC) was little more than a toy or IBM knowing that the mainframe would always reign supreme.[43]

Knowledge Access

Even though capturing knowledge is the objective of the knowledge repository, other projects focus on providing access to knowledge or facilitating its transfer among individuals. These projects are sometimes referred to as corporate "Yellow Pages," and are internally focused with the intent of making knowledge more visible and accessible. Yellow Pages map and categorize knowledge and expertise in an organization, allowing identification of expert knowledge sources.

An approach that simulates knowledge access is **data mining,** which is the process of analyzing data warehouses for "gems" that can be used in management decision making. It identifies previously unknown relationships among data. Typically, data mining refers to the process of combing through massive amounts of customer data to understand buying habits and to identify new products, features, and enhancements. Data mining can enrich CRM systems such as Ritz Carlton's Class described in Chapter 1.

Knowledge Environment

Another type of internally focused knowledge management initiative is aimed strictly at culture, seeking to establish an environment conducive to knowledge creation, transfer, and use. This includes projects that are intended to build awareness and cultural receptivity to knowledge, initiatives that attempt to change behavior relating to knowledge, and attempts to improve the knowledge management process. One consulting firm encouraged creation and distribution of management knowledge by changing its appraisal system so that contributions to the firm's structured knowledge repository were made a significant factor in compensation decisions.

Knowledge Assets

The fourth type of initiative is internally focused on managing knowledge as an asset, sometimes referred to as intellectual capital. These initiatives attempt to treat knowledge as a balance-sheet asset to persuade investors of the value of the firm's intellectual capital and direct attention toward the effective or ineffective use of intellectual capital over time.

▶ MEASURING THE VALUE OF KNOWLEDGE MANAGEMENT

No knowledge management effort is likely to be maintained unless it provides some evidence of financial return to the organization. As the number of knowledge management projects undertaken grows, so does the pressure to measure the value of those efforts. If the acquisition and management of knowledge cannot be tied directly to bottom-line results, such projects are likely to be abandoned. As the

---

[43] We are indebted to a reviewer for this example.

director of knowledge management at McKinsey & Company observed, "The point of a knowledge-based strategy is not to save the world; it's to make money."[44]

The question of valuation is central to the Internal Revenue Services' (IRS) concerns that some U.S. firms are underreporting tens of billions of dollars because they are stashing their intellectual property abroad to shelter income from the overseas sales of intellectual property. Firms with valuable patents and trademarks, especially a number of software and pharmaceutical companies, are establishing a subsidiary in a tax haven such as Bermuda or the Cayman Islands. The offshore subsidiary buys the intellectual property at an arguably low price and collects royalties from the overseas sales of the parent company's products. Although all royalties are reported back to the IRS, only the portion of them that is transferred back to the parent is subject to U.S. taxes. The remainder of the royalties reside untaxed in the subsidiary. They can be used for overseas expansion or transferred back to the parent under more financially opportune circumstances. To carry forward its case against companies adopting this strategy, the IRS first must determine how to value royalties on intellectual property.[45]

Several methods have been advanced to assess the value of knowledge management, intellectual capital, and their relative value to the firm; none has been widely adopted or proven entirely satisfactory, and none relies on traditional accounting methods or permits common-size analysis of knowledge management efforts and intellectual capital at competing firms. Three common methods to assess the value of knowledge management are project-based measures, the intellectual capital report, and valuation of knowledge capital.

Project-Based Measures

The most common method examines the success or failure of specific projects by some metric that is supposed to be improved through leveraging knowledge. A firm might assess whether production or sales increased, or whether costs and cycle times were reduced. Sometimes called "measurement by anecdote," this technique identifies specific benefits derived from knowledge management projects. Anecdotes are easy to understand, require little expense to gather, and provide good publicity. Inherent in project-based measures is the belief that knowledge adds value, and that specific firm-wide measures are expensive and unnecessary. Some examples of this approach include the following:[46]

- *Enhanced effectiveness.* The technical support function in one computer firm undertook a number of knowledge management initiatives that reduced the volume and cost of support calls from dealers. Through identifying patterns in support calls, the team preempted many potential

[44] Brook Manville and Nathaniel Foote, "Strategy As If Knowledge Mattered," *Fast Company* (April–May 1996), p. 66.

[45] Glenn R. Simpson, "A New Twist in Tax Avoidance: Firms Send Best Ideas Abroad," *The Wall Street Journal* (June 24, 2002), pp. A1, A10.

[46] David DeLong, Tom Davenport, and Mike Beers, "What Is a Knowledge Management Project?" working paper, Ernst & Young Center for Business Innovation (February 17 1997), available at http://www.businessinnovation.ey.com/mko/pdf/KMPRES.PDF.

problems by alerting customers to frequently asked questions and providing solutions through a discussion database.

- *Revenue generation from existing knowledge assets.* By managing patents
  more effectively, Dow Chemical saved $4 million in its first year of a
  review program and expects to generate more than $100 million in
  licensing revenues that might otherwise have been forgone.

- *Increased value of existing products and services.* To enhance the value
  of its generic computer-aided design software, one developer began
  including applications designed especially for the energy and chemical
  industries with its products. Embedding industry-specific knowledge
  into the software reduces design time for customers in those industries,
  significantly differentiating the software from competitors.

- *Greater organizational adaptability.* Filtering, synthesizing, and interpreting competitive intelligence can improve a firm's ability to react to
  external changes. Threatened by a Japanese competitor that was under-
  pricing them by 50 percent, a major auto parts supplier created a competitive intelligence system to capture a predefined cost model of the
  business. Using that information, the supplier was able to quickly reposition itself in the market in response to the strategic threat.

- *More efficient reuse of knowledge assets.* Ernst & Young's Center for Business
  Knowledge tracks the number of consulting engagements in which knowledge captured from previous projects is reused. One performance measure
  for the firm's consultants is the amount of reusable knowledge created.

- *Reduced costs.* Chevron saved $150 million in annual fuel and power
  expenses through internal knowledge sharing on energy management.

- *Reduced cycle time.* Hoffman-LaRoche reduced filing time for FDA
  approval for new drugs from 18 months to 90 days, and obtained FDA
  approval, normally requiring at least three years, in 9 months. In the
  pharmaceutical industry, a single day's delay can represent up to $1 mil-
  lion in lost revenues.

Intellectual Capital Report

A widely known approach to measuring intellectual capital is the one developed at
Skandia, a Swedish insurance company.[47] The Skandia methodology (see Figure
11.10) attempts to define the market value of a company by differentiating between
traditional balance-sheet measures of equity and intellectual capital, then further
divides intellectual capital into two categories: (1) human capital, which exists in
the minds of individuals: their knowledge, skill, experience, creativity, and innovation; and (2) structural capital, which includes both (a) organizational capital, the
infrastructure supporting human capital (IS, internal processes, proprietary software and documentation), and traditional forms of intellectual property (patents,

[47] Leif Edvinsson and Michael S. Malone, *Intellectual Capital* (New York: HarperCollins, 1997).

Skandia Intellectual Capital Framework

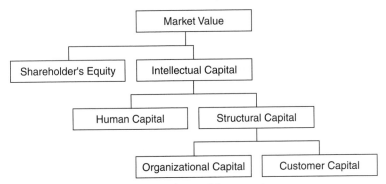

FIGURE 11.10 Skandia intellectual capital framework.

Source: Leif Edvinsson and Michael S. Malone, *Intellectual Capital* (New York: HarperCollins, 1997), p. 52.

trademarks, and copyrights); and (b) customer capital, the relationships, satisfaction, longevity, price sensitivity, and financial well-being of long-term customers.

These classifications are used to develop a set of measures for progress in managing knowledge. In its "Intellectual Capital Report," published as a supplement to its annual report, Skandia identifies 111 indexes in the following five different groups: (1) financial focus, including income per employee and market value per employee; (2) customer focus, including number of customer visits, satisfied customer index, and lost customers; (3) process focus, including administrative error rate and IT expense per employee; (4) renewal and development focus, including training per employee, the ratio of R&D expense to administrative expense, and a "satisfied employee index;" and (5) human focus, including a "leadership index," rate of employee turnover, and IT literacy among employees. Determining a fair market value for such assets, however, remains problematic.

Valuation of Knowledge Capital

If measuring the value of intellectual capital can be considered conventional in any sense, perhaps the most conventional approach was proposed by Paul Strassmann, a former IS executive in government and industry, consultant, and author. "Knowledge capital" is Strassmann's term for the value a customer places on goods or services over the cost of sales and cost of capital (i.e., the surplus value of corporate knowledge in excess of traditional accounting measures). Strassmann contends that techniques such as those used by Skandia fall short because the data derived cannot be used as an acceptable valuation of assets on the stock market.[48]

Rather than working from the bottom up and estimating the value of knowledge assets to determine intellectual capital, Strassmann works from the top down, examining the capacity of firms to generate additional revenue based on the value added to processes through knowledge. He emphasizes that the costs of acquiring knowledge and the revenue-generating potential of knowledge are unrelated. The

[48] Paul A. Strassmann, "The Value of Knowledge Capital," *American Programmer* (March 1998), pp. 3–10.

value of intellectual capital lies in its use, not in its cost. Thus, any value added through knowledge is worth only what investors are willing to pay for it.

Traditionally, knowledge assets are reflected in financial reports only after a merger or acquisition at a substantial premium over book value. At that point, such assets are recognized as "goodwill." Allowing companies to record knowledge capital as part of shareholder equity, according to Strassmann, would generate balance sheets that more closely reflect corporate value.

Knowledge capital is the amount an investor is willing to pay for intangible assets, in excess of the cost of capital, for a risk-adjusted interest in the future earnings of the company. Investors cannot differentiate between the price of capital for financial or knowledge investments because those investments are intermingled. "Management value added" is what is left over after all costs have been fully accounted. Determining management value added requires subtracting an allowance for the costs of shareholder equity and other adjustments to correct for income taxes from after-tax profits. Knowledge capital then becomes management value added divided by the cost of capital. This relationship makes it possible to prepare common-size balance sheets for any firm by adding a line item called knowledge capital on the asset side, and increasing (or decreasing) shareholder equity by the same amount.

▶ CAVEATS FOR MANAGING KNOWLEDGE

Following such a broad survey, it seems appropriate to conclude with a few caveats. First, recall that knowledge management is an emerging discipline. Viewing knowledge management as a process rather than an end by itself requires managers to remain flexible and open-minded.

Second, the objective of knowledge management is not always to make knowledge more visible or available. Like other assets, it is sometimes in the best interests of the firm to keep knowledge tacit, hidden, and nontransferable. Competitive advantage increasingly depends on knowledge assets that are difficult to reproduce. Retaining knowledge is as much a strategic issue as sharing knowledge.

Third, knowledge can create a shared context for thinking about the future. If the purpose of knowledge management is to help make better decisions, then it should focus on future events. Through the use of multiple scenarios, organizations can create "memories of the future." The goal is not to know the future, but rather to know what projections influence long-term strategy and short-term tactics.[49]

Finally, people lie at the heart of knowledge management. Establishing and nurturing a culture that values learning and sharing of knowledge enables effective and efficient knowledge management. Knowledge sharing—subject, of course, to the second caveat already described—must be valued and practiced by all employees for knowledge management to work. The success of knowledge management ultimately depends on a personal and organizational willingness to learn.

[49] Liam Fahey and Laurence Prusak, "The Eleven Deadliest Sins of Knowledge Management," *California Management Review*, 40, 3 (1998), pp. 265–276.

▶ FOOD FOR THOUGHT: DIGITAL MILLENNIUM COPYRIGHT ACT

The recent Napster case raised controversial issues long surrounding the practice of copyrighting. A decade ago, the Audio Home Recording Act (1992) was passed in the United States to prevent serial copying. Although the act protected intellectual property, it also confirmed the freedom to copy music for personal use. In 1998, the more stringent Digital Millennium Copyright Act (DCMA) passed with the active support of the entertainment industry. The DCMA makes it a crime to circumvent copy protection, even if that copy protection impairs rights established by the Audio Home Recording Act.

Violations of DCMA are being vigorously prosecuted. In July 2001, Dmitry Sklyarov, an employee of the Moscow-based software company, ElcomSoft, was criminally charged in the United States when he attended a conference to promote his company's software. A range of ElcomSoft protection-cracking products are available at their Web site, including software designed to break the copy protection in Adobe eBook so that legal owners can recover lost passwords, make backups, and copy books to Palm handhelds. Sklyarov, a Russian national, was held without bail until December 2001, and was facing a five-year prison sentence and a $500,000 fine until he agreed to testify against ElcomSoft.

Supporters of DCMA argue that ElcomSoft profits from the sale of the cracking software. Selling the software is clearly in violation of DCMA, and in doing so, the employee and his company become pirates. DCMA supporters argue that the only reason that this criminal activity is considered acceptable is because it occurs in a digital environment, where the hacker ethos penetrates so deeply that the theft of intellectual property is not only accepted, but promoted. Yet, they argue, the only way that the electronic content industry can flourish is if intellectual property is respected and protected.[50]

However, many others decry the actions taken against ElcomSoft and DCMA itself. One of the loudest voices is that of the Electronic Frontier Foundation (EFF). The EFF and others think that DCMA protects intellectual property rights at the expense of technological research and innovation, as well as the broader public interest. Critics of the law believe that while it protects the creative work of software writers, entertainers, and musicians, it fails to recognize a large and vibrant "public domain" where ideas should be freely shared.[51] Many argue that fair use in a digital world includes that rights to make backup copies, translate content into different formats, "time-shift" audio or video when making copies for later playback, or "space-shift" audios, videos, or software by copying to blank CDs, multiple personal computers, or portable players.

---

[50] P. Seybold, "ElcomSoft Supporters Miss the Point," available at http://www.planetebook.com/main-page.asp?webpageid=196 (accessed June 27, 2002).

[51] Phyllis Plitch, "The Legal Theorist," *The Wall Street Journal* (May 13, 2002), pp. R12, R14.

A number of other legal concerns with the ElcomSoft case have also been raised. It is frequently admitted by even the proponents of DCMA that the wording of the law is vague about what is "fair use" in digital environments. Further, the ElcomSoft software enables the making of at least one backup copy that is allowed by "Fair Use" under Russian copyright law.[52]

▶ SUMMARY

- Knowledge management is related to information systems (IS) in three ways: (1) information technologies make up the infrastructure for knowledge management systems; (2) knowledge management systems make up the data infrastructure for many IS and applications; and (3) knowledge management is often referred to as an application of IS.
- Data, information, and knowledge should not be viewed as interchangeable. Knowledge is more valuable than information, which is more valuable than data because of the human contributions involved.
- The two kinds of knowledge are tacit and explicit.
- For many reasons, it is advisable to manage knowledge. These reasons include benefits derived from sharing best practices, the need to respond to globalization and rapid change, organizational downsizing, the need to manage information and communication overload, controlling knowledge embedded in products, and leveraging knowledge to gain competitive advantage.
- Knowledge management is a dynamic and continuously evolving process that involves knowledge generation, capture, codification, and transfer.
- Knowledge transfer modes are socialization, externalization, combination, and internalization.
- Knowledge management projects are not as technology-oriented as information technology projects.
- The value of knowledge management programs can be measured using project-based measures, the intellectual capital report, or the valuation of knowledge capital. None of these approaches are widely adopted or totally satisfactory.

▶ KEY TERMS

combination (p. 293)
communities of practice
 (p. 287)
data (p. 276)
data mining (p. 296)
data warehouse (p. 295)
explicit knowledge (p. 278)
externalization (p. 293)
information (p. 276)

intellectual capital (p. 275)
intellectual property
 (p. 275)
internalization (p. 293)
knowledge (p. 277)
knowledge capture (p. 284)
knowledge codification
 (p. 284)

knowledge generation
 (p. 284)
knowledge management
 (p. 275)
knowledge map (p. 291)
knowledge transfer (p. 284)
socialization (p. 293)
tacit knowledge (p. 278)

[52] Lisa Rein, "And Justice for Adobe," O'Reilly Network (July 24, 2001), available at http://www.oreillynet.com/cs/user/view/wlg/505 (accessed June 25, 2002).

► DISCUSSION QUESTIONS

1. The terms *data, information*, and *knowledge* are often used interchangeably. But as this chapter discussed, they can be seen as three points on a continuum. What, in your opinion, comes after knowledge on this continuum?

2. What is the difference between tacit and explicit knowledge? From your own experience, describe an example of each. How might an organization manage tacit knowledge?

3. What are the steps in the knowledge management process? What IT would you prescribe for each step?

4. How do knowledge maps aid an organization?

5. Do you think that the Digital Millennium Copyright Act is the type of legislation that should be enacted to protect intellectual property? Why or why not?

6. PricewaterhouseCoopers has an elegant, powerful intranet knowledge management system called Knowledge Curve. Knowledge Curve makes available to its consultants and auditors a compendium of best practices, consulting methodologies, new tax and audit insights, links to external Web sites and news services, online training courses, directories of in-house experts, and other forms of explicit knowledge. Yet, according to one of the firm's managing partners, "there's a feeling it's underutilized. Everybody goes there sometimes, but when they're looking for expertise, most people go down the hall."[53] Why do you think that Knowledge Curve is underutilized?

CASE STUDY 11-1

MCKINSEY AND COMPANY

McKinsey and Company is perhaps one of the best-known management consulting firms in the world. Founded in 1926, McKinsey built a reputation for creative and innovative strategic solutions for clients. The success of this firm is in part due to a narrow focus on problems and issues only relevant to senior managers, its primary clientele. At one point, an estimated 80 percent of its business was repeat business from former clients. Its Web site sums up the firm as follows:

> The nature of the problems we help clients address has changed over the years and has reflected both differences in the relationships between large companies and their governments and the sophistication of management. McKinsey consultants designed the initial organization of NASA (U.S.), advised the Vatican (on its banking system), developed the Universal Product Code (U.S.), specified the systems supporting Frankfurt's stock exchange, and helped the Treuhandanstalt privatize East German companies.

Given the breadth and depth of this work, the intellectual tradition at McKinsey is very different from what one finds in a university or in a consulting firm that concentrates on a single problem or industry. It is a tradition that first celebrates the complexity and the

[53] Thomas Stewart, "The Case Against Knowledge Management," *Business 2.0* (February 2002), p. 81.

differences of management challenges, and then presses for practical answers based on both analysis and experience. It is a tradition that recognizes the importance of being able to reach out to colleagues wherever they are in the world.

McKinsey and Company has built an extensive knowledge management system. The McKinsey philosophy of knowledge is described on its Web site.

> Among consulting firms there are very different approaches to building and sharing knowledge. Some believe knowledge of a company or an industry introduces a backward-looking bias into their thinking and instead rely entirely on their consulting skills, e.g., interviewing, coaching, or counseling. Others build depth in a single function or industry and believe their expertise is the primary value they bring to a client. Some rely on a few people, e.g., gurus, to develop a single "big idea," e.g., reengineering, which the rest apply through codified processes. Others try to build capability and expertise throughout their consulting staff.
>
> We take the position:
>
> - That knowledge per se is of limited value until people and consulting skills (not merely processes) combine to make it valuable.
> - That both perfection and creativity should result from our knowledge (and our clients').
> - That it is in the intersections of different kinds of knowledge that truly creative and valuable insights often occur.
> - That those intersections are more likely in a team-based, integrative approach to problem solving enhanced by both a culture of collaboration and a commitment to impact.

McKinsey and Company began their investment in managing knowledge after a 1971 internal study determined that even though the consultants were excellent generalists, they often lacked deep industry knowledge or specialization needed to meet clients demands. As a result, McKinsey consultants were encouraged to develop continuously and to supplement their general knowledge with deep knowledge in an industry or specialty. Ultimately, 15 virtual centers of competence were established to develop consultants and to ensure a consistent knowledge base. Management systems were developed to reward practice development. Building on its culture of self-governance and individual initiative, industry and functional networks played significant roles in the way the company negotiated and staffed engagements and developed its people.

The knowledge management system is described on the Web site as follows:

> While some kinds of knowledge can be "codified" and "applied," most of them—the most valuable for the kinds of problems top management faces—exist only in people's heads. A consulting firm thus needs its people—not databases—to collaborate. "Knowledge management" is relatively easy. The culture and values that support it are much harder.

McKinsey's consultants share their knowledge and personally collaborate in ways that most organizations and most other consultants find remarkable. We invest in this core competence in several ways:

- Through office transfers and practice development meetings we help each of our consultants build his or her personal networks within McKinsey.
- We look for evidence that the partners responsible for a client have brought others into the team who have depth in an industry or function.

- We avoid any kind of accounting, e.g., making our industry or functional practices profit centers, that would discourage collaboration.
- As stated earlier, we grow our own offices and develop a sense of "one-firm" in all our people.
- We have invested heavily in the information technology and people (researchers, experts) that can support, but not replace, collaboration.

The knowledge infrastructure included technological as well as nontechnical initiatives. By the 1980s, the firm was actively encouraging consultants to publish their key findings in newspapers, prestigious business magazines, and trade books. Doing so required major investments of time and resources. By 1987 a committee reviewed the knowledge infrastructure, and the Knowledge Management Project recommended the firm build a common database of knowledge accumulated from client work in the practices, hire a full-time practice coordinator for each area responsible for the quality of input and assisting consultants with access, and establish career paths for deep specialists that parallel those available for generalists.

The result was an examination of the Firm Practice Information System (FPIS). This database of client engagements typically archived each project, but was overhauled to provide increased accessibility and reliable information useful for current engagements. A Practice Development Network (PDNet) was also built to manage documents representing core knowledge of each practice. Finally, a Knowledge Resource Directory (KRD) was published for internal use with a list of all firm experts and key documents. This directory became instantly indispensable to many consultants.

In the 1990s, the leadership at McKinsey again reevaluated the company's knowledge infrastructure. One partner suggested, in a case study published by Harvard Business School, that:

> Too many people were seeing practice development as the creation of experts and the generation of documents in order to build our reputation. But knowledge is only valuable when it is between the ears of consultants and applied to clients' problems. Because it is less effectively developed through the disciplined work of a few than through the spontaneous interaction of many, we had to change the more structured "discover-codify-disseminate" model to a looser and more inclusive "engage-explore-apply-share" approach. In other words, we shifted our focus from developing knowledge to building individual and team capability.

Discussion Questions

1. What is the goal of a knowledge management system for a company like McKinsey and Company? How well does its knowledge management system meet this goal?

2. "Traditional" knowledge management systems involve four steps: generation, capture, codification, and transfer. How do you think the McKinsey system implements each of these steps? How is that implementation different from the "engage-explore-apply-share" philosophy mentioned by the manager at the end of the case?

3. How should McKinsey integrate the Web and its advantages in the area of collaboration and communication in their future knowledge management strategies?

Source: Adapted from C. Bartlett, "McKinsey and Company: Managing Knowledge and Learning," Harvard Business School case 396-357 (1996); and McKinsey and Company, available at www.mckinsey.com (accessed October 28, 1999).

CHAPTER 12

USING INFORMATION ETHICALLY[1]

On December 26, 1990 the Wall Street Journal carried an article headlined "Coming Soon to Your Local Video Store: Big Brother." The report chastised Blockbuster Video for its plan to sell customer movie preference information to direct mailers and other companies for the purpose of targeted marketing campaigns. Although legality was not at issue, since the law had allowed similar sales of customer data, the article cited many sources that voiced concerns about ethical issues.[2]

The basic principle is that information collected for one purpose shouldn't be used for another purpose without an individual's consent. Many companies regularly sell their customer lists, but Blockbuster is one of a small fraction using sophisticated computers to keep records of each individual's transactions. Its database promises to raise some especially difficult privacy issues; for the same reason it should be such a gold mine for direct mailers: Video choices are among the most revealing decisions a consumer makes.

Federal law forbids video stores to disclose the names of movies its customers rent. But the law permits stores to tell direct marketers "the subject matter" of movies a customer has rented. Blockbuster—whose members constituted one out of six U.S. households at the time—contended its database was legal because it monitored only video categories, not specific titles. Selling lists of mystery movie renters to mystery book clubs, children's movie renters to toy stores, etc., promised valuable information to direct marketing firms concerned with targeting expensive direct mail campaigns. As Allan Caplan, the Blockbuster vice president overseeing the database project, told the Journal, "We not only will know their tastes in movies—we'll know their frequency and that will give us a little more information about their lifestyle."[3]

As in the case of Blockbuster, information collected in the course of business can create valuable competitive advantage. But ethical questions concerning just how that

[1] The author wished to acknowledge and thank Arthur J. Ebersole, MBA 1999 for his help in researching and writing early drafts of this chapter.

[2] Miller, M.W. "Coming Soon to Your Local Video Store: Big Brother," *Wall Street Journal*, December 26, 1990, pp.9, 10.

[3] Miller, Ibid.

information will be used and by whom, whether they arise inside or outside the organization, can have powerful effects on the company's ability to carry out its plans.[4] As computer networks and their products come to touch every aspect of people's lives, and as the power, speed, and capabilities of computers increase, managers are increasingly challenged to govern their use in an ethical manner. No longer can managers afford to view information systems (IS) as discrete entities within the corporate structure. In many cases, IS are coming to comprise much of the corporation itself.

In such an environment, managers are called upon to manage the information generated and contained within those systems for the benefit not only of the corporation, but also of society as a whole. The predominant issue, which arises due to the omnipresence of corporate IS, concerns the just and ethical use of the information companies collect in the course of everyday operations. Without official guidelines and codes of conduct, who decides how to use this information? More and more, this challenge falls upon corporate managers. Managers need to understand societal needs and expectations in order to determine what they ethically can and cannot do in their quest to learn about their customers, suppliers, and employees and to provide greater service.

Before managers can deal effectively with issues related to the ethical and moral governance of IS, they need to know what these issues are. Unfortunately, as with many emerging fields, well-accepted guidelines do not exist. Thus, managers bear even greater responsibility as they try to run their businesses and simultaneously develop control methods that meet both corporate imperatives and the needs of society at large. If this challenge appears to be a matter of drafting operating manuals, nothing could be further from the truth.

In a society whose legal standards are continually challenged, managers must serve as guardians of the public and private interest, although many may have no formal legal training and, thus, no firm basis for judgment. This chapter addresses many such concerns. It begins by elaborating the most important issues behind the ethical treatment of information. Next this chapter expands upon the definition of ethical behavior and introduces several heuristics which managers can employ to help them make better decisions. This is followed by a discussion of some newly emerging controversies that will surely test society's resolve concerning the increasing presence of IS in every aspect of life.

This chapter takes a high level view of ethical issues facing managers in today's environment. It focuses primarily on providing a set of frameworks the manager can apply to a wide variety of ethical issues. Omitted is a specific focus on several important issues such as social justice (the impact of computer technology on the poor or "have-nots," racial minorities, and third world nations) nor is there a discussion of social concerns that arise out of artificial intelligence, neural networks, and expert systems. Although these are interesting and important areas for concern, in this chapter the objective is to provide managers with a way to think about the issues of ethics and privacy concerns. The interested reader

---

[4] Hasnas, J. and Smith, J. "Ethics and InformationSystems: The Corporate Domain." Working paper, 1998, p. 2.

may wish to seek out one of a number of sources for dozens of articles and books on this area of IS management (such as www.isworld.org).

▶ CONTROL OF INFORMATION

In an economy that is rapidly becoming dominated by knowledge workers, the value of information is tantamount. Those who possess the "best" information and know how to use it, win. The recent trend in computer prices has meant that high levels of computational power can be purchased for relatively small amounts of money. While this trend means that computer-generated or stored information now falls within the reach of an ever-larger percentage of the populace, it also means that collecting and storing information is becoming easier and more cost effective. Although this circumstance certainly affects businesses and individuals for the better, it also can affect them substantially for the worse. Consider several areas in which the control of information is crucial. Richard O. Mason, in an article published in MIS Quarterly,[5] identified four such areas, which can be summarized by the acronym PAPA: privacy, accuracy, property, and accessibility (see Figure 12.1).

Privacy

Many consider privacy to be the most important area in which their interests need to be safeguarded. **Privacy** is often defined as "the right to be left alone." [6] It pertains the authorized collection, disclosure and use of personal information. Employers can monitor their employees' e-mail and computer utilization while they are at work, even though they have not historically monitored telephone calls. Every time someone logs onto one of the main search engines, a "cookie" is placed in their hard drive so that these companies can track their surfing habits. A **cookie** is a message given to a Web browser by a Web server. The browser stores the message with user identification codes in a text file that is sent back to the server each time the

Area	Critical Questions
Privacy	What information must a person reveal about one's self to others? What information should others be able to access about you—with or without your permission? What safeguards exist for your protection?
Accuracy	Who is responsible for the reliability and accuracy of information? Who will be accountable for errors?
Property	Who owns information? Who owns the channels of distribution, and how should they be regulated?
Accessibility	What information does a person or an organization have a right to obtain, under what conditions, and with what safeguards?

FIGURE 12.1 Mason's areas of managerial concern.

[5] Mason, Richard O. "Four Ethical Issues of the Information Age" MIS Quarterly, 10(1), March 1986.
[6] Warren, Samuel D. and Louis D. Brandeis, "The Right to Privacy," Harvard Law Review, (4:5), December 1890, 193-200.

browser requests a page from the server.[7] Currently this information is used only to target advertising, but its future use depends on the discretion of managers. Their view is formed in part by how much competitive advantage this knowledge can create. Do customers have a right to privacy while searching the Internet? Courts have decided that the answer is no, but as society moves ahead, the right to monitor customer habits will be affected by how managers decide to use the information that they have collected.

Governments around the world are grappling with privacy legislation. Not surprisingly, they are using different approaches for ensuring the privacy of their citizens. The United States' (US') sectoral approach relies on a mix of legislation, regulation, and self-regulation. Examples of the US' relatively limited privacy legislation include the 1974 Privacy Act that regulates the US government's collection and use of personal information, and the 1998 Children's Online Privacy Protection Act that regulates the on-line collection and use of children's personal information. In contrast to the US' sectoral approach combined with strong encouragement of self-regulation by industry, the European Union relies on comprehensive legislation that requires creation of government data protection agencies, registration of data bases with those agencies, and in some cases prior approval before processing personal data.

Because of pronounced differences in governmental approaches, many US companies were concerned that they would be unable to meet the European "adequacy" standard for privacy protection specified in the European Commission's Directive on Data Protection that went into effect in 1998. This Directive prohibits the transfer of personal data to non-European Union nations that do not meet the European privacy standards. Many US companies believed that this Directive would significantly hamper their ability to engage in many trans-Atlantic transactions. However, the US Department of Commerce (DOC) in consultation with the European Commission developed a "safe harbor" framework in 2000 that allows US companies to be placed on a list maintained by the DOC. The US companies must demonstrate through a self-certification process that they are enforcing privacy at a level practiced in the European Union.[8]

The Online Privacy Alliance of Washington, D.C., an industry coalition backed by trade groups and such companies as The Walt Disney Co., Proctor & Gamble, Time Warner Telecom, and IBM, offers its own set of Web privacy guidelines, including the following:

- Have and implement a privacy policy that gives consumers notice, choice, and the ability to correct inaccurate data
- Ensure data security
- Get parental consent before collecting or reselling personally identifiable information from children under the age of 13

[7] Webopedia, http://www.webopedia.com/TERM/c/cookie.html, downloaded 6/28/02.

[8] U.S. Department of Commerce, "Safe Harbor Overview," http://www.export.gov/safeharbor/sh_overview.html, downloaded July 15, 2002

Accuracy

The accuracy of information assumes real importance for society as computers come to dominate in corporate record-keeping activities. When records are inputted incorrectly, who is to blame? In a case in Florida, a family whose bank had recently changed from a paper bookkeeping system to a computer-based system found that a mortgage payment that had been made was not credited. As the family attempted to pay the mortgage in subsequent months, the system rejected the payments because the mortgage was listed as past due. After a year of "missing" payments, the bank foreclosed on the house.[9] While this incident may highlight the need for better controls over the bank's internal processes, it also demonstrates the risks that can be attributed to inaccurate information retained in corporate systems. In this case, the bank was responsible for the error, but it paid little—compared to the family—for its mistake. While they cannot expect to eliminate all mistakes from the online environment, managers must establish controls to ensure that situations such as this one do not happen with any frequency.

Over time it becomes increasingly difficult to maintain the accuracy of some types of information. While a person's birth date does not typically change (my grandmother's change of her birth year notwithstanding), addresses and phone number often change as people relocate, and even their names may change with marriage, divorce, and adoption. The European Union Directive on Data Protection requires accurate and up-to-date data, and tries to make sure that data is kept no longer than necessary to fulfill its stated purpose. Keeping data only as long as it is necessary to fulfill its stated purpose is a challenge many companies don't even attempt to meet.

Property

The increase in monitoring leads to the question of property. Now that organizations have the ability to collect vast amounts of data on their clients, do they have a right to share data with others to create a more accurate profile of an individual? And if they do create such consolidated profiles, who owns that information which in many cases was not divulged willingly for that purpose? Who owns images that are posted in cyberspace? With ever more sophisticated methods of computer animation, can companies use newly "created" images or characters building upon models in other media without paying royalties? Mason summarizes the issues,[10]

> Any individual item of information can be extremely costly to produce in the first instance. Yet once it is produced, that information has the illusive quality of being easy to reproduce and to share with others. Moreover, this replication can take place without destroying the original. This makes information hard to safeguard since, unlike tangible property, it becomes communicable and hard to keep it to one's self. It is even difficult to secure appropriate reimbursements when somebody else uses your information.

[9] Mason, Richard O. "Four Ethical Issues of the Information Age" *MIS Quarterly,* 10(1), March 1986.
[10] Mason, Ibid.

Accessibility

In the age of the information worker, accessibility becomes increasingly important. Would-be users of information must first gain the physical ability to access online information resources, which broadly means they must access computational systems. Recent trends in computer hardware prices have greatly lowered the barriers to entry on this account. Second and more importantly, the user must gain access to information itself. In this sense, the issue of access is closely linked to that of property. While major corporations have benefited greatly from the drop in computer prices, the same benefit only now is beginning to filter through the rest of society. Looking forward, the major issue facing managers is how to create and maintain access to information for society at large. As our society moves toward a service- or knowledge-based economy, managers whose organizations control vast quantities of information will have to weigh the benefits of information control against societal needs to upgrade the knowledge bases of individuals or knowledge workers.

▶ NORMATIVE THEORIES OF BUSINESS ETHICS

The landscape changes daily as advances in technology are incorporated into existing organizational structures. IS are becoming omnipresent as companies look to decrease costs, increase efficiency, and build strategic competitive advantages. Increasingly, however, these advances come about in a business domain lacking ethical clarity. Because of its newness, this area of IT often lacks accepted norms of behavior. Companies encounter daily quandaries as they try to use their IS to create and exploit competitive advantages.

Managers must assess current information initiatives with particular attention to possible ethical issues. Because so many managers have been educated in the current corporate world, they are used to the overriding ethical norms present in their traditional businesses. As Conger and Loch observed, "People who have been trained in engineering, computer science, and MIS, frequently have little training in ethics, philosophy, and moral reasoning. Without a vocabulary with which to think and talk about what constitutes an ethical computing issue, it is difficult to have the necessary discussions to develop social norms."[11]

Managers in the information age will need to translate their current ethical norms into terms meaningful for the new electronic corporation. In order to suggest a workable framework for this process, consider three theories of ethical behavior in the corporate environment that managers can develop and apply to the particular challenges they will face. These normative theories of business ethics—stockholder theory, stakeholder theory, and social contract theory—are widely applied in traditional business situations. They are "normative" in that they attempt to derive what might be called "intermediate level" ethical principles: principles expressed in language accessible to the ordinary business person, which can be applied to the concrete moral quandaries of the business domain.[12] Below is a definition of each theory followed

[11] Conger, S. and Loch, K.D. "Ethics and Computer Use," *Communications of the ACM* (38:12), December 1995, pp. 31,32.

[12] Hasnas and Smith, 1998, p. 5.

by an illustration of its application using a recent business example, the Blockbuster Video case outlined at the beginning of this chapter.

Stockholder Theory

According to **stockholder theory,** stockholders advance capital to corporate managers who act as agents in advancing their ends. The nature of this contract binds managers to act in the interest of the shareholders: i.e., to maximize shareholder value. As Milton Friedman wrote, "There is one and only one social responsibility of business: to use its resources and engage in activities designed to increase its profits so long as it stays within the rules of the game, which is to say, engages in open and free competition, without deception or fraud."[13]

Stockholder theory qualifies the manager's duty in two salient ways. First, managers are bound to employ legal, nonfraudulent means. Second, managers must take the long view of shareholder interest: i.e., they are obliged to forgo short-term gains if doing so will maximize value over the long term.

Managers should bear in mind that stockholder theory itself provides a limited framework for moral argument because it assumes the ability of the free market to fully promote the interests of society at large. Yet the singular pursuit of profit on the part of individuals or corporations cannot be said to maximize social welfare. Free markets can foster the creation of monopolies and other circumstances that limit the ability of members of a society to secure the common good. A proponent of stockholder theory might insist that, as agents of stockholders, managers must not use stockholders' money to accomplish goals that do not directly serve the interests of those same stockholders. A critic of stockholder theory would argue that such spending would be just if the money went to further the public interest.

The stipulation under stockholder theory that the pursuit of profits must be legal and nonfraudulent would not limit Blockbuster's plan to sell "broad-based, general" information about clients, because such sales do not violate privacy laws. Moreover, the plan would appear to satisfy the test of maximizing shareholder value because it potentially generates new revenues. On the other hand, if customers stopped renting movies from Blockbuster because they disliked the company's plans to use their personal information in this manner, any lost revenues would weigh against managers' success in meeting the ethical obligation to work toward maximizing value.

Stakeholder Theory

Stakeholder theory holds that managers, while bound by their relation to stockholders, are entrusted also with a fiduciary responsibility to all those who hold a stake in or a claim on the firm.[14] The term "stakeholder" is currently taken to mean any group that vitally affects the survival and success of the corporation or whose interests the corporation vitally affects. Such groups normally include stockholders, customers, employees, suppliers, and the local community, though other groups may also be considered stakeholders, depending on the circumstances. At its most

[13] Friedman, M. *Capitalism and Freedom.* University of Chicago Press, Chicago, 1962, p. 133
[14] Hasnas and Smith, 1998, p. 8..

basic level, stakeholder theory states that management must enact and follow policies that balance the rights of all stakeholders without impinging upon the rights of any one particular stakeholder.

Stakeholder theory diverges most consequentially from stockholder theory in affirming that the interests of parties other than the stockholders play a legitimate role in the governance and management of the firm. As a practical matter, due to the high transaction costs entailed in canvassing all of these disparate groups, managers must act as their agents in deriving business solutions that optimally serve their respective interests. Thus, in most cases stakeholders' only real recourse is to stop participating in the corporation: Customers can stop buying the company's products, stockholders can sell, etc.

Viewed in light of stakeholder theory, the Blockbuster plan begins to present more complex ethical issues. Chief among these is how much benefit accrues to stakeholders from an intrusion into clients' privacy. Blockbuster's shareholders stand to gain, but what would be the effects on other stakeholders? Apparently, the only group that stands to lose is the client group itself. Moreover, consumers considered more broadly might benefit by receiving better-targeted advertising to replace traditional mass-marketing campaigns. Also, consider the fact that Blockbuster's policy is publicly known, and clients do have recourse: They can stop patronizing Blockbuster, or ask the company to suppress the sale of their own individual information. In general terms, Blockbuster's plan would not violate ethical standards as they are understood under stakeholder theory, unless it could be shown that the costs to clients outweighed the benefits within the larger stakeholder group.

Social Contract Theory

Social contract theory derives the social responsibilities of corporate managers by considering the needs of a society with no corporations or other complex business arrangements. Social contract theorists ask what conditions would have to be met for the members of such a society to agree to allow a corporation to be formed. Thus, society bestows legal recognition on a corporation to allow it to employ social resources toward given ends. This contract generally is taken to mean that, in allowing a corporation to exist, society demands at a minimum that it create more value to the society than it consumes. Thus, society charges the corporation to enhance its welfare by satisfying particular interests of consumers and workers in exploiting the advantages of the corporate form. The corporation must conduct its activities while observing the canons of justice.[15]

The social contract comprises two distinct components: the social welfare term and the justice term. The former arises from the belief that corporations must provide greater benefits than their associated costs or society would not allow their creation. Thus, the social contract obliges managers to pursue profits in ways that are compatible with the well being of society as a whole. Similarly, the justice term holds that corporations must pursue profits legally, without fraud or deception, and avoid activities that injure society.

[15] Hasnas and Smith, 1998, p. 10.

Social contract theory meets criticism because no mechanism exists to actuate it. In the absence of a real contract whose terms subordinate profit maximization to social welfare, most critics find it hard to imagine corporations losing profitability in the name of altruism. Yet, the strength of the theory lies in its broad assessment of the moral foundations of business activity.

Applied to the Blockbuster case, social contract theory would demand that the manager ask whether the plan to sell client information could compromise fundamental tenets of fairness or social justice. If customers were not apprised of the decision to sell information about themselves, the plan could be seen as unethical. It would not seem fair to collect information for one purpose and then use it for another, without informing the parties concerned. If, on the other hand, the plan were disclosed to customers, and if it were clear its implementation would net a benefit to society, the plan could be considered ethical.

While these three normative theories of business ethics possess distinct characteristics, they are not completely incompatible. All offer useful metrics for defining ethical behavior in profit-seeking enterprises under free market conditions. They provide managers with an independent standard by which to judge the ethical nature of superiors' orders as well as their firms' policies and codes of conduct. Upon inspection, the three theories appear to represent concentric circles, with stockholder theory at the center and social contract theory at the outer ring. Stockholder theory is narrowest in scope, stakeholder theory encompasses and expands upon it, and social contract theory covers the broadest area. Figure 12.2 summarizes these three theories.

A similar situation to the Blockbuster case occurred when DoubleClick, a leading Internet advertisement company, announced its plans to merge its vast database of user navigational history with that of user's offline spending habits.

Theory	Definition	Metrics
Stockholder	Maximize stockholder wealth, in legal and nonfraudulent manners.	Will this action maximize long-term stockholder value? Can goals be accomplished without compromising company standards and without breaking laws?
Stakeholder	Maximize benefits to all stakeholders while weighing costs to competing interests.	Does the proposed action maximize collective benefits to the company? Does this action treat one or more of the corporate stakeholders unfairly?
Social contract	Create value for society in a manner that is just and nondiscriminatory.	Does this action create a "net" benefit for society? Does the proposed action discriminate against any group in particular, and is its implementation socially just?

FIGURE 12.2   Three normative theories of business ethics.

DoubleClick provides the sites of members of its DoubleClick Network with advertisements. It then monitors the viewing of these advertisements through cookies. From cookies, DoubleClick obtains "clickstream data" about the sites visited by a user, the time spent at these sites, and any purchases made by the user at the sites. DoubleClick has extensive Internet navigational histories for identified users. With its purchase of Abacus Direct Corporation in November 1999, it acquired a database with information about the spending habits of more than 88 million people derived from more than two billion offline purchases. Even though it was a complete reversal of its previously stated privacy policies, DoubleClick was going to merge these two powerful databases. A suit filed by Electronic Privacy Information with the Federal Trade Commission, coupled with a public uproar, caused DoubleClick to back down from its proposed merger.[16]

Living.com, a furniture retailer on the Internet made a very public decision not to sell its customer information. Living.com ceased doing business and filed for bankruptcy protection in the fall of 2000. But, while their customer data could be considered an asset and therefore sold to help pay off their debts, managers at Living.com and the U.S. government officials working with them agreed that their customer information was private and it would be inappropriate to sell it for use by someone other than Living.com.

▶ EMERGING ISSUES IN THE ETHICAL GOVERNANCE OF INFORMATION SYSTEMS

Pick up the newspaper almost any day of the week and it will include ethical concerns in the corporate environment. Such privacy issues as the surveillance of employees and their e-mail messages frequently make headlines. How should managers deal with these issues? Managers are rarely expert in better-known areas of ethical concern, much less the issues emerging in the information economy. This section highlights several such areas with an eye to exposing those on which managers should focus their attention.

There are two distinct spheres in which managers operate. The first involves the outward transactions of the business and focuses on the customer. To elaborate, consider the issue of privacy raised by the Blockbuster case from the perspective of the consumer, and what steps businesses are taking to ensure the ethical use of information. The second sphere includes the issues related to managing employees and information inside the corporation. This includes topics in internal surveillance and monitoring, the denigration of and bifurcation of IS jobs, and the problems related to the rigidity of IS in the workplace. Figure 12.3 shows these relationships.

In an age where the Internet and e-mail have become omnipresent, many companies have begun to question the efficacy of such technology in the workplace.

[16] Jones, Day, Reavis & Pogue, "DoubleClick and the Privacy Wars," May 2001, 1(1), http://www1.jonesday.com/files/tbl_s31Publications%5CFileUpload137%5C139%5CDouble_Click_Privacy.pdf, downloaded 6/28/02.

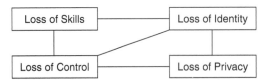

FIGURE 12.3   Some causal connections between identified areas of ethical concern.
Source: Adapted from Fernando Leal, "Ethics is Fragile, Goodness is Not," *Information Society: New Media, Ethics and Postmodernism,* Springer Verlag, 1995, p. 79.

Seeking to improve productivity, firms increasingly look to leverage IS to their fullest extent. While e-mail and the Internet have replaced traditional communications and research channels, some companies are seeing corporate networks clogged with excessive traffic, often personal in nature, which leads to lesser productivity gains than anticipated. To combat unauthorized uses of e-mail systems and Internet access, managers are turning to programs that monitor employees' online activities.

A recent Wall Street Journal article cited software companies, including Content Advisor of Somerville, Massachusetts, and Secure Computing Corporation of San Jose, California, whose products allow client companies to monitor or restrict the access of employees to certain Internet sites and to prevent them from conducting private business on company time. While the intention may seem both ethical and in the best interest of business, in practice the reverse may actually be true. In many cases employees are not informed that they are being monitored or that information gleaned is being used to measure their productivity. In these cases, monitoring appears to violate both privacy and personal freedoms.[17]

The use of monitoring and surveillance software highlights an increase in the level of control that employers can exert over employees. As employees become aware of these activities, productivity and morale may fall. While the central issue remains with privacy, other potential effects should concern managers, such as undue stress on employees. This issue may seem peripheral, but as technology further intrudes into the workplace and shapes working conditions, its importance can only increase.

Environmental issues previously were the domain of HR professionals and organizational behaviorists. Today, managers must be concerned with creating a work atmosphere amenable to IS. Ethically speaking, managers must address worker health in an increasingly regimented atmosphere. IS by their nature are inflexible. Jobs associated with computer systems demand rigor. As systems come to dominate corporate life, there is an increased risk of sacrificing individuality. Managers rethink job requirements and increase workloads, and depend upon our ability to generate mistake-free work. In an environment where small mistakes can be costly, employees feel greater stress. Managers must be alert to these fundamental changes in the working environment. Ethically, they are obliged to consider the welfare of workers. If, as they create employment opportunities and write job descriptions, managers set out to limit individuality, enforce conformity, and

---

[17] Conklin, J.C., "Under the Radar: Content Advisor Snoops as Workers Surf Web," *The Wall Street Journal,* October 15, 1998, p. B8.

increase demands, they violate their ethical responsibilities as understood under all three normative theories considered in this chapter.

In addition to managing internal ethical concerns, managers must be aware of their relationships with customers. Net purchasers surveyed believed Net retailers should post their policies about how they will use private information. Mary J. Culnan noted in CIO magazine that the ease with which consumer information is collected over the Internet makes purchasers increasingly uneasy. "People are balking at giving their information on the Web in a lot of cases because the organization has not made a good case for why they should," Culnan wrote. "If there are no benefits or if they aren't told why the information is being collected or how it's being used, a lot of people say 'Forget it.'"[18] As customers increasingly appreciate the power new technologies put in the hands of retailers, they become skeptical about the wisdom of providing personal information in transacting business online.

Recently the FTC made strides toward requiring Web retailers to more fully disclose how they will use customers' private information. The FTC's efforts to foster fair information practices for Net commerce mesh with Mason's PAPA framework. To protect the integrity of information collected about them, federal regulators have recommended allowing consumers limited access to corporate information databases. Consumers thus could update their information and correct errors. Many consumer advocacy groups are arguing for requirement that retailers cannot use personal information unless the customer "opts-in," or specifically gives the retailer permission to use the information. The default practice now is "opting-out," or using the information unless the customer specifically tells the retailer that his or her personal information cannot be used or distributed. In 2000, Federal legislation was passed requiring states to allow registrants to "opt-in" their driver license information.

Many Internet industry groups have instituted their own codes of practice in an attempt to avoid regulation. Such companies as TRUSTe Inc. and the Better Business Bureau are licensing members who agree to abide by stringent privacy policies. Compliance earns a medal that can be displayed on the member's Web site. Transgressors are removed from the program. By creating enforceable standards, the government has begun institutionalizing ethical behavior within corporate IS departments.

Information privacy guidelines must come from above: from the CEO, CIO, and general management. Employees must learn about these issues early in their tenure with a firm to avoid incurring serious problems with FTC oversight.

▶ FOOD FOR THOUGHT: ETHICS AND THE INTERNET

Much debate has been given to privacy and ethics on the Internet. The fact that the Internet crosses state and country boundaries makes these issues extremely complex. Different cultures, laws, customs, and habits of people from different countries ensure that each geographical region polices the Internet in very different ways.

---

[18] "Saving Private Data" *CIO Magazine*, October 1, 1998.

As a result, managers face challenges in navigating their organizations through the murky waters of ethical use of the Internet.

One area of debate is free speech and censorship. On the Internet, the balance between free speech and censorship is difficult to pinpoint. On the one hand, the First Amendment of the U.S. Constitution guarantees freedom of speech, but that is a United States law, not an international law. The Internet crosses international boundaries, making it a difficult issue to manage. Accompanying freedom of speech is the burden of responsibility. Do Web sites that host materials of questionable ethics have the responsibility to make sure only appropriate visitors have access to that information? For example, a Web site with pornography is clearly unsuitable for children. Who is responsible to make sure children do not see it? The Web author? The Web site host? The site where the children access the Web, such as their school or library? Or the children's parents and guardians. In this evolving world of the Internet, the issues of controlling access, censorship, free speech, and responsibility must be reexamined. The astute manager has thought out these issues and addressed them prior to launching the company Web site.

An Internet Code of Ethics is an issue of much debate by the International Federation of Information Processing (IFIP). IFIP is a nongovernmental, nonprofit umbrella organization for national societies working in the field of information processing. Established in 1960 as part of the United Nations Educational Scientific and Cultural Organization (UNESCO), IFIP has members from all over the world and maintains friendly connections to specialized agencies of the UN System and nongovernmental organizations. This organization's objectives are to help computer professionals and systems designers become aware of the social consequences of their work, to develop criteria to determine the extent to which the public is served with computers, and to encourage designers and users to take human needs into account when making system choices.

IFIP is leading the charge for a discussion of a code of ethics for Internet governance.[19] But consensus among individuals in the United States has not been reached, much less between individuals in different countries. There is general agreement among virtually all IS professionals that safeguarding minors and protecting human dignity is necessary. Virtually all countries have some law or policy related to these dimensions. But beyond that, there is emotional debate on most issues. A well-circulated list of guidelines for computer ethics has been developed by the Computer Ethics Institute. Figure 12.4 summarizes these as the Ten Commandments of Computer Ethics.

Security and Controls

At one end of the spectrum of issues relating to security and control of the Internet is the discussion of issues such as the ones presented earlier: protecting organizational data from unauthorized hackers and undesirable viruses. Managers go to great lengths to make sure their computers are secure from unauthorized insider

---

[19] See, for example, IS World Web site, www.isworld.org for information on IFIP.

1. Thou shalt not use a computer to harm other people.
2. Thou shalt not interfere with other people's computer work.
3. Thou shalt not snoop around in other people's files.
4. Thou shalt not use a computer to steal.
5. Thou shalt not use a computer to bear false witness.
6. Thou shalt not use or copy software for which you have not paid.
7. Thou shalt not use other people's computer resources without authorization.
8. Thou shalt not appropriate other people's intellectual output.
9. Thou shalt think about the social consequences of the program you write.
10. Thou shalt use a computer in ways that show consideration and respect.

FIGURE 12.4 Ten Commandments of Computer Ethics.

Source: Arlene Rinaldi, Florida Atlantic University, 1998, http://wise.fau.edu/netiquette/net/ten.html verified on September 20, 2000.

access, such as an employee seeking data he or she is not authorized to have, and outsider access, such as a hacker who seeks to enter a computer for sport or for malicious intent. At the other end are issues primarily about privacy and protecting individual rights.

Technologies have been devised to manage the security and control issues. Figure 12.5 summarizes three types of tools. These tools, such as firewalls, passwords, and authentication routines, restrict access to information on a computer by preventing access to the server on the network. They provide warning for early discovery of security breaches, limit losses suffered in case of security breaches, analyze and react to security breaches (and try to prevent them from reoccurring), and recover whatever has been lost from security breaches.[20]

Future approaches to security and privacy may include a combination of software and hardware. Microsoft, in partnership with a number of companies including Intel and AMD, is proposing a major initiative called Palladium. The Palladium initiative promises to combine public key cryptography and special microprocessors to make the Windows operating system more secure and to move privacy and security to a new level.

Managers must be involved in decisions about security and control measures because these issues can affect business decisions. For example, a firewall that limits access to an internal network, or intranet, may cause the failure of a work-at-home program a manager seeks to put in place. The firewall may be built in such a way as to completely eliminate gaining access. Likewise, an encryption/decryption system may make future business decisions more expensive because all future applications would have to be built in a manner to accommodate the cryptology. That additional expense may tip the scales against a future business application the manager sought to implement.

[20] J. Berleur, P. Duquenoy, and D. Whitehouse, "Ethics and the Governance of the Internet," IFIP-SIG9.2.2 white paper, September 1999.

Hardware system security and control	Firewalls	A computer set up with both an internal network card and an external network card. This computer is set up to control access to the internal network and only lets authorized traffic pass the barrier.
	Encryption and decryption	Cryptography or secure writing ensures that information is transformed into unintelligible forms before transmission and intelligible forms when it arrives at its destination.
Network and software security controls	Network operating system software	The core set of programs that manage the resources of the computer or network often have functionality such as authentication, access control, and cryptology.
	Security information management	A management scheme to synchronize all mechanisms and protocols built into network and computer operating systems and protect the systems from authorized access.
	Server and browser software security	Mechanisms to ensure that errors in programming do not create holes and trapdoors which can compromise websites.
Broadcast medium security and controls	Labeling and rating software	The software industry incorporates Platform for Internet Content Selection (PICS) technology, a mechanism of labeling web pages based on content. These labels can be used by filtering software to manage access.
	Filtering/blocking software	Software that rates documents and websites that have been rated and contain content on a designated filter's "black list" and keeps them from being displayed on the user's computer.

FIGURE 12.5   Security and control tools.

Source: Adapted from J. Berleur, P. Duquenoy, and D. Whitehouse, "Ethics and the Governance of the Internet," IFIP-SIG9.2.2 white paper, September 1999.

▶ SUMMARY

- Due to the asymmetry of power relationships, managers tend to frame ethical concerns in terms of refraining from doing harm, mitigating injury, and paying attention to dependent and vulnerable parties. As a practical matter, ethics is about maintaining one's own, independent perspective about the propriety of business practices. Managers must make systematic, reasoned judgments about right and wrong, and take responsibility for them. Ethics is about decisive action rooted in principles that express what is right and important and about action that is publicly defensible and personally supportable.

- PAPA is an acronym for the four areas in which control of information is crucial: privacy, accuracy, property and accessibility.
- Three important normative theories describing business ethics are: (1) Stockholder Theory (maximizing stockholder wealth), (2) Stakeholder Theory (maximizing the benefits to all stakeholders while weighting costs to competing interests, and (3) Social Contract Theory (creating value for society that is just and nondiscriminatory).
- Issues related to the ethical governance of information systems are emerging in terms of the outward transactions of business that may impinge on the privacy of customers and electronic surveillance and other internally-oriented personnel issues.
- Security looms as a major threat to Internet growth. Businesses are bolstering security with hardware, software and communication devices.

▶ KEY TERMS

accessibility (p. 311)
accuracy (p. 310)
cookie (p. 308)
privacy (p. 308)
property (p. 310)
social contract theory (p. 313)
stakeholder theory (p. 312)
stockholder theory (p. 312)

▶ DISCUSSION QUESTIONS

1. Private corporate data is often encrypted using a key, which is needed to decrypt the information. Who within the corporation should be responsible for maintaining the "keys" to private information collected about consumers? Is that the same person who should have the "keys" to employee data?

2. Lotus Development Corporation launched its Marketplace product in 1990. The product was a marketing database of 120 million U.S. consumers, with demographic information based on publicly available information. Each consumer had personal information, such as name and mailing address. But the value proposition for the product was in the fact that it combined several publicly available databases and the result was a database that made assumptions about lifestyle, income, family and marital status, and several other demographic categories. It was intended to give companies a comprehensive database of individual spending habits for direct-mail marketing using otherwise unthreatening databases. A grassroots outcry on the Internet resulted in over 30,000 letters and phone calls from individuals who wanted their names deleted from the product. The negative press Lotus received, combined with the flood of letters from consumers who were concerned about invasion of privacy, caused Lotus to cancel the project In this case, the resulting database showed patterns of spending and placed consumers into categories which reflected personal data the consumers felt was private. But many organizations these days collect individual information, including your credit card provider, your bank, your creditors, and virtually any retail store in which you use a credit card or other identifying customer number. Who owns the information that is collected? Do you, the person who initially provided information to the collector? Or the collecting organization that spent the resources to save the information in the first place?

3. Consider arrest records, which are mostly computerized and stored locally by law enforcement agencies. They have an accuracy rate of about 50 percent—about half of them are inaccurate, incomplete, or ambiguous. These records often are used by others than just law enforcement. Approximately 90 percent of all criminal histories in the United States are available to public and private employers. Use the three normative theories of business ethics to analyze the ethical issues surrounding this situation. How might hiring decisions be influenced inappropriately by this information?

4. The European Community's Directive on Data Protection that was put into effect in 1998 strictly limits how database information is used and who has access to it. Some of the restrictions include registering all databases containing personal information with the countries in which they are operating, collecting data only with the consent of the subjects, and telling subjects of the database the intended and actual use of the databases. What effect might these restrictions have on global companies? In your opinion, should these types of restrictions be made into law? Why or why not?

CASE STUDY 12-1

ETHICAL DECISION MAKING

Situation 1

The secretarial pool is part of the group assigned to Doug Smith, the Manager of Office Automation. The pool has produced very low quality work for the past several months. Smith has access to the passwords for each of the pool members' computer account. He instructs the pool supervisor to go into each hard drive after hours and obtain a sample document to check for quality control for each pool member.

Discussion Questions

1. If you were the supervisor, what would you do?
2. What, if any, ethical propositions have been violated by this situation?
3. If poor quality were found, could the information be used for disciplinary purposes? For training purposes?
4. Apply PAPA to this situation.

Situation 2

Kate Essex is the supervisor of the customer service representative group for Enovelty.com, a manufacturer of novelty items. This group spends its workday answering calls, and sometimes placing calls, to customers to assist in solving a variety of issues about orders previously placed with the company. The company has a rule that personal phone calls are only allowed during breaks. Essex is assigned to monitor each representative on the phone for 15 minutes a day, as part of her regular job tasks. The representatives are aware that Essex will be monitoring them, and customers are immediately informed when they begin their calls. Essex begins to monitor James Olsen, and finds that he is on a personal call regarding his sick child. Olsen is not on break.

Discussion Questions

1. What should Essex do?
2. What, if any, ethical principles help guide decision making in this situation?
3. What management practices should be in place to ensure proper behavior without violating individual "rights"?
4. Apply the normative theories of business ethics to this situation.

Situation 3

Jane Mark was the newest hire in the IS group at We_Sell_More.com, a business on the Internet. The company takes in $30 million in revenue quarterly from Web business. Jane reports to Sam Brady, the VP of IS. Jane is assigned to a project to build a new capability into the company Web page that facilitates linking products ordered with future offerings of the company. After weeks of analysis, Jane concluded that the best way to incorporate that capability is to buy a software package from a small start-up company in Silicon Valley, California. She convinces Brady of her decision and is authorized to lease the software. The vendor e-mails Jane the software in a ZIP file, and instructs her on how to install it. At the initial installation, Jane is asked to acknowledge and electronically sign the license agreement. The installed system does not ask Jane if she wants to make a backup copy of the software on diskettes, so as a precaution, Jane takes it upon herself and copies the ZIP files sent to her onto a set of floppies. She stores these floppies in her desk drawer.

A year later the vendor is bought by another company and the software is removed from the marketplace. The new owner believes this software will provide them with a competitive advantage they want to reserve for themselves. The new vendor terminates all lease agreements and revokes all licenses upon their expiration. But Jane still has the floppies she made as backup.

Discussion Questions

1. Is Jane obligated to stop using her backup copy? Why or why not?
2. If We_Sell_More.com wants to continue to use the system, can they? Why or why not?
3. Does it change your opinion if the software is a critical system for We_Sell_More.com? If it is a noncritical system? Explain.

Situation 4

In a recent court case, the rock band Metallica sued Napster for allowing the illegal copying and distribution of its copyrighted songs. At the Napster site, music fans can swap songs over the Internet without charge. The fans can search for their favorite songs by song title or artist name and then download the MP3 song files onto their own computers. Metallica is not only concerned that their work is being illegally copied and distributed, but also that other artists are being deprived of royalties. Napster argues that its sites offers unknown musicians a very affordable means of competing against huge corporate conglomerates in making their work known to potential fans worldwide. Thousands of artists have approved Napster's distribution of their music. Napster can also help fans who legally bought an album to download an MP3 copy to play through a computer or to compile play lists from various CDs. The challenge for Napster is to screen out infringing uses of their site. But, Napster neither knows the contents of files that its users are sharing nor monitors its users' activities. The Digital Millennium Copyright Act ("DMCA") states that an Internet service provider like Napster has no duty to monitor or seek facts showing infringing activities. The only way Napster can know about infringements is through a claim of infringement from a copyright holder. Once it is alerted, Napster can block access for those accused of the infringement.

Discussion Questions

1. Do you think that Napster should be allowed to continue its operations as it has in the past? Why or why not?
2. Do you think that Metallica's suit is justified? Why or why not?
3. What, if any, ethical principles help guide decision making in this situation? Do you think it is ethical to copy files from the Napster site? Explain.

Source: Adapted from short cases suggested by Professor Kay Nelson, University of Utah. The names of people, places, and companies have been made up for these stories. Any similarity to real people, places, or companies is purely coincidental.

Glossary

activity based costing (ABC) Costing approach that counts the actual activities that go into making a specific product or delivering a specific service.

administrator An employee who "takes care of" a computer or a number of computers. Administrator duties typically include backing up data (and restoring it if it is lost), performing routine maintenance, installing software upgrades, troubleshooting problems, and assisting users.

allocation Funding systems that recover costs based on something other than usage, such as revenues, login accounts, or number of employees.

ANSI X12 The name of the standard used by EDI applications to allow a software program on one computer system to relay information back and forth to a software program on another computer system, thus allowing organizations to exchange data pertinent to business transactions.

application A software program designed to facilitate a specific practical task, as opposed to an operating system that controls resources. Examples of application programs include Microsoft Word, a word processing application; Lotus 1-2-3, a spreadsheet application; and SAP R/3, an enterprise resource planning application.

application service provider (ASP) An Internet-based company that "rents" the use of an application to the customer through their Web site. In return, the ASP provides not only the software, but the infrastructure, people, and maintenance to run it.

architecture Provides a blueprint, translating business strategy into a plan for IS that combines hardware, software, data, and network components; The strategy implicit in hardware, software, data, and network components.

asymmetric encryption Type of encryption that uses differentiated keys, called public keys and private keys.

authentication A security process in which proof is obtained to verify that the users are truly who they say they are.

automate Technology replaces the human worker. *See* **informate.**

backsourcing Returning to an "in-sourced" status.

Balanced Scorecard Methodology that focuses attention on the organization's value drivers (which include, but are not limited to, financial performance).

bandwidth The rate at which data can travel through a given medium. The medium may be a network, an internal connection (say from the CPU to RAM), a phone line, etc. For networks and internal connections, bandwidth is typically measured in terms of Megabytes per second (MB/sec) or Gigabytes per second (GB/sec).

bit A "binary digit"; the smallest unit of data as represented in a computer. A bit can take only the values 0 or 1.

bricks-and-clicks The term used to refer to businesses with a strong business model both on the Internet and in the physical world.

broadband Telecommunication in which a wide band of frequencies is available to transmit information. Because a wide band of frequencies is available, more information can be transmitted in a given amount of time.

business continuity plan (BCP) An approved set of preparations and sufficient procedures for responding to a variety of disaster events.

business diamond A simple framework for understanding the design of an organization, linking together the business processes, its values and beliefs, its management control systems, and its tasks and structures.

business reengineering The fundamental rethinking and radical redesign of a business process to achieve dramatic improvements in performance.

business strategy A well-articulated vision of where a business seeks to go and how it expects to get there.

business to business (B2B) Using the Internet to conduct business with business customers. *See* **business to consumer.**

business to consumer (B2C) Using the Internet to conduct business directly with consumers of goods and services. *See* **business to business.**

byte Eight bits. A byte can be thought of as a "character" of computer data.

central processing unit (CPU) The computer hardware on which all computation is done.

centralized IS organization Brings together all staff, hardware, software, data, and processing into a single location; Best for standardizing and focusing on IT specializations.

chargeback Funding method by which IT costs are recovered by charging individuals, departments, or business units based on actual usage and cost.

chief information officer (CIO) The senior-most officer responsible for the information systems activities within the organization. The CIO is a strategic thinker, not an operational manager. The CIO is typically a member of the senior management team and is involved in all major business decisions that come before that team, bringing an information systems perspective to the team.

chief knowledge officer (CKO) Individual in charge of building and maintaining a knowledge management infrastructure and creating a knowledge culture.

chief technology officer (CTO) Senior IS officer who often works alongside the CIO and is responsible for tracking and advising on emerging technologies Must have enough business savvy and communication skills to create an organizational vision for new technologies, as well as to oversee and manage the firm's technological operations and infrastructure.

client A software program that requests and receives data and, sometimes, instructions from another software program usually running on a separate computer.

client/server A computing architecture in which one software program (the client) requests and receives data and, sometimes, instructions from another software program (the server) usually running on a separate computer. In a client/server architecture, the computers running the client program typically require less power and resources (and are therefore less expensive) than the computer running the server program. In many corporate situations, a client/server architecture can be very cost effective.

coaxial cable (coax) A kind of copper wire typically used in networking. An inner wire is surrounded by insulation, which is surrounded by another copper wire and more insulation.

combination Knowledge transfer from explicit knowledge to explicit knowledge.

commerce server A suite of software components designed to create and manage Web storefronts.

communities of practice Groups that are composed of workers who share common interests and objectives, but who are not necessarily employed in the same department or physical location, and who occupy different roles on the organization chart.

complementor One of the players in a co-opetitive environment. It is a company whose product or service is used in conjunction with a particular product or service to make a more useful set for the customer. *See* **value net.**

cookie A message given to a Web browser by a Web server. The browser stores the message with user identification codes in a text file that is sent back to the server each time the browser requests a page from the server.

co-opetition A business strategy whereby companies cooperate and compete at the same time.

core capability Firm's ability used to create competitive advantages that cannot be easily duplicated over time.

corporate budget Funding method in which the costs fall to the corporate P&L rather than levying charges on specific users or business units.

cost leadership strategy A business strategy in which the organization aims to be the lowest-cost producer in the marketplace. *See* **differentiation strategy** and **focus strategy.**

customer relationship management (CRM) The management activities performed to obtain, enhance, and retain customers. CRM is a coordinated set of activities revolving around the customer.

cycle plan A project management plan that organizes project activities in relation to time. It identifies critical beginning and end dates and breaks the work spanning these dates into phases. The general manager tracks the phases in order to coordinate the eventual transition from project to operational status, a process that culminates on the "go live" date.

dashboard Management tool that provides a snapshot of metrics at any given point in time.

data Simple observations of the state of the world; mere facts.

data mining The process of analyzing data warehouses for "gems" that can be used in management decision making. It identifies previously unknown relationships among data. Typically, data mining refers to the process of combing through massive amounts of customer data in order to understand buying habits and to identify new products, features, and enhancements.

data warehouse A collection of data designed to support management decision making. Data warehouses contain a wide variety of data that is used to create a coherent picture of business conditions at a single point in time.

database A collection of data that is formatted and organized to facilitate ease of access, searching, updating, addition, and deletion. A database is typically so large that it must be stored on disk, but sections may be kept in RAM for quicker access. The software program used to manipulate the data in a database is also often referred to as a "database."

database administrator (DBA) The person within the information systems department who manages the data and the database. Typically this person makes sure that all the data that goes into the database is accurate and appropriate, and that all applications and individuals who need access have it.

debugging The process of examining and testing software and hardware to make sure it operates properly under every condition possible. The term is based on calling any problem a "bug"; therefore, eliminating the problem is called "debugging."

decentralized IS organization Scatters hardware, software, personnel, data, and operation components in different locations to address local business needs.

decision models Information systems-based model used by managers for scenario planning and evaluation. The information system collects and analyzes the information from automated processes, and presents them to the manager to aid in decision making.

differentiation strategy A business strategy in which the organization qualifies its product or service in a way that allows it to appear unique in the marketplace. *See* **cost leadership strategy** and **focus strategy.**

digital cash (Alternatively called e-cash) The nearest equivalent to cash transactions on the Internet. While it can be used for purchases of any size, it was designed specifically for small-ticket transactions.

digital signature A digital code applied to an electronically transmitted message used to prove that the sender of a message (e.g., a file or e-mail message) is truly who she claims to be.

digital subscriber line (DSL) A technology used for connecting users to the Internet. The connection is typically offered by a telephone company or other independent company to homes and businesses that desire direct, all-the-time access. DSL subscribers are able to use the Internet without dialing up to a server, and the connection is usually of higher speed than dial up lines.

e-business (electronic business) Any business activities done electronically within or between businesses. Many use this term to specifically refer to business activities done over the Internet.

e-channel The chain of relationships between companies and customers and between companies and their partners/resellers.

e-commerce (electronic commerce) Transacting business electronically, typically over the Internet or directly with an EDI system.

economic value added (EVA) Valuation approach that accounts for opportunity costs of capital to measure true economic profit and revalues historical costs to give an accurate picture of the true market value of assets.

e-learning Using the Internet to enable training, learning, and knowledge transfer. E-learning includes distance learning, computer-based training (CBT), on-demand learning, and Web-based training.

electronic data interchange (EDI) The direct computer-to-computer transfer of business information between two businesses that uses a standard format.

electronic funds transfer (EFT) The business transaction of sending payments directly from a customer's bank account to a vendor's bank account electronically.

electronic immigration Foreign outsourcing of software development and computer services.

e-marketplaces A special application of the Internet that brings together different companies to buy and sell goods and services. Sometimes called "net-markets" or "virtual markets."

encryption The translation of data into a code or a form that can be read only by the intended receiver. Data is encrypted using a key or alphanumeric code, and can be decrypted only by using the same key.

enterprise resource planning (ERP) software A large, highly complex software program that integrates many business functions under a single application. ERP software can include modules for inventory management, supply chain management, accounting, customer support, order tracking, human resource management, etc. ERP software is typically integrated with a database. ERP software is a type of enterprise system.

enterprise system A comprehensive software package that incorporates all modules needed to run the operations of a business.

Ethernet A standard for local area networks. Ethernet specifies software protocols and hardware specifications for creating a LAN to interconnect two or more computers. There are three common versions of

Ethernet: 10Base-T, which provides for bandwidths of up to 10 Megabits per second; 100Base-T, which provides 100 Megabits per second; and Gigabit Ethernet, which provides 1 Gigabit per second.

explicit knowledge Objective, theoretical, and codified for transmission in a formal, systematic method using grammar, syntax, and the printed word. *See* **tacit knowledge.**

externalization Knowledge transfer from tacit knowledge to explicit knowledge.

extranet A network based on the Internet standard that connects a business with individuals, customers, suppliers, and other stakeholders outside the organization's boundaries. An extranet typically is similar to the Internet, however it has limited access to those specifically authorized to be part of it.

federalism A structuring approach that distributes power, hardware, software, data, and personnel between a central IS group and IS in the business units.

fiber optic (or optical fiber) A data transmission medium (and technology) that sends data as pulses of light along a glass or plastic wire or "fiber." Fiber-optic technology is capable of far greater bandwidth than copper technologies such as coax.

file transferring Transferring a copy of a file from one computer to another on the Internet.

firewall A security measure that blocks out undesirable requests for entrance into a Web site and keeps those on the "inside" from reaching outside.

focus strategy A business strategy in which the organization limits its scope to a narrower segment of the market and tailors its offerings to that group of customers. This strategy has two variants: cost focus, in which the organization seeks a cost advantage within its segment; and differentiation focus, in which it seeks to distinguish its products or services within the segment. This strategy allows the organization to achieve a local competitive advantage, even if it does not achieve competitive advantage in the marketplace overall. *See* **cost strategy** and **differentiation strategy.**

full outsourcing An enterprise outsources all its IT functions, from desktop services to software development.

functional view The view of an organization based on the functional departments, typically including manufacturing, engineering, logistics, sales, marketing, finance, accounting, and human resources. *See* **process view.**

gigabit (Gb) One billion bits.

gigabyte (GB) One billion bytes.

graphical user interface (GUI) The term used to refer to the use of icons, windows, colors, and text as the means of representing information and links on the screen of a computer. GUIs give the user the ability to control actions by clicking on objects rather than by typing commands to the operating system.

groupware Software that enables a group to work together on a project, whether in the same room or from remote locations, by allowing them simultaneous access to the same files. Calendars, written documents, e-mail messages, discussion tools, and databases can be shared.

hard drive A set of rotating disks used to store computer data. Since hard drives typically have much greater capacity than RAM, they are often also referred to as "mass storage."

hierarchical organization structure A type of organizational form that is based upon the concepts of division of labor, specialization, and unity of command.

hypercompetition A theory about industries and marketplaces that suggests that the speed and aggressiveness of moves and countermoves in any given market create an environment in which advantages are quickly gained and lost. A hypercompetitive environment is one in which conditions change rapidly.

HyperText Markup Language (HTML) The language used to write pages for the Internet. It was created by a researcher in Switzerland in 1989, and is part of an Internet standard called the HyperText Transport Protocol (the "http" at the beginning of Internet addresses), which enables the access of information stored on other Internet computers. "Hypertext" itself is another name for the "links" (or "hyperlinks," "hot links," or "hot spots") found on Web pages.

informate A term coined by S. Zuboff to imply the situation when workers are provided with access to a variety of information that allows them to go beyond the requirements of a job to understand the larger picture and more abstract concepts. The alternative to informate is automate, where the tasks done are simply put on a computer to increase speed and accuracy and to cut costs. Informate, on the other hand, means to bring out the information aspects of the job to assist in assessment, monitoring, and decision making.

information Data endowed with relevance and purpose; data in a context.

information model A framework for understanding what information will be crucial to the decision, how to get it, and how to use it.

information resource The available data, technology, people, and processes within an organization to be used by the manager to perform business processes and tasks.

information superhighway U.S. Vice President Al Gore coined the term to describe the vision of a communications network that carries high-speed information all over the world. It encompasses voice, data, telephony, cable television, satellite systems, and other conduits of information.

information system (IS) The combination of technology (the "what"), people (the "who"), and process (the "how") that an organization uses to produce and manage information.

information systems (IS) strategy The plan an organization uses in providing information services.

Information Systems Strategy Triangle The framework connecting business strategy, information system strategy, and organizational systems strategy.

information technology (IT) All forms of technology used to create, store, exchange, and use information.

infrastructure Everything that supports the flow and processing of information in an organization, including hardware, software, data, and network components.

instant messaging (IM) An Internet protocol (IP)–based application that provides convenient communication between people using a variety of different device types.

integrated services digital network (ISDN) A standard for transmission of digital signals over ordinary telephone lines at up to 128 kilobits per second.

intellectual capital The knowledge that has been identified, captured, and leveraged to produce higher-value goods or services or some other competitive advantage for the firm.

intellectual property Allows individuals to own their creativity and innovation in the same way that they can own physical property. Owners can be rewarded for the use of their ideas and can have a say in how their ideas are used.

internalization Knowledge transfer from explicit knowledge to tacit knowledge.

Internet The system of computers and networks that, together, connect individuals and businesses worldwide. The Internet is a global, interconnected network of millions of individual host computers.

Internet checking Service that provides merchants with the ability to accept checks over the Internet.

Internet service provider (ISP) A company that sells access to the Internet. Usually, the service includes a direct line or dial-up number and a quantity of time for using the connection. The service often includes space for hosting subscriber web pages and e-mail.

intranet A network used within a business to communicate between individuals and departments. Intranets are applications on the Internet, but limited to internal business use. *See* **Extranets.**

JAVA An object-oriented programming language designed to work over networks and commonly used for adding features into Web pages.

joint applications development (JAD) A version of RAD or prototyping in which users are more integrally involved, as a group, with the entire development process up to and, in some cases, including coding.

kilobit (kb) approximately 1 thousand bits (i.e., 1024 bits).

kilobyte (kB) approximately 1 thousand bytes (i.e., 1024 bytes).

knowledge Information synthesized and contextualized to provide value.

knowledge capture Involves continuous processes of scanning, organizing, and packaging knowledge after it has been generated.

knowledge codification The representation of knowledge in a manner that can be easily accessed and transferred.

knowledge generation Includes all activities that discover "new" knowledge, whether such knowledge is new to the individual, the firm, or to the entire discipline.

knowledge management The processes necessary to capture, codify, and transfer knowledge across the organization to achieve competitive advantage.

knowledge map A list of people, documents, and databases telling employees where to go when they need help. A good knowledge map gives access to resources that would otherwise be difficult or impossible to find. Maps may also identify knowledge networks or communities of practice within the organization. A knowledge map serves as both a guide to where knowledge exists in an organization and an inventory of the knowledge assets available.

knowledge repository A physical or virtual place where documents with knowledge embedded in them, such as memos, reports, or news articles, are stored so they can be retrieved easily.

knowledge transfer Involves transmitting knowledge from one person or group to another, and the absorption of that knowledge.

legacy system Older, mature information system (often 20–30 years old).

list server A type of e-mail mailing list to which users subscribe, and when any user sends a message to the server, a copy of the message is sent to everyone on the list. This allows for restricted-access discussion groups. Only subscribed members can participate in or view the discussions, since they are transmitted via e-mail.

local area network (LAN) A network of interconnected (often via Ethernet) workstations that reside within a limited geographic area, typically within a single building or campus. LANs are typically employed so that the machines on them can share resources such as printers or servers and/or so that they can exchange e-mail or other forms of messages (e.g., to control industrial machinery).

mainframe A large, central computer that handles all of the functionality of the system.

managerial levers Organizational, control, and cultural variables that are used by decision makers to affect changes in their organizations.

marketspace A virtual market where the transactions taking place are all based on information exchange, rather than the exchange of goods and services.

matrix organization structure A type of organization structure that assigns workers to two or more supervisors in an effort to make sure multiple dimensions of the business are integrated.

megabit (Mb) 1 million bits.

megabyte (MB) 1 million bytes.

mobile workers Workers who work from wherever they are.

modem A device that translates a computer's digital data into an analog format that can be transmitted over standard telephone lines, and vice versa. Modems are necessary to connect one computer to another via a phone line.

net present value (NPV) Valuation approach that accounts for the time value of money by discounting the costs and benefits for each year of the system's lifetime using the present value factor.

netcentric architecture Intranets that build upon Internet connections and use standard browsers. Also called Web-centric.

network externality The concept that the value of a network node to a person or organization in the network increases when another joins the network.

networked organization structure A flexible, adaptive organizational form in which formal and informal communication networks connect all parts of the company.

newsgroup A type of electronic discussion where the text of the discussions typically is viewable on an Internet or intranet Web page rather than sent through e-mail. Unless this page is shielded with a firewall or password, outsiders are able to view and/or participate in the discussion.

open-sourcing The process of building and improving "free" software by an Internet community.

operating system (OS) A program that manages all other programs running on, as well as all the resources connected to, a computer. Examples include Microsoft Windows, DOS, and UNIX.

options pricing Valuation approach that offers a risk-hedging strategy to minimize the negative impact of risk when uncertainty can be resolved by waiting to see what happens.

Oracle A widely used database program.

organizational strategy The organization's design, as well as the choices it makes that define, set up, coordinate, and control its work processes.

organizational systems The fundamental elements of a business, including people, work processes, structure, and the plan that enables them to work efficiently to achieve business goals.

outsourcing The purchase of a good or service that was previously provided internally. It is a business arrangement in which third-party providers and vendors manage the information systems' activities. In a typical outsourced arrangement, the company finds vendors to take care of the operational activities, the support activities, and the systems' development activities, saving strategic decisions for the internal information systems personnel.

password A string of arbitrary characters that is known only to a select person or group, used to verify that the user is who he says he is.

payback analysis Simple, popular method that determines the payback period, or how much time will lapse before accrued benefits overtake accrued and continuing costs.

peer-to-peer Allows networked computers to share resources without a central server playing a dominant role. Napster used a peer-to-peer architecture.

personalization The selective delivery of content and services (such as specific product and service offerings, advertising, coupons, and other promotions) to customers and prospective customers.

portal Easy-to-use Web sites that provide access to search engines, critical information, research, applications, and processes that individuals want.

privacy The right to be left alone.

process An interrelated, sequential set of activities and tasks that turns inputs into outputs, and have a distinct beginning, a clear deliverable at the end, and a set of metrics that are useful to measure performance.

process view The view of a business from the perspective of the business processes performed. Typically the view is made up of cross-functional processes that transverse disciplines, departments, functions, and even organizations. *See* **functional view.**

productivity paradox The failure of massive investment in information technology to boost productivity growth.

project A temporary endeavor undertaken to create a unique product or service.

project management The application of knowledge, skills, tools, and techniques to project activities in order to meet or exceed stakeholder needs and expectation from a project.

protocol A special, typically standardized, set of rules used by computers to enable communication between them.

prototyping An evolutionary development method for building an information system. Developers get the general idea of what is needed by the users, and then build a fast, high-level version of the system as the beginning of the project. The idea of prototyping is to quickly get a version of the software in the hands of the users, and to jointly evolve the system through a series of cycles of design and build, then use and evaluate.

random access memory (RAM) Computer memory that can be accessed at random, read from, and written to by the CPU. Sometimes also called "main memory," it is typically used to store currently running programs and their data. RAM requires power to maintain data.

rapid application development (RAD) This process is similar to prototyping in that it is an interactive process, in which tools are used to speed up development. RAD systems typically have tools for developing the user, reusable code, code generation, and programming language testing and debugging. These tools make it easy for the developer to build a library of a common, standard set of code that can easily be used in multiple applications.

reengineering The management process of redesigning business processes in a relatively radical manner. Reengineering traditionally meant taking a "blank piece of paper" and designing, then building, a business process from the beginning. This was intended to help the designers eliminate any blocks or barriers that the current process or environment might provide. This process is sometimes called BPR, Business Process Redesign or Reengineering, or Business Reengineering.

return on investment (ROI) Percentage rate that measures the relationship between the amount the business gets back from an investment and the amount invested using the formula ROI = (Estimated lifetime benefits – Estimated lifetime costs)/Estimated lifetime costs.

SAP The company that produces the leading ERP software. The software, technically named "SAP R/3," is often simply referred to as SAP.

scalable Feature that refers to how well a hardware or software system can adapt to increased demands.

search engine A program that searches the Internet (or an intranet or individual site) for specified keywords.

secure electronic transaction (SET) Protocol for secure payments for online credit-card transactions that uses mutual authentication.

secure server Server that utilizes encryption technology to protect the privacy of transmitted data by converting plain text into encrypted text before it is transmitted.

secure sockets layer (SSL) A protocol for encrypting Web transactions that authenticates the merchant's identity.

security validators Web sites that validate the security level of other sites, and provide a "seal of approval" that a particular Web site is protected.

selective outsourcing An enterprise chooses which IT capabilities to retain inhouse and which to give to an outsider. Areas include Web site hosting, business process application development, help desk support, networking and communications, and data center operations.

server A software program or computer intended to provide data and/or instructions to another software program or computer. The hardware on which a server program runs is often also referred to as "the server."

silo Self-contained functional unit such as marketing, operations, finance, and so on.

smart card A plastic card with an embedded microchip that can be loaded with data and used for telephone calling, electronic cash payments, and other applications. It can be periodically "recharged" for additional use.

social contract theory A theory used in business ethics to describe how managers act. The social responsibilities of corporate managers include considering the needs of a society with no corporations or other complex business arrangements. Social contract theorists ask what conditions would have to be met for the members of such a society to agree to allow a corporation to be formed. Thus, society bestows legal recognition on a corporation to allow it to employ social resources toward given ends.

socialization Knowledge transfer from tacit knowledge to tacit knowledge.

stakeholder theory A theory used in business ethics to describe how managers act. This theory suggests that managers, while bound by their relation to stockholders, are entrusted also with a fiduciary responsibility to all those who hold a stake in or a claim on the firm, including employees, customers, vendors, neighbors, etc.

stockholder theory A theory used in business ethics to describe how managers act. Stockholders advance capital to corporate managers who act as agents in advancing their ends. The nature of this contract binds managers to act in the interest of the shareholders, i.e., to maximize shareholder value.

strategic alliance An interorganizational relationship that affords one or more companies in the relationship a strategic advantage.

supply chain management (SCM) An approach that improves the way a company finds raw components it needs to make a product or service, manufactures that product or service, and delivers it to customers.

symmetric encryption The sender and recipient use the same special "key" to encrypt and decrypt the data.

systems development life cycle (SDLC) The process of designing and delivering the entire system. SDLC usually means these 7 phases: initiation of the project, requirements definition phase, functional design phase, technical design and construction phase, verification phase, implementation phase, and maintenance and review phase.

tacit knowledge Personal, context-specific, and hard to formalize and communicate. It consists of experiences, beliefs, and skills. Tacit knowledge is entirely subjective and is often acquired through physically practicing a skill or activity. *See* **explicit knowledge.**

TCP/IP Pair of connection-oriented protocols. TCP (transmission control protocol) establishes a connection between processes on different host computers before data is transmitted, while IP (Internet protocol) defines a connectionless service through which data is delivered from computer to computer.

telecommuting Combining telecommunications with commuting. This term usually means individuals who work from home or other convenient locations instead of commuting into an office. However, it is often used to mean anyone who works regularly from a location outside her company's office.

T-form organization An organizational form in which conventional design variables—such as organizational sub-units, reporting mechanisms, flow of work, tasks, and compensation—are combined with technology-enabled components, such as electronic linking, production automation, electronic workflows and communications, and electronic customer/supplier relationships.

thick client A full function stand-alone computer that is used, either exclusively or occasionally, as a client in a client/server architecture. Thick clients are typically standard PCs equipped with disk drives and their own copies of commonly used software.

thin client Computer hardware designed to be used only as a client in a client/server architecture. Thin clients are also referred to as NCs (Network Computers) or NetPCs (Network PCs), and typically lack disk drives, CD ROM drives, and expansion capability.

total cost of ownership (TCO) A technique that attempts to comprehend all the costs associated with owning and operating an IT infrastructure.

total quality management (TQM) A management philosophy in which quality metrics drive performance evaluation of people, processes, and decisions. The objective of TQM is to continually, and often incrementally, improve the activities of the business toward the goal of eliminating defects (Zero Defects) and producing the highest quality outputs possible.

transaction processors Service that allows merchants the ability to stay out of Internet transaction entirely. This service is ideal for merchants who wish to sell products on the Internet and do not want to worry about handling any of the credit card information themselves.

value net The set of players in a co-opetitive environment. It includes a company and its competitors and complementors, as well as their customers and suppliers, and the interactions among all of them. *See* **complementor.**

value-added network (VAN) An independent third-party company that provides connection and EDI transaction forwarding services to customer companies using EDI.

virtual corporation A temporary network of companies who are linked by information technology to exploit fast-changing opportunities.

virtual organization An organization made up of people living and working from anywhere in the world. The virtual organization may not even have a company headquarters or company building, but functions much like any other organization. Employees typically use an information systems infrastructure to

communicate, collaborate, and carry out company business.

virtual private network (VPN) A private data network that makes use of public telecommunication infrastructures such as the Internet, maintaining privacy through the use of a tunneling protocol and security procedures.

virtual team Geographically and/or organizationally dispersed coworkers who are assembled using a combination of telecommunications and information technologies to accomplish an organizational task.

virtual terminal An Internet interface that acts in place of a credit card swipe machine.

wide area network (WAN) A computer network that spans multiple offices, often dispersed over a wide geographic area. A WAN typically consists of transmission lines leased from telephone companies.

wireless architecture Environment maintaining a data connection from a remote network using a wireless technology. Also called mobile architecture.

World Wide Web (WWW) A system for accessing information on the Internet via the use of specially formatted documents. WWW is used interchangeably with the term "Internet."

zero time organization An organization designed around responding instantly to customers, employees, suppliers, and other stakeholder demands.

Index

04893192